Hitler's Justice

Hitler's Justice

The Courts of the Third Reich

·

Ingo Müller

Translated by
Deborah Lucas Schneider

Harvard University Press
Cambridge, Massachusetts

This book was originally published as *Furchtbare Juristen: Die
unbewältigte Vergangenheit unserer Justiz,* by Kindler Verlag,
copyright © 1987 by Kindler Verlag GmbH, Munich.

This book is printed on acid-free paper, and its binding materials
have been chosen for strength and durability.

Library of Congress Cataloging-in-Publication Data

Müller, Ingo.
  [Furchtbare Juristen. English]
  Hitler's justice: The courts of the Third Reich / Ingo Müller;
translated by Deborah Lucas Schneider.
     p.   cm.
  Translation of: Furchtbare Juristen.
  Includes bibliographical references and index.
  ISBN 0–674–40418–1 (alk. paper)
  1. Justice, Administration of—Germany—History.
2. Judges—Germany—History.   3. National socialism.
I. Title.
KK3655.M8513   1991
347.43—dc20
[344.307]   90–39068
                                                         CIP

To my friends and colleagues
Dian, Diemut, Fritz, Gerd, Hans-Ernst, Heinrich, Helmut,
Joachim, Johannes, Martin, Peter, Rudolf, Sven,
Ulrich, Waldemar, and Werner

Contents

III · The Aftermath

Introduction
by Detlev Vagts

This English-language edition of Ingo Müller's book offers the general reader an opportunity to survey the history of the German legal system during Hitler's rule, as well as before and after it. It tells a depressing tale, one that reminds us how fragile the safeguards of a civilized society can be in face of the powers of darkness. It is particularly significant for judges and lawyers, who will be led to consider how much resistance a legal system can put up against rampant misrule. It complements studies of the German medical and psychiatric professions during this period. As one reads about the hesitant manner in which postwar Germany dealt with this past, one asks: What should have been done? How much punishment, how much housecleaning, of legal personnel would have been appropriate?

An introduction to this work should accomplish three tasks. First, it needs to explain to the English-speaking reader some things about the German legal system—things the author could assume an audience of educated German lay people would understand. Second, it should point out more explicitly what aspects of this history are enveloped in controversy in Germany nowadays, as distinguished from those elements on which there is general agreement. Third, it should indicate the various ways in which American and British lawyers have been involved, directly or indirectly, with the history that is set forth here.

Elements of the German Legal System

People are often tempted to assume that the German legal system is very much like the American and British systems. Similar-sounding terminology helps to disguise differences. In fact, one quickly sees when attending a German trial how different the systems are in many respects. To complicate the matter, it is easy to swing to the opposite error: to conclude that they differ on all points and, in particular, that a civil law system such as the German provides none of the safeguards for the accused that the Anglo-American system offers. The following brief description of the German system is designed to provide a bit of clarification. Although it is written in the present tense, it applies (except where otherwise indicated) not only to the legal framework in use today, but to the arrangements that prevailed under the Weimar and Nazi regimes as well.

The German legal system comprises three levels of regular courts. At the ground level, there are two courts. One is the *Amtsgericht,* here translated as "Petty Court." It functions as a trial court with a jurisdiction that is limited to the less serious cases, both civil and criminal. More important cases are tried in the first instance before a *Landgericht,* here translated as "County Court." The County Courts also operate in some cases as the courts to which appeals from the Petty Courts may be taken. From the County Courts, appeals go to the *Oberlandesgericht,* or "Court of Appeals." Each of these courts is designated by the name of the town or city where it sits. For historical reasons, the Court of Appeals for Berlin is termed the *Kammergericht* (literally, "Chamber Court"). The court of final appeal was called the *Reichsgericht,* or "Supreme Court." It was renamed the *Bundesgerichtshof,* or "Federal Supreme Court," after World War II. At the same time, the function of deciding upon the compatibility of legislation with the new constitution was separately assigned to the *Bundesverfassungsgericht,* or "Federal Constitutional Court." Germany also operates specialized court systems for labor law, administrative law, tax law, and social security matters. During the Third Reich, there existed a so-called People's Court (*Volksgerichtshof*) and other special courts for the speedy and brutal disposition of political offenses.

These courts are constituted somewhat differently from their counterparts in the United States and Britain. The courts of first instance, as well as the Courts of Appeal, are staffed by several judges, so that important trials are presided over by a panel rather than by a single judge. American and British lawyers are familiar with the practice according to which appellate courts sit in panels. The German practice is different, in that a panel remains of the same composition for protracted periods rather than rotating from week to week. And the panels are characteristically divided into civil and criminal groupings. The panels produce written opinions, but these do not bear the authors' names; and there are no dissents. There are official publications of the opinions of the German Supreme Court, divided into criminal and civil series. Some opinions of lower courts are unofficially published and commented upon in legal journals. While German lawyers reject the Anglo-American view of the binding effect of precedent, the opinions of the Supreme Court are regarded as very important guides to the law.

German courts have always functioned without a jury in the Anglo-American sense. Some German trials are held before professional judges only. Others are held before panels composed of regular judges and lay persons. The latter are not legally trained; however, unlike Anglo-American jurors, they are not chosen at random but are deliberately selected for their supposed judiciousness, and serve for long periods of time. Instead of receiving instructions on law from the judge and supposedly dealing only with questions of fact, the lay persons and judges deliberate together.

German judges, like their British and American counterparts, are trained at law schools alongside students headed for private practice or business or government work. But their later career path is different, branching off immediately after formal legal education. Thus, German judges are not chosen for the bench after experience in the private bar but work their way up through the judicial system, starting as assistants in the Petty Courts and working toward a post on the Supreme Court. Their career path is thus much like that of the lifetime civil servant. It is a matter of conjecture whether judges on the Anglo-American model would have resisted Nazi incursions any better than German jurists did. In several instances the newly created Federal Constitutional Court, composed of specially appointed noncareer judges, has been able to distance itself from the Nazi past of the judiciary more successfully than have the regular courts.

With respect to German lawyers, too, one must be alert to differences from Anglo-American patterns. Preparation for the profession begins with attendance at a university; law students come directly from high school (*Gymnasium*) to legal studies. Unless they are interested in pursuing an academic career, they generally do not acquire a doctorate but proceed through two examinations, which are set by the state authorities and not by the universities. An obligatory period of clerkship with courts, practicing lawyers, and government agencies completes the training. Some lawyers become "notaries"—a term that may evoke false comparisons in the American mind, since Americans know notaries only as routine wielders of rubber stamps, whereas their functions in Germany include many of those entrusted to office lawyers or solicitors in the United States and Britain. German lawyers are somewhat constrained in their representation of the accused in criminal cases by the greater investigatory and examining role assigned to the judiciary and prosecution. Still, in the Weimar period quite a few lawyers succeeded in establishing themselves as important political trial counsel.

The German trial is, as a consequence of these differences, quite different from an American or British proceeding. A German criminal trial does not begin with an indictment by a grand jury but grows out of the investigatory proceedings of the state's attorney. Under the so-called legality principle, a German state's attorney who receives convincing evidence that a crime has been committed is required to institute proceedings. "Prosecutorial discretion" is alien to German theory. Whereas a British or American trial, when conducted before a jury, must start at the beginning (since the jurors are as new to the case as the spectators), a German trial starts with the file. The trial is kept much more tightly under control by German judges, who do most of the examining of witnesses and call for documentary evidence. They are not the relatively passive umpires between contesting attorneys that one sees in courtrooms in the United States, and somewhat less often in Great Britain. Occasionally, a criminal case is tried before an appellate court—as in the case of the Reichstag fire trial, which was tried before the Supreme Court itself.

To some degree, the German legal system under the Weimar Republic had elements of federalism; under the Federal Republic, it has even more. One should not assume, however, that German federalism has the same features as its Canadian and American counterparts. Under Weimar, the governments of the constituent states (*Länder*) had significant powers with respect to the appointment of judges, law professors, and other legal functionaries. They were headed by governors who presided over cabinets much like prime ministers. In Weimar Germany, Prussia was by far the largest and most important *Land*. Nazism abolished the autonomy of these units and divided Germany into regions presided over by *Gauleiter* chosen by the Führer. The autonomy of the *Länder* was enhanced in the constitution of the Federal Republic. Prussia disappeared as an entity; that part which fell to the Federal Republic was divided into several *Länder*. German criminal and civil statues apply across the entire nation, as do the rules of civil and criminal procedure.

The German system of laws is supposed to be organized in general, all-encompassing codes. The most significant of these are the Civil Code, the Commercial Code, the Criminal Code, the Civil Procedure Rules, and the Criminal Procedure Rules. All of these date back to the turn of the century or earlier. Efforts to draft a new People's Civil Code during the Nazi period proved to be abortive. The National Socialist statutes considered in this book were not, in general, integrated into the respective codes but

were treated as separate pieces of legislation which the courts had to rec-
oncile with the rules of the codes as best they could. It has been difficult
under the Federal Republic, as well, to preserve even a semblance of code-
based cohesion in the German legal system.[1]

Controversies about German Legal History

As is the case with other parts of recent German history, there is considerable controversy about many aspects of the events this book recounts.
The historical study of National Socialist law was first characterized by a
stream of books written by those who had participated in that life and
who sought to justify what they had done. There followed a variety of
writings by the succeeding generation of German lawyers, whom older
colleagues accused of being eager to drag down the generation of their
fathers and to convict them of collusion in evil.

The controversies concern four basic issues, each of which this book
takes a position on, though sometimes only inferentially and implicitly.
The first is: What was the collective contribution of the German legal
profession to the taking of power by the National Socialist regime and its
retention of that power for twelve years? As the book makes clear, the
author believes that contribution was substantial. There are those who
challenge that assessment and who doubt that even a very different legal
system or different profession would have made much difference. They
would note that the legal community, unlike the medical profession, did
not as an entity stand to gain much from National Socialism. To pursue
the comparison, they might add that, unlike doctors, lawyers did not provide the basic driving racist ideas which constituted the core of Nazi thinking—that lawyers merely refuted various objections to Nazism without
providing its underlying convictions.

The second question is the matter of individual lawyers' responsibility
for what happened. Obviously, this will vary from case to case. The book
provides examples from both ends of the spectrum. One sees the bloodthirsty ranting of Roland Freisler, presiding officer of the People's Court,
captured in a film so vile that the Nazis omitted presenting it to the public
lest the reaction be one of revulsion. One sees the opportunism of Carl
Schmitt as he betrays his Jewish friends and praises Hitler's murder of his
Nazi partners and miscellaneous others, including Schmitt's own former

1. The reader will see references to the *Reichsgesetzblatt* in the endnotes. This was an
official publication containing the texts of laws arranged in chronological sequence, not according to subject matter. The *Reichsgesetzblatt* thus resembles the U.S. Statutes at Large and
the British Public General Acts.

patron. And at the other end, one sees the defiant resignation of Professor Anschütz and a few other acts of courage. In between, one observes a parade of jurists who rather passively go along. In fact, there were quite a few lawyers and judges specializing in corporate and commercial matters who seldom if ever got their fingers dirty with the work described here. Readers will have to try to incorporate into their judgment on the behavior of X or Y as an individual some sense of the German environment of the 1920s and 1930s, so different from that of Britain and the United States in the 1990s. Nazism arrived at the end of a long period of upheaval: the military disaster of 1914–1918, the inflation of the early 1920s, the depression of 1930–1933, and constant political instability and street violence. All of these made Germans more susceptible to Hitler's promises. The United States, in contrast, has only McCarthyism with which to calibrate the hysteria and the fear that prevailed in Germany from 1933 to 1945; and McCarthyism involved no death sentences (other than those of the Rosenbergs) and only a fraction of the dismissals that took place in the Reich in the 1930s. Britain has been fortunate in having had no such major purge during its modern history.

The third complex of issues concerns the extent to which the postwar Federal Republic did justice to what had happened before, making good the losses of the persecuted as well as it could and punishing those malefactors who had sunk the lowest in carrying out Hitler's orders and wishes. The author presents a variety of cases in which the victim received little or nothing and in which the malefactors continued unscathed to retirement or a natural death. It is hard to find a comparison to use as a measure for what the Federal Republic did or failed to do. The German Democratic Republic (East Germany) did quite a lot more than the Federal Republic to punish and remove from office those who had committed crimes in the service of the Nazi state; however, it did very little for the victims of that state, in particular for the victims of Hitler's anti-Semitism. It could not match the wealthier western state's liberality and did not try. Of course, neither of the two German republics was entirely a free actor, and the victorious occupying powers get a good deal of the credit or blame for what went on there. One can also look to some other cases in which new and more democratic regimes came to power in the wake of military dictatorships—Greece, Argentina, and Uruguay, for example. Or one can look at the post-1945 purges of collaborators in other European countries. In terms of punishing the oppressors and compensating the victims, few of these states have done an impressive job.

Then there is the question of continuity: Is the Federal Republic still much the same sort of legal edifice it was during the Third Reich? Observers from other countries tend to see the new Germany as a civilized state. It is a party to the European Convention on Human Rights, submitting its system of justice to external scrutiny. It has abolished the death penalty. Its prisons are less brutal than many American and some British institutions. Its Federal Constitutional Court applies rather stringent tests to the products of the legislature. A foreigner who has visited Germany at regular intervals notices the gradual diminution of the authoritarian tone of civil servants—police officers, railroad conductors, and so on—in their dealings with the citizenry. On the negative side, one notes the imposition of rules barring Communists from government jobs and the restrictions on defense counsel introduced in the wake of the terrorist operations since 1970. These are, in a sense, reminiscent of actions undertaken by the Nazi regime. But they may also be taken as stemming from the perception that the Weimar Republic did not defend itself strongly enough against the antidemocratic forces that sought its downfall. It is from the same causes that Germany has enforced rules against neo-Nazi propaganda, against the denial of the "Holocaust," for example—rules that would not pass muster under the First Amendment in the United States.

On each of the above questions, the author sets forth a great deal of evidence in such a form that the reader can arrive at a personal judgment as to the answer.

British and American Involvement with German Law

Nazism came as a shock to those American lawyers, a small minority, who kept in touch with major developments abroad. Although American jurists were never as intimately involved with German law as they were with the British, they had respect for the traditional German legal system. In particular those Americans who thought that Anglo-American legal thinking was too pragmatic, disorganized, and antitheoretical looked to Germany for inspiration. References to such thinkers as Savigny and Jhering were sprinkled throughout the American literature. Karl Lewellyn studied in Berlin and derived inspiration for his later redrafting of American commercial laws from the German codes. This respect dissolved as Americans became aware of what the Nazis were doing to (and through) the German legal system. The image of what was going on in Germany was largely shaped by the writings of émigrés, and there was little response from defenders of the new regime. British lawyers seem to have been less attracted than Americans by the orderliness of German legal theory. The most fa-

mous example of German influence on British legal writing is that of the
medieval legal historian Otto von Gierke upon his counterpart Frederic
Maitland.

Even while the war was in full swing, Britain and the United States
began to formulate ideas about what was to be done after victory. Lawyers
sensed a need to do something about the German legal system, which had
gone drastically wrong somewhere. They recognized that while legal reform would not be enough to build a better, safer German society, the
establishment of legal restraint was vitally necessary. Part of that reform
entailed the removal of the Nazi personnel who had made Hitler's law.
(The book shows how limited the results of that purge were.) An American court, following up on the Nuremberg case in chief, tried a number
of Nazi judges and prosecutors and passed substantial penalties upon
them. Another part entailed the reformation of the body of law itself.
Military Government Law Number 1 set about this task. It declared a
number of laws abrogated as Nazi products. It next declared that no German law should be applied if it "would cause injustice or inequality" by
favoring a person because of Nazi party membership or discriminating
against any person on account of race, nationality, religious belief, or opposition to Nazism. It went on to say that "interpretation or application
of German law in accordance with National Socialist doctrine, however or
whenever enunciated, is prohibited." Decisions of German courts or agencies interpreting law in a Nazi way were no longer to be used as references.
And such laws enacted in the Hitler period as had not been voided were
to be interpreted in accordance with "the plain meaning of the text and
without regard to objectives or meanings ascribed in preambles or other
pronouncements." Other provisions forbade resort to the "sound consciousness of the folk" or the infliction of cruel or unusual punishments.
In this legislation, the Allies recognized the responsibility incurred by the
German courts in hastening the Nazi legislative process by moving ahead
of the output of the law- and decree-making authorities.

But the ardor for de-Nazification did not last long. The reasons for this
slackening are various. Part of it related to personnel changes. The people
with the bitterest experience of Nazism and its consequences went home
and were replaced by routine bureaucrats. There developed a sense of urgency about reviving the German economy and, through the Marshall
Plan, integrating it with the other European economies. This seemed to
imply noninterference with the personnel and structure of the German
state and business systems. The Berlin airlift, the suppression of all parties
other than the Communist party in the German Democratic Republic, the

putsch in Czechoslovakia, and other ominous acts beyond the Iron Curtain gave rise to a willingness to overlook the past in the interests of building up West Germany as a bulwark against Stalinism. Klaus Barbie was not the only beneficiary of this trend. The means used in the early de-Nazification efforts seemed abhorrent to the Allies as well as the Germans. The questionnaires used to ferret out those with Nazi pasts intruded deeply into individuals' past private lives. Punishment for acts covered by at least apparent state authority seemed unfairly retroactive. There was something out of tune about the Allied military government law that forbade future cruel and unusual punishments—yet permitted the death penalty for inflicting them.

American and British theorists were stirred by the challenge of National Socialism to law. The history of Nazi courts became the focus of new battles between positivists and those who found the ultimate basis of justice somewhere else. A famous exchange between H. L. A. Hart of Oxford University and Lon Fuller of Harvard[2] focused on a case in which a German woman was prosecuted after 1945 for having denounced her husband to the Nazis as a defeatist, in order to get him out of the way so that she could pursue a new love affair. Her action was consistent with wartime Nazi law. But was that really "law"? The question arose when one considered the source of the legislation. Does a law have to be compatible with basic moral conceptions in order to be truly law? Or is it enough that the body or person exercising control has said that is its or his will? The Anglo-American debate proceeded at a rather abstract level. On that plane, it was not necessary to delve into some of the issues of positivism that this book brings to the surface. Were the Nazi statutes really law despite the fact that they had been passed under the 1933 Enabling Act, which had been obtained by Hitler through the exclusion of Communist deputies from the Reichstag and the exertion of enormous pressures on the voters and the deputies? Was legislation invalid because it failed to respect the limitations inherent in the provisions of the Weimar constitution granting emergency powers? Was a mere informal indication of the Führer's wishes enough to create law—as in the case of the euthanasia campaign? The Nazis had themselves paid a certain amount of attention to these questions; some writers had given the answer that Nazism was revolutionary and that it obtained its legitimacy through that very revo-

2. H. L. A. Hart, "Positivism and the Separation of Law and Morals," *Harvard Law Review* 71 (1958), 593–629; and Lon Fuller, "Positivism and Fidelity to Law," *Harvard Law Review* 71 (1958), 630–672.

lutionary act. It is a separate question to ask whether German judges can legitimately claim for themselves that they acted in a positivistic way, merely declaring the law that there was. This book provides much evidence for the proposition that many judges went beyond the bounds of what they had to do and strove to anticipate the underlying will of the Führer.[3]

3. The author gratefully acknowledges the helpful comments of John Langbein on an early draft of this Introduction.

· I ·

Prologue

"Time to Raise an Outcry": German Judges Oppose the Forces of Reaction

In the first half of the nineteenth century members of the legal profession, including numerous judges, continued to uphold the spirit of the Enlightenment, forming the backbone of resistance to Metternich's reactionary policies. Their strivings for an independent legal system free from state controls were part of the general struggle for civil liberties. One of the judges whose democratic attitudes brought him into inevitable conflict with the authorities was E. T. A. Hoffmann, who was also a composer and celebrated writer. As a judge of the Prussian Supreme Court *(Kammergericht)* and member of a "commission for the investigation of treasonable contacts and other subversive activities," he had dared to criticize the police for prosecuting an alleged demagogue named "Turnvater Jahn" and declared publicly that the proceedings were illegal. He even went so far as to represent Jahn in his suit against the leader of the police action, von Kamptz, since, in Hoffmann's opinion, "not even the highest government officials are above the law; rather, they are subject to it like every other citizen."[1] A reminiscence of the affair has been preserved in literary form: in the "Knarrpanti" episode of his satirical tale "Master Flea," Hoffmann included a depiction—only thinly disguised—of contemporary police methods, "a whole web of arbitrary acts, blatant disregard for the law, [and] personal animosity."[2]

Knarrpanti, the leader of the investigation described in the tale, is clearly modeled on Hoffmann's real-life adversary von Kamptz, and his methods are a caricature of the political "justice" typical of (but not unique to) his day: "When reminded that, after all, a crime had to have been committed for there to be a criminal, Knarrpanti opined that once the criminal was identified, it was a simple matter to find out what his crime had been. Only a superficial and careless judge would . . . not be able to slip into the inquest some small lapse or other on the defendant's part that would justify the arrest."[3] The publication of this satire led to disciplinary sanctions against Hoffmann; the charge was, appropriately enough, "revelation of court secrets." However, his trial never reached a conclusion. Hoffmann died on July 25, 1822; von Kamptz went on to become minister of justice in Prussia in 1832.

As a judge, E. T. A. Hoffmann was by no means an exceptional figure. Some of the leading opponents of the suppression of liberty were members of the legal profession, and fully one fourth of the members of the National Assembly in Frankfurt in 1848 were judges and jurists.[4] One delegate, Benedikt Waldeck, a judge at the Secret High Court in Berlin who was a lifelong enemy of Prussian despotism and an advocate of popular rights, was imprisoned for six months in 1849 for alleged high treason. Later, as a member of the Prussian parliament, he became a leader of the Independents and one of the most resolute opponents of Bismarck's crypto-absolutism. The extent to which he was revered by the local population was apparent at his funeral: in the Berlin of 1870, the procession of 20,000 people represented an extraordinary demonstration of mass feeling.[5] In Münster a judge at the Court of Appeals, Jodokus Donatus Temme, even ran for election to the National Assembly while serving a term in prison, and was promptly elected. It was impossible to convict him on a charge of high treason, but after a disciplinary hearing he was removed from office without pension and emigrated to Switzerland.[6]

Although such judges were not isolated figures, neither did they represent the legal system as a whole. Bismarck himself, first as Prussian prime minister and later as chancellor of the Reich, used the legal system unscrupulously as a weapon in internal political disputes. In these disputes he was able to rely on a new institution, the Office of Public Prosecutions (*Staatsanwaltschaft*), which was created in 1849 on the French model. It had at first seemed to the Liberal party to offer hopes of a more independent judiciary, since it replaced the inquisitorial form of trial of the absolutist era, but it soon proved to be "one of the reactionary bureaucracy's most effective weapons."[7] Since the Office of Public Prosecutions had a monopoly on the bringing of criminal charges and since its prosecutors were civil servants forced to obey the instructions of their superiors, the government could use the legal system against political opponents at will. During the Prussian constitutional crisis of 1860–1866 members of the liberal Progressive party made the acquaintance of this form of political justice, just as the followers of the Catholic Center party were to do later during the *Kulturkampf* ("struggle for civilization") between 1872 and 1886. All of them had reason enough to complain of "the outrageous partiality of the bench."[8]

Again and again, however, protests against political misuse of the legal system came from judges themselves. As early as 1844 Heinrich Simon, judge at the Municipal Court in Breslau, had pointed to state manipulation of the courts and prophesied, "The Prussian judiciary, hitherto so exalted, will fall . . . and the ruins of this institution will come crashing down upon the Prussian throne and upon the civil liberties of the Prussian people." A year later Simon resigned from his office with a noteworthy remark to the king: "Only something that offers resistance can provide support."[9] For the leading role he played in the revolution of 1848, he was sentenced in absentia to life imprisonment. After his death in exile in Switzerland, the liberal newspaper *Nationalzeitung* wrote in its obituary: "The German people have lost one of their greatest citizens . . . The lives of men such as Heinrich Simon point to the coming of a better future."[10]

In postrevolutionary parliaments, too, politically minded judges remained a liberal element. The Prussian Chamber of Deputies of 1862, in which 230 Liberals were opposed by only 11 Conservatives, was called "the District Judges' Parliament" because it included a great number of judges. This assembly waged a persistent battle for years against the reactionary Prussian regime during the *Kulturkampf* mentioned above. Bismarck referred acidly in those days to "district judges and other revolutionaries," and was not far off the mark. Many judges had a revolutionary past, and when the Supreme Court *(Reichsgericht)* was founded in 1879, even its first president, Martin Eduard von Simson, who was known for his loyalty to the regime, was said to have participated in an armed student uprising in March 1848.[11] Although their election to parliament caused many judges to shift their loyalties toward the government, some of them continued to create serious difficulties for Bismarck. Carl Twesten, for example, a municipal judge in Berlin, became known as the author of a series of pamphlets attacking reactionary politics in Prussia ("Friend, Now It Is Time to Raise an Outcry!"). As a member of the state parliament, he had exposed government manipulation in the assignment of judgeships and had faced criminal charges, even though the constitution guaranteed the right of free speech in parliament. After a tense debate between Twesten and Bismarck, the delegates voted: 283 censured the penalization of the courageous judge, whereas Bismarck could enlist only 35 on his side.[12]

· 2 ·

The Enforcement of Conformity

After the founding of the German Empire in 1871 and above all after 1878, when Bismarck, now promoted to chancellor, shifted his base of support in the Reichstag from the National Liberal party to the Conservatives, he initiated a series of ultraconservative measures to purge the judiciary of its more progressive members. The number of existing courts was drastically reduced and many of the oldest judges were sent into early retirement—the generation, that is to say, whose political thinking had been influenced by the revolution of 1848 and the constitutional crisis of the sixties. Since in the following decade no judgeships became vacant, whoever aspired to a seat on the bench had to undergo an eight- to ten-year probationary period as an assistant judge, in addition to the years already spent as a law student and the required four-year period as a judicial trainee without pay.[1] An assistant judge on probation had to work without the guarantee of judicial independence. This influenced future judges decisively in several respects. First of all, they were inevitably recruited from a certain social class, since only the very wealthy could afford what amounted to a twenty-year training period. (And until 1911, admission to candidacy for the judiciary in Prussia was limited to those who could make a deposit of 7,500 marks and demonstrate that they possessed the annual income of 1,500 marks "appropriate to the practice of the profession.")[2] In addition, judges could be dismissed at any time during their training and assistantship. This period offered ample opportunity to observe the candidates, to remove those elements associated with the opposition, and to suppress every liberal tendency. The only candidates who survived this ceaseless scrutiny were those who were loyal and compliant to a particularly high degree—those who, in other words, accepted the existing social and political order unconditionally.

The abolition in 1878 of all political limitations on admission to the bar had an indirect effect on the judiciary: judges with a liberal orientation could now escape the political pressure by resigning from office and working as attorneys.

State supervision of judges did not end with their appointment for life, however. Vacancies at high levels tended to be filled with public prosecutors of tested mettle. In contrast to judges, such men had been civil servants required to accept and follow instructions from their superiors in the government, who had learned in long years of service to obey. As "political appointees" the prosecutors could be sent into retirement at any time without explanation; for this reason, only one type of man tended to last in the profession—namely, the highly conservative new type of civil servant with extreme loyalty to authority. In his *History of Bourgeois Society,* Leo Kofler has provided a striking description of the thinking and behavior typical of this group: "A formalistic emphasis on duty, a false concept of honor (false because it led to a constant and often tragic conflict with life), spinelessness combined with a tendency to heroic posturing, rationalized sentimentality, and—a Prussian haircut."[3] Although public prosecutors constituted only about 8 percent of the higher ranks of the legal system, at the turn of the century the majority of presidents of higher courts were former prosecutors.[4] It was not until 1889 that the number of judgeships began to be increased, and the entire judiciary toward the end of the nineteenth century had as its preceptors and leaders those men who had been assistant judges during the eighties. The model for civil servants and public prosecutors was the officer in the reserves, that link between the liberal bourgeoisie and the feudal military state who developed into a symbolic figure of the Second Empire. "The liberal privy councillor had to disappear from the civil service," observed the historian Eckart Kehr, "and he disappeared with amazing speed . . . The inconsistency in this system lay in the fact that it could no longer do without the bourgeoisie to fill all the existing positions in the civil service and the army, but it allowed promotions to middle-class officials and officers only when they had renounced their bourgeois attitudes and taken on the neo-feudal way of thinking."[5]

Despite all the submissiveness toward state authority which has just been described, judges did remain formally independent of the government, unlike civil servants and military officers. And this was something they were made to feel. They ranked far below members of other branches of the government in social standing, as demonstrated by the fact that Jews, who were barred from entering the civil service and the army, were granted admission to the judiciary. Another example was the practice of awarding decorations, in which judges were classed with middle-level civil servants. The judiciary reacted to such discrimination not with protest and dissent, as one might expect, but rather with increased conformity, as if to prove that it merited greater confidence. This only speeded up the "metamorphosis from liberal dignitaries to officers in the reserves."[6]

Bismarck's personnel policies soon bore fruit. When the persecution of socialists began, the working classes came up against a judiciary which had largely closed ranks. The Social Democrats were questioning the existing political order, but judges identified themselves with it to such a degree that in a large number of criminal trials they were accused of dispensing "class justice"—a devastating but accurate criticism. It became almost obligatory for leaders of the workers' movement, from August Bebel and Wilhelm and Karl Liebknecht to Rosa Luxemburg, to stand trial for high treason.

Legal thinking in the days of the empire was dominated by a rigid theory of positivism that was supposedly free of all partisan taint and that claimed to have liberated the law "from the chains of doctrinaire politics."[7] Its main proponents, however, were well aware of the political significance of their theory when they issued warnings against democratic ideas ("every step in this direction would be a danger to the empire")[8] and propagated a "value-free" system of legal tenets. In the judgment of historian Heinrich Heffter, "Behind the neutral mask of positivism, the partisanship for the existing order of the constitutional monarchy is obvious."[9] The formalism favored by the positivist way of thinking and its strict refusal to go beyond the existing order increased judges' intellectual dependence on the state. "Independence in the administration of justice?" asks the legal sociologist Ernst Fraenkel in regard to the actions of judges of that era. "In theory no one ever doubted it; in practice no one ever strove for it."[10]

Nevertheless the old order, apparently so firmly established, was showing signs of decline long before the kaiser abdicated. As parliamentary influence on legislation grew, the initiative for new laws came more and more frequently from the Reichstag instead of from the government bureaucracy, and the judiciary reacted with loud antiparliamentary criticism. In the *Deutsche Richterzeitung,* the journal of the German Federation of Judges, leading figures expressed their "conviction that the administration of justice is being ruined by politics," that "logical argumentation . . . is not useful in parliaments," and that the activities of the legislative branch were characterized by "the most blatant dilettantism."[11] The judiciary as a whole stood solidly behind the monarchy, and when one of the men who spoke for the bench, Judge Max Reichert, proclaimed, "What the army is at our borders, our decisions must be within them!"[12] it was almost superfluous. The analogy was already valid. Even this, however, could no longer turn back the tide of history.

The Judges of the Weimar Republic

When the German Empire came to an end and a republic was declared by a Social Democrat, it was a terrible blow to the members of the judiciary who had been loyal monarchists. "Every majesty has fallen," lamented the chairman of the Federation of Judges, Johannes Leeb, "including the majesty of the law." In the laws of the republic he saw a "spirit of deceit," "a bastardized law of party and class."[1] All the same, the judiciary received guarantees of continuing independence and immunity from dismissal, while those judges whose conscience would not permit them to serve the republic instead of the kaiser were offered early retirement by the government, with full consideration of their material needs. Less than 0.15 percent of judges took advantage of this opportunity, however.[2]

In 1926 the president of the Supreme Court, Dr. Walter Simons, looking back on the time of the upheaval, commented: "In our country the judiciary of the monarchy entered the new state as a whole. The judges have placed themselves in the service of the new republic and sworn an oath of loyalty to the republic. They certainly have striven to keep that oath, but they would not and could not change their spirit under the new regime." Simons added, not without pride, that "judges are conservative."[3] The majority of them were now allied with the *Deutschnationale Volkspartei* (German National Popular party) at the right-wing end of the political spectrum; they kept their distance from the republic and continued to take what remained of the old values as their point of orientation. They were quite willing to accept the version of the end of the First World War favored in conservative circles, in which an army unbeaten in the field was defeated solely by sabotage on the home front (the notorious *Dolchstosslegende,* or "legend of the stab in the back"). They devoted themselves to eliminating this "enemy within."

Carl Schmitt—who can aptly be characterized as the "state thinker" of the Third Reich—was the first to make this polarized attitude of "friend or foe" respectable in scholarly circles. In 1927, in his book *Der Bergriff des Politischen* (The Concept of the Political), he expressed as no one else had how conservatives then understood politics. In his view, "the specifically political decision on which political actions and motives are based" was "the distinction between friend and foe." Its purpose was to characterize "the most extreme degree of intensity in a connection or a separation," for a political foe is "precisely that other, that alien being, and it suffices to identify his nature to say that he is existentially an other, an alien in a particularly intensive sense, so that in extreme cases conflicts with him are possible which can be decided neither by a previously determined general norm nor by the verdict of a third party who is not involved and therefore impartial"—that is, by neither law nor judicial decorum. According to this doctrine, the concepts of "friend, foe, and struggle" acquire "their real significance through the fact that they exist in a framework of the real possibility of physical killing."[4]

Schmitt had not invented this distinction, but had simply made use of his particular talent for putting the spirit of the times into words. Soon after the "revolutionary explosions set off in the muddy trenches of World War " (in the words of Otto Kirchheimer),[5] the courts set out to make this distinction between friend and foe. This did away with the distinction between loyal opposition and treason which had been one of the great achievements of the nineteenth-century legal system. The extent to which this occurred in Germany is demonstrated by the legal repercussions of two major political upheavals in the early years of the Weimar Republic: the declaration of the Socialist Republic in Munich in 1919, and the Kapp putsch of 1920.

The first prime minister of the People's Republic of Bavaria (*Volksstaat Bayern*), Kurt Eisner, an Independent Socialist, had proclaimed the republic in Munich in November 1918. On February 21, 1919, as he was on his way to the Bavarian parliament, he was murdered. Two weeks later a new government was formed by the Majority Socialist Johannes Hoffmann, but Eisner's supporters had been so radicalized by the assassination that they proclaimed the *Räterepublik*, the revolutionary government of workers' councils, on April 7. On April 14 the communists took over the government (the "second revolutionary republic"), forming a Red Army, and a Red Guard that was intended to take over the duties of the police. When not quite two weeks later the national government sent in troops "to restore order," the workers' government was already close to collapse under the pressure of its own internal disputes. Nevertheless, the government troops, operating under martial law, carried out so many murders and executions among the workers in Munich that their action amounted to a genuine bloodbath. Wilhelm Hoegner, then a public prosecutor in Bavaria, reports 1,100 deaths.[6] After this "white terror" ended, courts of martial law were set up in Bavaria and staffed with civilian judges; these courts continued to exist for all practical purposes even after martial law was lifted on July 19, 1919, and the tribunals were officially renamed "Bavarian People's Courts."[7] All the leaders of the revolutionary government who had survived the period of military intervention were summoned before this court in Munich and charged with high treason. According to official information later supplied to the Reichstag, the court sentenced one defendant to death and 2,209 to terms of imprisonment. Out of the total of 6,080 years of imprisonment imposed, 4,400 were actually served.[8]

The Kapp putsch of March 1920, the most serious instance of treason in the fourteen-year existence of the Weimar Republic, presents a striking contrast. Although the putsch forced the national government to flee from Berlin, brought the country to the brink of civil war, and resulted in the execution of two hundred people by firing squads, only one of its leaders was found guilty afterward, and he was given the minimum sentence: five years' confinement in a fortress (*Festungshaft*). [*Festungshaft*, the mildest form of sentence in the German legal system of that time, was a form of specifically "honorable arrest" (*custodia honesta*) in which the prisoner lost none of his privileges as a citizen (*bürgerliche Ehrenrechte*), such as the right to serve as an elected official, as a legal guardian, and as a witness in certain cases.—*Translator.*] At first, investigations were opened into 507 cases of suspected criminal offenses,[9] but an amnesty passed on August 4, 1920, led to the dropping of charges against most of the accused.[10] After several leaders of the putsch had been allowed to flee the country and Kapp had died in prison awaiting trial, the charges against General Ludendorff were also dropped, leaving only three men to face trial before the First Criminal Panel of the Supreme Court. These were the former chief of police in Berlin, Traugott von Jagow ("minister of the interior" in the Kapp cabinet), von Wangenheim ("minister of agriculture"), and a confidant of Kapp's named Dr. Schiele. The court then dropped the charges against von Wangenheim and Schiele, so that only von Jagow was actually sentenced.[11]

Besides the glaring disparity between the number of sentences passed, the two cases present a number of interesting contrasts. The amnesty law, for example, had been specifically worded to cover only those who had participated "in a treasonable undertaking against the national government," and thus excluded the leaders of the socialist republic in Bavaria who had led an uprising against a state government and were already serving their sentences. "Instigators or leaders of such an undertaking" were excluded from the general amnesty, however, so that several of the insurrectionists had to be classified as "followers" in order to qualify. These included General von Lettow-Vorbeck, who had placed the members of the provincial government of Mecklenburg under arrest and ordered several executions, and also Mayor Lindemann of the city of Kiel, who had served as governor of the province of Schleswig-Holstein during the putsch.[12] In the Munich trials, on the other hand, a tailor from the town of Rosenheim, whose sanity was clearly questionable and who after his sentencing sent an appeal for clemency to King Ludwig of Bavaria (although Bavaria had long since ceased to have a king), was promoted to a leader in the treasonable activities there.[13] Thus it emerged that the workers' republic in Bavaria had more than 2,200 "leaders," whereas the Kapp putsch was found by the courts to have had virtually no leaders at all.

In determining the sentences of political criminals, the courts customarily gave considerable weight to character and "motivation"; the relatively comfortable sentence of confinement in a fortress could be granted only when the accused had not acted from "dishonorable motives." Whereas 97 percent of the republicans sentenced in Munich were found to have had such dishonorable motives,[14] in von Jagow's trial even government prosecutor Ebermayer stressed the accused's "undoubtedly noble motives," and the judgment itself spoke warmly and enthusiastically of the way von Jagow had responded "to Kapp's summons . . . under the banner of selfless love for the fatherland."[15] Von Jagow was pardoned after three years. He then began a series of appeals to regain his right to a government pension as former chief of police and as president of the state government of Prussia under the monarchy. The pension had been canceled in accord with paragraph 7 of the Prussian Disciplinary Code, which prescribed the loss of either office or pension if an official was sentenced to more than one year in prison. After both the County Court and State Supreme court in Berlin had rejected his appeal, the third civil senate of the Supreme Court ordered the government of Prussia to pay the convicted insurrectionist the full amount of his president's pension retroactively.[16] In recognizing von Jagow's claim, the court argued that the original verdict in his criminal trial had not specifically named the loss of his office—and thus the loss of pension rights—as a part of the sentence. Such a specific mention would have been completely absurd, however, since the disciplinary code automatically provided for the loss of office if the verdict was guilty. General von Lüttwitz, the military leader of the putsch, even had the right to his pension granted retroactive to the time of the revolt itself, in spite of the fact that he had left his troops without permission after the putsch had failed and had fled to Sweden with a false passport.[17]

A widow in Kiel, on the other hand, whose husband had responded to the national government's appeal for help in opposing the coup and had been killed, was refused a pension. The decision of the Reich Pension Court of January 27, 1925, observed that it was the duty of "the police and, if necessary, the armed forces . . . to maintain public order" (although in this case it was the armed forces themselves that had created disorder with the putsch). Therefore, the deceased himself had to assume "responsibility for any damage or loss caused by his death," and all claims of his surviving relatives were thereby forfeited.[18] The county court in Schwerin even ruled after the putsch that the insurrectionists' executions of striking workers had not been illegal, since they had had "a lawful basis" in "the chancellor's Regulation No. 19 at the time."[19]

The Courts and the Nazi Movement

The courts had a first opportunity to show their sympathy with the young National Socialist German Workers' party (NSDAP) in the trial of Hitler and eight other Nazis after the attempted "beer hall putsch" of November 8–9, 1923.

The year 1923 was probably the most turbulent year of the Weimar Republic. Inflation had reached a peak. France had marched into the Ruhr region, and German nationalists were offering bitter resistance to the occupying troops. In the states of Saxony and Thuringia, the Social Democrats had formed coalition governments with the Communists. In Küstrin, special units belonging to the so-called Black *Reichswehr* attempted a coup. [These were army units formed secretly in violation of the Treaty of Versailles; see below.—*Translator.*] And in Bavaria, radical right-wing groups, such as the SA, the *Bund Oberland,* and the "Reich War Flag" were planning a march on Berlin to depose the government. [SA stands for *Sturmabteilung,* the "storm troopers" of the Nazi party.—*Translator.*] Bavaria proclaimed a state of emergency in which Gustav von Kahr was named as "State Commissar General." Since von Kahr was a monarchist and Bavarian separatist, it was feared that Bavaria might try to secede from the republic, and Chancellor Stresemann declared a state of emergency for the entire country. Von Kahr then refused to surrender his executive powers to the commander of the army in Bavaria, General von Lossow, and instructed the national troops stationed in the state to take their orders from the Bavarian government. He was determined to send troops to Berlin after invading Saxony and Thuringia and deposing the popular-front governments there headed by the Social Democrats. Only after the national government sent troops into Saxony and Thuringia and deposed these governments itself did von Kahr abandon his plans for a coup. This provided the immediate background for the beer hall putsch, since abandoning the coup was a move of which the radical right, and above all Adolf Hitler, then active in Munich, did not approve. On November 8 he and a band of armed supporters broke into a beer hall meeting where von Kahr was speaking. Firing a shot at the ceiling, Hitler declared the Bavarian government, the national government, and President Ebert deposed. The Bavarian politicians present in the hall made a show of going along with Hitler's demands, but after being allowed to leave they issued orders to put down the revolt. On November 9 a march to the large Field Warlords' Hall organized by radical rightist groups was stopped,[20] and Hitler and eight of his followers were arrested and charged with high treason. This trial opened on February 24, 1924, before the Munich People's Court. It had been preceded by a battle over jurisdiction between the central government and Bavaria, since legally the trial should have taken place before the State Court for the Protection of the Republic, in Leipzig. The Bavarian government wanted to hold the trial in Munich and offered a deal: if the national government agreed to transfer jurisdiction to Bavaria, the Bavarians would then agree, once the trial was over, to dissolve the People's Courts, which were unconstitutional.[21]

The trial before the Munich *Volksgericht* amounted to a display of strength by the radical right. The court failed to admonish the speakers when the national government was called a "Jew government" and its members "November criminals" (a reference to the declaration of the republic in November 1918). The president of the country was ridiculed as a "mattress engineer," and the defendants were permitted to describe everything in Berlin as *ver-Ebert und versaut*. [This phrase contains an untranslatable pun on the name of President Friedrich Ebert. The German word *Eber* means "boar," and the colloquial verb *versauen* contains the word *Sau* ("sow"), a term of abuse. *Versauen* means to make a complete mess of something. *Ver-Ebert and versaut* thus means "Ebert-ized and ruined."—*Translator.*] One of the defendants, Ernst Pöhner, a justice of the Bavarian Supreme Court and former chief of police in Munich, said openly during his testimony, "If what you are accusing me of is treason, then I've been at it for the last five years."[22]

The judgment handed down on April 1, 1924, acknowledged that all the defendants had "been guided in their actions by a purely patriotic spirit and the noblest of selfless intentions," and continued: "All the accused . . . were convinced, to the best of their knowledge and belief, that they had to act to save the fatherland . . . For months, even years, they had taken the position that the treason of 1918 required atonement through an act of liberation." The court therefore refused to deprive them of their citizens' privileges and sentenced Hitler and his comrades-in-arms Pöhner, Kriebel, and Weber to the minimum of five years' confinement in a fortress ("the minimum sentence provided for by law is already very ample . . . and constitutes a sufficient atonement for their crime"). It also imposed a fine in the ludicrous amount of 200 marks, since the portion of the law in question, paragraph 9 of the Law for the Protection of the Republic, provided that "every person found guilty of high treason is to receive a fine as well. The amount of the fine is not limited." The same law stated: "In the case of foreign nationals, the court must issue an order for deportation. Infringement of the deportation order is punishable by imprisonment."

In their decision, the judges offered Hitler the prospect of being paroled after serving only six months and of being able to consider the remaining four and a half years a suspended sentence. They did this in spite of the fact that the Nazi leader had already been given a suspended sentence for disturbing the peace and was still on probation; legally the court was required to revoke the suspension and sentence Hitler to serve the full time. As for the deportation order required in the case of a foreign national (Hitler was an Austrian citizen), the court specifically rejected it, stating, "In the case of a man whose thoughts and feelings are as German as Hitler's, the court is of the opinion that the intent and purpose of the law have no application."

Five of the other defendants, including the subsequent chief of staff of the SA, Ernst Röhm, and the subsequent minister of the interior, Wilhelm Frick, got off with fifteen months' fortress arrest and fines of 100 marks apiece. General Ludendorff—who was always addressed by the court as "Your Excellency" out of respect for his rank—was acquitted; once again, just as in the case of the Kapp putsch, the judges were willing to believe that "he was present at the site of the events"—in full uniform—"by pure chance."[23]

The degree of comfort in which Hitler and his party comrades spent the six months of their sentence at the fortress of Landsberg (which had been lavishly fitted out for Count Arco-Valley, the aristocratic assassin of Kurt Eisner) has been vividly described by the British historian Alan Bullock: "They ate well—Hitler became quite fat in prison—[and] had as many visitors as they wished . . . Emil Maurice acted partly as Hitler's batman, partly as his secretary, a job which he later relinquished to Rudolf

Hess, who had voluntarily returned from Austria to share his leader's imprisonment . . . On [Hitler's] thirty-fifth birthday, which fell shortly after the trial, the parcels and flowers he received filled several rooms. He had a large correspondence in addition to his visitors, and as many newspapers and books as he wished. Hitler presided at the midday meal, claiming and receiving the respect due to him as leader of the Party."[24]

In many trials in the years that followed, the courts continued to take the Nazi side of the ongoing political struggle, sometimes openly, sometimes behind the façade of legal maneuvers. One example was the trial of Nazi supporter General Litzmann, who at a public meeting in Dresden on May 27, 1930, concerning the Treaty of Versailles had shouted, "Unfortunately we lack the secret tribunals to wipe out the signers of this treaty." The court dropped the charges against him after he testified that this had been merely a slip of the tongue: he had actually meant to say that the "signatures" should be wiped out.[25]

In an inquiry into the activities of the subversive organization "Consul," the senior prosecutor Niethammer claimed, in spite of the fact that numerous "executions" by radical right-wing groups had come to light, that the slogan "Traitors will be dealt with by the Vehm" merely referred to "social ostracism." [In medieval Germany, "courts of the Vehm" were secret tribunals that frequently meted out death sentences. Like the yellow badges required to be worn by Jews for purposes of identification, the Vehm was one of the medieval practices revived by the Nazis.—*Translator.*] On the other hand, a Munich worker who had carried a sign saying "Workers, burst your chains!" at a demonstration was sentenced to five months in prison for "incitement to class hatred."[26] In another case a Nazi official named Kremser, who had claimed that the president's appeal for support in the signing of the Young Plan was "just as deceitful" as that of the German representatives at the surrender of 1918, was acquitted by the District Court of Glogau, on the grounds that the revolution of 1918 had been "perjury and treason."[27] [The Young Plan of 1929 revised the arrangements for payment of the German war reparations.—*Translator.*] Goebbels was also acquitted by the court in Berlin-Charlottenburg after he had labeled the members of the government "traitors to the people," "hirelings of international finance," and "deserters to the French." Another court in Hannover in 1930 had already declared his accusation of corruption on the part of Prussian premier Otto Braun to have been made "in the pursuit of legitimate interests."[28]

Judges also clearly aligned themselves with the Nazis in cases of clashes between their armed troops and supporters of the Weimar Republic. After one SA attack on members of the "Iron Front" (the paramilitary organization of the Social Democrats and trade unions) in Alfeld, for example, the Great Criminal Chamber of the Hildesheim County Court handed out prison sentences ranging from six to eight months to the National Socialists, while the Social Democrats were given twelve to twenty-four months and in one instance a penitentiary sentence for defending themselves.[29]

The courts of the Weimar era were not characterized solely by favorable treatment meted out to defendants from the radical right and by persecution of supporters of the republic and Communists, however. There was also the occasional but blatant and unmistakable anti-Semitic tone of the decisions of various courts, up to and including those at the highest level. The anti-Semitism was usually combined with hostility to republican ideas, as exemplified by the notorious phrase "Jew republic." The line of the Erhardt Brigade song, "We don't need any Jew republic! Shame, Jew republic!" was so popular in radical right-wing circles that it led to countless criminal charges, for the Law for the Protection of the Republic of July 21, 1922, had made it an offense "publicly to vilify the constitutionally established form of government."[30] [The Erhardt Brigade was a mutinous unit that attained notoriety in the Kapp putsch and in the reconquest of the Ruhr region in 1920. Former members of the unit murdered foreign minister Walter Rathenau in 1922.—*Translator.*] But after several lower courts had found that "Jew republic! Shame, Jew republic!" constituted such a vilification, the Supreme Court reversed these decisions on June 22, 1923, with a hair-splitting argument reflecting both anti-Semitic and antirepublican attitudes:

> The expression "Jew republic" can be used in different senses. It can designate the particular form of democratic republic which was "constitutionally established" by the Weimar National Assembly; it can also include the entire form of government which has existed in Germany since the violent upheaval of November 1918. It can denote the new legal and social order in Germany which was brought about in significant measure by German and foreign Jews. It can also denote the disproportionate power and disproportionate influence which, in the opinion of many citizens, a small number of Jews, relative to the total population, actually wields. The sense in which the accused used the expression "Jew republic" is not precisely established. It has not even been specifically determined that the accused vilified the constitutionally established form of government of the Reich, but only that they vilified the presently existing form of government.[31]

Judge Beinert of the Petty Court in Wernigerode put it even more clearly than the Supreme Court in a judgment of March 6, 1924, in which he himself came to the defense of a nationalistic newspaper editor and his associates: "The German people are coming to recognize more and more that the Jews bear the heaviest guilt for our misery. There can be no thought of improving the lot of our people if we do not crush the power of the Jews . . . The ideas put forth by the accused did not endanger our public order; far from it. Even the best men of our nation share this view." [32] When Prussian premier Otto Braun was characterized by a German Nationalist politician named Elze as a "shameless Judas Iscariot" and a man of "abysmal lack of character," the local court in Halle saw this as "the pursuit of legitimate interests" and found in favor of acquittal. [33] Finally, by February 1930, even the Supreme Court could no longer find anything libelous in the statement, "The Jew Rathenau is not a traitor." [34]

After a Jewish landlord in Berlin named Nordheimer had been called a "German swine" several times by one of his tenants, a foreigner, he gave the tenant notice and went to court to try to get him evicted. The Central Berlin Petty Court rejected the landlord's case, however, with the startling argument: "Despite his German citizenship, the plaintiff does not fall into the category of persons popularly connoted by the word 'German.'" [35] Prominent Jewish figures in government, who were favorite targets of Nazi propaganda attacks, were refused protection from libel by the courts, in opinions that were frequently more insulting than the original statements. The Nazi speaker Bernhard Fischer, for example, had claimed at a public meeting: "Chief Grzesinski [of the Berlin police] is a Jew bastard. He is the illegitimate son of a maid who worked for a Jew. Every person has his history written in his face." Fischer was at first found guilty of libel, but in his appeal before the country court of Neuruppin he was acquitted on September 1, 1932. The court admitted that the manner in which the accused had attacked the chief of police represented "the limit of what can be tolerated in debate between political parties," but it could not "recognize in the claim that someone was of illegitimate Jewish background any expression of contempt." [36]

When the last major trial of a group of Nazis accused of treason began before the Fourth Criminal Panel of the Supreme Court, which was responsible for political crimes, any remaining doubts about the attitude of most judges toward the National Socialist movement were removed. Between September 23 and October 4, 1930, the Supreme Court deliberated upon the case of three army officers stationed in Ulm (their names were Scheringer, Ludin, and Wendt) who had tried to create Nazi cells in various garrisons and to influence soldiers not to shoot at Nazis in the case of a new putsch attempt, but rather to refuse to obey orders or even to intervene on the Nazis' side. The trial received a great deal of publicity when the only witness called by the court to testify whether the NSDAP planned the violent overthrow of the government was Adolf Hitler. Hitler was thus given an opportunity to deliver a two-hour harangue before the Supreme Court. And even though the outcome of another trial was still pending in which Hitler himself was accused of spreading Nazi propaganda in the army, he was allowed to give sworn testimony on what amounted to a medieval "oath of purification."

When undersecretary Erich Zweigert of the Ministry of the Interior wanted to present as evidence a memorandum giving clear proof of various Nazi crimes and putsch plans, the judges refused to consider it, since this question (which they had sought to answer by summoning Hitler to testify) was "not of central importance for reaching a decision in the present case." Although Hitler's two-hour polemic against democracy was illegal under the Law for the Protection of the Republic, the court offered no objection. He was even permitted to make an undisguised threat: "When our movement is victorious, then a new Supreme Court will be assembled, and before this court the penalty will be exacted for the crime of November 1918. Then you may be sure heads will roll in the sand." [37]

The existing Supreme Court hastened to offer a reassuring interpretation of Hitler's words in its decision, stating that Hitler had "in mind that National Socialist court which would exercise its functions after coming to power in a legal manner." This "legality," which Hitler had guaranteed "in unambiguous words," appeared plausible to the court, since "Germany's growing sympathy with the popular liberation movement" made it "completely unnecessary" for him to consider "an illegal course." In a total reversal of its usual dry and reasoned style, the Supreme Court described Hitler's appearance with open enthusiasm: "The roars of Hitler's supporters who had assembled in the square outside to cheer him could be heard even inside the courtroom. Many people among the press and public were passionate in their defense of the accused, who were after all comrades of the witnesses and whose views the witnesses agreed with on many points. The great success of the National Socialists in the last [Reichstag] election, which they achieved shortly before the main trial opened, influenced the verdict of those associated with the trial and the public in favor of the accused." [38]

After this, it was hardly surprising that the three Nazi defendants got off with the mild sentence of eighteen months' imprisonment in a fortress, a judgment in which the Supreme Court attested to their "good intentions," "unblemished past record," "good qualities," and "noble motives." [39]

In the fall of 1931 the "legality" to which Hitler had sworn, and which the court was so willing to believe in, was revealed by a Social Democratic memorandum to be a fiction: the memorandum exposed the "legality" oath of the Nazi leader as obvious perjury. For the years 1930–31 alone, it documented 1,184 cases of Nazi violence, with 62 persons killed and 3,209 injured; in addition, that there had been 42 disrupted meetings, 26 attacks on trade union headquarters, and many desecrations of cemeteries.[40] Nevertheless, the courts persisted in their refusal to recognize the violent character of the National Socialist movement. In November 1931, after state legislature elections in Hessia, the police even seized a complete collection of detailed plans for another Nazi putsch. These "Boxheim Documents" showed that the Nazis had learned a lesson from their previous failures. The plans provided for a takeover of the entire government by the SA, the death penalty for all strikers and anyone refusing to comply with SA orders, the seizure by the SA of all private property, the introduction of compulsory military service from the age of sixteen, and numerous other unconstitutional actions. The admitted author was a young judge in Hessia, Dr. Werner Best. Hitler claimed to have had no knowledge of the documents. Even before proceedings were opened, the highest public prosecutor in the country, Reich prosecutor general Karl Werner, announced that it was doubtful whether the charge of high treason could be made at all, because the plans foresaw a Nazi seizure of power only in the event of a Communist uprising.[41] The preliminary investigation was lengthy, and on October 12, 1932, the Fourth Criminal Panel of the Supreme Court dropped the charges against Best "for lack of evidence regarding the accusation of high treason."[42] Judge Best, who had been only temporarily suspended from office, was not even removed from the bench. (During the Third Reich he rose to become chief counsel of the Gestapo and later Reich minister to occupied Denmark.)

The Decline of the Rule of Law

The support and preferred treatment accorded accused criminals who had acted from "nationalist" motives had disastrous political consequences, for they encouraged the radical right and undermined the confidence of the supporters of democracy. However, the related erosion of the law itself proved to have even more serious consequences.

According to the Treaty of Versailles, which was officially part of the corpus of German law and stood even above the constitution, the rearmament of Germany was subject to rigorous limitations. The law contained exact provisions concerning the equipment and training of the German army, which was not to exceed a strength of 100,000 men.[43] Yet the "new old army" (in the words of its chief, Hans von Seeckt) used every possible means to increase its strength, so as to be able to undo "the shameful decree of Versailles" with military force, should the opportunity present itself. It established illegal units (the Black *Reichswehr* mentioned above), included "volunteers" in maneuvers, maintained secret arsenals, and even built up an illegal air force. In all of these undertakings, the army leaders used clearly conspiratorial tactics. To ensure that their forbidden activities would not be "betrayed" to the Inter-Allied Military Commission, which the victors had set up in a supervisory capacity, they arranged to have suspected informers murdered. The civilian authorities, who were well informed about the illegal rearmament under way, covered up these assassinations to the best of their abilities. Nonetheless it was impossible to prevent some of these murders from coming to light, and legal investigations had to be opened. The killers' defense attorneys—some of whom went on to highly successful careers in the Third Reich—regularly entered a plea for acquittal, arguing that the accused had acted "in self-defense" and on behalf of the government, which was forbidden to take action by the peace treaty.

The doctrine that "defense of the state" or "national emergency" justified the defendants' actions had already been denounced long before by the prominent professor of constitutional law Georg Jellinek as "merely another way of stating the principle that might makes right."[44] But courts accepted it, up to and including the Supreme Court, which recognized at least in principle that belief in the existence of a state of national emergency could justify breaking the law. Yet at the same time the courts had eliminated the need for such a justification and shown that the government was by no means condemned to inaction when the illegal doings of the army became known.

The courts of those years presided over the trials of thousands of pacifists and republicans, who were accused of treason after exposing the army's unlawful activities. During the Weimar Republic, twice as many people were convicted of treason every year as in the entire thirty-two years preceding the First World War.[45] The legal scholar Emil Julius Gumbel characterized the simple and arrogant argumentation underlying these verdicts as follows: "(1) A Black *Reichswehr* has never existed. (2) It was disbanded long ago. (3) Anyone who mentions it is a traitor."[46] Virtually every prominent pacifist in Germany became a victim of this kind of treatment from the courts, including the two German Nobel peace laureates Ludwig Quidde and Carl von Ossietzky.

The Social Democratic party had pointed to the political consequences of such decisions as early as 1924. The Social Democratic members of the Reichstag warned the government that "administration of justice in this manner presents a danger to the republic, insofar as it enables subversive and monarchist organizations to amass weapons without giving that part of the population which supports democracy the possibility to defend itself or to insist on respect for the law."[47] The way these tactics also undermined the legal foundations of the government was even more serious. After the Supreme Court had recognized "defense of the state" as a justification for murder, the Frankfurt law professor Hugo Sinzheimer lodged an accurate protest against "the monstrous principle which this decision has dared to propose": "Such a decision does more than merely damage the legal order which judges are called upon to protect. This decision destroys it."[48]

The extent to which the Supreme Court helped destroy the rule of law becomes clear when the decisions involving nationalist "executions" are linked with the convictions of pacifist journalists for treason. The Supreme Court, with its own particular gift for suggesting connections, printed two decisions right next to each other in Volume 62 of its opinions; the first one again recognized "defense of the state" as a justification for a crime,[49] while the second found two journalists, Berthold Jacob and Fritz Küster, guilty of treason in what became known as the "pontoon case." The journalists had published an article entitled "The Temporary Volunteers' Grave in the Weser" in a pacifist journal called *Das andere Deutschland* (The Other Germany).

On March 31, 1925, during army maneuvers, eighty-one soldiers had drowned near Veltheim as they were attempting to cross the Weser River. Jacob had concluded from the obituaries published in two newspapers, *Der Jungdeutsche* (The Young German) and *Wiking* (Viking), giving some victims' civilian professions but no military ranks, that the group had included at least eleven temporary volunteers. This stood in contradiction to the public assurances of minister of defense Gessler and chancellor Hans Luther that there were no temporary volunteers. On the basis of three opinions from the Ministry of Defense on the necessity for keeping the existence of the illegal volunteers secret, the court sentenced Küster as author and Jacob as responsible editor to nine months' fortress arrest on March 14, 1928. The crucial passage of the decision, frequently cited later, ran: "Loyalty to his own country is required from every citizen. Protecting the welfare of his country is his first duty, whereas the interests of a foreign country must be disregarded. The observance and implementation of existing laws can occur solely through resort to the government institutions existing for this purpose."[50]

Alert legal experts recognized at the time just how far the Supreme Court had gone in perverting justice with its fatal message that the (presumed) interest of the state stood above the law. By implication, even the most heinous crimes were not punishable if they were committed in the interest of the state, while legal actions were punishable if they ran counter to it. Thomas Mann commented that such legal doctrines "ought to be left to fascist dictators,"[51] and law professor Gustav Radbruch had already warned in 1929 that with the help of the "national defense" doctrine, one could also justify the activities of "fascists who might attempt to rescue the state by force from the permanent emergency of its 'democratic-liberal' constitution."[52] In fact, the last chapter of Hitler's *Mein Kampf* was entitled "The Right of Self-Defense," and the emergency "Enabling Act" of 1933, called by Carl Schmitt "the temporary constitution of the Third Reich,"[53] was officially named the "Law to Remove the Danger to the People and the Reich."

In general, one may say that the doctrine of "national emergency" came to be used as a justification for everything the National Socialist regime did. The decision handed down in the "pontoon case" was repeatedly hailed as a "courageous step" which had "contributed to the victory of the new concept of the state over the letter of the law."[54] The fundamental legal principle of Nazi dictatorship—"Whatever benefits the people is right"—had been established by the highest courts in the land five years before the Nazis seized power, and National Socialist legal theorists liked to point later to the decisive role played by the venerable Supreme Court in creating "the new legal order, which has as its sole standard the welfare and security of the German people."[55]

· II ·

The German Legal System from 1933 to 1945

· 4 ·

The Reichstag Fire Trial

On January 30, 1933, the aging President Hindenburg appointed Adolf Hitler chancellor and requested him to form a coalition government. Hitler named a "national revolutionary" cabinet consisting of nine ministers with either a right-wing nationalistic orientation or no party affiliation, and only three Nazis—apart from Hitler himself, Wilhelm Frick as minister of the interior, and Hermann Göring as minister without portfolio. In actual fact, the Nazis were in a far stronger position than appeared at first sight, however. After the army, the Prussian police constituted the second-largest armed force in the country, and since the Nazis had "purged" it of virtually all democratic elements in the summer of 1932 and placed it under the command of Göring (who at the same time was acting minister of the interior in the Prussian state government), the Nazis had more power concentrated in their hands than the nine conservative ministers together. On the day after Hitler's appointment, Hindenburg gave him the authority to dissolve the Reichstag and call for new elections. In practical terms, the dissolution of the legislature enabled the Nazis to issue emergency decrees according to Article 48 of the constitution and thus create a dictatorship, for the Reichstag could have invalidated all such measures had it still been in office. Only five days after coming to power Hitler's government issued the "Decree for the Protection of the German People," [1] which required political organizations to report all meetings and marches in advance and allowed the police to forbid meetings, demonstrations, and pamphlets at will—and this in the middle of an election campaign! Three weeks later, on the evening of February 27, just when the campaign was at its height, the Reichstag building went up in flames. Shortly after the fire broke out, Marinus van der Lubbe, an unemployed Dutch construction worker, was arrested not far from the site.

Virtually every other circumstance connected with the Reichstag fire is still in dispute today, and there is scarcely any other topic debated so heatedly by historians. The two camps into which this question has divided the experts are by now so furiously embroiled that the various allegations, defamations, and calumnies have themselves become the subject of lawsuits. The only matter on which the authorities agree is that van der Lubbe played a role in setting the fire. There is considerable evidence to support the view that it was not the work of a single person, however.[2]

Hurrying to the scene, the Nazi leaders quickly agreed that it must be the work of the Communists, who wanted to give the signal for an uprising. This version, which the Nazis proceeded to disseminate, had nothing to back it up. The "evidence," such as the documents supposedly found at Karl Liebknecht House, the Communist party headquarters, proved to be such an obvious forgery that it had to be withdrawn. There was much more to support the plausible theory published by the Communists in their *Brown Book on the Reichstag Fire and Hitler's Terror*[3]—namely, that the Nazis themselves were responsible for the arson. Today it is extremely difficult to determine to what extent the official investigation led by Göring was slanted toward presenting the fire as the work of a group, so as to be able to fix the blame on the Communists. However, such an attempt would in all likelihood have boomeranged—as the Nazis must have realized—and would have directed suspicion back on themselves. Undersecretary Herbert von Bismarck of the Prussian Ministry of the Interior, is supposed to have surmised in the presence of officers of the Berlin Fire Department "that the Nazis themselves" were "the perpetrators of the fire," and to have found confirmation of this view in the behavior of Hitler, Göring, and Goebbels during a conference on the very same night.[4] Later, an old World War I comrade of Göring's is supposed to have bragged to a group of pilots about having set the fire.[5]

Today historians and objective witnesses concur that the Communists and Social Democrats can be ruled out as possible perpetrators. The speed with which the National Socialists proceeded to use the fire to their own advantage suggests at the very least that the roundup of political opponents beginning the same night had been planned well in advance. The question of who profited from the burning of the Reichstag pointed automatically to the Nazis, since it offered them the opportunity and excuse to abolish the existing parliamentary democracy. And last but not least, they had cloaked all of their previous putsch attempts in the guise of an "emergency defense plan" to hinder a Communist uprising. Whether or not they were in fact behind the Reichstag fire, it was the long-awaited signal for action. In an unprecedented move, the offices of the Communist party were occupied, its assets seized, and its leaders arrested. The lists of those to be arrested, obviously prepared ahead of time, included not only Communists, however, but also Social Democrats, pacifists, and leftist writers—that is to say, political foes of every stripe.

By the next morning, February 28, the Reichstag Fire Decree ("Decree for the Protection of the People and the State") was published, one of the main legal foundations of National Socialist rule.[6] It offered the government, at the height of the election campaign, not only further powers to shut down the presses of the left-wing parties, to forbid every publication by the opposition, to break up campaign rallies, and to arrest opponents at will; it also annulled almost all of the basic rights guaranteed by the constitution. Also, during the same night, the decree prohibiting "disloyalty to the German people and treasonable activities" was formulated, which increased the penalties for treason and betrayal of military secrets and intentionally blurred the distinction between criticism of the government and treason. The mere spreading of "rumors or false reports"—such as the allegation that the Nazis had set fire to the Reichstag—was now a treasonable offense. Among the "treasonable activities" to which severe penalties were attached, there now numbered the "production, dissemination, or storing of writings" that called for uprisings or strikes or that were "in other ways treasonable."[7]

In this manner, every voice of protest and every attempt at resistance in the face of the terror after the Reichstag fire were quashed "entirely legally." The fire represented the decisive development on the way to the actual takeover, since Hitler was far from having acquired unlimited powers on being appointed to head the government. To begin with, he was merely the twenty-first chancellor of the postwar era; the Nazis seized total control only by means of a series of putsch-like actions, the most important of which were the decrees following immediately upon the Reichstag fire. In retrospect, the Enabling Act proved to be only a consistent further step in the unfolding of events.

After the government had instituted a gigantic propaganda campaign to spread the theory of the planned Communist uprising, it naturally had to come up with further "perpetrators" in addition to van der Lubbe. On February 28, the Chairman of the Communist party delegation in the Reichstag, Ernst Torgler, had presented himself at police headquarters after reading in the morning papers that he was suspected of arson. On March 9, Georgi Dimitrov, Blagoi Popov, and Vassily Tanev, three Bulgarian exiles who had been living in Berlin under assumed names, were arrested on suspicion of complicity. The journalist Carl von Ossietzky, who had been taken into "preventive detention" on the night of the fire, was also originally included as an accessory to the crime.[8] The evidence assembled by Rudolf Diels, then chief of the political police, from the unreliable statement of a police informer and a false photograph was so obviously trumped up, however, that the chief public prosecutor was forced to drop the charges against him. Van der Lubbe, Torgler, Dimitrov, Popov, and Tanev were detained pending their trial; Paul Vogt, a judge of the Supreme Court, was placed in charge of the preliminary investigation. The case was assigned to the Fourth Criminal Panel of the Supreme Court in Leipzig, which was responsible for cases of high treason; this was the same senate that had found Ossietzky guilty in the *"Weltbühne* trial" (*World Stage* trial)[9] and had allowed Hitler to swear his legality oath in the trial against the three army officers from Ulm.

The preliminary investigation took a one-sided course from the start. Judge Vogt carefully followed his instructions not to search among the Nazis for any possible conspirators, and as they waited for the trial, the accused were subjected to various hardships not prescribed in the penal code, such as being kept chained day and night for the entire six-month period, on Vogt's orders.[10]

Only after many requests did Dimitrov obtain permission to be released from his chains for half an hour each day. So much pressure was put on his attorney, a man named Wille, that he eventually gave up the case. Numerous offers of foreign attorneys to represent the defendants were refused, although allowing foreigners to participate in the trial would have been perfectly legal. Finally the defense was taken over by court-appointed attorneys, who had the full confidence of the judges, if not their clients. Judge Vogt remained in close contact with the Prussian state government, and urged the need for ensuring that "reliable" judges were assigned to the panel that would hear the case.[11]

A week before the trial, which was scheduled to open on September 21, an independent commission met in London to investigate the circumstances of the fire; it was composed of eight prominent jurists, and the inquiry was followed closely by the press. The commission reached the conclusion that van der Lubbe could not possibly have set the fire on his own, that the accused Communists had nothing to do with it, and that the other conspirators should probably be sought in the National Socialist camp.[12] Afterward a "countertrial" took place in London simultaneously with the actual trial. In mock courtroom proceedings a great deal of testimony was heard, including some from prominent Germans who had had to flee abroad to escape Nazi persecution. The judgment reached by this group and published on December 20, 1933, stated: "(1) Lubbe did not act alone. (2) There is grave suspicion that the arson was ordered and carried out by National Socialist circles. (3) The Communists are not guilty. (4) The law of February 28, 1933 (the "Reichstag Fire Decree"), is invalid. (5) Conviction of Torgler would evoke worldwide protest."[13]

In addition to abolishing most of the basic rights guaranteed by the Weimar constitution, the Reichstag Fire Decree had imposed the death penalty for arson, treason, and several other crimes. A further law of March 29 concerning the imposition and implementation of the death penalty applied specifically to crimes "committed in the period between January 31 and February 28."[14] For such crimes, this law also permitted the government to pass a sentence of death by hanging, which was considered a particularly dishonorable form of execution. In this way the "legal" framework was created which would make it possible to execute the Reichstag arsonists.

The main trial began on September 21 in the large courtroom of the Supreme Court in Leipzig. Senior Public Prosecutor Werner and County Court Judge Parrisius, who later became deputy chief prosecutor at the "People's Court" (*Volksgericht*) during the war, acted as counsel for the prosecution. On October 10 the trial was moved to Berlin, into the undamaged room of the Budget Committee in the Reichstag itself, in order to convene for six weeks at the scene of the crime.

Among the witnesses called to give evidence by the prosecution were Joseph Goebbels, who had been named Reich minister of propaganda in March, and Hermann Göring, who had in the meantime advanced to become premier of Prussia. The high points of the trial were the verbal exchanges between the quick-witted defendant Dimitrov and the two Nazi leaders. Even the usually self-controlled Göring began to lose his composure on the witness stand. When Dimitrov asked him whether the investigation of the fire had not been designed to erase all traces that might lead in another direction, Göring offered a furious denial that simultaneously proved Dimitrov's point: "For me it was a political crime and I was also convinced that the criminals had to be looked for in your Party. Your Party is a Party of criminals which must be destroyed! And if the hearing of the Court has been influenced in this sense, it has set out on the right track."

As the dispute went on, Göring's temper went further and further out of control: "I shall tell you what is known to the German people. The German people know that you are behaving insolently here, that you came here to set fire to the Reichstag. But I am not here to allow you to question me like a judge and to reprimand me. In my eyes you are a scoundrel who should be hanged."

By this point at the very latest, Dr. Bünger, the presiding judge and president of the panel, ought to have intervened and warned the witness that he could not be permitted to insult the accused in this manner and even threaten him with the gallows. However, Bünger reprimanded not Göring, but the defendant: "Dimitrov, I have already told you not to make Communist propaganda here. That is why you should not be surprised if the witness is so agitated. I most strictly forbid this propaganda! You can only ask questions referring to the trial."

The debate escalated even further. When Dimitrov replied to Göring's explanations with a smile and the words "I am highly pleased with the reply of the Prime Minister," Bünger intervened again, saying, "Whether you are pleased or not is quite immaterial. Now I deprive you of the right to speak." When Dimitrov persisted that he wished "to put one more question relevant to the trial," Bünger became clearly nervous and repeated, "I deprive you of the right to speak," while Göring shouted, "Get out of here, you scoundrel!" Dimitrov turned one last time to the witness, saying mildly, "You are probably afraid of my questions, Mr. Prime Minister?" At this point Göring finally exploded: "Be careful, look out! I shall teach you how to behave—just come out of the courtroom! Scoundrel!" Instead of reprimanding Göring for this unveiled threat, the judge resorted to a procedure not yet included in the regulations and barred Dimitrov from the court for three days: "Dimitrov is . . . barred for three days! Remove him at once!" [15]

It was obvious to every unprejudiced observer and to the members of the international press present at the trial during these scenes how nervous the Nazi leadership had become, and it was impossible to overlook how the court was hopelessly failing to meet the Nazis' expectations and simultaneously to preserve a shred of its own dignity in the public eye.

The considerable amount of testimony presented offered no evidence that the Bulgarian exiles had participated in setting the fire. In the end, the prosecution itself was forced to enter a plea for their acquittal, but the chief public prosecutor demanded the death penalty for Torgler and van der Lubbe.[16] The case assembled against Torgler in the course of the trial, however, had been revealed as a web of vague suspicions combined with the fiction—propagated by the Supreme Court even in the days of the Weimar Republic—that the Communist party was always planning a revolution and that every Communist activity thus constituted a preparation for treason. Pamphlets calling for a united front and a "struggle outside the institutions" and carrying Torgler's signature were the sole evidence the prosecution could muster for the charge of "continued treason." But try as they might, the prosecutors could not establish any connection between Torgler and the burning of the Reichstag. And as far as van der Lubbe was concerned, the evidence had shown that he had once been a member of the Communist party in Belgium, but that he had resigned long ago and could not be proved to have had any contact whatsoever with Communists in Germany.

Dimitrov, Popov, and Tanev received the expected acquittal, and Torgler could not be convicted. In spite of the fact that all the Communist defendants had been cleared, however, the judges still managed the difficult feat of laying the blame for the fire on the Communists in their written opinion: "Even though . . . the defendants Torgler and the Bulgarians could not be convicted as accessories, nonetheless no doubt exists as to the camp in which these accessories were to be found . . . The burning of the Reichstag was undoubtedly a political act. The enormity of the crime—that is to say, of the means—points to the importance and violence of the goal. This can only have been the seizure of power . . . The crime can only be the work of radical left-wing elements, who hoped to exploit it for the purpose of overthrowing the government and the constitution, and seizing power . . . The Communist party has proclaimed such treasonable goals as its program. It was the party of treason."

In contrast, the court sought to dispel the obvious suspicion that the arsonists had been the Nazis themselves: "As Minister Goebbels correctly stated in his testimony, the National Socialist party could already be assured of success in the upcoming elections before March 5, due to its already dominant position and swift growth. It had no need to improve its election prospects by means of a crime. The party's ethical principles of restraint preclude the very possibility of such crimes and actions as are ascribed to them by unprincipled agitators."[17]

What the members of the court had obviously failed to note was that in the election of March 5, 1933, the National Socialists—despite the muffling of the left, massive manipulations, brutal acts of violence against the Communists, and ceaseless propaganda—had won only 43.9 percent of the vote and had failed to gain a clear majority. They could in no way have been "assured of success." Given the terror that NSDAP had unleashed on the whole country in 1933, the hundreds of murders and thousands of illegal arrests, the crushing of all opposition and ruthless suppression of freedom, the court's reference to the party's "ethical principles of restraint" sounded almost like satire.

The remaining defendant, van der Lubbe, was condemned to death "for high treason in combination with arson for the purposes of agitation." Since this sentence was possible only with the aid of an *ex post facto* law, the judges felt that justification was necessary. Thus, they argued that the Enabling Act had given the government the power to make laws, including ones that would alter the constitution. [Officially entitled the "Law to

Remove the Danger to the People and the Reich" the Enabling Act of March 23, 1933, gave the government emergency powers to circumvent the legislature.—*Translator.*] Beyond this, however, the death sentence for van der Lubbe did not constitute a breach of the fundamental principle "no punishment without law" (*nulla poena sine lege*), since this referred solely to whether an action was punishable or not, and arson had been a punishable offense even before the Reichstag fire. In this case the only retroactive provision of the law was an increase in the penalty, and this could be altered by the government at any time without violating constitutional principles. Otto Kirchheimer, an authority on constitutional law who later emigrated to the United States, wrote in 1935: "Only with the help of such murderous interpretations were the executions of political opponents possible." His prediction that "the jurists of the Third Reich— theorists and practitioners—would one day be called to account" for them[18] proved to be false, however.

Opinion about the decision was divided and remains so to this day— presumably because, among other reasons, the government appeared dissatisfied with the result. The official organ *Nationalsozialistische Parteikorrespondenz* (National Socialist Party Correspondence) spoke of a "clear miscarriage of justice,"[19] and the Nazi newspaper *Völkischer Beobachter* (People's Observer) reported the decision under the headline: "Last Attempt to Overcome an Outmoded Legal System: A National Socialist Germany Will Know What Conclusions to Draw."[20] Hitler later referred in private to the trial's "laughable outcome."[21] In the face of these reactions, the court's decision must appear as a courageous act of resistance to those in power at the time, and it is presented as such in virtually all of the legal literature on the subject.

It should be realized, however, that the reactions of the National Socialists were hypocritical in the extreme. The public prosecutor—a civil servant bound to follow instructions from the government—had pleaded for acquittal of the three Bulgarians himself; and given the magnitude of the Reichstag fire trial, it is inconceivable that he would have made this decision without consulting higher authority. It is known that the trial was discussed in several cabinet meetings. The trial received so much international publicity that the Third Reich was forced not to deviate too far from internationally accepted legal standards; one purpose of it, after all, was to prove that the accusations about the illegality of the new German regime were false. The proceedings were clearly on a different level from those at the "People's Court" later; but nonetheless, in its preparation and handling of the Reichstag fire case, the German Supreme Court permitted polemics against the Communists, kowtowed to the new rulers in their written opinion, and imposed a flagrantly illegal death sentence on Marinus van der Lubbe. As the Berlin County Court ruled forty-seven years later, this constituted a "political perversion of justice" to the advantage of the National Socialists.[22]

5

Jurists "Coordinate" Themselves

The German Federation of Judges

In his New Year's greetings to his associates in the first 1933 issue of the *Deutsche Richterzeitung* (German Judicial Journal), the chairman of the German Federation of Judges, Karl Linz, had expressed his fear that positive developments were hardly to be expected that year: "rather, all signs point to new attacks and new struggles to maintain the rule of law and an independent legal system."[1] The federation of Judges had always protested alterations in the system under the republic and had fought against "the intrusion of politics into the administration of justice." In 1926 the president of the Supreme Court, Walter Simons (who had been appointed on the suggestion of a Social Democratic minister of justice by a Social Democratic president), even went so far as to dispute the suitability of Social Democrats for the judiciary in general, since they lacked the necessary objectivity.[2] The judges' organization feared nothing so much as democrats getting the upper hand through "preferential treatment of supporters of the parties making up the cabinet."[3]

In a number of decisions the existence of sympathy with the National Socialist movement had become too obvious to be overlooked; however, the appointment of Hitler as chancellor did not meet with undivided approval among judges. Chairman Karl Linz feared the new government might introduce measures "placing in question the security of judges' tenure in office and the independence of the courts."[4] The behavior of the Nazi party leadership after various party members had been placed on trial gave these fears a very real basis in fact.

The majority of German judges soon resolved their doubts, however, in spite of the "Decree for the Protection of the German People" and the "Decree for the Protection of the People and the State" (also known as the Reichstag Fire Decree), by means of which, as we have seen, the government had abrogated in coup-like fashion large parts of the constitution. And despite the terror tactics of the SA during the March election campaign of 1933 and the putsch-like maneuvers enabling the SA to take control of the police in most German states, the governing board of the Federation of Judges issued a declaration on March 19 expressing approval of "the will of the new government to put an end to the immense suffering of the German people" and offered its cooperation in the "task of national reconstruction": "May German law hold sway in German domains! German judges have always been loyal to the nation and aware of their responsibility." The declaration ended with the assurance: "German judges place their full confidence in the new government."[5]

This confidence would not easily be shaken. On April first, as part of a concerted action against Jews, the state ministries of justice suspended from duty all Jewish judges, public prosecutors, and district attorneys, and this was followed on April 7 by the "Law for Restoration of the Professional Civil Service" decreeing the permanent removal from the civil service of all judges and other officials who were Jews, Social Democrats, or otherwise "politically unreliable."[6] Nevertheless, although this was tantamount to destroying the independence of the courts, Linz announced after an audience with Hitler on precisely this seventh of April: "We have placed everything in his hands with complete confidence. The chancellor was clearly in agreement with out remarks and assured us that he would continue to maintain the independence of judges, even though certain measures would be necessary. We may therefore rest assured that the regulations contained in the law on the civil service will be dropped again as soon as possible."[7]

These servile words were the extent of the protest ventured by the Federation of Judges on the removal from office of its numerous Jewish members—643 in Prussia alone. A number of people were quite glad to see the Social Democrats go, and the banning of the Republican Federation of Judges was received in judicial circles with great satisfaction. Only very few Social Democrats had succeeded in becoming judges in the fourteen years of the republic in any case, and it was even more difficult for them to rise to the higher ranks. Among the 122 judges belonging to the various panels of the Supreme Court, only one, Hermann Grossmann, was a Social Democrat, and he was the sole member of this court to be dismissed in April 1933 for political unreliability.[8]

While the governing board of the national federation was still engaged in tactical attempts to preserve its independence by ingratiating itself with the new regime, on April 21 its largest state organization, the Association of Prussian Judges and Public Prosecutors, came out with an appeal to its members "to enter the front line of Adolf Hitler's ranks and join the Federation of National Socialist Jurists, for unconditional solidarity is a necessity for the success of our struggle." [9]

The board of the national federation hesitated a little longer, but more and more state organizations followed the Prussian lead. The Oldenburg Judges' Association voted to disband itself on April 29; on May 10 the officers of the Association of Supreme Court Judges resigned on "for the purposes of coordination" (Gleichschaltung); and on May 21 the Saxon Association of Judges and Public Prosecutors placed itself "jubilantly and dutifully under the leadership of the people's chancellor, Adolf Hitler." [10] At this point the leaders of the national organization finally sent a telegram to the "leader of jurists in the Reich" (Reichsjuristenführer), Hans Frank, declaring in its own name and the name of its member organizations in the various states "its entrance as a body into the Federation of National Socialist Jurists" and acknowledging "the leadership of chancellor Adolf Hitler." [11]

That this patronage would have consequences for the workings of the legal system was made clear only two weeks later in a declaration passed by delegates to a meeting of the national organization: "The German Federation of Judges sees as its main task . . . the cooperation of all judges in the revision of German law . . . Free of all shackles, as befits the Germanic ideal, judges must remain beyond the reach of the spirit of trade unionism and narrow professionalism." [12] As long as the federation's publication, the Deutsche Richterzeitung was permitted to exist—it was later absorbed by the official government organ Deutsche Justiz—it became a forum for judges' proposals as to what form the revision of the law should take. One example was Supreme Court judge Erich Schultze's suggestion as early as 1933 that there should be severe penalties for "betrayal of the race . . . that is, in short, the interbreeding of Germans with members of certain races named by law." [13] A further clear sign of how far "coordination" had proceeded was the oath taken at a mass meeting held in front of the Supreme Court building during the first national convention of jurists in Leipzig in October 1933: 10,000 lawyers swore, with their right arms raised in the Nazi salute, "by the soul of the German people" that they would "strive as German jurists to follow the course of our Führer to the end of our days." [14]

There had been a few jurists among the "old guard" of the National Socialist movement: one of the "martyrs of the movement" killed during the march to the Feldherrnhalle on November 9, 1923, had been a judge at the Bavarian Supreme Court, and another of the judges from the same court was a codefendant of Hitler's at the ensuing trial. In general, however, lawyers as a professional group had been underrepresented in the party. And among those who rose to prominence in the Third Reich, there were only a handful of "old" Nazis: Judge Werner Best, author of the "Boxheim Documents," after 1933 chief counsel of the Gestapo, and Reich minister to occupied Denmark during the war; attorney Hans Frank, who became minister without portfolio in the national cabinet in 1934, president of the Academy for German Law, and after 1939 governor general of occupied Poland; attorney Roland Freisler, made a senior official at the Prussian Ministry of Justice in 1933 and at the national ministry in 1934, and from 1942 president of the People's Court; Hans Kerrl, Prussian minister of justice in 1933–1934 and afterward Reich minister for church affairs until his death in 1941; and finally Otto Thierack, a public prosecutor who first became minister of justice in Saxony in 1933, then vice-president of the Supreme Court, then president of the People's Court in 1936 and after 1942 Reich minister of justice.

During the Third Reich, as in previous years, the courts remained the domain of those who had been right-wing German nationalists. Freisler and Thierack were the only out-and-out Nazis who obtained key posts in the legal system. All the other highest officials, including Franz Gürtner, the minister of justice who died in 1941, his undersecretary Schlegelberger, Supreme Court president Bumke, and Reich prosecutor general Karl Werner, had been either members or sympathizers of the *Deutschnationale Volkspartei* (German National People's Party). All of them had attained high office in the days of the Weimar Republic. The Third Reich had merely taken them over, and they embodied a continuing tradition in German law extending from the empire through the republic to the government of the Führer. Although their actions in the twelve years of the Third Reich may have been frequently prompted by opportunism, ambition cannot have been a motive. Their careers had been made before.

The Highest Judge

Erwin Konrad Eduard Bumke was born to affluent parents—his father was a physician—on July 7, 1874, in the Pomeranian town of Stolp. After finishing his schooling, completing his university studies with a doctorate in law, and passing the two-stage German bar examination, he obtained a position as judge at the County Court in the city of Essen.

Since he was intelligent, ambitious, financially independent, and also strictly conservative in his political views, Bumke's career advanced swiftly. As early as 1907 he became a provisional assistant at the Office of Judicial

Affairs (*Reichsjustizamt*)—which would later be known as the Ministry of Justice—and by 1909 he was appointed to the rank of privy councillor there. After serving in the First World War, at the end of which he held the rank of captain in the militia, he returned to the ministry, now under a democratic government, and was made head of a department in 1920. In this capacity he drafted several emergency decrees that had a profound effect on German law and, according to critics at any rate, threw the conduct of criminal trials back to the days before the Enlightenment. When Supreme Court president Walter Simons took early retirement in 1929, Bumke was named to succeed him. At the same time he became presiding judge of the Third Criminal Panel of this court, president of the Combined Panels, and chairman of the State Court for the German Reich.[15] After Chancellor von Papen had ousted the Social Democratic government of the state of Prussia on July 20, 1932, the Supreme Court under Bumke's leadership first held up deliberation of the suit the Social Democrats had filed against this move, and then issued a scandalous decision declaring the eviction of the government to be legal for the most part. This move created favorable conditions for the National Socialist takeover: when Hitler became chancellor and appointed Hermann Göring as acting minister of the interior in the Prussian government, Göring thereby became head of the Prussian police, which had played such an important role in the power struggles of the Weimar Republic. As has been mentioned, this police force was by 1933 already largely "purged" of democratic elements and was prepared for the coming internal political battles.

In December 1932, Judge Bumke received yet another promotion when he was named deputy to *Reichspräsident* Hindenburg; this was largely an honorary title, but it made him—according to official protocol, at least—the second most important man in the country. When the Nazi takeover followed and the tactics to intimidate its opponents grew more and more brutal, Bumke is said to have been "most deeply concerned" and to have been thinking about resigning."[16] Yet he was never indignant enough to take a public stand against what was happening, even though he was far from the sort of man to swallow everything without protest. In a letter to the State Chancery, he had once actually threatened to resign. This letter contained the courageous words, "It is almost more than I can bear to think that my name will be connected with a period in the history of the Supreme Court which means its downfall." Bumke's protest was not directed against the dismissal of his Jewish colleagues on the bench, however, or against the "coordination" of the legal system with Nazi principles, or against the murder of opponents of the regime. And the letter was not written in 1933, but in January of 1932—to protest the plans contained in Chancellor Brüning's economy measures for limiting the extremely high pensions of retired Supreme Court judges to a maximum of 12,000 marks a year. For Bumke at that time, it was "almost an impossibility to remain the highest judge of a government which has departed so far from legal principles as would be the case if the law to reduce pensions were to pass." [17]

After the Nazis had had time to consolidate their rule and after "law and order" had returned to the Third Reich, Bumke, who had been a member of the German National People's Party, joined the NSDAP in 1937. Only a year later he was awarded the golden party badge. Bumke enjoyed Hitler's confidence to such a degree that not only was he made chairman of the "Special Panel" ("the Führer's Court," as it proudly called itself), which dealt with all of the special appeals lodged in the Führer's name in criminal cases; in addition, a special decree of July 4, 1939, exempted him from retirement at the age of sixty-five, allowing him to remain in office for another three years or even longer. Bumke proved to be worthy of such confidence in every respect, as we shall see. For now, it suffices to mention his extreme interpretation of the Race Laws, his "correction" of other courts' valid verdicts, and his participation in a meeting of the leaders of the German legal system to discuss the procedures for the mass murder of the handicapped. On April 20, 1945, as the U.S. Army was taking Leipzig, Judge Dr. Dr. Hon. Erwin Bumke committed suicide.

The State Thinker

Carl Schmitt was born on July 11, 1888, in Plettenberg in the Sauerland. His father was a merchant. After studying law in Berlin, Munich, and Strassburg under Max Weber and others, he wrote a thesis on a topic in criminal law and received a doctorate from the University of Strassburg. In 1916 he completed his *Habilitation* (a further examination qualifying a candidate for the rank of full professor), also in Strassburg, and became a full professor of public law at the University of Greifswald in 1921. In 1922 he moved to the University of Bonn and in 1926 to the Commercial College of Berlin. He owed his appointment to a professorship at the University of Cologne in 1933 largely to the efforts of a Jewish colleague, Hans Kelsen, whose views on political theory were the antithesis of Schmitt's. Soon afterward Schmitt took the lead in driving Professor Kelsen out of the university. [18] When the Social Democratic Prussian government filed a suit with the Supreme Court against its ouster by Chancellor von Papen in July 1932, Schmitt was placed in charge of the national government's case, and he went on to become a close political friend and adviser of Papen's successor in office, General von Schleicher. After the Nazis seized power, Göring, who was all-powerful in Prussia, obtained a chair for Schmitt at the University of Berlin and named him a Prussian privy councillor. Schmitt turned his back on the former conservative friends who had furthered his career and joined the Nazi party on May 1, 1933, barely escaping the ban on new members that went into effect for several years. The writer Ernst Niekisch has provided an excellent psychological portrait of Schmitt containing a comment on this move: "Hitler had barely got in, when Schmitt was ready: he slipped through the gates of the Third Reich just before they closed, so that he could not be overlooked when they needed a star jurist. Schmitt always managed to be a nose ahead of political developments, to an amazing degree. As a result he became something like the intellectual 'billeting officer' of the movement, coming in and setting up camp with such prudence and foresight that he earned the gratitude of the movement at every stage of the bourgeois restoration, while at the same time he always secured an advantageous position for himself."[19] Within the Nazi organization known as the *Rechtswahrerbund* (Federation of the Guardians of the Law), Schmitt chaired the section of university professors; he served as editor of several scholarly journals and monograph series. Above all, however, as the teacher of Ernst Forsthoff, Ernst Rudolf Huber, and Theodor Maunz, the leading National Socialist professors of constitutional law, he was the originator of the "new" doctrine in this field.

To be sure, Schmitt could never completely shake off his past. Radical Nazi circles never forgave him the close contacts he had had with Jewish scholars: not only some of his benefactors but also some of his students had been Jews. The SS and its newspaper *Das Schwarze Korps* (The Black Corps) remained suspicious of his Catholicism and "reactionary" past association with chancellors Brüning and von Schleicher. The 1942 edition of the Brockhaus Encyclopedia, which had been "coordinated" to reflect Nazi thinking, noted that some of the privy councillor's writings were "not always free of contradictions; in addition they contain strikingly frequent shifts of position, so that objections to his 'situational jurisprudence' have been raised." Nonetheless, this official assessment recognized "Schmitt's achievement in contributing through his work to the undoing and destruction of outmoded and useless systems."

No one could argue with that. Carl Schmitt had always been the anti-democratic, conservative constitutional lawyer *par excellence,* a circumstance which explains his swift rise to prominence before and during the Third Reich as well as the strong influence he continued to exert afterward.

Although both friend and foe testified repeatedly to his "brilliance," Schmitt's obsessive need to adapt to his surroundings led him to commit numerous painful lapses during the Nazi era. His essay "The Führer as the Guardian of Justice,"[20] which is his legal and moral justification of the murders committed between June 30 and July 2, 1934, in the wake of the "Röhm putsch," is occasionally cited as a prime example of the depths to which German legal scholarship could sink. The lack of character evinced by this attempt to ingratiate himself with the killers was made all the more appalling by the fact that his onetime friend and mentor Kurt von Schleicher and von Schleicher's wife were among the victims.

When a number of intellectuals were stripped of their German citizenship and their books were burned, Schmitt's comment was: "German intellectuals like these we can do without . . . Germany has spit them out for all time."[21]

His anti-Semitic rantings were even worse, if anything. Already in 1933 he published as a gesture of obeisance to the National Socialists a book entitled *State, Movement, People,* in which he claimed, "Someone not of our kind may make every effort to appear a critical and penetrating thinker; he may read books and write books; yet he thinks and understands in different terms, because he is of a different kind, and his every significant thought remains determined by the existential conditions of his kind."[22] In 1936 Schmitt organized a conference on the subject of "Jews in the Fields of Law and Economics," at which he proclaimed, "The Jew's relationship to our intellectual work is parasitical, tactical, and commercial . . . Being shrewd and quick, he knows how to say the right thing at the right time. That is his instinct as a parasite and born trader."[23] When someone in the audience pointed out that the Jewish law professor Friedrich Julius Stahl—a leader of the Prussian conservatives and one of the most important antidemocratic political thinkers of the nineteenth century, from whom many of Schmitt's own doctrines were derived—had made genuine contributions to German legal scholarship, Schmitt replied, "When it is pointed out again and again that this man was subjectively honest, that may be right, but I must add that I cannot see into the soul of this Jew and that we have no access at all to the innermost nature of Jews. We are aware only of the disparity between them and our kind. Once you have grasped this truth, then you know what race is."[24] "The constitutional theorist of the new Reich," as Schmitt like to be called,[25] had outdone virtually everyone else in grasping the connections between intellect and race. In his opening address to the conference mentioned above, he objected strenuously to the way Jewish German emigrants had characterized "the magnificent efforts of *Gauleiter* Julius Streicher as unintellectual."[26] [The Nazis divided Germany into regions, each known as a *Gau*. The *Gauleiter* was the regional Nazi party leader.—*Translator.*]

When Schmitt fell slightly out of favor in 1936 and lost his top office in the Nazi Federation of the Guardians of the Law, he once again displayed his opportunism in his choice of a research topic. Leaving the field of constitutional law, the legal analogue of domestic policy, he shifted his interest to international law, the analogue of foreign policy. Until 1945 his published papers were devoted almost exclusively to this field. Previously he had supported the dictatorship and had attempted to justify the Nazis' seizure of power and the suppression of "the enemy within" the borders of Germany. Now, as Hitler prepared to conquer Europe, and later, when the Germans occupied half of it, he developed a doctrine justifying the subjection of neighboring peoples, the legal concept of *Grossraum*. [*Grossraum* translates literally as "large area," and in National Socialist thinking is related closely to the concept of *Lebensraum*. It refers to the territory outside the borders of Germany which the Nazis claimed as their natural sphere of influence.—*Translator.*] "The new ordering concept of a new international law is our concept of the Reich, [which] is capable of acquiring influence reaching into Central and Eastern Europe and of repelling interference by powers alien to the territory and the *Volk*. The Führer's deed has given political reality, historical truth, and a great international future to the ideas of our Reich."[27]

Once the great international future had turned into the political reality of unconditional surrender (to powers alien to the territory and the *Volk*, no less), the Americans placed *Grossraum*-theorist Schmitt in a detention camp and even debated making him a defendant at the Nuremberg war crimes trials. However, the prosecutors apparently thought it would be more advantageous to make use of Schmitt's notorious opportunism in order to discredit a witness summoned by the attorneys who were defending Ernst von Weizsäcker, a senior official in the foreign ministry. This witness was Erich Kaufmann, Schmitt's former teacher, a German nationalist, and a Jewish professor of constitutional law.[28] Schmitt did not disappoint his new masters. He provided quotations from Kaufmann's writings in which Kaufmann glorified war and dreamed the dream of *Grossraum*. After this the value of Kaufmann's testimony was considerably diminished. Schmitt was released from detention and promised to withdraw "into the security of silence." Nonetheless, back home in Plettenberg, he published a few writings, partly to justify his earlier publications and to convert his contributions to Nazi rule into a subtle form of "resistance." In so doing he did not shrink from massive falsifications: one of the main authors of the "national defense" doctrine brazenly claimed that he had "never participated . . . in the talk about the 'state emergency.'"[29] Later, federal chancellor Kurt Kiesinger never denied a report of the newspaper *Frankfurter Rundschau* that at the time of the "grand coalition" government (1966–1969), Schmitt was his "secret adviser in matters of constitutional law" and that Kiesinger was in the habit of conferring with a small group in Plettenberg that included the theorist of "national defense."[30] In 1948 it had not been possible to celebrate Schmitt's sixtieth birthday with appropriate ceremony, and instead of a *Festschrift* there was merely a little book dedicated to him on the occasion: *Imagery in the Texts of Works by Johann Sebastian Bach.*[31] However, the fat *Festschrift* volumes for his seventieth[32] and eightieth birthdays[33]—the latter entitled *Epirrhosis,* which means "enthusiastic agreement" in Greek—included contributions from every postwar German authority on constitutional law; it documented the esteem in which Carl Schmitt and his antidemocratic doctrines were held even by the legal scholars of the Federal Republic.

Schmitt, who died in 1985, had much in common with Erwin Bumke. Both numbered among Germany's most respected jurists prior to 1933, and both were highly cultivated men: Schmitt had a great fondness for Bach's organ music, and Bumke is said to have been a talented violinist. Both were conservative and German nationalists in their thinking; both longed for an authoritarian government and sympathized openly with the Nazis, while supposedly detesting them in private. And finally, among their legal colleagues, neither the president of the Supreme Court nor the celebrated constitutional scholar was exceptional in sympathizing with the Nazis. On the contrary, they were quite representative of the rank and file of less prominent judges, public prosecutors, law professors, and—to a lesser extent—attorneys. This is shown by events during the process of "coordination": soon after Hitler became chancellor, every trace of opposition was crushed. The sympathy demonstrated by German jurists with the rise of the National Socialist movement, from its beginnings to the seizure of power, was at most only temporarily clouded by the brutality of the "coordination."

6

The Legal System during the State of Emergency

The Decree for the Protection of the People and the State promulgated immediately after the Reichstag fire declared a state of emergency; thus, it represents not only the foundation of National Socialist rule but also the end of Germany as a constitutional state. Carl Schmitt, the theorist of the state of emergency, had claimed as early as 1922 that it gave the government powers which were "in principle without limits—that is to say, [it suspended] the entire existing order": "Once this state of emergency has been declared, it is clear that the constituted authority of the state continues to exist, while the law is placed in abeyance . . . The decision exempts that authority from every normative restraint and renders it absolute in the true sense of the word. In a state of emergency, the constituted authority suspends the law on the basis of a right to protect its own existence."[1] This passage shows that such ideas were developed long before the Third Reich. Conservative German theories of constitutional law had always reflected a fascination with authoritarian government, and, in Schmitt's words, "the nature of state authority is revealed most clearly in the state of emergency. Here the decision making and the legal norm diverge, and . . . authority proves that it need not have a basis in law in order to establish justice."[2]

The burning of the Reichstag had provided an excuse for declaring a state of emergency; it was a fiction, however, since whether or not the fire had been set by the Nazis themselves or by van der Lubbe on his own or even by the Communists, it had in no sense created a true emergency situation. But an "emergency" had to be conjured up in order for the Nazis to be able to issue their emergency decree, allegedly to prevent the Communist uprising for which the fire was to have been the signal. The preamble of the Reichstag Fire Decree declares accordingly, "As provided for by Article 48, paragraph 2 of the constitution, the following is decreed to defend the state against Communist acts of violence . . ." What was actually decreed was the loss of all personal rights during the Third Reich. The freedom of the individual, the inviolability of the home from unwarranted search, the privacy of the mails, freedom of speech and assembly, the right to form organizations, and even the right to own property were suspended "until further notice." "Further notice" did not come until May 8, 1945, as it turned out, for the decree remained in effect until canceled by the military government of the Allies.

The linking of the decree with the purported Communist threat was designed to give it the appearance of legality; the Weimar constitution permitted emergency decrees only to deal with narrowly circumscribed situations, so that the Nazis could not have written "for the purpose of crushing political opposition" into the preamble (at least not before February 1933). However, the courts and government administrators grasped both the true purpose of the Reichstag Fire Decree and the fact that its preamble was not to be taken too literally. They soon began to apply it not only to Communists but also to anyone or anything that could be considered political opposition in the broadest sense or an annoyance to the new regime. The Prussian Supreme Court (*Kammergericht*) even forbade lower courts to determine whether the provisions of the decree were actually met in specific instances. The court ruled that the decree had lifted all "federal and state limitations on police measures" and that all actions taken by the police served the general purpose of combatting Communist threats, "whereby the question of whether they were appropriate or necessary is not subject to investigation by the court."[3] And as early as 1933, the County Court of Berlin developed the handy rule that "all attacks on public safety and order" were to be "considered Communist in the broadest sense."[4]

The courts came up with more and more variations of the "Communist threat" in order to be able to apply the Reichstag Fire Decree to all actual or presumed opponents of the Nazis. In the Münsterland, for example, the governor had made use of it to ban all church youth group activities. When several members of a Catholic youth organization nonetheless persisted in going on outings and playing sports together, they were charged with violating paragraph 4 of the decree (infringement of official regulations). The County Court of Hagen found them not guilty,[5] but the State Supreme Court reversed the decision, ruling that "this kind of emphasis on [religious] divisions carries within it by nature the seeds of a subversion of the German people, and every such subversion represents a potential furtherance of Communist aims and support of its goals." [The word *Zersetzung*, translated here as "subversion," literally means "disintegration" or "dissolution" and was a key National Socialist term applied to the effect of all opposition.—*Translator.*] Since one might think that Catholics were immune to the godless doctrine of Communism and even opposed to it, the court felt compelled to point out the danger inherent in their activities: "Such a public display of personal opinion or belief can all too easily become an encouragement to Communists, Communist sympathizers, or persons currently of unsettled political allegiance, who would then develop and spread the opinion that the National Socialist state did not have the people behind it."[6]

Using this interpretation of the "indirect Communist threat," the courts justified the actions taken by the authorities against, among others, the Lutheran Confessional Church (Prussian Supreme Court decision of May 3, 1935),[7] opponents of vaccination (Reich Supreme Court, August 6, 1936),[8] a charitable organization called the Home Mission (Administrative Court of Württemberg, September 9, 1936),[9] and Protestant societies for the care of the sick (Administrative Court of Baden, January 9, 1938).[10] However, since it was difficult to make it clear to the general population why a Communist threat "in the broadest sense" might be posed by outspoken anti-Communists (and also why the supposed danger was not receding with each wave of arrests), the courts soon dispensed with mention of the preamble altogether. In the decision cited above, the Administrative Court of Württemberg ruled in September 1936 that the decree served "to protect the state not only against all Communist threats but also against all dangers to its continued existence and to public safety and order, from whatever source they may come." The judges at this court saw such a danger to the continued existence of the state in the bylaws of a privately supported home for children which provided that, should its board of sponsors ever have to disband, its assets would go to the Home Mission. The local representative to the state legislature had instructed the board to change the bylaws to make the beneficiary the *Nationalsozialistische Volkswohlfahrt* (National Socialist People's Welfare Association). Thereupon the board took its case to the Administrative Court, claiming that its bylaws could pose no possible threat to the state. The court thought otherwise. The claim was dismissed on the grounds that "the protection of public order and safety in today's state also includes safeguarding the general interests of our social order," and that limits on government infringement of individual rights no longer existed.[11]

In this manner the courts legitimized the disbanding of organizations, the banning of meetings, the seizure of assets, arrests, and the imposition of fines and prison sentences to such a degree that the courts' very existence came to be meaningless. By refusing to protect citizens against government regulations, they gave the police a free hand, while at the same time granting the police the sole right to define what was legal. A dissenting opinion on the most trivial subjects imaginable could be blown up into a case of "enmity to the state." A man with a fleet of taxicabs in Leipzig, for example, was a director of the Taxicab Owners' Cooperative and had disagreed with the Ministry of Traffic about how the profession ought to be organized. At the request of the police, his permit was revoked. He then brought suit against this act of the authorities, arguing that just because he had his own opinion about how the taxi business ought to be run, that did not make him an enemy of the state. The second time the case was heard on appeal, the Munich Court of Appeals informed him of his lack of rights: "The constitutional provisions mentioned in the [Reichstag Fire] Decree have been stripped of their previous meaning entirely as regards the rights of individuals against the police . . . The previously existing legal protection . . . regarding actions of the police is therefore set aside."[13]

The police on the one hand and scholars and administrators of the law on the other agreed that political matters should not come under review by the courts. In addition, the courts did what they could to extend the definition of "political" until it applied to almost everything. The Kiel Court of Appeals, for example, made a political affair out of a series of newspaper articles that had allegedly discredited the medical profession and damaged its prestige. In the court's view, the newspaper had "acted against the tendencies and aims of the leaders of the state in public health policy."[14] The Stettin Court of Appeals declared that the car accident of an SA man did not fall under its jurisdiction, since "every action performed by an SA man or member of the National Socialist Drivers' Corps in the course of his duties occurs under the aegis of the National Socialist Party" and should thus be "judged as political action in the broad and general sense."[15] In the case of the taxicab owner mentioned above, the Munich Court of Appeals had already given a sufficient explanation of how just how broad the term "political" had become: "In the struggle which the German people must wage today to maintain its existence, there no longer exists an unpolitical sphere of life." The "creative" interpretation of the Reichstag Fire Decree and its universal application by the courts sometimes went too far even in the eyes of Nazi leaders. No less a figure than Dr. Werner Best, chief counsel for the Gestapo, felt obliged in 1938 to criticize the way the decree was being used: if the courts could not reach a solution any other way, they would fall back on "interpreting the doctrine of danger to the state in a manner so excessively broad" that it occasionally led to "internal inconsistencies in their reasoning."[16]

7

Treason and Treachery:
Political Opposition and the Courts

In the first few months of the National Socialist regime, the SA and SS as well as local Nazi party and police officials arrested and tortured many people in disfavor—labor leaders ("Communists"), intellectuals, and politicians of the Weimar era—more or less at will, and by way of settling old accounts. [The SS, meaning *Schutzstaffel* or "security units," were originally founded as Hitler's black-shirted personal bodyguards and eventually grew into the elite armed units of the Nazi party.—*Translator.*] The arrests were usually made in the name of the Reichstag Fire Decree, but frequently occurred without any legal justification whatsoever. The chief of the political department of the police (renamed in 1934 the Secret State Police—the *Geheime Staatspolizei,* or "Gestapo" for short) at that time was Rudolf Diels. After the war ended and Diels had been "de-Nazified," he described the atmosphere in Berlin: "In those March days every SA man was 'on the heels of the enemy'; each knew what he had to do. The *Stürme* [storm troopers] cleaned up the districts . . . Not only Communists but anyone who had ever expressed himself against Hitler's movement was in danger . . . In those March days the concentration camps around Berlin were set up. News was received of camps near Oranienburg, Königswusterhausen, and Bornim . . . 'Private prisons' were set up in various parts of the city. The 'bunkers' in Hedemann- and Vosstrasse became hellish torture chambers." And according to Diels, activities in the rest of the country were similar: "The unleashing of the Berlin storm troopers had an electrifying effect on the most remote parts of the country. In many cities where police power had been handed over to the local SA leaders they began a revolution."[1]

After several weeks of this unrestrained reign of terror, the national leaders began trying to regain control and reestablish their sole authority. On July 25, 1933, the Prussian minister of justice declared an amnesty for all crimes committed by members of the SA and SS in an excess of zeal "on the occasion of the end of the National Socialist Revolution." At this time the "unofficial" concentration camps were supposed to be either turned over to the established authorities or closed down. In the peat-bog camps Papenburg and Esterwegen, the SS guards were replaced by troops of police from Berlin. In January 1934 a memorandum sent by Gestapo headquarters to all its branch offices pointed out that even in cases of preventive detention certain formalities, such as issuing a written order, had to be observed: "Whereas in the early days of the takeover it was possible to overlook this because the protection of the state against the plots and machinations of its enemies required quick measures unhampered by formal regulations, today the instructions issued must be strictly observed." Gestapo chief Diels included an unmistakable warning in the memorandum: "Anyone failing to do so will be called to account for misuse of authority and restriction of liberty."[2]

During the Third Reich, there was considerable competition in the effort to track down and crush the "enemy within," the political opposition. Not only did government agencies compete with the gangs of the SA, the SS, and—at least to begin with—the nationalistic veterans' organization *Stahlhelm* ("Steel Helmet"); even within the government, there was competition between the police and the criminal justice system. In an ordinance issued to all state governments, the Reich minister of the interior emphasized that preventive detention was purely a police measure for the protection of public safety and order; under no circumstances should it be "used as a 'punishment'—that is, as a substitute for a sentence passed by a court of law or by the police, and its duration must not be fixed at the outset." In addition, it was "in principle . . . not permissible to order a person to be taken into preventive detention instead of starting criminal proceedings against him."[3]

To make matters even more complicated, jurisdiction over political offenses was shared by no less than three different courts: the Supreme Court (the *Reichsgericht*, which was replaced as the court of first instance by the People's Court, the *Volksgerichtshof*, on April 24, 1934); the Courts of Appeal; and the "Special Courts," the *Sondergerichte*. Created on March 21, 1933, the Special Courts had jurisdiction over all crimes listed in the Reichstag Fire Decree:[4] violations of all directives of the national government; incitement to such violations that caused public danger; high treason; arson; sabotage; aggravated insurrection; and aggravated breach of the peace. They were also responsible for violations of the Decree to Protect the Government of the National Socialist Revolution from Treacherous Attacks[5]: unauthorized use of Nazi uniforms and badges, and making false claims or misrepresentations designed to damage the repute of the government or the National Socialist party. However, the Special Courts had jurisdiction over all these offenses only insofar as they did not come under the jurisdiction of the Supreme Court or a Court of Appeals.

Until the People's Court was established, the Supreme Court was the first and only instance for cases of treason and high treason. If the Reich prosecutor general considered a particular case to be of minor importance, however, he could delegate it to the chief prosecutor of the state involved, who would then bring it before a Criminal Panel of a Court of Appeals. In the last analysis, the Reich prosecutor general thus had the power to decide whether a case would come before the Supreme Court or a Court of Appeals.

Since it was important for the courts to prosecute only the right sort of criminals, a whole series of laws and decrees passed after the Nazis seized power specified that the penalties for political offenses were to be increased; at the same time, a generous amnesty was provided for offenses committed "during the national revolutionary struggle of the German people, in preparation for this revolution, or in the struggle for the German homeland."[6] In addition, a County Court judge named Dietrich argued that the "national aim" should be generally recognized as grounds for immunity. He referred to the decisions of the Supreme Court based on the doctrine of "national emergency," which suggested such a line of reasoning. Of course, judges should hand down fair decisions, "but objectivity finds its limits in the German understanding of the law when the national security is placed in doubt"; every judge is "a son of his country" and as such must "place the vital interests of the nation unconditionally above what is formally the law." Judge Dietrich issued a passionate appeal to his colleagues on the bench: "Eliminating the last traces of the enemy within is undoubtedly a part of the restoration of German honor. German judges can participate in this task through generous interpretation of the penal code."[7]

From 1933 to 1935, cases of Communist and socialist resistance to the regime were delegated as far as possible to the Courts of Appeals with their panels of five professional judges. Their sentences offered a greater appearance of legitimacy than did the abbreviated proceedings of the Special Courts, and the deeds of the regime's political opponents could be more easily presented as "ordinary criminal activities." The authorities were hardly placing their cause at risk when they left their opposition on the left to the regular courts: the judges of the Weimar period had offered sufficient evidence of their "loyalty to the state" where Communists, pacifists, and republicans were concerned. It was thus simple enough for the courts to continue in their established manner in political cases after 1933. The Supreme Court, for example, could cite a previous decision word for word when it said it was well known to the courts that "the Communist party of Germany . . . [aims] with all means at its disposal to eliminate the existing constitution of the Reich and the states and to set up in its place by way of the dictatorship of the proletariat a Communist government on the Russian model."[8] After January 30, 1933, the courts continued to find numerous Communists guilty of trying to eliminate "the existing constitution of the Reich," although in actual fact the Nazis had already eliminated most of the constitution themselves with the Reichstag Fire Decree of February 28 and the Enabling Act of March 24. Between January 30, 1933, and the establishment of the People's Tribunal, the majority of offenses found to fulfill the conditions of "preparation for high treason" had been committed before the Nazis seized power; almost two thirds of the ninety-one verdicts of high treason involved "older cases"[9]—that is to say, activities from the Weimar period. In these decisions, the Supreme Court was "protecting" a democratic government which had long since been eliminated by the ruling National Socialists.

After the Communist party was outlawed, the courts had to alter their policy only to the extent that now any activity which could have profited the Communist party even remotely—including accepting members' dues or distributing newspapers—was classified as "preparation for high treason." On March 14, 1934, the Fourth Criminal Panel of the Supreme Court found a worker guilty of the "crime of preparing a treasonable undertaking," because in June 1933 he had acted as a courier and carried mail to the nearest Communist party office. The court argued once again that "the goal of the party leaders now working underground" remained "the establishment of a soviet republic on the Russian model in Germany."[10]

Once the Social Democratic party had also been banned (on June 22, 1933), the courts extended the same treatment to its members, as well as to members of the Socialist Workers' party, a group which had split off from the Social Democrats in 1931. It did not help the Social Democrats at all that they had resigned from the Socialist Workers' International on March 30 and had even voted approval of the government's foreign policy program on May 17.[11] Their organizations were destroyed, and their members persecuted, arrested, and driven into exile. Once the party had been banned, the Supreme Court regarded it as "public knowledge" that the aims of the Social Democratic party were treasonable, without the slightest evidence ever having been produced. In the case of three Social Democrats who were found guilty of having contacts with the leaders of their party in exile in Prague and of having distributed leaflets in Germany, the court remarked: "The fact that the activities of the Social Democrats who have fled abroad are intended to prepare the violent overthrow of the constitution, which has been guaranteed by the new government with the support of the entire population, is obvious to anyone who has to do with these matters." [12] (The judges actually meant the Weimar constitution!)

All the activities of the Socialist Workers' party were also "clearly treasonable" in the opinion of the Supreme Court, though no formal evidence was entered: where the aims of this party were concerned, the court simply took over the routine phrases originally developed for the Communists. When three party members were found "guilty of authorship or publication of writings in accord with the aims of the Socialist Workers' party and also, through their activities as officers of party organizations, guilty of the crime of preparing a treasonable undertaking," the court declared: "[The Socialist Workers' party's] aims extend just like those of the German Communist party to violent revolution, overthrow of the government, the dictatorship of the proletariat, and the creation of a workers' and peasants' republic on the Russian model." [13]

The courts accepted the views of leading Nazi jurists that no privileges could be granted to political opponents in the Third Reich and that, on the contrary, they should be considered "the most vicious of criminals." As a result, the courts drastically increased the penalties for such offenses. Officially, offenses committed before January 20, 1933, came under the old paragraph 86 of the Criminal Code, which provided only fortress arrest or imprisonment for convicted traitors, and the more severe punishment of a penitentiary sentence only when the accused had acted from "base motives." However, even during the days of the Weimar Republic the crime of "preparation for high treason" had, as a rule, been punished with the mild and honorable form of fortress arrest solely in the case of "nationalist" offenders, whereas Communists were seldom granted this privilege. [14] After the Nazis seized power, sentences were limited to prison and penitentiary; not a single case of fortress arrest for left-wing opponents of the regime is documented. Under the influence of new laws that provided for penalties up to and including the death sentence for opposition to the national government, the courts assumed in every case that the accused Communists or Social Democrats had acted from "base motives" and sentenced them to prison or penitentiary terms without exception.

Such severe sentences came to seem plausible enough in the light of the campaign being waged by the government; largely in order to justify its suppression of the political opposition, it magnified the danger of Communist resistance out of all proportion. In June 1933 the chief of police in Bremen sent a secret communication to "Party Comrade Dr. Freisler" in which he advocated "ordinances of the utmost stringency on a national level, the establishment of summary courts of justice, and the death penalty for all illegal Communist activities," in order to put down the Communist resistance supposedly increasing at an alarming rate "all over the country." Freisler, at that time an official in the Prussian ministry of justice, replied that he was already paying "particularly close attention to the activities of the German Communist party" because of the reports reaching him from public prosecutors.[15] After a meeting on July 22, 1933, the chief public prosecutors of the different states urged subordinates to increase their vigilance. The chief public prosecutor of Breslau called for the criminal justice system to "move promptly, swiftly, and with the most drastic measures against all enemies of the National Socialist state," and on August 8 his colleague in Naumburg instructed the public prosecutors working under him always to cooperate with the appropriate officials of the Nazi party.[16]

The hysteria was unfounded, for at no time could one of the workers' parties have represented a real danger to the new regime. They were not prepared to wage a fight from underground, and the traditionally moderate German working class rejected terrorist tactics. The "monstrous crimes" referred to repeatedly in government pronouncements or court decisions were usually small acts of kindness toward the victims of violence or attempts to expose the truth about the Nazi regime. The German Communist party was officially outlawed before the elections of March 1933, even before the banning of the Social Democrats. (The bourgeois parties were eventually forbidden by the so-called Law against the Formation of New Parties of July 14, 1933.)[17] After the offices of the Communists had been closed, their leaders arrested, and Communist newspapers banned, Communists all over the country tried to keep regional or at least local organizations intact. Illegally printed newspapers were passed from hand to hand; leaflets were occasionally distributed, and collections taken on behalf of political prisoners. Naturally all of this had to take place in the greatest secrecy. The close watch kept on most Communists made it difficult to accomplish anything which might have a public effect, such as painting political slogans on walls or raising a red flag on a factory chimney, except now and then.

Nevertheless, during the first year of National Socialist rule the courts had their hands full trying to hear all the cases against Communists and Social Democrats. The Hamm Court of Appeals found no fewer than 300 people guilty of "Communist agitation" in the three months between October 15 and December 15, 1933: 124 for producing, distributing, or storing Communist leaflets; 46 for agitating on behalf of the "Revolutionary Trade Union Opposition"; 7 for collecting party dues; and 2 for "concealing property of the Communist party."[18] In August 1933, 91 members of the Socialist Workers' party and its affiliated youth organization were found guilty of high treason and given prison and penitentiary sentences totaling more than 110 years.[19] The zeal of the offices of public prosecution reached such heights in the first few months of Nazi rule that the government found it necessary to include minor offenses of the opposition in the Law on the Granting of Immunity, passed on August 7, 1934. The core of the new law was an amnesty "for offenses committed in an excess of zeal for the National Socialist cause,"[20] but it also covered petty offenses against the party such as "insults to the Führer and chancellor" or "written or verbal offenses against the welfare and repute of the nation." On the basis of this amnesty, 414,407 cases were disposed of in Prussia alone, including 238,832 in which sentence had already been passed.[21]

Even after this partial amnesty, however, the judicial persecution of the Nazis' political opponents continued. The mere lists of the trials involving Social Democrats fill page after page of the *Deutschland-Berichte,* reports published by the party leaders in exile. In Berlin between May 1934 and April 1935, ten trials against 112 Social Democrats resulted in sentences totaling 114 years in penitentiary and 120 years in prison. In July 1935 Hamburg, 150 members of the Social Democratic party were tried at the same time.[22] They were accused of having tried to build up the party again, although in fact most of them had only collected or donated money for the families of party members who were in concentration camps or prisons. The Communists were able to summarize the results of three years of persecution under the Third Reich at the so-called Brussels Conference in October 1935, the first conference held by the German Communist party after it had been banned. (The conference actually took place near Moscow; for camouflage reasons, rumors that it would be held in Brussels were deliberately circulated.) There it was reported that 393 members had been murdered, 21 sentenced to death, 21 to life imprisonment, and 860—including 73 women—to penitentiary and prison terms amounting to 3,980 years.[23]

After 1935 the Special Courts began to play a larger role in the persecution of political opponents, and their sentences were usually even more draconian. In the "Ruhr Trial" in Dortmund against 34 members of the Socialist Workers' party, chief defendant Eberhard Brünen was sentenced to 15 years in a penitentiary. And in another trial which also took place in 1935, the Special Court of Hamm tried 18 members of the Socialist

Workers' youth organization at one time; the defendants, all minors, were given a total of 90 years in a penitentiary.[23]

Such long sentences began to set new standards for the regular courts. In a whole series of trials in 1935, the Hanseatic Court of Appeals attempted to deal with Communists who had established new local organizations in Oldenburg, Delmenhorst, and Wilhelmshaven and who had tried to maintain some of their old contacts. Roughly a dozen decisions of about fifty pages each covered such questions as what had happened to a typewriter belonging to the Communist party and who was hiding it; who had placed a wreath on the grave of the revolutionaries killed in Wilhelmshaven in 1919; who had later placed a red ribbon on the wreath with the inscription "We are thinking of you and continuing the struggle! Our victory is assured!"; and whether one of the defendants had collected the sum of two reichsmarks for the "Red Relief" or donated it out of his own pocket.[25]

The sentences imposed for such trifling offenses ranged from six months in prison to the legal maximum of three years in a penitentiary. A defendant named Haase, found guilty by the court of "having given an illegal Communist newspaper, namely either the *Red Front* or the *Red Flag,* to Waldorn for ten pfennigs (cents) in May or June 1933, and of having bought an illegal newspaper from Brand in July for nine pfennigs," received a sentence of one year in prison for "aiding and abetting the preparation for high treason." The defendant Anna Sathemann's act of "laying a plain wreath" (that is, without a red ribbon) on the revolutionaries' grave was also interpreted as aiding and abetting the preparation for high treason, and for this she was sentenced to seven months in prison.[26] The courts repeated over and over again the same formulaic phrases that "all activity after March 5, 1933, which aimed at reestablishing the Communist party in Germany" must be considered "objectively as preparation for high treason," "since at this time the entire Communist party apparatus had been shut down by the National Socialist government. Throughout the entire country the party's offices were closed, all of its officials who could be located were in preventive detention, and the entire party was outlawed . . . Therefore, all activity after March 5 could only be illegal."[27] The Hanseatic Court of Appeals noted dutifully: "According to the established interpretation of German courts, every activity on behalf of the German Communist party serves to prepare the violent overthrow of the government and the constitution of Germany. In consequence, every activity on behalf of the German Communist party or its affiliated organizations such as the Revolutionary Trade Union Opposition or the Red Relief is to be considered as preparation for high treason and a punishable offense. Once the German Communist party had been crushed following the burning of the Reichstag, once its leaders had been arrested and its assets seized, there could be no doubt in the mind of anyone within the Reich about its legal status."[28] What the court meant by this, however, is not so much what was legal as what those in power could dictate, for the legal situation was in fact such that the constitution referred to had been violated by the Nazis, in part rescinded by decree and in part simply ignored; no one knew how much of it was still in effect, and opinion at the time was divided about the extent to which it had been superseded by the "national revolution."

The decisions in such cases continued as a rule to be couched in the traditional language of the higher courts—that is, in a dispassionate and impartial tone largely free of Nazi polemics. Nonetheless, this should not disguise the fact that the Courts of Appeals made a substantial contribution to legitimizing the persecution of the Nazis' political opponents. They repeatedly expressed the view that the illegality of the Communist party was proved by the fact that Communists were being prosecuted; they concurred that anyone donating money for political prisoners—even if the collections were taken for purely humanitarian reasons and not for the party as such—thereby endorsed the treasonable aims of the party; and they imposed extremely harsh sentences. All of these circumstances taken together gradually blurred the distinction between the Special Courts and the Courts of Appeals. The regular courts' decisions may have had more appearance of legality; they were written in more neutral language, and in general these courts paid more attention to formalities. But otherwise the results differed so little from the verdicts of the Special Courts that newspapers referred several times to "proceedings before the Special Court of the Hanseatic Court of Appeals, in the panel for high treason."[29] The difference between the criminal panel of the regular court and the Special Court had become so small, in spite of the different judges in each and their very different titles, that journalists were not aware of it and the press censors did not even bother to correct the error.

· 8 ·

Purges at the Bar

Accounts of the power and influence wielded by Jews in the Weimar Republic have usually been grossly misleading. In actual fact the percentage of Jews in the population of Germany declined steadily from the late nineteenth century onward, shrinking from 1.2 percent in 1871 to 0.76 percent in 1930.[1] The figure of more than 3 percent frequently mentioned by the National Socialists was entirely inaccurate.[2] Other conservative politicians besides the Nazis also alluded to the supposed influence of Jews in the government with vastly exaggerated figures. In a speech delivered in May 1933, the German ambassador to the United States and former chancellor Hans Luther attributed the anti-Semitic mood in Germany to the fact "that almost 50 percent of civil servants were Jews," and Hitler told American journalists in the summer of 1933 that he had found 62 percent of government posts filled by Jews.[3]

The truth was that Jews were underrepresented in the civil service: they constituted 0.16 percent of all government employees. In politics the situation was similar, so that the slogan "Jew Republic" bore no relation to the facts. Approximately 250 ministers served in the twenty different postwar cabinets of the Weimar era; of these a total of six were Jewish, and only two of them actively practiced their faith.[4] The numerous forms of discrimination faced by Jews, including their long exclusion from the civil service, had led them to enter the unrestricted professions, so that their numbers among writers, editors, merchants, physicians, and lawyers were in fact significantly greater than their percentage of the total population. This was true above all in the field of law, where the lifting of all restrictions on admission to the bar made the private practice of law one of the most attractive careers for educated Jews. According to official statistics, 4,394 of the 19,500 members of the bar in Germany were of Jewish background—that is to say, about 22 percent. In major cities the percentages were even higher: in Berlin in 1933 the figure stood at about 60 percent, and in Vienna before 1938 supposedly 80 percent of all attorneys in private practice were Jewish.[5] The *Deutscher Anwaltsverein* (Association of German Attorneys) had a largely Jewish leadership, and men such as Max Hachenburg, Martin Drucker, Max and Adolf Friedlaender, Julius Magnus, and Max Alsberg had contributed to a strong and independent bar through their commentaries on the law and work in professional organizations. The attorneys and legal sociologists Ludwig Bendix, Sigbert Feuchtwanger, and Ernst Fraenkel made fundamental contributions to an understanding of the German legal system, while men such as Felix Halle, Max Hirschberg, Hans Litten, Philipp Loewenfeld, Rudolf Olden, and Alfred Oborniker set high standards as defense counsel in criminal trials during the Weimar era. In addition, a number of leaders of the labor movement were Jewish lawyers, among them men such as Hugo Haase, Karl Liebknecht, Paul Levi, Kurt Rosenfeld, and Alexander Obuch. Prominent Jewish attorneys, such as Alfred Apfel and Rudolf Olden, also numbered among the leaders of pacifist organizations.

Jewish attorneys had represented the liberal element in the German legal system since the profession of attorney had been freed of the restrictions that had continued for a time to apply to the civil service. When the historian Karl Dietrich Bracher observes that "attorneys . . . in large numbers proved to be virtual pillars of support for democracy in the Weimar era, in contrast to the courts,"[6] he is referring above all to Jewish attorneys. This group embodied, better than almost any other section of the population, all the qualities and attitudes which the National Socialists particularly hated. A careful reading of Hitler's frequently quoted venomous outbursts against the legal profession reveals that they were directed less at judges than at attorneys, and especially at "those Jewish shysters."[7] As Jews, pacifists, socialists, committed democrats, and supporters of the legal system of the republic, they were a thorn in the Nazis' side for many reasons, and many of them were affected by more than one category of the Nazi law restricting admission to the bar. The Law for Restoration of the Professional Civil Service (passed April 7, 1933), which decreed that political undesirables and "non-Aryans" were to be dismissed from public service, had a parallel in a law regulating membership in the bar which took effect on the same day. According to this law, attorneys of "non-Aryan" descent could be excluded, and lawyers who "had been active in a Communist sense" were excluded from the bar without exception. The only attorneys who were exempted from the "Aryan clause" were those who had been admitted to a bar association before August 8, 1914, who had performed military service during the First World War, or who were the fathers or sons of men killed in that war. On the basis of this law, 1,500 attorneys were deprived of their right to practice, most of them for "racial" reasons.[8] A decree was then issued guaranteeing all those remaining not only "full enjoyment of their professional rights," but also to each individual the "title to the respect owing to him as a member of his professional community."[9]

That these assurances did not apply to the 2,900 Jewish attorneys who were still permitted to practice soon became evident, however. Local bar associations, whose policies had now been "coordinated" with those of the government, began to announce new guidelines for membership. They established binding criteria for acceptable professional conduct, as they still do today, and provided a basis for disciplinary proceedings, according to which an attorney could be disbarred, if necessary. The Bar Association of Berlin declared that establishing or maintaining a law firm with partners of both "Aryan" and "non-Aryan" descent was unethical.[10] The Bar Association of Düsseldorf decreed that is was a violation of professional standards for anyone to take over the practice of an attorney whose membership in a bar association had been revoked, to employ former "non-Aryan" attorneys, or to take over their clients. It concluded with the sweeping statement: "Every professional contact with disbarred, non-Aryan attorneys is a violation of standards."[11] After the Federation of National Socialist German Jurists had voted to "expose" all "Aryans" who allowed themselves to be represented by a "non-Aryan" attorney, the newspaper *Hessische Volkswacht* on August 28, 1933, published a list, including the file numbers and attorneys' names, of thirty litigants "who possessed the audacity to engage Jewish attorneys."

The Prussian minister of justice Hans Kerrl had already requested all presiding judges at the Courts of Appeal under his jurisdiction "urgently to recommend to all Jewish notaries in their own interest to refrain from practicing their profession for the time being," since "maintenance of public order and safety will be seriously endangered if in their legal affairs Germans must continue to be confronted with documents which have been written or notarized by Jews."[12] [A *Notar* in Germany must have a law degree.—*Translator.*] On July 4, 1933, the city council of Tilsit passed a vote of urgency to give no more cases to the German Nationalist attorney and notary Dr. Jacoby, because he had expressed sympathy for a Jewish colleague at a bar association meeting.[13] The regional legal associations (which were organized on a private and voluntary basis) demanded that any remaining Jewish attorneys resign. And the *Juristische Wochenschrift* (Legal Weekly Journal), the prestigious publication of the Association of German Attorneys, issued "guidelines on publishing policy" announcing that they would continue to print only "contributions from persons who are Aryans," and that books "written by non-Aryans or published by a non-Aryan publisher" would no longer be reviewed.[14]

Above and beyond such harassment, restrictions, and discrimination, Nazi party circles continued to press for a complete exclusion of Jews from the legal profession. As early as the spring of 1933, the Federation of National Socialist German Jurists had solemnly vowed it would "never cease to demand that Jews must be utterly excluded from all forms of legal life."[15] Yet in early 1938 Professor Erwin Noack, the inspector general of the federation (which had in the meantime been renamed the Federation of National Socialist Guardians of the Law), issued a report on the "de-Semitization of the German legal profession"; according to this report, 1,753 Jews still remained among the 17,360 attorneys in the country.[16] This "intolerable" situation was finally resolved by the fifth decree for administering the Law on German Citizenship of September 27, 1938: it revoked the right to practice of all remaining "non-Aryan" attorneys and demoted them to the rank of "Jewish legal advisers," who were permitted to act only on behalf of Jewish clients. However, former Jewish attorneys did not have an automatic right even to this status, which could be revoked at any time. In addition, the number of such advisers and the places where they were allowed to practice were restricted. Noack commented, "The Jewish adviser may under no circumstances be consulted in the role of guardian of the law or as fulfilling a function similar to that of an attorney. He is nothing more than a representative of the interests of a Jewish party. The law can be upheld only by judges and attorneys as officers of the courts. The solution chosen by the legislators is a fitting ideological compromise. The German guardian of the law for the German! The Jewish adviser for the Jew! Once again German lawyers can take pride in the title of attorney!"[18]

Every conceivable measure was undertaken to make life as difficult as possible for the disbarred attorneys. In 1935 the Law to Prevent Abuses in the Practice of Law was passed—and remains in effect today; at that time, it was aimed at keeping disbarred attorneys from circumventing the regulations.[19] Since the bar associations had declared it a violation of professional ethics to take over "non-Aryan" firms, their owners could not sell the once flourishing practices. When it also became illegal to employ disbarred Jewish attorneys in subordinate positions such as office manager or legal assistant, those who had lost their former livelihood had virtually no way of earning a living. Even the possibility of working privately as a crammer or tutor for law students was eliminated. On November 25, 1935, the Reich's minister of education issued an ordinance: "It constitutes an offense against the dignity and prestige of the universities if students of German descent take instruction from tutors of Jewish or Jewish-related descent. I will deal with offenders according to the disciplinary regulations for students of April 1, 1935." He also announced that he had included a new provision in the examination regulations for students of economics, business, and business education, making admission to the examination dependent on the candidate's assurance that he had not been instructed by a Jewish tutor; in the same ordinance he requested the minister of justice, under whose jurisdiction the examination of law students fell, to establish a corresponding regulation.[20]

Being a "German guardian of the Law," a station in life on which some attorneys greatly prided themselves, supposedly meant more than merely representing the interests of one party in a disagreement. The distinction between "guardian of the law" and "Jewish advocate," which was repeatedly stressed in bar association pronouncements on professional ethics, was supposed to make the difference clear.[21] The Supreme Court observed in this connection: "The freedom of activity once granted in accordance with the principle of free exercise of a profession [is] now rescinded . . . The attorney has become the holder of a public office."[22] Whether attorneys were now referred to as "servitors of the law," "institutes of public law," or "agents of the law," all these terms served the purpose of reminding them of "the combined virtues of the civil servant: loyalty, obedience, and reliability."[23] "From this role as an agent of the law it follows that the attorney—. . . despite the private nature of his relationship to his client—has the same special obligation to the state which characterizes the position of the civil servant."[24] Such a position "bearing a resemblance to government service" turned out to have practical consequences for the daily practice of the profession, particularly in those cases in which the state had an interest. Above all, the perceived role of the defense attorney in criminal trials underwent a fundamental change. "As counsel for the defense, the attorney has taken up a position closer to the state and the community," the minister of justice notified the legal profession in a statement entitled "Letter to Lawyers." "He has become a member of the community of guardians of the law and lost his earlier position as a one-sided representative of the defendant." He continued with an unmistakable threat: "Whoever cannot accept this completely and unconditionally in his own mind and be ready and willing to act upon it at all times should not don the robes of a German attorney or appear in the role of defense counsel."[25]

The attorneys themselves may have tried to preserve much of their independent status. However, the repeated assurances of their spokesmen (such as Reinhard Neubert, the president of the Reich Bar Association), emphasizing the attorney's "exercise of a state function" and disparaging his former freedom as "a distortion from the liberal era," tended to have exactly the opposite effect.[26] When President Leupolt of the Dresden Bar Association stressed the struggle of "genuine German attorneys true to the German view of their profession" against "the domination of liberal Jewish attitudes in legal life," and when he reminded them that an attorney's duty toward his client "is limited by his duties . . . toward society," he was in effect calling for abolition of the profession's freedom and independence.[27]

At a meeting which left a marked impression on minister of justice Otto Thierack, Hitler informed him that the attorney must become "a person representing the state," "like the judge." Thierack then wrote to Neubert "that the position of the attorney in the legal life of Germany will have to have an entirely different orientation in the future, probably toward the state."[28] What this "coordination" meant for the conduct of trials came to be expressed in the term "unanimity of aim" on the part of the lawyers and judges participating in them. Developed by German legal scholars, it was explained by Heinrich Henkel, a professor of criminal law, as follows: "By freeing ourselves from the notion of parties [to a lawsuit], we free ourselves from the liberal notion of a trial as a conflict of aims, an unleashing of a struggle to find the truth, which by its very nature as a conflict between two parties makes finding the truth difficult. We thus become free to set against the liberal system of opposing forces a new order, in which the participants have a unanimity of aim."[29] In the view of the prominent right-wing defense attorney Dr. Alfons Sack, judges, public prosecutors, and defense attorneys should be "comrades on the legal front . . . fighting together to preserve the law . . . The coordination of their tasks must guarantee their practical cooperation and comradeship . . . Just as the new trial no longer represents a conflict between the interests of an individual and the state, now the legal participants should regard their tasks no longer as opposed to one another, but rather as a joint effort infused with a spirit of mutual trust."[30]

Sack had already given an indication of what such "comradely cooperation" looked like in his defense of Ernst Torgler, the leader of the Communist party delegation in the Reichstag. And the sad culmination of this development came later in the actions of the specially selected defense counsel at the People's Court, who frequently delivered speeches against the defendants they represented. The defense attorney for General Hoeppner, for example, who was accused of participating in the conspiracy to assassinate Hitler on July 20, 1944, expressed horror at his client's actions and closed by demanding the death penalty for him.[31]

Again and again, however, the courts had to deal with attorneys who refused to adapt to "the requirements of the new era." In an edict of January 19, 1943, the minister of justice criticized the repeated failures of attorneys to carry out "their professional duties, particularly in the area of political opinion."[32] Soon after passage of the above-mentioned Law on Requirements for Continued Admission to the Bar, which prescribed the dismissal of attorneys who "had been active in a Communist sense," a number of attorneys who had defended Socialists or Communists were disbarred. But since the law was completely vague as to what constituted activity " in a Communist sense," an administrative decree was necessary to clarify that representation and defense of members of the Communist party accused of crimes were in fact such an activity only "if this is justified by the particular circumstances, in particular the frequency of such defense or representation, the manner in which it is conducted, or the circumstances in which the case was taken on."[33] This nebulous "clarification" created a state of affairs in which any more than half-hearted attempt to defend a person accused of a politically related offense could lead to revocation of an attorney's right to practice. However, it was the legal profession's own disciplinary committees that brought about full "coordination" of the status of attorneys and civil servants, and in the vanguard was the "Court of Honor" attached to the Supreme Court, which functioned as the final arbiter of professional conduct. The Supreme Disciplinary Court of Reich had already found it necessary to place civil servants on an equal footing with members of the Nazi party in order to enforce their total obedience to the party line. In this case, its decisions could at least make reference to the institution of the professional civil service with its increased duty of loyalty to the government. In the case of the legal profession, however, where neither historical tradition nor the law itself prescribed such duties, the Court of Honor derived the analogy to the civil service simply from the oath which every new attorney had to swear according to paragraph 19 of the Attorney's Code: "I swear to remain loyal to Adolf Hitler, the leader of the German nation and people, and conscientiously to fulfill the duties of a Germany attorney." In the judgment of the Court of Honor, this "established a particular and direct relationship of loyalty to the head of state on the part of German attorneys, which is also binding with regard to constitutional law." Whether a given attorney had actually taken this oath or not was declared by the court to be "immaterial, [since] for all German attorneys the identical rights and duties apply."[34]

After the duty of attorneys had been construed to mean they must be particularly loyal followers of the Führer, the courts interpreted every appearance of coolness toward the regime as a breach of professional standards. One attorney who failed several times during appearances at court to return the Nazi salute—which was not required—was called to a disciplinary hearing; the committee took a lenient view that the omission had not been intentional, but resulted rather from an "understandable indifference," and let him off with a warning. The Court of Honor increased the penalty to a formal censure, however, since witnesses' testimony allegedly left "no doubt that the defendant had on many occasions intentionally failed to offer or respond to the 'German' salute." This behavior, linked with the circumstance "that the conduct of the defendant has attracted attention in a negative sense and tended to diminish the prestige of German guardians of the law in the eyes of the rest of the community, required an increase in the penalty imposed by the court of first instance." [35]

Another attorney who had "consciously and of his own volition" refused to vote in the Reichstag elections of March 1936 as a protest against Gestapo persecutions was actually disbarred; the Court of Honor ruled that "the special duty of loyalty to the Führer, which influences the general rights and duties of citizens, raises the expectation that attorneys will show themselves to be loyal followers of the Führer in all major political decisions of the leaders of the German state . . . Through his failure to participate in the election, not only did he give evidence of his own lack of loyalty to other members of the community, but also this conduct of the defendant was such as to raise doubts about the solidarity of the German legal profession and its commitment to the Führer and the state." [36] Of course, merely voting in an election was not sufficient; one also had to vote correctly. A further attorney who had dared to vote "no" in the referendum on the annexation of Austria was also disbarred by the Court of Honor, since "the general rights and duties of the attorney as a citizen and the particular duty of loyalty toward the Führer demanded of him by law require that he loyally aid the Führer in all major political decisions." The defendant had failed in this duty with his negative vote, although, as the court specifically observed, it could not be established that he had cast this vote "in a provocative manner." The court also emphasized several times that it had no reservations about violating the principle of secret elections. Once the attorney's vote had become known, "nothing stood in the way of scrutinizing his conduct with regard to professional ethical standards." [37]

The same duty of loyalty required attorneys to accede to all other wishes of the regime. One attorney continued to consult a physician to whose treatment she owed her life, although she had acquired "knowledge that Dr. M. was a member of the Jewish race." Here the Court of Honor took the view that "in spite of all sympathy with her situation . . . her exclusion from the legal profession must be the consequence." [38]

Finally, in March 1943, the final step in this series was taken to place attorneys on an equal legal footing with civil servants. The profession's own disciplinary institutions were eliminated and supervision of attorneys' conduct was handed over to the jurisdiction of the disciplinary courts responsible for supervising judges, where rulings were made directly on the basis of the laws applying to the civil service.[39]

9

Nazi Jurisprudence

An essential role in the decline of law during the Third Reich was played by law professors at German universities. They provided a philosophical cloak for the Nazis' arbitrary acts and crimes, which would otherwise have been clearly recognizable as unlawful. There was virtually no outrage perpetrated by the Nazis which was not praised during the regime as "supremely just" and defended after the war by the same scholars, with equally dubious arguments, as "justifiable" or even "advisable" from a legal point of view.

Since after the war the leading legal thinkers either kept their professorships or were soon reinstated—that is, continued to direct the course of legal studies—and since the current generation of law professors has been recruited almost exclusively from the ranks of their most acquiescent students, there has been only scanty research on the contribution of jurists to Nazi terror. It is almost impossible to overestimate this contribution, however, for it was in the writings of these scholars that the judges of the Third Reich found guidelines for their verdicts and lethal interpretations. This occurred more and more as the increasingly vague wording of laws ceased to provide a precise foundation on which decisions could be based.

Even prior to 1933, conservative law professors had openly sympathized with the National Socialist movement. In 1930, for example, the Nazi members of the Reichstag proposed an outrageous amendment to the Law for the Protection of the Republic which would have classed advocacy of conscientious objection and disarmament, along with any claim that Germany had been responsible for the world war, as "military treason" and would have provided the death penalty for all of them. This proposal, which would also have established "vilification of war heroes, living or dead," "betrayal of the race," and "disparagement of national symbols" as capital crimes,[1] was received enthusiastically by several noted legal scholars. Georg Dahm applauded the "courageous renunciation of all definitions" as to what constituted such crimes,[2] and Johannes Nagler felt that at last an effective means had been found to combat "defeatism of all kinds." In his eyes the amendment did not go far enough, however: he proposed adding severe penalties for negligent treason as well, and "perhaps even negligence in the aiding and abetting of treason."[3]

On April 7, 1933, all professors of law who were Jews and those few who were not conservatives were driven from their universities in humiliating circumstances. With one stroke, 120 of the 378 scholars who had been teaching at German law schools in 1932 were dismissed—that is to say, almost a third of the total number, the great majority of them for racial reasons.[4] Their positions were now vacant for promising untenured faculty colleagues with a "nationalistic orientation." Count Gleispach, an Austrian expert on criminal law who was highly regarded in Germany, had already been given an honorary professorship in Berlin after disciplinary sanctions were imposed on him in Vienna in 1931 for National Socialist agitation. Now in 1933, in Prussia alone, Hermann Bente, Georg Dahm, Ernst Forsthoff, Heinrich Henkel, Heinrich Herrfarth, Fritz von Hippel, Ernst Rudolf Huber, Max Kaser, Karl Larenz, Siegfried Reicke, Paul Ritterbusch, Karl Siegert, Gustav Adolf Walz, Hans Julius Wolff, and Hans Würdiger were also appointed to professorships.[6] Most of them were young, barely over thirty, and continued to teach until the late 1960s. (By 1939, fully two thirds of the faculty at German law schools had been appointed in or after 1933.) A few scattered liberals who had not been dismissed following "restoration of the permanent civil service" resigned from their universities and withdrew into "inner emigration." One of the rare documents of moral courage and integrity in that era is the letter of Gerhard Anschütz, professor of public law at Heidelberg, requesting early retirement. Anschütz wrote to the minister of education in the state of Baden that he was unable to muster the intellectual "solidarity with new German constitutional law as it is now taking shape," which would be necessary to train law students "in accord with the intent and spirit of the current government."[7]

By contrast, the Association of German Institutions of Higher Education, which spoke for the universities, greeted the "rise of the new German Reich" as a "fulfillment of their longings and confirmation of their undying and heartfelt hopes."[8] Once the law faculties of the country had lightheartedly parted company with their Jewish and (Social-)democratic colleagues, they boldly set about throwing overboard achievements fought for and won in Europe during centuries of struggle: the requirements that legal learning be disinterested, objective, and autonomous. Scholars were more than willing to return to the role of handmaiden which had characterized the profession in the Middle Ages and to accept a system of values imposed on them from the outside. National Socialism had long since recognized, in the words of Bernhard Rust (minister for universities, schools, and popular education), that "scholarship [is] completely impossible without a foundation of values."[9] Carl Schmitt applied this doctrine to the specific case of legal scholarship: "The whole of German law today . . . must be governed solely and exclusively by the spirit of National Socialism . . . Every interpretation must be an interpretation according to National Socialism."[10]

The anti-Enlightenment spirit of the new regime found favor among law school faculties, whose members were largely antirepublican, antidemocratic, and authoritarian in attitude. Not only the newest appointees, who owed their promising careers to the personnel policy of the Nazis, but also established professors were astoundingly productive during the early years of the Third Reich in helping to shape a "National Socialist legal system." They saw it as their task to bring about a "coordination" of the legal profession's thinking parallel to the "coordination" of legal institutions which had already occurred. In this effort, some of the older full professors strove to outdo their young colleagues in demonstrations of nationalistic fervor. Wilhelm Sauer, for example, who had been appointed to his professorship in 1919, published in the respected journal *Archiv für Rechtsphilosophie* (Archive for Legal Philosophy) in 1933 an exhortation "to extol the Führer as a figure of light and a hero who is leading the German soul out of the depths into the light, showing it the safe path to Valhalla, to God the Father in the true German homeland, setting an example of this Gothic life to his own brothers, offering them help to help themselves, so that all Germans may become brothers before God the Father."[11]

In this flood of publications, lectures, manifestos, and proposed amendments to existing laws, both the fiery avowals of loyalty to the Führer, to a nationalistic order, and to racial homogeneity, and the development of "completely new" legal methods, ways of thinking, and interpretations managed to disguise only with difficulty the fact that all these usually meant turning back the clock and eradicating every trace of civilization and historical progress from German law. Citing Goebbels' famous remark that the task of National Socialism was "to erase the year 1789 from German history," legal scholars began to indulge in polemics against human rights, guarantees of individual rights vis-à-vis the state, limitations of state powers, and restraints on the state's right to impose punishments. In this area, as Friedrich Schaffstein, one of the up-and-coming talents of

Nazi jurisprudence, remarked in his inaugural lecture as a professor in January 1934, there was a lot of work to be done: "Almost all the principles, concepts, and distinctions of our law up to now are stamped with the spirit of the Enlightenment, and they therefore require reshaping on the basis of a new kind of thought and experience." [12]

Most of the hallmark achievements of constitutional government—the subjection of state authority to law, equality of all citizens before the law, and certain inviolable individual rights—had already been done away with during the "National Socialist revolution." Nonetheless, for a broad spectrum of the population the concept of the "constitutional state" long retained its positive connotations, and traditionally this was understood to mean a government which was subject to law—that is, liberal constitutionalism. In the early years of the Third Reich, a discussion thus arose in which legal thinkers attempted to clarify what the correct stand was on the issue of the constitutional state. Ernst Forsthoff, who had referred to the constitutional state as the "prototype of a society without honor and dignity," [13] attacked Otto Koellreutter's use of the term as an "error in terminology" [14] that encouraged liberal associations. And Carl Schmitt issued a warning that if the term was used at all, such usage should be aimed only at illustrating how its meaning had changed and should occur only in combinations such as "the German constitutional state," "the National Socialist constitutional state," or better yet, "the German constitutional state of Adolf Hitler," [15] for "we do not determine what National Socialism is according to a preexisting concept of the constitutional state, but rather the reverse; the constitutional state [is determined] according to National Socialism." [16] Political theorists vied with one another in coining new combinations such as "the national constitutional state" [17] or "real constitutional state," [18] a contest in which Roland Freisler demonstrated the most active imagination. He compared the "National Socialist constitutional state" with "the concentrated might of the people, as only concentrated firepower could stop a tank attacking the front lines." [19] Metaphors such as these made it clear that there would be no carryover of earlier civil libertarian ideas about freedom, and that the formal constitutional state, the "mere state under the law," [20] would be replaced by a "more profound idea of legality" [21]—namely, "that the state and the law acquire an identical meaning for the *Volk*." [22] During the whole controversy, however, the participants were fundamentally agreed on the main point: "At issue was not the thing itself, but only its name." [23]

German jurists were particularly united in their rejection of the constitutional democracy of the "formalist era." It embodied for them a "degenerate from of bourgeois constitutionalism," [24] and its fundamental notions—democracy, liberalism, equality before the law, and tolerance of differing political opinions—were "opposed and repellent to our own German world view."[25]

The most important specific application of the principle of constitutionalism to the administration of justice is judges' independence and their obligation to the law alone. But since the Nazi dictators, despite their hectic legislative activity, were unable to alter all laws overnight, their problem was to commit the judiciary to a new and flexible attitude, depending on whether a particular statute stemmed from the old republic or was a new one of the Führer's. The Law for Restoration of the Professional Civil Service had already done away with judges' security of tenure, since it allowed the government to dismiss from office all judges who were politically undesirable, or not "Aryan," or who would not undertake "to support the national state at all times and without reservation." Furthermore, judges could also be removed from office without such reasons being given, even "if the conditions required for this by existing laws are not met."[26]

The dismissals which followed the passing of the law reinstituting the permanent civil service represented a decisive step in purging the courts of undesirables. But the law had a further, virtually incalculable effect on the "coordination" of the legal profession owing to the way it also intimidated those judges who were not directly affected by it. German law professors now informed them that "in the interest of consistent government, certain limits must be imposed" on the autonomy of the courts.[27] There should be no mistaking the fact "that the rule that a judge's sole obligation is to the law now means something different from what it used to,"[28] for "we seek an obligation which is more reliable, more vital, and deeper than the misleading obligation to the letter of thousands of paragraphs, which can be twisted."[29]

In the future, decisions should be handed down only by "one who lives in his people, feels with his people, and seeks justice where it is born, in the healthy common sense of the people."[30] A judge's "true nature and racial identity" ought to "make him part of the community which creates the law and make him an existential member of it";[31] it should also make him a person who acts "on his convictions in a harmony of feeling and will with all his legal comrades."[32] The judge's labors should "not [be] constricted by arbitrary decisions or by a formalistic and abstract principle of stability of the law; rather [they should] find clear lines and, . . . wherever necessary, their limits through the legal views of the people that have found expression in the law and that are embodied by the Führer."[33] The ideal of the rational, dispassionate judge propagated since the Enlightenment was suspect in the eyes of jurists of this ilk. "Abstract and normative thinking" appeared to them as an "expression of helplessness, rootlessness, and debility."[34] The new judge should decide his cases "not on the basis of an analytical investigation of their elements, but only as wholes, concretely, after grasping their essence."[35] The "rationalistic dissection" of the facts of a case and "the distortion of its essential nature"[36] that resulted from an unprejudiced approach—these were ideas they rejected completely. After all, the new form of law was "not to be arrived at by logical reasoning alone, . . . but instead was to be felt and experienced by a member of the *Volk* by virtue of his close ties to it."[37] A judge should therefore approach a case with "healthy prejudice" and "make value judgments which correspond to the National Socialist legal order and the will of the political leadership."[38] This kind of jurisprudence stood above the "typically exaggerated liberal fear of miscarriages of justice";[39] an "emotional, value-laden, and overall approach"[40] and an "overall view of the nature of the law"[41] would guarantee that judges reached correct decisions. It was probably Justus Hedemann who best expressed the emotionality of the new direction in legal thinking in his remarks entitled "Truth in the Law": "And [let there be] no guardian of German law who is not gripped, at least in great moments, by that seriousness of purpose, who pales at any labor, and who does not hear from beyond the course of his labors, now near, now far, the waters gushing from the fount of truth."[42]

Such irrational phrases about the "rootedness" of the jurist "in the substance, the spirit of the *Volk*,"[43] and about his "proper place in a national order based on racial unity, to which the jurist and his intellectual labors belong as well,"[44] had a concrete background which was revealed in Erik Wolf's warning to judges: "In the everyday practice of law, genuine National Socialism is certainly best represented where the idea of the Führer is silently but loyally followed."[45] Judges were "liberated" from their obligation to the law only to be constrained by an incomparably more restrictive "obligation to the main principles of the Führer's government,"[46] a step which in the last analysis had the effect of making "the judge a direct servant of the state,"[47] or, as Freisler put it in one of his inimitable metaphors, "The law is the bated breath of life, . . . but the guardian of the law must be the soldier at the front of the life of the nation."[48]

National Socialist polemics were directed not only against every effort to make the criminal code more humane, but also and equally against its constitutional foundations, particularly the principle *nulla poena sine lex* ("no penalty without law"). This fundamental principle sums up several limitations of the state's power to impose punishments: nothing may be prohibited retroactively (only an act which was punishable at the time it was committed may be punished); nothing may be prohibited by analogy (only what the wording of the law specifically declares to be punishable is punishable); nothing may be left unclear (the statute must be worded precisely and must make it possible to recognize what is a punishable offense and what is not); and finally the right to impose punishments must be granted exclusively to an independent judiciary, since any system of justice can be undermined if sanctions are permitted to exist outside it. Every single component of this fundamental legal principle was quickly abolished during the Third Reich. Retroactive punishment became possible with passage of the Law on the Imposition and Implementation of the Death Penalty, the so-called Van der Lubbe Law, and more than twenty other statutes and ordinances of the Nazi era also contained provisions for retroactive penalties.[49] A possibility for sanctions outside the criminal courts was created by the institution of "preventive detention," over which the police had sole control. And finally the prohibition against declaring an act criminal by analogy was eliminated in June 1935 by the rewording of paragraph 2 of the Criminal Code: "That person will be punished who commits an act which the law declares to be punishable or which deserves punishment according to the fundamental principle of a criminal statute or healthy popular opinion."[50]

Ernst Niekisch hits the nail on the head when he calls the legal analogy an "insidious arrangement" created for the sole purpose "of sending every unyielding opponent to the penitentiary, even though no law whatsoever exists against which he has offended."[51] Nevertheless, the significance of this piece of legislation is often overestimated today. Of course—as Roland Freisler pointed out approvingly—it enabled "the judge to punish every lawbreaker, even if his particular crime was not specifically mentioned by law, something which until then had been difficult and only partially possible through broad interpretation of the limits of sentencing."[52] However, in practice the new paragraph 2 played only a small role in the courts. This was due primarily to the efforts of jurists who had long since developed a theory of criminal law and a number of procedural tools which made rewriting of the criminal code in fact unnecessary.

There was, of course, no area of the law which National Socialist ideas failed to permeate eventually; even such apparently apolitical fields as landlord and tenant law, commercial law, and trade and industrial law were "fertilized" with Nazi legal thinking. The consequences of this new jurisprudence emerge most clearly, however, in criminal law, an area which allows the state the firmest grip on its citizens and where, for this reason, the notion of the stability of law has traditionally been most sharply defined. Whereas since the time of the Enlightenment efforts had been directed toward making the dividing line between lawful and unlawful acts as clear as possible, professors of criminal law in the Third Reich openly acknowledged it as their chief task to blur this line to the point of invisibility. The primary aim of criminal law was "to protect the community of the *Volk* from criminals," and this protective function supplanted what had been the foremost principle of the constitutional state: "Today everyone will recognize that the maxim 'No crime without punishment' takes priority over the maxim 'No punishment without law' as the higher and stronger legal truth" (Carl Schmitt).[53]

Just as from an authoritarian point of view criminal law was not designed "to protect the rights of the individual against the state . . . , but rather to protect the state from the individual,"[54] National Socialist criminal law was "less concerned with the clarity of statutory provisions than with material justice."[55] Stability of law and protection of individual rights were thrust aside in favor of this mystical "material justice," which could supposedly be grasped only through "an overall view of its essential nature." For this reason, laws ought to be formulated purposely in vague and fuzzy wording: "General provisos, admission of analogy, recognition of healthy popular opinion as a source of law, and admission of direct and immediate recognition of what is just . . . are criteria of National Socialist criminal law."[56] The concomitant loss of stability of law was quite intentional, for, as Carl Schmitt noted, "In the decisive case of political crime, the use of norms and procedures merely means that the Führer's hands are tied, to the advantage of the disobedient."[57] There was even some discussion of whether a criminal code could not be dispensed with entirely: "The recognition that it is impossible for individual legal norms to cover all possible cases suggests that it would be preferable to do without a list of specific offenses and to provide the judge with guidelines in the form of a few general principles, according to which he must determine the criminal nature of an offense."[58] The fact that it would then become impossible for an individual "to comprehend the law and to calculate its consequences" was expressly welcomed by the professor of criminal law Heinrich Henkel as a desirable aim, since uncertainty about the possible repercussions of an act would increase the pressure to conform. Therefore, the saying ought no longer to run, "What is not forbidden is allowed, but rather: What is not allowed is forbidden."[60]

As a result, this new kind of criminal jurisprudence was no longer concerned with determining whether an action was prohibited by law or not, since according to Reich minister of justice Gürtner, "National Socialism replaces this concept of formal illegality with the concept of material illegality . . . Hence, the law renounces its claim to be the sole source for determining what is legal and illegal."[61]

What did it in fact amount to, this notion of "material illegality" that was cited repeatedly and supposed to be understandable only in terms of a "world view determined in the last analysis by experience and faith?"[62] Criminal law professor Wilhelm Sauer had already worked this out in 1921: "Behavior is unlawful when its general tendency in the judgment of jurisprudence does more harm than good to the state and its members."[63] From this conservative, statist position it was only a small step to Edmund Mezger's succinct definition: "Materially unlawful activity is activity counter to the German National Socialist world view."[64]

A widely known maxim in those days, which every law student had to learn by heart, taught that the chief aim of criminal law, the "protection of German society," would be achieved "by eliminating individuals who are degenerate or otherwise lost to society and by allowing petty offenders who can still perform useful social functions to atone."[65] This maxim revealed the two areas on which National Socialist criminal jurisprudence concentrated its efforts: developing a disciplinary code for the German citizen "derelict of his duty," and finding means to destroy the enemy, the deviant "other," a group to which "degenerate" criminals were also assigned. And it was by no means true, as one might suppose, that only the most extreme Nazis among the criminal law experts emphasized the more aggressively punitive area of "tactical law" for the "protection of society," while the older school of conservatives tended to turn to the "disciplinary" side. On the contrary, an Official Criminal Law Commission composed chiefly of conservatives and chaired by Reich minister of justice Gürtner placed the idea of "protection" at the center of their ideas about a future Criminal Code, whereas it was the Reich Law Bureau of the Nazi party which stressed the "duty of allegiance to the *Volk.*"[66]

"Protective" law aimed to "purge society of inferior individuals"[67] and stressed that "the particular obligation of criminal law is to the negative, defensive side of protection. Its ultimate function is to exterminate."[68] The notion of "protection" was not directed solely—or even primarily—at "degenerate criminals," but above all at opponents of the system, since the view of criminal law as a "law of war" led to the conclusion that "obviously the goal of this law is not merely to resist the opponent, but to annihilate him."[69] The privileged treatment of political offenders—previously guaranteed by the criminal code and from which Hitler had profited himself during his trial for high treason—was now not just abolished, but in fact turned into its opposite: as Roland Freisler explained, "There is no place in National Socialism for the recognition of political offenses. This would be tantamount to classifying the offender as a decent and respectable adversary, and this is not possible under National Socialism." Political opponents were branded as particularly reprehensible criminals: "For the enemy of the state and the community of the *Volk* there is only one course in prosecution and sentencing: unflinching severity and, if necessary, total annihilation."[70] In Gürtner's words, there "could be no doubt" that the German people had never shown "any sympathy" for the recognition of political offenses, "for the traitor has always been regarded everywhere as the most heinous of criminals."[71]

In order to be able to decide whether "unflinching severity" or "total annihilation" was called for, legal scholars developed a system of criminal punishment which closely resembled existing disciplinary procedures for the civil service and the armed forces and which was based on an increased loyalty owed to the state and its leaders. A long tradition (which continues to the present day) decrees that such disciplinary procedures are less concerned with exacting expiation from a civil servant for a particular misdeed than with establishing whether his "overall behavior" permits his remaining "in the circle of his colleagues." In precisely this manner the criminal law of the Third Reich was now to attempt to judge whether a "member of the *Volk* could still be tolerated by society" or whether, depending on the prognosis for his future behavior, he should be removed from society, either temporarily or permanently. And like disciplinary law, which was feudal in origin and still hardly touched by the spirit of the Enlightenment, the criminal law of the Nazi era was characterized by categories of "wrongdoing" based on vague and feudalistic moral values such as "honor," "loyalty," and "duty." The legal scholars of the Law Bureau of the Nazi party developed the following guidelines for criminal offenses:

> National Socialist criminal law must be based on the duty of loyalty to the *Volk:* loyalty is the highest duty of the *Volk* and therefore a moral duty in National Socialist and German thinking. In German thinking there is a harmony between moral values, a sense of duty, and a sense of justice . . . According to these principles a violation of the duty of loyalty necessarily leads to the loss of honor. It is the task of the National Socialist state to require just expiation from the disloyal, who by their disloyalty have renounced their membership in the community. Just punishment serves to strengthen, protect, and safeguard the community, but also serves to educate and improve the criminal who is not yet lost to society.[72]

Nazi theorists of criminal law had begun early to equate crime with "disloyalty," "violation of duty," and "treason." In addition to the particular gravity assigned to it, a criminal offense represented a breach of duty toward the community; George Dahm took the view that even simple theft constituted an act of disloyalty toward the Führer and the *Volk*.[73] Of course, a breach of loyalty could be committed only by someone who owed loyalty—that is to say, a member of the community. Thus, Friedrich Schaffstein called for a "consolidation of the *Volk*" as a prerequisite for this new criminal law to be redefined along the lines of disciplinary law. A criminal should be made "the subject of study in criminal law solely in terms of his necessary ties as a member of society, not as an individual, but as a member of the *Volk*."[74] The contribution of jurisprudence to this consolidation would consist in pointing out the right path to members of the *Volk*. Hans Welzel, who always stressed the "constructive ethical force of criminal law," saw its foremost task to be impressing "enduring values" firmly upon the German consciousness: "Loyalty toward the *Volk*, the Reich, and its leaders, obedience to the authority of the state, readiness to defend one's country, truthfulness in oaths, sexual decorum, respect for the life, health, and freedom of others, honesty with regard to others' property, probity in financial dealings, and so on."[75] German professors of criminal law generally liked to regard themselves as educators of the populace. Wilhelm Sauer declared that "a healthy criminal law [must] have the highest ethical values pulsing through it, to keep popular sentiment healthy, particularly in a moral sense, and to contribute to the improvement and advancement of the *Volk*."[76] It was Hans Welzel's hope that criminal law "would raise the ethical attitudes of all members of the community."[77]

It followed that punishment was seen above all as a loss of honor, and that a sentence imposed on a convicted criminal represented "a moral judgment on his attitudes as a member of the *Volk*."[78] Scholars came out early in favor of penalties which would have the effect of a pillory or exposure to public shame; one example was the "declaration of dishonor," which went far beyond the loss of a citizen's privileges and included a ban on becoming a farmer, manager of a business, shop steward, legal guardian of a minor or incompetent, lay magistrate, or soldier. Georg Dahm even went so far as to demand a form of penalty which would in effect declare the convicted criminal outside the protection of the law: "He may no longer participate in legal transactions, and it appears inevitable that his legal status as a member of a family is forfeited as well."[79] However, even the stigmatizing effect of "normal" criminal penalties ought to be increased, it was thought, since "every real punishment is a loss of honor."[80] The purpose would be "to give visible expression to the dishonor and disesteem" in which such an individual is held by the community."[81] A penitentiary sentence would mean not only the loss of freedom under more severe conditions, but also "the severest form of dishonor." Only when the criminal had expiated his guilt would he be permitted to stand "once more in rank and file with all the other members of the *Volk*." [83]

"Absolution" of this kind was possible only in limited measure, however—a point on which Nazis and old-style conservatives agreed. For criminal law professor Friedrich Oetker (who like many of his colleagues is still regarded in the postwar literature as a "liberal" of that period), it was clear that "whoever forgets his place in the ranks, whoever commits an assault on the community of the *Volk* or refuses to obey its laws [is] . . . an enemy of the people." [84] And in the eyes of the committed National Socialist Count Gleispach, an "attack on the foundations of national life" represented the gravest kind of disloyalty: "The German who transgresses against the community itself in this manner . . . commits treason." [85]

The consequences of the verdicts "enemy of the people" or "traitor" were obvious, for "certain of the most serious crimes preclude the reintegration of the criminal into society by their very nature, even if in a given instance the education and resocialization of the culprit as they used to be understood appear possible." [86]

As a result, the purpose of a trial now became not so much to determine whether the accused had broken a law, but rather "whether the wrongdoer still belongs to the community"; [87] the criminal trial was supposed to be "an evaluation and segregation of types." [88] A decisive characteristic of National Socialist theory was that emphasis was placed less on the act committed than on the "criminal personality." Legal scholars developed categories of "characteristic criminal types" for use in the rewriting of laws and decrees; these "types," which were determined by "simple and popular distinctions," came to play an ever greater role, from the law against dangerous habitual criminals, the decree concerning protection against juvenile criminals, and the decree on violent crimes and "antisocial parasites" to the new version of the murder laws, which stated: "Murder is punishable by death." All of these laws, which prescribed the death penalty as a possible or as a mandatory sentence, proceeded on the assumption that murderers are born, not made.

A half-hearted attempt to maintain the traditional principle of guilt—that is, the principle according to which a person is punished not for what he is, but for what he has in fact done—was made by Edmund Mezger in the form of his doctrine of "culpability in the conduct of one's life." [89] This concept was designed to force the "law of criminal types" into the old mold of the principle of guilt, since it maintained that "antisocial outsiders, who are a burden to the community and who merit punishment not so much on the basis of single actions as for their antisocial . . . existence," should supposedly not be punished because they are antisocial but because they had become so through "culpable conduct of their lives." However, the dominant view of that time was long past the stage of being willing to accept this kind of hair-splitting. Geog Dahm objected that "even judges experienced in dealing with life and people trained in criminology" would not be able "to determine the roles played by personal guilt and fate in a person's life." Should a judge, he asked rhetorically, "seriously consider whether a defendant with twenty or thirty previous convictions is responsible for having become what he is, and whether his heredity or personal guilt is the actual cause of the crime? It is precisely in such a case that the death penalty fulfills the intention of the law, if the lawbreaker had no other possibility than to become a criminal." [90]

Since at that time two basic types of criminal punishment—the penalty intended to protect society if a defendant was found unfit to stand trial, and "retribution" if he was guilty—led to the same result in both instances, namely the death penalty, it would have been superfluous in any case to inquire into the motives and causes of an action. The courts certainly tended to take this view. For example, the Supreme Military Court (*Reichskriegsgericht*), which has been praised in recent years for its supposedly model constitutional stance, determined on January 24, 1940, that "the particular circumstances of the army and the requirements of wartime make it necessary to treat defendants of diminished responsibility no differently from those who are fully responsible in the sense of the law." [91]

The essential features of Nazi theory in criminal law were developed above all at the law school of the University of Kiel, where personnel policy had led to the assembling of an incomparable Nazi faculty, including Georg Dahm, Ernst Rudolf Huber, Karl Larenz, Karl Michaelis, Friedrich Schaffstein, and Wolfgang Siebert. They provided the judicial system with the intellectual basis for its murderous interpretations. The pithiest summary of these principles is probably the program contained in Schaffstein's *Politische Strafrechtswissenschaft* (Political Theory of Criminal Law). This work also demonstrates that the antirepublican spirit of many court decisions in the Weimar era created a foundation enabling Nazi leaders to twist criminal law at will and make it an instrument for cementing their power.

One doctrine in particular made is possible for judges even in the Weimar Republic to disguise breaches of the law contained in their own decisions as "interpretation." This was the "teleological method" of interpretation developed by professor of criminal law Erich Schwinge, a method of "teleological concepts" which encouraged judges to identify a particular ideological meaning and intent underlying a given law and then to use this "intent" to undermine the wording of the law as such.

One crass example of this method has already been mentioned in the verdict of the court against Hitler after his attempted coup in Munich. Although the law clearly required his deportation as a foreign national, "the meaning and intent of the requirement" prevented its application in the case of "a man whose mentality is as German as Hitler's." This kind of "interpretation" served effectively to counteract the intentions of the democratic legislative branch of the Weimar government; during the Third Reich, "the will of lawmakers" could be carried out to a far greater extent than could actually be expressed in the wording of the laws themselves. Although the Supreme Court never admitted officially the degree to which it was practiced, such a method of interpretation led, as Schaffstein rightly concluded, to an "abandonment of the liberal notion of the separation of powers and to a neglect of the principles of stability of law and predictability in favor of other new legal values."[93]

The recognition of "defense of the state" as a justification for breaking the law made it possible for the courts to let the most serious crimes up to and including political assassinations go unpunished. The emphasis on motives, general tendencies, previous convictions, and character of a defendant—rather than the objective and verifiable circumstances of a particular act—made the criminal justice system flexible and often permitted the courts to circumvent the provisions laid down by law in favor of penalties they deemed "appropriate."

The numerous "scientific" approaches to criminal law developed by right-wing scholars in the 1920s and 1930s, such as the doctrine of "criminal types" and inflated pseudo-scholarly concepts such as "material crime," "creative interpretation," "teleological method," and "grasp of essences," were even more sinister than the formal step finally taken by the Nazi government of recognizing the principle of analogy in judging a defendant. The approaches suggested by Nazi legal theorists led to the same result in a less obvious manner, providing the courts with the means to subvert justice and commit judicial murder.

10

Civil Servants Become the Führer's Political Troops

Soon after radical purges had removed "non-Aryans" and the politically unreliable from the ranks of the civil service, a flood of scholarly articles began to appear concerning the new understanding of the civil servant's duty of loyalty to the government. The commentaries on the professional civil service laws of the Weimar era had always stressed the political neutrality of government employees, in order to prevent them from becoming politically attached to the democratic system. Now, however, the status of the civil servant was suddenly redefined as "inherently political."[1] It was not a sufficient demonstration of loyalty if "the civil servant takes it upon himself to observe the law loyally"; what was now required of him was that he live "with the Führer in the inner conviction that he is the focal point of the state."[2] At first, the Law for Restoration of the Professional Civil Service had demanded "merely" that he uphold "the national state unconditionally at all times." However, this duty of loyalty was redefined and increased by the wording of the Law on the Civil Service of 1937, which required that he "uphold the National Socialist state unconditionally at all times and that he be guided in his every action by the fact that the National Socialist German Workers' party, through its indissoluble ties with the *Volk,* embodies the concept of the German state."[3]

The scholarly commentaries on this law outdo one another in making the demands on the loyalty of civil servants more and more sweeping: "The civil servant's inner ties to the Führer and thus to the party [should be] an indispensable prerequisite for his appointment."[4] For Ernst Rudolf Huber, the minimum requirements for appointment were "unqualified identification with the National Socialist world view" and "unconditional commitment to the Führer," since "we will not reach a state of affairs in which it goes without saying that every administrative act and every judicial decision is based on unerring instinct and an emanation of the spirit of the *Volk*, until civil servants are thoroughly steeped in the national world view."[5]

It was the task of the disciplinary institutions to ensure that the behavior of civil servants came close to reaching this ideal; the final court of appeal was the Supreme Disciplinary Court (*Reichsdisziplinarhof*, later changed to *Reichsdienststrafhof*) attached to the Supreme Court and under the leadership of Supreme Court president Bumke. Even before the new law took effect, this court had defined the "legal nature" of the civil service as "loyalty, obedience, and conscientious performance of duty" and had referred to civil servants as "the political troops of the Führer in the area of administration."[6] The Supreme Disciplinary Court had already done much to pave the way for the new law by interpreting many details of civil service law—that is to say, the individual civil servant's lack of rights—as seemed "appropriate" and "in accord with the principles of the National Socialist state." In one "creative" decision (meaning that it violated the letter of the law), the court determined that violations of professional duty by civil servants no longer fell under a statute of limitations, and that a government employee had no right to see the file of reports kept on him by his superiors. Article 129 of the Weimar constitution, which had never been formally revoked, guaranteed this right to every civil servant; the Supreme Disciplinary Court found, however, that this article conflicted "with the basic principles of National Socialism," and thus that it had "ceased to be valid, though there had been no express legal disposition, at the time of the National Socialist revolution."[7] Furthermore, the right of a civil servant to respond to criticism by his superiors in writing was found to be "irreconcilable with the principle of the Führer's leadership" and therefore no longer in effect. It was not even sufficient in the view of this court that a civil servant "recognize the authority of the National Socialist state and demonstrate this conviction in both his professional and private life"; beyond that, it was expected that he would "promote and carry out to the best of his ability . . . the wishes of the government leaders and the National Socialist party."[8]

The court regarded as examples of the most severe dereliction of duty, which had to be punished by dismissal from the civil service, the fact that one government employee had failed "to display flags from his apartment on appropriate occasions and was also not in possession of a swastika flag,"[9] or that another "had not offered the German salute in the prescribed form to be observed by every civil servant," since "this avowal of loyalty to the Führer numbers among his foremost duties."[10] In other cases, the court took the view that a government employee who in 1935 still patronized a department store owned by Jews,[11] borrowed money from a Jew,[12] or acceded to his French-born wife's wishes to send their son to a school in France rather than Germany failed in his duty to such a degree that he could "no longer belong to the civil service."[13]

When one civil servant expressed his aversion to the local candidate Alfred Rosenberg by voting "no" in the parliamentary elections of April 10, 1938, and in the simultaneous referendum on the annexation of Austria, and later did not attempt to deny that he had so voted, he was dismissed from office. The Supreme Disciplinary Court rejected his appeal to be reinstated on the grounds that "full and unconditional support for the Führer" demanded of every civil servant by the law must "also be expected in the exercise of his election and voting rights . . . though elections are still free and secret even now, the freedom to vote . . . finds its natural limits in the special position of the civil servant in the National Socialist state . . . For the civil servant, just as for the party member, it goes without saying that he must express his loyalty to the Führer by declaring himself in favor of the reunification of Austria with the German Reich brought about by the Führer."[14]

The "special" duties of loyalty owed to the state by civil servants as construed by the courts led to a situation in which every defendant's appeal to supposedly still existing freedoms or rights could be interpreted as a "misuse" of such freedoms. The degree to which their behavior became totally regulated as a result is illustrated by the following case.

A civil servant—who was by no means an opponent of the National Socialists but had been "a champion of the national cause for years"—had refused to participate in the "Winter Relief Fund" (*Winterhilfswerk*), a collection for charity mounted yearly by the Nazis with a great deal of accompanying propaganda. In the ensuing disciplinary proceedings, he protested that he regularly donated large sums of his income to charity and furthermore the contributions to the Winter Relief Fund were voluntary—as the authorities always stressed. This protest alone was sufficient demonstration to the Supreme Disciplinary Court that the man had no place in the civil service of the Third Reich. In its decision of June 15, 1937, the court gave him a severe dressing-down: "He still has notions about his freedom, according to the crassest form of the liberalist view . . . Freedom to him means the authority to refuse to carry out all duties not explicitly prescribed by law, as he himself sees fit. He has refused to participate in a community undertaking, because he wishes to show that no one [can] compel him to"; however, precisely this attitude signified a "reprehensible abuse of the freedom granted him by the Führer in his reliance on the German spirit."[15]

· 11 ·

Creation of the Concentration Camps

"Our criminal friends have also taken note that since 1933 a fresher and healthier wind has been blowing in Germany. There is no more sentimentality in our penitentiaries and prisons."[1] The Nazi "prison reform program" described by undersecretary Roland Freisler in these brisk words was assured of wide support among the middle class from the beginning. The previous liberal reforms first put forward by progressive jurists at the turn of the century, and later implemented by the Weimar government at least in part, had always met with considerable opposition from most judges and public prosecutors. In 1932, for example, the judges and public prosecutors of Prussia had presented a program of alleged "economy measures" which in fact would have represented a drastic tightening of prison conditions, including stricter discipline, increased work demands, and a reduced diet.[2]

Some theorists of criminal law with authoritarian leanings also argued in favor of stricter treatment of criminals, on the grounds that "the idea of retribution is too deeply rooted in popular thinking about justice for it to be eliminated by rationalistic theories in the foreseeable future."[3] It was ironic that the German section of the International Union of Criminologists, an organization originally founded by liberal jurists committed to social reforms in order to improve treatment of prisoners, became a forum for the "new" conservatives. At the annual conference in 1932, members who already openly espoused the Nazi cause spoke out about the concern which the relaxation of prison regulations in the 1920s had caused them: "If one imagines the trend continuing for another thirty to forty years, then we will have no punishment left at all."[4]

According to the "Principles of Criminal Punishment" adopted in 1923, prisoners were supposed "to be made accustomed to order and work, and strengthened in character so that they do not become repeat offenders." Paragraph 48 indicted how this goal was to be achieved: "Prisoners are to be treated seriously, justly, and humanely. Their sense of honor is to be respected and strengthened."[5] There had been an outcry from conservative jurists over such "bleeding heart" notions, and, as was to be expected, the reformulation in 1934 of the principles on which prisons were to be run was dominated by the concepts of atonement, retribution, severity, discipline, and order. The new version of paragraph 48 now ran: "The restriction of the prisoner's liberty is a penalty through which he shall atone for the wrong he committed. The conditions of imprisonment shall be such that they represent a considerable hardship for prisoners and create lasting resistance to the temptation to commit further crimes even in those who are not accessible to reeducation. Prisoners are to be trained in discipline and order, made accustomed to work and fulfillment of duty, and strengthened in character."[6]

In actual practice, these principles were expressed in the repeal of all modern improvements in the treatment of criminals and a return to the old ways of compulsion. Committees once created to oversee fair treatment of prisoners were disbanded and prison libraries closed. The right to receive packages was abolished; the right to lodge complaints about prison conditions was limited; and passes for prisoners to leave prison temporarily were revoked.[7] "All abuses of the previous system" had been corrected, reported the governor of the Plötzensee prison: "Smoking is no longer permitted anywhere. On visitors' days prisoners are no longer allowed to greet relatives with a kiss or handshake. The right to lodge complaints has been dealt with in such a manner that nothing may now go outside the prison walls . . . The new government has intentionally arranged things so that a prison sentence represents a hardship and is experienced as such."[8]

The total number of inmates in prisons and penitentiaries rose sharply after 1933. According to official statistics, on April 1, 1934, there were 64,000 in Prussia alone; in 1929 there had been fewer than 30,000. In the whole of the Reich there were some 150,000 people in penal institutions in 1934.[9] This large figure had resulted to a considerable degree from the government's criminalization of the political opposition. Between 1935 and 1937, there were more political criminals who had been tried and sentenced than there were in "preventive detention."[10] Three fourths of the 2,300 inmates in the large Waldheim prison near Chemnitz were "politicals"; in Hamburg-Fuhlsbüttel and Bautzen, with 1,200 each, the percentage was two thirds, and in the Remscheid-Lüttringhausen penitentiary it was half of 1,400. There were 1,520 inmates in the Güsteckerdorf penitentiary and the Benninghaus and Aplerbeck prisons of the city of Dortmund, all of them imprisoned for political reasons. The prisons of

Koblenz, Neuwied, Hönningen, and Heimbach were also filled entirely with "politicals."[11]

Above and beyond the crowding and harsh discipline in prisons which were usually old and in need of repair, the inmates suffered from an inadequate diet. Between 1931 and 1935, the average yearly sum spent on a prisoner dropped from 1,228 to 725 marks, and the sum spent on food was cut by half.[12] At the same time, the working hours in penitentiaries were raised from eight to ten, and the hour allotted to daily recreation was replaced by an hour of strenuous military drills. The results were weight loss, exhaustion, and increased susceptibility to disease, particularly digestive disorders. In 1935, as a consequence of the substandard diet, nearly all the inmates of the large female penitentiary Jauer in Lower Saxony were suffering from stomach and intestinal problems; and since all fresh fruits and vegetables had been gradually eliminated from the menu and the remaining, monotonously unvarying meals were prepared without seasonings, prison inmates began to develop a disgust for food, a symptom which prevented them from consuming adequate nourishment despite their hunger pangs. This undernourishment led to the development of furuncles, skin rashes, and metabolic disturbances in many of them, and did nothing to alleviate the hygiene problems in the already hopelessly overcrowded institutions.[13] The prison in Hannover, which had been built to house 600 inmates, contained approximately 1,200 in 1935; the Jauer penitentiary held 800 women instead of the planned 250, and three women were placed in the cells designed for solitary confinement. At the Luckau penitentiary, where prisoners slept in large dormitories, 32 of them shared one bucket as a chamber pot, and fresh underwear was handed out every two weeks; at Jauer it was once a month.[14]

The sanitary conditions existing in these institutions stood in grotesque contrast to the prison guards' obsession with order; they insisted that beds be made with tight corners and not a single wrinkle, although the sheets were stiff with dirt, and chamber pots had to be scrubbed and polished until they shone.[15] This was part of the military regimen in penal institutions, which also demanded that prisoners salute and "report" at every turn. In the Brandenburg penitentiary, inmates were required to give the guard a military salute even when they wished to step out of a room with chamber pot in hand; refusal to comply or too casual a salute was punished with solitary confinement.[16]

A training course for judges and public prosecutors on the topic "Treatment of Prisoners" was accompanied by an article in the *Rheinisch-Westfälische Zeitung* on the Münster penitentiary, one of the largest in the Reich. The newspaper reported on July 5, 1935: "Particularly striking is the discipline, which has become considerably more severe and rigorous. Prisoners must obey with military precision and carry out the orders given without protest. Those who remain insubordinate are soon tamed with even stricter confinement, which in some circumstances can include being placed in irons."

It was the catastrophic overcrowding of existing institutions which made swift measures to create additional space necessary. As early as the summer of 1933 the "Emsland camps" Börgermoor, Esterwegen, and Neusüstrum were constructed as concentration camps and filled with 4,000 political prisoners.[17] The plan was to have the inmates remove the peat and then farm the enormous but agriculturally useless peat bogs of the Emsland region. Gradually a chain of fifteen camps was created along the Dutch border. The Esterwegen camp, to which many of the prisoners of the original "unofficial" concentration camps were sent, became part of the official system of large, central concentration camps and soon was the second-largest in all Germany after Dachau. In this "peat-bog camp," where numerous prominent politicians and intellectuals of the Weimar Republic suffered inhuman treatment (including the Social Democrats Theodor Haubach, Julius Leber, and Wilhelm Leuschner; the Communist deputies to the Reichstag Theodor Neuberger and Bernhard Bästlein; and the Nobel Peace Prize laureate Carl von Ossietzky), young candidates for the SS received their training in how to run concentration camps. The careers of Koch and Loritz, the later commandants of Buchenwald and Sachsenhausen, began in Emsland.[18]

In 1934 Emsland camps Börgermoor, Neusüstrum, and Oberlangen came under the administration of the Ministry of Justice; they were supposed to be built up into model institutions of National Socialist criminal punishment. At the eleventh congress of the International Union of Criminologists, which took place in Berlin in 1935 under the chairmanship of Supreme Court president Bumke, they were presented as outstanding examples of what could be done with modern techniques of resocializing criminals. The majority of delegates from abroad allowed themselves to be taken in, although the exiled leadership of the Social Democratic party had sent each participant a revealing memorandum entitled *Tendencies Developing in German Penal Institutions*.[19] Otto Kellerhans, governor of a prison in Switzerland, wrote a laudatory report for the *Schweizer Zeitschrift für Strafrecht* (Swiss Journal of Criminal Law): "The camp personnel consists of bright young people who all make a positive impression. What has been achieved in the bogs of the Ems in the few years since construction began is impressive and amazing."[20] Nonetheless, the "bright young people" running what was the largest and supposedly most up-to-date

penal institution in the Reich were not trained officials of the prison system, but rather SA and SS units specially recruited for service in concentration camps. In addition, as time went on, personnel from the older,
unofficial camps were transferred to the new one, so that the administrators of the Ministry of Justice could soon proudly report that 468 "veterans of the SA" and 70 SS men had "found a place in the ministry's
service."[21] The former commandant of the concentration camp at Oranienburg, SA standard bearer (regimental leader) Emmanuel Schäfer, was
named as the new governor and promoted to the rank of senior official in
the prison service. After Schäfer received permission from the ministry "to
deviate from prison regulations," he introduced such concentration-camp
measures as beatings, deprivation of food, confinement in complete darkness, and capricious humiliations, thus improving this "model institution"
of prison reform.[22]

"Protecting the Race"

The "racial purity of the German people" had been a central concern of the National Socialist Party since its founding, and Hitler's *Mein Kampf* is above all a warning about the dangers of "mingling higher and lower races."[1] Helmut Nicolai, the legal philosopher who became the party architect for the "entire new construction of the Third Reich," published his book *The Doctrine of Racial Laws* (*Rassengesetzliche Rechtslehre*) in 1932; in it he declared that "the most important task of legal policy" was the "struggle against racial dishonor," since "law originates in the racial soul of the people it governs."[2] Thus, it was only consistent that at the first annual conference of law professors after the Nazis' seizure of power, which took place in September, 1933, in Leipzig, the question of "racial laws" dominated the discussion. Heinrich Stoll, a professor of civil law at the University of Tübingen, delivered a report on the consensus of those assembled that "the concept of race is closely linked to the concept of law, and precisely for this reason the law represents not the work of man, but rather God's sacred order."[3]

It remained unclear how the much maligned "mingling of races" was to be prevented, however, since ideas about how the term "race" was to be understood were vague in the extreme. The chief ideologist of National Socialism, Alfred Rosenberg, had presented some preliminary propositions in 1930 in his major work *The Myth of the Twentieth Century* (*Der Mythos des zwanzigsten Jahrhunderts*): "Marriages between Germans and Jews should be forbidden . . . Sexual intercourse, rape, and so forth between Germans and Jews should be punished according to the severity of the case by seizure of assets, deportation, penitentiary, and death."[4] As already mentioned, the Nazis had proposed to the Reichstag that the March 13, 1930, Law for the Protection of the Republic be amended so as to prescribe the death penalty for military treason and betrayal of the

Volk; this amendment also declared "betrayal of the race" (*Rassenverrat*) to be a crime. Either a penitentiary sentence or, in serious cases, a sentence of death was to be passed on anyone "who contributes or threatens to contribute to the racial deterioration and dissolution of the German people through interbreeding with persons of Jewish blood or the colored races."[5]

After Hitler had obtained the chancellorship, however, the subject proved to be legally far more complicated than had initially been supposed. The Prussian minister of justice Hanns Kerrl and his undersecretary Roland Freisler did propose in their memorandum "National Socialist Criminal Law," which they submitted to the party in September 1933, that marriages and extramarital sexual contact between "those of German blood" and "members of racially alien communities" be considered punishable offenses, along with "offenses against the honor of the race" and "endangerment of the race."[6] But these suggestions found little positive echo in the Reich Ministry of Justice, for technical legal reasons. The ministry replied that before a decree could be passed making sexual intercourse between members of different races an offense, it would first be necessary to declare it "an obstacle to marriage"—that is, to make marriages between such persons illegal. Officials at the ministry were not willing to take responsibility for such a far-reaching decision, which would also have created a stir outside Germany; it would have to be made at the very highest level. In addition, they pointed out that criminalization of sexual contact might have most unfortunate results: "Extortion, denunciations, and so forth by partners from a broken relationship or third parties would not only occur in frightening numbers, but they would also . . . assume a particularly repellent form."[7]

Denials of the Right to Marry

In the following years, discussion of the "racial issue" became increasingly limited to the categories of "those of German blood" and Jews. The legal debate on the advisability and possible form of a "protection of the race" law with criminal penalties continued; to start with, the only consensus reached was that first "a legal barrier to marriage" was to be established, "and based on this, every form of sexual interbreeding between Jews and those of German descent was to be made criminal."[8] In the meantime, however, officials entitled to perform marriages (judges and civil servants in registry offices) began anticipating these laws, which had not yet been passed. Although paragraphs 1303 *et seq.* of the Civil Code recognized only the "classic" obstacles to marriage of close blood relationship and an already existing marriage, an increasing number of officials began refusing to perform marriage ceremonies between "those of German blood and Jews on the grounds of "general national principles," such as had already been expressed in the Law for Restoration of the Professional Civil Service. On January 17, 1934, Reich minister of the interior Frick even found it necessary to send a formal memorandum to all officials under his jurisdiction instructing them to respect the limits of the "Aryan laws" more carefully and to perform official acts, such as marriage ceremonies, when the legal conditions were satisfied, even if such laws "perhaps appear not to conform fully to National Socialist views."[9] The Supreme Court also determined, citing Frick's memorandum explicitly, that "mixed marriages" were not illegal and that lower courts must recognize this fact.[10]

Frick's memorandum and the Supreme Court decision met with no sympathy whatever from many registry officials of the civil service, which had been "coordinated" with Nazi party policy. In 1935 many more "mixed" couples were denied permission to marry, and in the summer of that year, several courts to which people appealed against such illegal practices decided in favor of the registrars. It was argued repeatedly that although the letter of the law did not prohibit "mixed marriages," they violated "the most important laws of the nation, which consist in cultivating German blood and maintaining its purity." "Mixed marriages" were therefore "immoral through and through."[11] The Wetzlar Petty Court conceded in one instance that "existing legal provisions do not forbid the marriage"; however, "this formal legal situation" retreated into insignificance in view of "the sum total of all official and semiofficial pronouncements by the government and the National Socialist party" on the subject. An appeal to the actual wording of existing laws, on the other hand, could in the eyes of the court arise only from a "typically Jewish and liberalistic moral and legal mentality."[12] The Petty Court of Königsberg found that a registry official could not refuse to perform such a marriage "if none of the legal obstacles to marriage is present," and these were "determined in full and in their limits" in the Civil Code. Its decision against the registrar was reversed by the County Court, however, which pointed out that the application of legal principles was justified not by the fact that they had been elevated to the status of laws, "but rather because they are established on the basis of generally held convictions about what is right." The existing status of the law in 1935 should "not lead to the erroneous conclusion that a form of behavior condemned on the basis of generally held convictions is still permissible and may even be sanctioned by a court of law. No one can be in any doubt that marriage between a Jew and an Aryan woman is contrary to the German understanding of what is right."[13] This sensational decision—which came, after all, from a court of review—was praised at the time by Carl Schmitt as "a model of truly creative legal practice," and "an example" for every "National Socialist upholder of the law."[14] Meanwhile, on July 26, 1935, Minister Frick had issued a new ordinance in which he announced that since the legal status of "the question of marriages between Aryans and non-Aryans" would be clarified shortly, both the publication of banns and the ceremonies in such cases should be "postponed until further notice."[15]

The promised legal clarification was announced at the "Reich Party Conference of Freedom" in Nuremberg on September 15, 1935. The Reichstag, which had been summoned there in haste for the purpose, passed the so-called Law for the Protection of German Blood and German Honor. Its first paragraph read: "Marriage between Jews and citizens of German or related kinds of blood is forbidden. Marriages contracted in violation of this rule are null and void."[16]

The Dissolution of "Mixed Marriages"

Forbidding marriages between Jews and "Aryans" did not solve the "problem" of the numerous already existing marriages of this kind.[17] The legal situation as such was clear. According to the Civil Code still in force, divorce was not a possible solution, since the law required one of the partners to have committed some wrong as grounds for it; and despite the strongest desire to assign blame, it was impossible to find a person guilty of wrongdoing in his or her parentage. Until a new law was passed dissolving all existing "racially mixed marriages," the only way to end such a marriage was to file a claim for annulment under paragraph 1333 of the Civil Code, which stated: "A marriage can be challenged by a spouse who at the time of its contraction was unaware of personal qualities in the other spouse, qualities that would have prevented a person from entering into the marriage had he had knowledge of the true circumstances and a proper understanding of the nature of marriage." An annulment on these grounds was virtually out of the question in "racially mixed marriages," however, since it could be granted only if the spouse filed a claim within six months of discovering the error, and was not permissible at all if the spouse with grounds for complaint had nonetheless "confirmed" the existence of the marriage through his behavior. Furthermore, one's "racial identity" was neither a "personal quality" nor something the non-Jewish spouse of a Jewish husband or wife was likely to have been unaware of at the time of the marriage.

Nevertheless, soon after the Law for Restoration of the Professional

Civil Service of April 7, 1933, had first established racial origin as a category with significant legal consequences, several journals printed articles by "courageous" jurists in favor of challenging the validity of "mixed marriages" in the courts.[18] They began by hastily advancing all sorts of arguments on the "significance of Jewishness," in order to declare it a "personal quality" after all. The next problem they had to face was the unlikelihood that this quality had remained hidden from the non-Jewish spouse, but even this proved not too difficult to surmount. Pointing out that "until recently . . . the belief was widespread in the population that the Jew different from the Aryan solely in his religion," and that very few Germans were aware of "the inner dimensions of the race question," one author argued that the non-Jewish spouse's ignorance about the significance of the quality should be treated in the same manner as ignorance of the quality itself. "If the Aryan spouse had recognized the significance of Jewishness," with all its negative consequences, he wrote, "then he would never have entered into the marriage."[19] This argument also covered the matter of timing, since the permitted six-month period for filing an annulment claim could now logically be considered to have begun only at the time when racial identity acquired such overwhelming significance—at the very earliest on January 30, 1933, but even better on April 7, the day on which it had become grounds for the dismissal of civil servants and attorneys.

One of the first courts to take over this dubious line of reasoning was the County Court of Cologne. In late 1933, in a decision positively dripping with anti-Semitism, the court proceeded as if it were self-evident that "the race to which a person belongs is among his chief personal characteristics." In this case the plaintiff had naturally been aware that his wife was Jewish, but this fact did not invalidate the claim for annulment, since "he had no knowledge of the essential facts" this identity entailed. Proof that this knowledge was lacking at the time the marriage took place—proof that was required by law in cases where a person claimed to have been deceived in the spouse's personal qualities—was not required, however; it could "not be demanded from the plaintiff, since it is unfortunately incontestable that until recently the significance of race, blood, and national identity in their full importance had become clear to only a minute percentage of the population, including even so-called educated circles." Although it could have become clear to this particular plaintiff by March 1933 at the very latest, since he had joined the Nazi party at that time, the court found that a "purely instinctual" racism was still not the same as "knowledge," and "firm knowledge of the error is necessary." Thus, the judges concluded, "in view of the plaintiff's merely average level of general education, it is reasonable to assume that he acquired a full knowledge of the circumstances only during the summer of 1933—that is to say, at a time which then fell within the six-month limit.[20]

Not all courts of that era were willing to go so far in what was obviously a perversion of justice. Their decisions were strikingly at odds. In several cases, the Prussian Supreme Court (*Kammergericht*) in Berlin left it "an open question" as to whether racial identity could be considered a "personal quality" at all, and it regularly refused to grant annulments of "mixed marriages" on the grounds that the permissible time limit had expired. As late as February 1934, this court informed a plaintiff who claimed to have recognized his Jewish wife's "true nature" in 1926 that for just this reason the six-month period had long since expired.[21] By contrast, the Court of Appeals in Karlsruhe found in favor of the plaintiff in a similar case, simultaneously recognizing race as a personal quality and dismissing the factor of time: "Today it has been recognized that the Jewish race differs considerably from the Aryan race with regard to blood, character, personality, and view of life, and that a connection and pairing with a member of this race is not only undesirable for a member of the Aryan race, but also injurious and . . . unnatural."[22]

The wave of similar decisions that followed, and that obviously ignored the prevailing law, began to make even leading Nazi jurists nervous. In November 1934, Roland Freisler, who would later become president of the People's Court, felt compelled to issue a public statement pointing out "that it is not the role of the judge to alter the existing laws of the nation," for if every judge were to deal with them as he saw fit and to "decide questions which [can] be solved only from the superior vantage point of the Führer," then "chaos and anarchy would replace unified leadership."[23]

After this harsh reminder to those courts whose activities on behalf of the National Socialist cause had gone too far to suit the party leaders, the question of how to handle the challenges to existing "racially mixed marriages" was passed on to the Supreme Court. The two decisions of the Prussian Supreme Court and the Karlsruhe Court of Appeals described above were reviewed in a decision of July 12, 1934. The highest court in Germany began by declaring membership in the Jewish race to be a "personal quality in the sense of paragraph 1333 of the Civil Code," thereby endorsing the first step in the perversion of justice. The court also confirmed the view of the lower courts that an error concerning the significance of racial differences was equivalent to ignorance of the racial difference itself. However, it was willing to recognize such an error only in exceptional cases, such as when "the Aryan spouse was influenced by church doctrines and unaware of the racial difference, assuming instead that the other spouse merely belonged to a different religion and the difference would be removed by a conversion to Christianity." With regard to the time limit, the court bowed to the views of Nazi radicals, observing that since a suit for annulment on racial grounds would have been futile before January 30, 1933, this fact would have had an "inhibiting" effect on potential plaintiffs before that date and would have prevented them from filing within the required period. Furthermore, a general knowledge of the significance of the racial error and the possibility of annulling mixed marriages could not be presumed to have existed with certainty until the racial clause of the civil service law went into effect.

This decision was a superb demonstration of tactics by the justices. On the one hand, they were able to please radical Nazi circles on three points, particularly by spelling out the principle "that in applying the law, the courts must take into account the existence of racial differences recognized by the state through passage of the Aryan laws." On the other hand, they also conformed to Freisler's demand that the limits of Nazi laws be respected, since they stressed that "the courts are not authorized to carry National Socialist views beyond the limits which the legislation of the National Socialist government has set for itself."[24]

The final word in this episode was the Marriage Law of July 6, 1938, which repealed paragraph 1333 of the Civil Code and definitely established the legality of annulling "racially mixed marriages." In any case, no such marriages had taken place subsequent to the Frick decree issued on July 26, 1935.

The Nuremberg Laws

While officials at the Ministries of Justice and the Interior were still busy trying to pass responsibility for formulating "racial hygiene laws" to each other, those committed to the Nazi program began to press for visible results. Roland Freisler was outraged by the delaying tactics of the lawyers in the Ministry of Justice and dictated a strongly worded protest to the minister into the minutes of a meeting of the Official Commission on Criminal Law: "I cannot tolerate the fact that no one in this group is willing to urge that measures to protect the race be included in the new criminal code . . . We are in danger of . . . betraying our fundamental convictions if we fail to include this provision."[26] And participants in a medical conference held to discuss "racial hygiene and current biological questions of heredity" sent a telegram to the Minister of the Interior in December 1934, demanding immediate passage of a law with draconic penalties "to prevent all further Jewish racial poisoning and contamination of German blood."[27] By this time, the two ministries had been able to agree on the wording of a bill to forbid "mixed marriages" and all extramarital sexual contact between Jews and "Aryans," but its passage did not appear imminent. At the same time, Nazi party demands on the subject were growing increasingly more urgent and radical, calling for such things as mandatory dissolution of "mixed marriages," and sterilization or even the death penalty for "dishonor to the race."

Then Hitler came to a decision—clearly on the spur of the moment—to conclude the "Party Conference of Freedom" in Nuremberg by assembling the Reichstag there to pass the appropriate laws and by announcing them at the closing rally. Ministry officials were hastily summoned the day before to formulate the bills on the basis of their previous deliberations; they then "improved" them after receiving Hitler's criticisms and settled on "compromises." Just in time for the final rally, the Reichstag passed the three "Nuremberg laws": a flag law, which established the swastika flag as the emblem "of the Reich and the nation"; a law on citizenship, which deprived all those "not of German blood" of their rights as citizens; and the "Law for the Protection of German Blood and German Honor." This last was the law which forbade, as has already been mentioned, marriages "between Jews and citizens of German or related kinds of blood," as well as "extramarital intercourse." In addition, Jews were prohibited from employing females under the age of forty-five in their households.

The origin of the idea, frequently met with today, that special importance should be attributed to the way the Nuremberg laws came to be passed—with the obvious aim of presenting them as Hitler's own brainchild—can be traced to undersecretary Franz Schlegelberger. At the Nuremberg War Crimes Trial Schlegelberger claimed that the Ministry of Justice had not participated in their passage and in fact had not learned of them until afterward.[28] However, it is not so crucial whether the wording finally decided upon was in fact "improvised a few hours in advance in grotesque circumstances on the backs of old menus in a beer hall,"[29] or whether the initiative lay "decisively with Hitler and his party advisers."[30] It is certain in any case that actual formulation of the laws had been preceded and prepared for by a wealth of debates, memoranda, and rough drafts in both the Ministry of Justice and the Ministry of the Interior. Legislative regulation of the situation was long overdue; the practice of the courts had already begun to anticipate it. The chief public prosecutor in Karlsruhe, for example, had notified the Ministry of Justice in 1935 that "within the jurisdiction of the Karlsruhe Court of Appeals, quite a large number of Jews . . . [have been] taken into preventative detention" for sexual offenses with "Aryans," although no corresponding provision of the Criminal Code existed as yet.[31] And finally, the Ministry of the Interior had itself announced on July 16, 1935, that the legal question of "mixed marriages" would soon be settled.

The Courts Deal with "Dishonor to the Race"

Of the three Nuremberg laws, it was above all the Law for the Protection of German Blood and German Honor which acquired significance for the courts. It prescribed penitentiary sentences for both partners if they married in defiance of the law, and punished "dishonor to the race" with either prison or penitentiary. In the latter case, only the male partner was to be punished, whether Jewish or "of German blood," while the female went free. The *Reports on Germany* published by the leaders of the Social Democratic party in exile had already characterized the "blood law" as "Streicher pornography in legal form."[32] (Julius Streicher, the Nazi *Gauleiter* in Nuremberg, was publisher of the viciously anti-Semitic and widely distributed weekly newspaper *Der Stürmer,* or *The Storm Trooper.*) However, it was the "scholarly penetration" of the meaning of these laws and their interpretation by the courts which revealed even clearer traits of sexual pathology.

To begin with, the law created a state of confusion. The courts were at a loss as to how to determine who was a Jew and just what constituted "extramarital intercourse." These questions were clearly so difficult to clarify that it took two full months of feverish activity before these key concepts could be defined and the accompanying decrees on administering the citizenship law and the "blood law" could be issued.

The first attempt to give a precise definition of the "chief enemy" of the Third Reich revealed the totally pseudoscientific nature of its racist doctrines and the charlatanism of the "scientists" associated with them. The definition also exposed the hollowness of the constantly reiterated claim that race as such was "not a political, but rather a biological concept."[33] The first administrative decree accompanying the Nuremberg citizenship law declared namely that a "Jew" was any person with three or four Jewish grandparents, and that a "Jewish crossbreed (first degree)" was anyone with two entirely Jewish grandparents. However, a "crossbreed" was to be considered a "Jew" in the full sense if he had been a member of a Jewish religious community at the time of the laws' passage or was married to a Jewish spouse.[34] Thus, racial categorization depended in such cases on the religion one practiced or on one's spouse; but the situation became even more confused if the "crossbreed" also happened to be a foreigner. The discussion of this situation in the most frequently cited commentary on the race laws—the commentary by Stuckart and Globke—shows to what absurd lengths legal scholars had to go to uphold the concept of "race" at all:

> While categorization as a Jew according to paragraph 5 section 1 is not affected by the Jews' nationality, according to paragraph 5 section 2 only those crossbreeds in the first degree otherwise meeting the conditions stated in paragraph 5 section 2 who possess German citizenship are to be considered Jews. Crossbreeds of foreign nationality thus remain crossbreeds even if in their case one of the conditions in paragraph 5 section 2a–b applies. If, however, a foreign crossbreed in the first degree acquires German citizenship through marriage to a Jew which would result in his categorization as a Jew were he already a citizen, then this result also applies to him. Conversely, however, a German crossbreed in the first degree who loses his German citizenship through marriage to a foreign Jew does not cease to be a crossbreed.[35]

In such instances, race was determined not by religion but by nationality.

In general, the whole question of racial categorization was beset with insoluble contradictions. Since paragraph 2 of the first administrative decree for the citizenship law declared that "a grandparent is to be considered entirely Jewish if he belongs to the Jewish religion," all grandparents "of German blood" who had converted to Judaism were "Jews." Thus, anyone with two such grandparents who himself attended services at a synagogue was classified as a "Jew." On the other hand, anyone with four half-Jewish grandparents was "of German blood" in the legal sense, since paragraph 5 section 2 of the law itself was concerned solely with the number of "entirely Jewish" grandparents. Commentaries on the race laws appealed to readers to remember that there should be "no confusion of the concepts of race and religion! Only the *race* of the grandparents is decisive!"[36] However, this failed to alter the fact that the wording of the law itself unmistakably declared religion (which was after all the only demonstrable criterion) as the crucial factor. Neither the combined efforts of the Nazi party's Race Office and the Heredity Office of the SS nor all the scientific jargon of the numerous university institutes for hereditary biology, race research, and anthropology could gloss over that.

The County Courts each had a panel of three judges who normally dealt with criminal cases; it was these panels, and not the Special Courts, that became responsible for decisions on violations of the race laws. And despite all reports from abroad that the laws were meeting with "outspoken rejection from the people,"[37] they went to work with alacrity. Once the term "Jew" had been defined, as described above, a debate arose in the legal journals over the term "intercourse." This difference of opinion was not settled even after the first administrative decree for the "Blood Law" had stated in paragraph 11 that "extramarital intercourse, in the sense specified in paragraph 2 of the law, is limited to sexual intercourse."[38] Up to this point, the law had used only the terms "cohabitation" (*Beiwohnung*), "coition" (*Beischlaf*), and "fornication" (*Unzucht*). Now there appeared in rapid succession a series of legal commentaries on the race laws, all offering different interpretations. The most radical came at first from Stuckart and Globke, who advocated prosecution even for "acts similar to intercourse, such as mutual masturbation."[39] But for some judges and authors of legal articles, even this was not sufficient. The County Court of Nuremberg-Fürth was more moderate, taking the view that in general usage "sexual intercourse" was understood to mean "coition," and that since the preamble of the law spoke of preserving "the purity of German blood," it made sense to consider only the act of coition itself an offense.[40] In this restrictive interpretation, the court stood more or less alone, however. The County Court of Augsburg, for example, convicted an "entirely Jewish" defendant, who had been caught in sexual intimacies with his girlfriend (although they had not performed actual coition), of "effected dishonor to the race." When reference was made to "sexual intercourse as such," the court argued, the phrase as generally used was understood to include "not only normal but also perverse" forms of intercourse. "Since the law aims at protecting the purity of German blood as far as possible, the will of the lawmakers must be seen as also making illegal all perverse forms of sexual intercourse between Jews and citizens of German or related kinds of blood. It is furthermore the intention of the relevant law to protect *German honor,* in particular the sexual honor of the citizen of German blood."[41]

The somewhat vague wording of the law itself and its broad interpretation by many courts caused numerous appeals to be filed with the Supreme Court, which now faced the task of clarifying the ambiguous terms. Four of the six criminal panels of the highest German court were occupied with cases of this nature. At the request of the first criminal panel, even the Grand Criminal Panel (consisting of the president and vice-president of the court and seven other judges, usually the heads of the criminal panels) had to consider the question of what sexual intercourse was. Every criminal panel had the right to call upon the Grand Panel when dealing with legal questions "of fundamental significance."[42] The most august body devoted to German criminal justice thereupon pronounced on December 9, 1935: "The term 'sexual intercourse' as meant by the Law for the Protection of German Blood does not include every obscene act, but is also not limited to coition. It includes all forms of natural and unnatural sexual intercourse—that is, coition, as well as all those sexual activities with a person of the opposite sex which are designed, in the manner in which they are performed, to serve in place of coition to satisfy the sex drive of at least one of the partners."

The court rejected the narrower interpretation of "sexual intercourse" as equivalent to "coition," arguing that

> it confronts courts with virtually insuperable obstacles in the admission of evidence and would require them to deliberate upon the most delicate issues. A broad interpretation is furthermore appropriate in view of the fact that the provisions of the law are meant to protect not only German blood but also German honor. This requires that in addition to coition, all such sexual manipulations—whether actively performed or passively tolerated—that have as their aim the satisfaction of one partner's sex drive in a manner other than the completion of coition, must cease between Jews and citizens of German or related kinds of blood.[43]

In this statement, the Supreme Court had taken up the most extreme of the positions represented at the time, thereby pointing the way for lower courts. In a further decisions on the "Blood Law," the Grand Panel elaborated on its general interpretation: "The courts to which the Third Reich has assigned responsibility for administering justice, can carry out this task . . . only if they do not remain glued to the letter of the law, but rather penetrate its inner core in their interpretations and do their part to see that the aims of the lawmaker are realized."[44] After this kind of invitation to the courts to increase the severity of the laws through their "interpretations," it was only to be expected that as time went on, lower courts and even some criminal panels of the Supreme Court would go even further in their "administration of justice." The greatest excess was committed by the Second Criminal Panel in its decision of February 2, 1939, based on the following case.

The defendant, who was "of German blood," had maintained a relationship with a Jewish woman for many years. It had been ascertained by the court of first instance, however, that "approximately from 1925 on" he had lost "in increasing measure the capacity and inclination" for coitus. Thus, the couple had given up sex ten years before the racial laws went into effect. For the County Court, there nevertheless could be no doubt "that the defendant maintained unnatural sexual relations with her until at least 1937, these activities taking the form of repeated masturbation, in her presence and with her knowledge." The court convicting him of "continued dishonor to the race." The Supreme Court had no fault to find with this conviction. Since "according to the manner in which it was performed," the activity had to represent intercourse "between" two persons of the opposite sex in order to count as a violation of the law, purely one-sided "misconduct of a sexual nature" was not sufficient as an offense in the panel's eyes. On the other hand, the panel observed that

> it ceases to be a case of purely one-sided activity . . . if the other party participates at least outwardly in some form or other, whether it be active or passive . . . Participation in the sense described above is in fact entirely possible, even if there is no physical contact between the participants. Physical contact is also not required by law. Neither the wording of the law, if normal linguistic usage is taken into account, nor its intent can imply the limitation that dishonor to the race can be effected only if one party touches the body of the other party. It would run counter both to healthy popular feeling and to the clear goals of German racial policy if such surrogate acts were to go completely unpunished, thereby creating, with regard to perverse conduct between the sexes, a new stimulus for violating the racial honor of the German people.

A summary of the principle set forth by the case was also placed by the justices at the head of the decision, as printed in the official collection of decisions: "Dishonor to the race according to paragraphs 2 and 5 section 2 of the Blood. Prot. L. can also be committed without physical contact between the participants."[45]

This decision naturally had the effect of a green light on the lower courts. Even though the Grand Panel had specifically emphasized that "not every obscene act" was to be equated with sexual intercourse, and the First Criminal Panel of the Supreme Court had even spelled it out as the principle of a decision ("Kissing is not sexual intercourse"),[46] this did not prevent the Hamburg County Court from treating kisses as "dishonor to the race." The accused in this case had pleaded in his own defense that he was no longer capable of sexual intercourse; that he had often suffered from nocturnal pollutions in his youth; that his sex drive was greatly weakened as a result of his war experiences; and that occasionally a mere embrace could cause him to ejaculate. The Sixth Criminal Chamber of the Hamburg County Court promptly turned all this information against him, regarding the kisses in question as "completed dishonor to the race." Since as a result of his particular physiological difficulties, kissing "took the place of normal sexual intercourse," the court sentenced him on September 26, 1938, to two years in a penitentiary.[47]

The courts soon ceased to pay any attention to the limitation that intercourse could occur only "between" two persons as well. Leon Abel, a fifty-seven-year-old "Jew and merchant," had been to a "German-blooded" physical therapist to have his stomach massaged. For the first treatment session, he had lain unclothed on the massage table, his lower body covered with a towel. A second session did not take place; as Abel was waiting in the therapist's office, the police entered and arrested him. During interrogation, the therapist never wavered in her assertions that she had noticed no signs whatsoever of sexual arousal in her patient. However, Abel himself had "confessed" under interrogation that he had been excited during the massage. The court must certainly have been aware of how such "confessions" were obtained. Many people convicted of "racial" sexual offenses reported after the war that the Gestapo had threatened—and by no means idly—that if no charges could be made to stick, they would simply send the accused to a concentration camp instead. One of the victims had twenty teeth knocked out after his arrest. In his book on the trials of accused "racial" sexual offenders in Hamburg, Hans Robinsohn cites the testimony of a "German-blooded" defendant who withdrew his previous confession at his trial. When asked why he had signed it in the first place, he replied that in the circumstances he would have signed anything, including his own death sentence.[48]

At his trial, Leon Abel also withdrew the confession extracted from him by the Gestapo, while the sole witness, the masseuse, maintained her position. Nonetheless, the court gave more weight to the confession before the Gestapo than to Abel's testimony during the trial. It sentenced him to two years in a penitentiary for having "attained sexual gratification with Miss M." and thereby "effecting . . . the crime of dishonor to the race, regardless of whether or not the witness [had] knowledge of it." The judges expressed their conviction that Abel had sought out the massage treatment solely "for lascivious purposes and to abuse women as objects of his sexual lust, regardless of whether or not they were aware of it." The exceptionally severe sentence was justified as follows: "As his perverse behavior to German-blooded women shows, the accused is an inferior human being. The offense in this case was committed approximately three years after the Nuremberg laws took effect. It represents an extraordinary piece of effrontery on the part of the accused to have dared, at this date, to abuse the witness as the object of his sexual lust."[49]

This kind of language was nothing out of the ordinary in decisions against Jews accused of "racial" sexual offenses. Courts considered offenses to be aggravated by certain circumstances—for example, that one defendant "practiced illegal intercourse with Miss J. after outbreak of the war, plotted by world Jewry to destroy Germany"; or that another, "as a Jew and French citizen, should and did know that his behavior represented an act of sabotage against the resistance of the German people."[50] In a further instance, the Hamburg County Court found that the romantic love affair of two young people who had written daily letters to each other during a five-week separation was "so grave and vile, that no mitigating circumstances can be found. It is a prime example of Jewish effrontery, Jewish contempt for German laws, Jewish lasciviousness, and Jewish unscrupulousness." The court sentenced the male partner in the affair (who was Jewish) to six years in a penitentiary.[51]

Some courts even made use of the appallingly harsh sentences passed elsewhere to justify even harsher verdicts: "It is a monstrous instance of shamelessness that in November 1937 a Jew, in full knowledge of the unbending determination of the German people to secure its future for all time by maintaining the purity of its blood, and in full knowledge of the severe sentences widely known . . . to be given to defilers of the race, spoke in the street to a girl clearly and immediately recognizable as being of German blood and made her his mistress."[52]

In theory, the race laws regarded the "German-blooded" men who had love affairs with Jewish women just as guilty of an offense as the male Jewish partners of "German-blooded" women. In fact, however, they received incomparably better treatment. They were allowed to plead mitigating circumstances with far greater frequency, and they received much lighter sentences. Three times as many Jewish defendants as "Aryans" were given penitentiary sentences.[53] Whereas the former were usually accused of having "seduced innocent girls of German blood" even when the women in question were prostitutes, any Jewish woman who became involved with a "German-blooded" man was assigned the greater portion of the blame. In one case, for example, the court concluded: "The witness B. is a lascivious, morally depraved Jewess who used her unchecked sexual appetite and ruthlessness to acquire a strong influence over the defendant."[54]

Within a short time, it became established practice—as the Frankfurt County Court noted on December 22, 1936—for courts "to impose a penitentiary sentence in all cases in which no particular circumstances can be recognized to mitigate the offense."[55] On the other hand, the Supreme Court had found that in the "crime of dishonor to the race," no mitigating circumstances could exist at all, since none were specifically mentioned in the law itself.[56] Thus, the considerably harsher sentence of a penitentiary term rather than a prison term was used in the so-called normal case—contrary to all the rules of ordinary legal interpretation. The Hamburg County Court spelled out the principle with startling frankness in a decision of December 14, 1938: "As a general rule, the court gives penitentiary sentences to Jews who have been found guilty of dishonoring the race. A penitentiary sentence generally appears indispensable to the court, because the Law for the Protection of the Blood represents a fundamental law of the German people, which is designed to guarantee the purity of the race."[57]

The courts consistently and repeatedly referred to the Law for the Protection of German Blood in terms such as a "fundamental law" or "one of the most important laws of the National Socialist state."[58] One of the most passionate commentators on the law reminded the courts that "dishonoring the race is a crime almost as abominable as the other great crimes against society—treason and high treason."[59] The more the courts were required to occupy themselves with cases of this kind, the more urgent the task of "preserving the purity of German blood" apparently came to seem to them. The judges of the chamber responsible for "racial" sexual offenses in Hamburg sentenced the defendants in the first few cases to two years in a penitentiary (even though the law would have allowed a sentence of one night in prison); by the end of 1938, however, the average sentence was four to five years in a penitentiary.[60]

The thoroughly vague concept of "racial identity," a brew concocted from elements of religion, citizenship, and heredity, led to numerous instances of confusion and misunderstanding, especially since membership in a particular population group was generally not evident from a person's appearance. In spite of all efforts to clarify the situation in the decrees accompanying the citizenship law, in practice it often remained unclear who was to be considered a Jew and who was not. And although in traditional legal thinking an error concerning one's own or sexual partner's "race" constituted an "error of fact" that automatically excluded the possibility of an existing "intent" (and therefore guilt as well), the courts now regularly treated it as an error of law that did not absolve the accused of responsibility.

In a trial before the Stettin County Court, a Jewish man pleaded in his own defense that he had thought his partner was half Jewish. The young woman had assured him that her mother was Jewish. The criminal chamber of the court thereupon found him not guilty, since "the defendant, acting on the plausible information given him by the girl, assumed that she was half Jewish. While the defendant's actions as such were irresponsible, he was nevertheless in error as to the circumstance which made them illegal." The chief public prosecutor of the Reich then entered an appeal against this decision, which was indeed overturned by the Fifth Criminal Panel of the Supreme Court. The justices observed,

> The crime of dishonor to the race, according to the meaning of paragraph 5 section 2 of the Law for Protection of the Blood, can . . . be committed only with intent. An indication of at least limited intent must be found for guilt to be established. Consequently, the Jew must at least have included the Ger-

man blood of the citizen in his limited intent, in order for him to be found guilty. However, a Jew who seeks extramarital relations with a German woman in Germany has the legal obligation conscientiously to seek information about the race to which she belongs. If he fails to obtain documentation concerning the citizen's parentage that would seem sufficient and reliable to a conscientious person, and if, in particular, he accepts an explanation from the girl about her supposedly Jewish parentage without further evidence, then the strong suspicion exists that the Jew has violated paragraph 2 of the Law for Protection of the Blood with limited intent, meaning that his actions were more than merely irresponsible.[61]

Decisions of this sort encouraged lower courts to require ever greater precautions on the part of Jews. Soon, even official documents ceased to be considered sufficient evidence. In one case, the defendant, B., had hired a housekeeper through the "situations wanted" column of the *Israelite Family News,* a newspaper in which only Jews were allowed to advertise. During the first interview, the applicant had presented a document issued by the chief of police in Dresden certifying that because her maternal grandfather was Jewish, she was a "Jewish crossbreed," exempted from the provisions of the race laws concerning Germans, and that "there were no objections to her employment in a Jewish household." B. thereupon hired her as his housekeeper, and subsequently began having sexual relations with her. He was charged with "dishonor to the race." The law itself, as everyone knew, prohibited sexual relations only between "Jews and citizens of German and related kinds of blood"; but the first decree concerning its administration contained a little-known paragraph that extended the ban to include relations between Jews and "crossbreeds of German nationality" with only one Jewish grandparent (called "crossbreeds in the second degree"). B. pleaded not guilty to the charge, explaining that he had relied on the accuracy of the official document and had no knowledge of the relevant paragraph 11 of the administrative decree. Nonetheless, the Sixth Criminal Chamber of the Hamburg County Court regarded this error as "insignificant in a legal sense," without even investigating whether B. could have avoided making it. Under German law, an unavoidable error with regard to the legal situation exonerates a person from all guilt, in principle, but during the Third Reich the courts were obviously blind to all mitigating circumstances. In this instance, the judges considered the offense compounded by the fact that the defendant had had sexual relations with previous housekeepers—long before the Nazi takeover: "It represents a grave offense that the accused had no inhibitions about using a German woman to satisfy his sexual desires and thus to violate the honor of the German people. It weighs far more heavily against him, however, that he is a vile Jew who has satisfied his sexual lust without inhibition over a long period by dishonoring German-blooded women and girls who were . . . placed in his care as employees or were as such economically dependent upon him."[62]

In violation of all principles of criminal law, the courts finally arrived at a point where every mistake about a person's parentage was treated as an "error of law." The daughter of a Jewish mother and a "German-blooded" father had taken part in Lutheran religious instruction at school. At the age of eighteen she fell in love with a young "German-blooded" technician, and they became engaged. The girl wished to make a formal conversion to Christianity at the time of her marriage, but at her mother's wish this was to be postponed until she attained her majority (which at that time was twenty-one). During the waiting period, the Nuremberg Laws went into effect, and the young man was arrested after his landlady denounced him to the police. He did not deny having sexual relations with his fiancée, but argued that she was not Jewish in the meaning of the race laws; at any rate, he had assumed that she counted as "German-blooded," since as a "crossbreed in the first degree" she was not a practicing member of the Jewish religious community. The County Court of Berlin nevertheless found him guilty of "dishonor to the race," a verdict upheld by the Second Criminal Panel of the Supreme Court. The panel argued that a person's membership in the Jewish religious community should "not be judged on the basis of the person's personal and inner convictions about the Jewish religion, but solely by external criteria." The girl had belonged to the Jewish religious community from birth and had never officially left it; "therefore, the external facts point to a violation of paragraph 5 section 2 of the Blood Protection Law."[63]

The fate of "crossbreeds in the first degree" was often decided by whether or not they were members of the Jewish religious community. If they were, the provisions of the Law for Protection of the Blood applied to them. If they had not been members at the time the citizenship law went into effect, then they were not considered to be "Jews." However, in a number of decisions, the Supreme Court developed a line of argument quite opposed to that of the above mentioned case: they declared it immaterial whether or not a crossbreed was "actually a member of the Jewish religious community in the real sense."[64] The high court considered application of the Blood Protection Law justified in any case in which someone had been "confirmed according to Jewish rites,"[65] had ever received Jewish religious instruction,[66] or even "failed to contest being listed among the membership of a synagogue."[67] On the basis of this somewhat arbitrary assignment to membership in the Jewish religious community,

the Supreme Court increased the number of potential "racial" sexual offenders far beyond the provisions of even the administrative decrees concerning the Blood Protection Law. Since it regarded the slightest connection to Judaism as evidence that someone was a member of the Jewish
religious community, many persons who had ceased to observe the Jewish
faith years earlier were transformed into "Jews" again in the eyes of the
law. In one case, even a "crossbreed" whose name had found its way onto
the list of members of the Jewish community "through an obvious over-
sight," in the opinion of the court of first instance (his mother was not
Jewish; he was not circumcised; he had not been raised in the Jewish faith
and did not practice it), was treated by the Supreme Court as a Jew subject
to the provisions of the Blood Protection Law. The court found sufficient
grounds for a verdict of guilty in the fact "that the accused at the time of
the crime must have realized the possibility that he had been entered in
the lists of the Jewish religious community at the time the citizenship law
was passed."[68]

By means of its arbitrary decisions, the Supreme Court enlarged not
only the group of those to be regarded as "Jews" but also the group identified as "Germans." On September 10, 1940, its First Criminal Panel declared all citizens of occupied Czechoslovakia to be Germans according to
the sense of the Blood Protection Law. The wording of the law was unambiguous, as has been shown: "Extramarital intercourse between Jews
and citizens of German and related kinds of blood is prohibited." Naturally, the only people who could be counted as "citizens" were, as paragraph 1 of the first administrative decree spelled out, "German citizens
according to the meaning of the Blood Protection Law." This meant that
while foreign Jews could be prosecuted for violation of the law, foreigners
"of German or related kinds of blood" could not. According to this administrative decree, the prosecution of a "foreign citizen" who happened
to be Jewish required the consent of the ministers of justice and the interior, in order to prevent diplomatic repercussions. This requirement was
misunderstood by the courts, particularly the Supreme Court, apparently
intentionally, to mean that even citizens of other countries were liable to
prosecution if they had affairs with Jewish women. The justices of the
highest German court had the following comment on the relationship of
a Czech national with a Jewish woman: "The defendant is an inhabitant
of the Protectorate of Bohemia and Moravia . . . The legal position of
these persons in relation to German citizens need not be investigated
here." The court chose to act as if the question were solely the procedural
one of whether or not the two ministers should be consulted, rather than
to cite the relevant law (which after all was titled the Law for the Protec-

tion of German Blood and German Honor), stating that only Germans could be punished for contact with Jewish women. The decisions continued:

> In no case can they be reckoned among those foreign nationals whose prosecution for a violation or infringement of the German Blood Protection Law is admissible only with the consent of the ministers of justice and the interior . . . The only persons who can be understood to be "foreign citizens" under the meaning of this decree are those who fall under the protection of a foreign government. Members of the Protectorate of Bohemia and Moravia do not number among such persons, since the protectorate belongs to the territory of the Great German (*grossdeutsche*) Reich; its members enjoy the protection of the Reich, even if they are not ethnic Germans.

The court thus upheld the conviction of a Czech national and the harsh sentence for "dishonoring the race."[69] In their obsessive determination to prosecute all Jews and those closely associated with them, the justices of the German Supreme Court appear not even to have realized that with such "legal principles," they were presuming to protect Czech "blood and honor" rather than German.

In order to ensure that every overture made by a Jew to a "German-blooded" woman would be punished, the Supreme Court even abandoned its time-honored and well-defined doctrine of "attempted crime." In cases where it is an offense to attempt a crime (felonies and those misdemeanors for which the law specifically declares an attempt to be a punishable offense), the problem is always to distinguish the attempt, which is punishable, from preparatory actions, which are not illegal in themselves. Traditionally the courts had defined the crucial moment as "the beginning of the attempt" to commit the crime, and such an attempt at commission was assumed to have begun only with such actions as "appear in the natural view of the matter to be constituent parts of the illegal act." This wording has been developed by Reinhard Frank, a commentator on criminal law, around the turn of the century,[70] and it had been used repeatedly by the Supreme Court in the following years. As late as 1920 the court had stressed that a crime could be considered to have been attempted only if an action with "the essential attributes of the crime" had begun; according to this definition, "every action which serves merely to make it possible or easier to commit a crime does not constitute part of an actual attempt."[71] These principles allowed the courts to make a relatively precise distinction between legal and illegal actions. In its decisions in cases of "racial" sexual offenses, however, the Supreme Court tossed them aside. On January 5, 1939, it deliberated upon the following case.

A Jewish electrician had spent the night at an inn in a small town in Poland. Toward evening he had called the chambermaid Elly C. to his room on a pretext, and had promised to give her two bracelets if she would sleep with him. The Supreme Court reported in its decision that the young woman "did not answer the accused and left the room. When she put the electrician's shoes, which she had polished, in front of his door the next day, he came out and asked her to come into his room. C. laughed, however, and went away."

This harmless incident had appeared sufficient grounds to the Sonnenberg County Court in Thuringia for convicting the electrician of "attempted dishonor to the race" and sentencing him to prison. The Fifth Criminal Panel of the Supreme Court upheld the conviction, since "an act represents attempted dishonor to the race if its direct connection with a sexual act . . . in the natural view makes it appear as a part of that act. It can thus be represented in the mere verbal invitation of the man to engage in racially dishonoring sexual intercourse, intended to follow at once . . . The circumstance that Elly C. did not agree to the intentions of the accused is legally immaterial, as is the circumstance that the accused . . . did not touch the girl."[72]

From then on, every attempt on the part of Jewish man to establish a relationship with a "German-blooded" woman was to be considered a punishable offense, since lower courts were obliged to follow the Supreme Court's redefinition of "an attempted crime" in their own decisions. Nevertheless, it was applied only to Jewish men, not to men "of German blood" who approached Jewish women. Finally, in 1940, the justices of the Second Criminal Panel managed to outdo even their colleagues of the Fifth Panel when it came to defining what constituted an attempt to commit a "racial sexual offense." This case involved a relationship between a Jewish man and a "German-blooded" woman that had come to an end before the Nuremberg laws took effect. The woman had ended the affair, but some of the man's belongings were still in her apartment. One evening he appeared at her apartment—obviously intoxicated—demanding to be allowed in to get his things. When she refused to open the door, he became enraged and broke a window. Thereupon he was charged with "attempted dishonor to the race," but was found not guilty by the Grand Criminal Chamber of the Berlin County Court. The court observed that "even if one were to assume that is was the defendant's intention to have sexual relations with K. again," there was no evidence "of action taken to carry out this intention, such evidence being required to convict him of having attempted the crime." Furthermore, there was no evidence "that a beginning had been made to carry out the planned crime" or that "the necessary close connection with regard to both time and space" existed between the defendant's behavior and the intention of sexual intercourse. However, the Supreme Court was by no means in agreement with this decision. It reversed the acquittal and called for a prison sentence for the defendant, since "if he wanted to be with her in her apartment at night, the possibility of immediately realizing his intention to have sexual intercourse with her existed as such, if the accused succeeded . . . in gaining admittance." For the new trial that would now be necessary, the Supreme Court justices instructed the County Court to look into the question of whether the man should not be charged with attempted rape as well.[73]

In cases where there was absolutely no possibility of charging a defendant with an "attempted racial sexual offense," the courts hit upon a different solution. On April 24, 1939, for example, the Second Grand Criminal Panel of the Frankfurt County Court gave the Jewish paint dealer Max Israel Adler a sentence of one month in prison—which was naturally not suspended—for "committing assault and a public insult." On January 7, 1939, at about eleven o'clock in the morning, in the center of Frankfurt, the defendant had committed the offense of looking across the street at the fifteen-year-old ("German-blooded") Ilse S., "if not importunately, then at least so as to attract notice." The "assault" mentioned in the decision consisted solely in a mere glance, which the court interpreted as follows: "The behavior displayed by the accused had a clearly erotic basis and could only have had the purpose of effecting an approach to the girl who interested him. This approach failed to occur only because the witness refused to cooperate and summoned the police to her aid. The behavior of the Jewish defendant toward a German girl expressed disrespect and contempt for the witness, since the accused clearly assumed that he could succeed in his attempt to approach her through his conspicuous behavior . . . This attitude toward a German girl's racial sensibilities, made evident to her through positive actions taken, represents a grave lack of respect for her sense of honor and is a punishable insult under the meaning of paragraph 185 of the Criminal Code. Even if the defendant pursued no further intentions with regard to the witness, his outward behavior at least could not be interpreted otherwise . . . He is thus punishable in this case in the same manner."[74]

Love Affairs and the Death Penalty

The Law for the Protection of German Blood contained no provision for the death penalty. Nevertheless, "dishonorers of the race" were on some occasions condemned to death. The legal possibilities were provided by certain other laws, such as the Law on Dangerous Habitual Criminals, the so-called Decree on Asocial Elements, and the Decree on Violent Criminals, which in certain cases called for increasing the normal sentence to a death sentence. Since only the Special Courts had jurisdiction over cases prosecuted under these laws, public prosecutors could manage to bring "racial sexual offenders" before these tribunals and demand the death penalty by cleverly combining the sexual charge with these other laws.

The Law on Dangerous Habitual Criminals, passed November 24, 1933, permitted a maximum sentence of fifteen years in a penitentiary for anyone who had committed three premeditated crimes of such a nature as to make the perpetrator appear a "dangerous habitual criminal."[75] A further law passed on September 4, 1941, provided further that "dangerous habitual criminals and sexual offenders are to receive the death penalty if the protection of society and the need for just atonement require it."[76] The Kassel Special Tribunal combined these two laws with the Blood Protection Law to achieve the desired result in the following instance.

Werner Holländer, a twenty-eight-year-old Hungarian, had studied engineering in Germany, passed his exams, and worked for various companies. Not until March 1941, when he applied for a job with the arms manufacturers Henschel & Son and was required to prove he was of "Aryan" descent, was it discovered that his parents were listed in old records of the Lutheran Church as "Israelites." Holländer had not paid particular attention to this, however, and had continued his relationship with a woman he had met at the university. In addition, he had had short-term affairs with several women "of German blood" in the years 1941–1942. In the eyes of the court, this made Werner Holländer, who had no previous criminal record, into a "dangerous habitual criminal," and it concluded: "For criminals of this kind, there can . . . be only one penalty, the death penalty." The judges did hold it in his favor that he had learned of his parentage only at a late date, but the fact that he then "began new sexual relationships with German women in several instances, despite clear knowledge of his fully Jewish identity, reveals his unscrupulousness and his criminal tendencies toward this kind of offense."[77]

This lethal interpretation had become possible only after a decision of the Fourth Criminal Senate of the Supreme Court on March 31, 1939, in the case of a Jewish sales representative who had been accused of having sexual relationships with several women "of German blood." The Leipzig County Court had found him guilty of "a continuing offense"—meaning that legally it was determined to be a single offense—because he "had committed all the actions on the basis of a single general and premeditated intent, as a Jew, to have extramarital sexual relations as long and as often as possible with women of German blood and German nationality."[78] The legal doctrine of the "continuing offense" had been developed in a series of decisions by courts, including the Supreme Court, for "acts which by their nature from a single whole." Its Fourth Panel, however, found the application of this doctrine, which tended to work in favor of defendants, unacceptable in cases of "racial sexual offenders," and reversed the lower court's decision. The concept of a "continuing offense" could be recognized, the panel found, "for embezzlement, for example, . . . as well as for numerous other offenses," and even "the fact that single actions may have involved different persons does not as a rule preclude the assumption that in terms of legal principle, the context of a continuing offense existed." Nevertheless, for "racial sexual offenses" there could be "in principle no assumption of a context of a continuing offense," since "healthy popular opinion contradicts it." It would be "incompatible with the particular nature of racial sexual offenses to assume that these misdeeds legally constitute a single action."[79]

After this decision, courts that were so disposed did not have to look far to find a way to punish repeated "racial sexual offenses" under the Law on Dangerous Habitual Criminals. The decision of the court in Kassel against Werner Holländer does not stand alone. Special Courts also sentenced "dangerous habitual criminals" to death, in Berlin on November 24, 1941,[80] and in Hamburg on May 29, 1942,[81] although the defendants were accused of nothing more than several love affairs.

In Nuremberg, the Special Court managed to combine the Decree on Asocial Elements with the Blood Protection Law, so as to assert its jurisdiction in a case involving Leo Katzenberger, leader of the Jewish community there. In a scandalous trial, the sixty-seven-year-old Katzenberger, owner of a chain of shoe stores until their "Aryanization" in 1938, was easily sentenced to death on the basis of the interpretation described above. He was still living in one of the buildings he had previously owned, where a woman named Irene Seiler had rented an apartment, as well as a small shop for her photography business. Katzenberger, who was still well-situated financially and who had been a friend of her father's, maintained a friendship with the thirty-year-old woman. A great deal of gossip and rumors began to circulate in the building, resulting in slander and libel, and in the spring of 1941 Katzenberger was charged with violating the race laws. Under interrogation, Leo Katzenberger and Irene Seiler remained steadfast in their assertions that nothing sexual had ever occurred between them, and there had certainly never been any sexual intercourse.

The main trial, which took place on March 13 and 14, 1942, aroused great public interest. The courtroom was crowded, and the president of the Court of Appeals, the chief public prosecutor, and many prominent members of the Nazi party were in attendance.[82] "Proof" of Katzenberger's guilt was provided by witnesses, who testified that on one occasion he had given Irene Seiler a bouquet of flowers and gone to a café with her, and that both of them smoked the same brand of cigarettes. It was further alleged that they had repeatedly shown fear when one was seen leaving the other's apartment, and that when someone called Mrs. Seiler a "Jew's tart" she had not protested. After the public prosecutor had placed evidence of this sort before the court and conferred with the presiding judge, he called for the death penalty under paragraph 2 and paragraph 5 section 2 of the Blood Protection Law, in connection with paragraphs 2 and 4 of the Decree on Asocial Elements.

The presiding judge, Dr. Oswald Rothaug, referred to Katzenberger several times in the course of the proceedings as a "syphilitic Jew" and an "agent of world Jewry" which was responsible for the war. That the court imposed the death penalty came as a surprise to no one. Irene Seiler was convicted of perjury—although the Blood Protection Law provided solely for punishment of the male partner and the first decree on its administration specifically stated that the woman involved could not be punished "for either participating in or abetting" the offense "or for false testimony while not under oath"—because she had taken an oath before testifying.

For Katzenberger's case, the Special Court developed several unconventional interpretations of the law. After determining that "the city and countryside are largely emptied of men," it concluded that Katzenberger had exploited the wartime situation, since "the defendant, when he continued to visit Seiler in her apartment until the spring of 1940, reckoned with the fact that . . . his intrigues would not be seen through at all, or only with difficulty." Since he had occasionally visited Mrs. Seiler in the evening, the court was able to claim in addition that he had exploited the nighttime blackout regulations. Now, the Decree on Asocial Elements made the death penalty contingent on conviction for a "crime against person, life, or property," and it was not an easy matter to reinterpret freely exchanged demonstrations of affection as bodily injury; furthermore, all commentaries on the Blood Protection Law stressed that violations did not represent a crime against the woman involved, but only against the "purity of German blood." The judges had no difficulty overcoming these obstacles, however: "The court is of the opinion that the actions of the defendant were designed with a certain purpose in mind and that they were part and parcel of his general conduct; they represent . . . a crime against the person . . . The Jew's dishonor to the race represents a grave attack on the purity of German blood; the racial attack is directed against the person of the German woman."

The death penalty, which in spite of everything was still a rarity in "racial" cases, was justified by the judges as follows: "Katzenberger had precise knowledge of the viewpoint of nationally minded Germans on the race question; he was well aware that his behavior was a slap in the face to national sentiment. Neither the National Socialist revolution of 1933 nor the proclamation of the Blood Protection Law in 1935, neither the action against Jews of 1938 [the so-called *Reichskristallnacht* or "Night of Shattered Glass'] nor the outbreak of war in 1939, sufficed to make him change his ways. The court holds that the only possible response to the defendant's frivolity . . . is the imposition of the death penalty."[83]

Although such death sentences did remain the exception in cases of "dishonor to the race," the imposition of long penitentiary sentences usually led to the same result. The court records in such cases regularly end with an entry stating that after serving his sentence, the prisoner was handed over to the Gestapo. As a rule, this was equivalent to a death sentence:

Reg. 6b crim. case 9/39 Frankfurt/Main:
Kaufmann, Julius, born 5/30/1897 in Vienna, full Jew, sentenced on 8/5/1939 to 2 years and 6 months penitentiary for dishonor to the race. After serving sentence, released to custody of Gestapo Frankfurt.

Reg. 6b crim. case 2/39 Frankfurt/Main:
Sternbach, Salomon, born 11/23/1903 in Wiesbaden, full Jew, sentenced to 3 years penitentiary on 3/28/1939. After serving sentence, released to custody of Gestapo Frankfurt.

Reg. 6b crim. case 10/39 Frankfurt/Main:
Neumark, Markus, born 4/9/1884 in Gross-Steinheim nr. Offenbach, full Jew, sentenced to 2 years and 3 months penitentiary for dishonor to the race. After serving sentence, taken into preventive detention.

Reg. 6b crim. case 17/38 Frankfurt/Main:
Blumenbach, Ludwig, born 1/16/1883 in Gelnhausen, full Jew, sentenced to 2 years penitentiary on 1/3/1939. After release from prison, transferred to custody of Gestapo Frankfurt.[84]

Loss of All Rights

The persecution of Jews, discrimination against them, and denial of their rights by the courts were not limited to imprisonment for violation of the race laws and dissolution of existing marriages. Resourceful judges discovered possibilities for depriving Jews of their rights in all areas of the law, even if no legal foundation for doing so existed. The pattern for the usual interpretations in such cases was established by the Supreme Court in the following case.

On February 24, 1933, the film production company Ufa had signed a contract with the (Jewish) director Eric Charell for the film rights to his novel *The Return of Ulysses*. Charell, who had also written the screenplay, was to direct the movie. The Ufa studio paid him the first installment of 26,000 marks on March 1, 1933, as stipulated in the contract. Five days later, however, the studio withdrew the contract, citing as a reason paragraph 6, according to which the agreement became null and void in the case of the director's death, illness, or a similar reason. The studio's suit to recover the money already paid to Charell was successful at every level. The final court of appeal, the First Civil Panel of the Supreme Court, found in favor of the film company in a decision which read in part:

> The earlier (liberal) view of personal rights made no fundamental distinction among human beings on the basis of sameness or difference in blood . . . According to the National Socialist world view, however, only individuals of German heritage (and those placed on an equal legal footing with them) should be treated as persons with full legal rights within the German Reich. This renews fundamental distinctions of the previous law on the rights of foreign subjects and leads to the reconsideration of notions which were recognized in former times through the distinction made between persons of full legal competence and those of limited competence. The degree of complete legal incompetence or lack of rights was formerly established when the legal existence of an individual had been completely annihilated; the concepts of "civil death" and "monastic death" drew their names from this comparison. When paragraph 6 of the manuscript contract . . . mentioned the possibility that Charell might "not be capable of carrying out his duties as director due to illness, death, or a similar reason," this is to be considered without reservation as equivalent to an alteration in the legal status of the individual as a result of racial policies recognized by law, to the extent that they prevent his carrying out his duties as director in a manner corresponding to death or illness.[85]

The concept of the "civil death" of Jews—long before their physical annihilation—was rarely so clearly articulated, but it did serve as the foundation for a variety of decisions by lower courts. On May 5, 1935, the Petty Court of Wanne-Eickel upheld the refusal of an SA man to pay the money he owed a Jewish merchant and rejected the latter's suit for payment, since National Socialists "refuse in principle to enter into commercial transactions with Jews."[86] The Mainz Petty Court declared the contract between a Jewish tutor and an "Aryan" student to be a "voidable legal transaction."[87] The Petty Court of Jena even went so far as to declare that contracts between "Jews and Jewish spawn" and a newspaper, agreements concerning the printing of advertisements, were null and void because they were "immoral."[88] The County Court of Nuremberg-Fürth voided the contract between an SS man and a Jewish creditor who had agreed to stand security for his debts, because the German-sounding name of the creditor amounted to a "malicious intent to defraud."[89] Other Jews were refused writs to attach the salaries of soldiers.[90] The fact that family members of a public servant shopped at a department store owned by Jews was accepted by the Supreme Labor Court as grounds for immediate dismissal.[91] The Berlin Petty Court took custody of adopted "Aryan" children away from Jewish parents, though it stipulated that the parents must continue to provide financial support for such children.[92] In divorce cases involving couples of "mixed race," the "Aryan" parent was always given custody of the children, even if this parent was the guilty partner,[93] despite a law which provided that as a rule custody was to be awarded to the innocent party.

In cases where Jewish tenants were refused renewal of their leases, some courts at first tried to bend the 1928 Law for Protection of Tenants to suit their own purposes. Paragraph 2 of this law stated that leases could be terminated only "if the behavior of the tenant is such that a continuation of the lease would represent an unreasonable hardship for the landlord," or if "the tenant is guilty of causing considerable annoyance to the landlord." Thus, if a Jewish tenant was quiet and gave no grounds for complaint, it was illegal not to renew his lease. However, on September 16, 1938, the Schöneberg Petty Court observed that "the personal qualities of the tenant" were also to be understood as part of his behavior, "since his actions are merely expressions of his personality." The court even managed to attach blame to the tenant for his own "racial qualities": "The fact that the tenant is a Jew does not mean that he is himself at fault in the normal sense. In the sense of paragraph 3 of the Tenant Protection Law, however, he is at fault. He is not only a foreign body within the community of the German occupants of the building; he also lacks the proper attitude required the membership in a German community."[94] Since the wording of the law itself offered not the slightest justification for such a decision, other courts were more outspoken and truthful, such as the County Court of Berlin: "The question is not one which can be resolved through an interpretation of the Tenant Protection Law, but is rather a question of ideology . . . Terminating the leases of Jewish tenants is . . . made difficult by the Tenant Protection Law and in certain cases impossible. This stands in opposition to the necessity for ending all associations with Jews in the community as quickly as possible . . . The fact that numerous Jews in Germany would become homeless if their leases are held to be terminable may be true, but does not alter the matter. These apartments will then be placed at the disposal of fellow Germans."[95]

On November 26, 1938, the Nuremberg Petty Court determined that the leases of Jewish tenants could be broken at any time without giving them the usual notice: "Since the Tenant Protection Law . . . is designed to serve the community of the German people, it can apply only to those who belong to the community of the German people or who are associated with it by reason of blood . . . Developments have shown that cohabitation by Germans and Jews has become an intolerable state of affairs. Fulfilling the terms of a lease is placed in jeopardy by the person of the tenant, by his membership in the Jewish race."[96]

As a rule, in decisions of this kind the courts openly admitted that the outcome was incompatible with the law. However, the opinion "that every measure directed against Jews could be decreed solely by the government," an opinion which was still widespread in 1935, was declared to be "incorrect" by the Berlin County Court in 1938.[97] Judges could be sure, certainly after the pogrom of the nationwide *Reichskristallnacht* at the very latest, that government leaders would approve every kind of discrimination against Jewish parties involved in lawsuits.

Employment contracts with Jews were often terminated in the same way leases were, although the laws for private employers, unlike those for government and civil service, contained no paragraphs on "Aryans." As early as April 21, 1933, the Labor Court of Frankfurt saw an "important justification" for the immediate dismissal of an orchestra leader in the fact that the café where he was employed could expect a customer boycott if he continued to work there.[98] A number of businessmen based their firing of Jewish employees in 1933 on their fear of financial losses. The Supreme Labor Court accepted this practice, noting that "the new attitude of the German people toward Jews created by the national revolution" made it necessary to determine in individual cases whether "circumstances exist and have been recognized" such that continued employment of a Jew could appear "so injurious or dangerous to the interests" of his employer "that it cannot fairly be expected of him."[99]

On the other hand, the same court found it *could* be expected of a Jewish notary that he should continue to employ his "Aryan" office manager, though his office had been closed following passage of the Law for Restoration of the Professional Civil Service of April 7, 1933, and there was now nothing for the manager to do.[100] In 1937 this court even refused to extend legal protection to Jewish employees in general, because "the racial principles espoused by the National Socialist party have found unmistakably wide acceptance even in large classes of society not associated with the party."[101] From 1938 on, as the degree to which Jews were being denied their rights began to increase rapidly, the labor courts gave their stamp of approval to every kind of tactic against Jewish employees. The County Labor Court of Koblenz denied them pay on national holidays;[102] the Labor Court of Frankfurt denied their right to paid vacations;[103] and the Supreme Labor Court arbitrarily reduced the old-age pensions that employers were required to pay them.[104] According to one decision of the Supreme Court, an employer was not entitled to stop paying all benefits to the widow of a deceased Jewish employee, but he could reduce them "according to the principle of good faith"; the amount of the reduction was to be determined by whether the widow herself was Jewish or not.[105]

The illegal terminations of employment contracts and leases and the numerous other instances of discrimination against Jews in civil suits were justified by judges who argued that every law was to be understood as containing the "unwritten proviso" that "Jews should receive no advantages."[106] They also noted that the legal position of Jews had by no means been fully and finally established yet: "The Nuremberg Laws were only a beginning. The process is not yet concluded."[107]

· 13 ·

The Courts and Eugenics

For the National Socialists, "purity of German blood" included not only "purity of the race" but also genetic health, for according to a brochure published by the Ministry of the Interior, "hereditary diseases in succeeding generations" would mean "the death of the people."[1] Hitler himself had already proposed a plan in 1927 in which newborn infants with physical or mental defects would simply be killed.[2] On July 14, 1933, a first step in this direction was taken with passage of the "Law for the Prevention of Hereditary Diseases," which provided for mandatory sterilization in cases of genetic disorders.[3]

The idea of killing people afflicted with hereditary defects or preventing them from having children was one which had been discussed in conservative circles before 1933,[4] and the Nazis had a foundation of previous work on which to build. Nevertheless, the fundamental tenor of this law was racist through and through, and its authors emphasized: "In maintaining the proper hereditary and racial health of the German people, the goal is to have at all times a sufficient number of genetically sound families with many children of high racial value. At the core of the idea of a healthy race is the notion of breeding. Future upholders of the law must be clear about the breeding aims of the German people."[5]

According to the first paragraph of the law, persons suffering from hereditary diseases were to be sterilized, if "the experience of medical science" suggested "with great probability" that any offspring of such persons would have "grave physical or mental defects." Declared as genetic diseases "under the meaning of the law" were feeblemindedness, schizophrenia, manic depression, epilepsy, degenerative chorea, hereditary blindness and deafness, severe physical deformities, and severe alcoholism. Application for sterilization could be made by the person affected, or by a legal guardian, medical officer, or head of a mental hospital. According to

paragraph 1 of an accompanying administrative decree, even the sterilization of children was possible.[6] Petitions for sterilizations were to be decided upon by special "Hereditary Health Courts" constituted for the purpose and attached to local petty courts; they would consist of a judge from
the petty court and two physicians, one of whom was to be "particularly
familiar with eugenics." Sessions were closed to the public; physicians appearing as expert witnesses before the court could not insist on professional secrecy and thus could not refuse to testify. The judgment in a case
before a Hereditary Health Court could be appealed to a Hereditary
Health Court of Appeals. Courts of the latter type were attached to every
Court of Appeals and consisted once again of a judge and two physicians.
They reached a final decision on the application, after which no further
appeals were possible. If the decision was in favor of sterilization, the person concerned was granted two weeks' time to have the operation performed voluntarily. Otherwise the sterilization would be performed "with
the aid of the police, and if necessary with the use of direct force."

Such operations were not without danger. The director of the University Hospital in Würzburg, Professor Gaus, worked out a "mortality coef-
ficient" of not less than 5 percent.[7] Given a total of approximately 350,000
sterilizations, one must reckon that the eugenics law claimed something
like 17,500 victims. This did not appear to affect the jurists and physicians
of the time unduly, however. Law professor Karl Binding and psychiatrist
Alfred Hoche, coauthors of the book *Sanction for Destroying Lives Not
Worth Living* (1920), had already dismissed the possibility of misdiagnosis
as of no great concern: "For family members the loss is naturally very
severe, but the human race loses so many members to errors that one more
or less hardly matters."[8]

The courts regularly treated as "major hereditary physical deformities"
such disorders as hemophilia, harelip, cleft plate, muscular dystrophy, and
dwarfism.[9] Severe alcoholism was viewed, in accordance with the most
widely cited commentary on the eugenics law, as "evidence of a certain
sort of inferior mental constitution."[10] The judges were only too glad to
defer to the "expertise" of Nazi medicine, which the journalist Hans-
Günther Thiele has summed up harshly but accurately as "unchecked cal-
lousness, evil, and bloodthirstiness that was uncontrolled and bureaucratic
at the same time."[11] Yet it is precisely the judgments of the "Health
Courts" that reveal the precarious grounds of these medical opinions—
especially the psychiatric opinions, which are the vaguest and least precise
of all.

Half of all cases heard were initiated on grounds of "congenital feeblemindedness"; in another 27 percent the diagnosis was "schizophrenia,"

and these two most frequent grounds for sterilization were also the most questionable. What constituted "congenital feeblemindedness" remained completely unclarified. On occasion the courts found slightly subnormal intelligence, retarded development, or congenital alexia (the inability to understand written words) grounds for sterilization.[13] The Hereditary Health Court of Appeals in Jena made it a principle that "the need to attend special schools always speaks for the presence of congenital feeble-mindedness."[14] But "feeblemindedness" was diagnosed not only in cases of low intelligence, but also in cases of "difficulty in understanding abstractions and in forming opinions, and an abnormal emotional and volitional sphere." The commentary written by Gütt, Rüdin, and Ruttke urged the jurists and physicians involved not to be overscrupulous in their judgments: "In numerous cases of asocial and antisocial, delinquent, or severely psychopathic debility, sterilization . . . can be recommended without reservation."[15]

The published surveys of decisions in this area confirm the degree of unconcern regarding the alleged existence of "congenital feeblemindedness"—as in the case of a precision-tool maker who had not only received high marks during his apprenticeship, but had also performed his work for years to the satisfaction of his supervisor.[16] In other instances, sterilization was recommended for a girl who had successfully graduated from a school for retarded children,[17] a working woman who had completed elementary school without repeating a grade and performed her job "to the complete satisfaction of her supervisors,"[18] a sailor who had graduated from a commercial high school without failing a grade,[19] and a laborer who had advanced to the rank of sergeant during the First World War.

This last case prompted the Hereditary Health Court of Appeals in Jena, in a decision on November 25, 1935, to revoke the sterilization order and to establish the following noteworthy guideline: "Successive promotions of a soldier in wartime speak against the presence of congenital feeble-mindedness."[20]

Shaky as the diagnoses of individual cases or conditions may have been at times, the decision about whether they were hereditary or not had an even flimsier basis. Even the leading geneticist of the day, Professor Hans Luxemberger, conceded that the classification of schizophrenia as a hereditary disorder was "no more than a working hypothesis." He added, however, that one could not wait until final proof had been established; after all, the practice of eugenics was "possible . . . even without an understanding of the genetic mechanism involved."[21] Gütt, Rüdin, and Ruttke also encouraged jurists to make do without proof of hereditary factors: "It is sufficient if the invisible predisposition to a disease has manifested itself only temporarily, or only in mild form, or to begin with only in a first attack or episode."[22]

If physicians were satisfied, then jurists were certainly not about to complain. The courts did not challenge medically doubtful claims, either. The Hereditary Health Court of Lyck in East Prussia, for example, ordered the sterilization of a young woman even though her deaf-mutism had resulted from two accidents and a severe ear infection, and the fact that she had given birth to a normal baby argued against the presence of a genetic disorder. In its decision of July 15, 1937, the court observed, "Although no further cases of deafness can be documented among blood relations, nevertheless the Hereditary Health Court is convinced on the basis of the medical specialist's opinion that it must be a case of hereditary deafness. After sterilization has been successfully performed, the woman X may marry the father of her child, the deaf-mute tailor Y, once he has also been sterilized."[23]

The vagueness of psychiatrists' expert opinions and the nonchalance with which "facts" were determined come to light in decisions that involved distinguishing between schizophrenia and other forms of mental illness. A forty-year-old architect, father of two healthy children, had been taken to a psychiatric hospital following a suicide attempt. The doctors first took him to be schizophrenic, but soon revised their diagnosis because he showed no sign of some typical schizophrenic symptoms, such as disturbances of attention and of focus in thinking and speaking. Since some of the symptoms observable in the architect, such as suicidal tendencies and anxious excitability, are also present in manic depressives, the Hereditary Health Court of Appeals in Zweibrücken, to which he had appealed his case, simply left open the question of whether he was suffering from schizophrenia or manic depression. The court took the latter to be more probable in view of "the petitioner's considerable gifts . . . which are alleged to occur with particular frequency in connection with manic depression as opposed to other forms of insanity." The completely contradictory medical evidence submitted led the court to conclude "that the mental illness . . . is either schizophrenia or manic depression. A precise diagnostic distinction is not necessary, however, since both disorders are hereditary disorders under the meaning of paragraph 1 of the Law for the Prevention of Hereditary Diseases." Both of the medical experts who testified had argued strongly against sterilization, because the patient was "a highly estimable person with very valuable intellectual and affective qualities and of high character, and such hereditary traits . . . deserve to be spared." This did not help the architect's cause, however, since the court objected that "the presence of valuable hereditary traits alone does not justify a rejection of sterilization."[24]

Although commentaries stressed that the decision whether or not to sterilize was to be based on the person "as a whole,"[25] the Hereditary Health Court of Appeals in Düsseldorf found it illegitimate to hold that "other factors compensate, as it were, for considerable deficiency in a single area." It conceded that one patient could "still make his way" in life despite his defective intelligence, but this was not the issue: "It must be taken into account that the aim of the law is not to protect him, but to guarantee the future of the German people."[26]

The Health Courts frequently misused the proceedings to classify "criminal types" as defined by Nazi theorists of criminal law. They introduced for this purpose the category of "moral feeblemindedness." This was not recognized as formal grounds for sterilization by the higher courts, but the frequency with which the sterilization orders of lower courts on such grounds were reversed on appeal shows that this kind of argumentation was widespread. Even though sterilization was not justified specifically on grounds of "moral feeblemindedness," however, the decisions were filled with moral outrage and condemnation of the persons in question. As in the case of most of the decisions dealing with "racial sexual offenses," the courts' fascination with the subjects' active sex lives was striking and barely concealed: "She reached sexual maturity while still a schoolgirl; at fourteen she entered into a sexual relationship . . . with a carnival man."[27] Or: "S. is undoubtedly an inferior psychopathic individual."[28] Another defendant "masturbated early, and also practiced mutual masturbation; he became sexually active at fourteen, and kept company with inferior types of girls day and night."[29] Moral condemnation was directed particularly at alcoholics. They failed to escape "punishment" by the Hereditary Health Courts even if they had managed to give up alcohol. The forms of assistance usually needed by former alcoholics to stay sober were turned into matters of reproach in themselves: "Z. is incapable of dealing with the consequences of alcoholism on his own. He is able to manage only with the support of his wife and teetotalers' groups. Thus, a condition of severe alcoholism . . . is present."[30] Yet even if someone had actually succeeded in overcoming his addiction without the aid of others, this did not help. "Even if K. has lived without alcohol for . . . seven months . . . under the pressure of his pending sterilization hearing, this does not eliminate the finding of severe alcoholism, which is present beyond doubt."[31] Since alcoholism alone was not sufficient grounds for sterilization, the courts had to find something to allow them to call it "severe alcoholism." In their eyes it was above all "asocial" or "immoral" behavior: "The patient threatens his family and spends all his money on drink. All this clearly establishes that Willi T. suffers from severe alcoholism."[32] The Hereditary Health Court of Appeals in Berlin noted indignantly that one alcoholic had sold his furniture—"bought with a special loan granted on the occasion of his marriage"—for drink and that he had later retracted his own application for sterilization, which had clearly been made under some duress. All of this, "his behavior in withdrawing the application . . . and the way he spent his money," left the court with only one conclusion to be drawn: severe alcoholism.[33] In general, alcoholism was regarded by the courts as the mark of an "unstable character," but since this in itself was no more grounds for sterilization than the mild form of the addiction, they fell back on circular reasoning. In cases of "unstable character"—for example, if an alcoholic had a criminal record or was "unrepentant" or "incorrigible"—the finding was to be severe alcoholism.

The task of imposing drastic sanctions on asocial and handicapped individuals without proceeding through criminal trials was clearly not an unpleasant one for the judges concerned. At the beginning of the war, after the number of hearings in connection with the eugenics law had become exorbitant, a decree was issued that reduced them considerably. As the bulletins of the SS Security Service reported, however, the suggestion was made "several times by judges that these proceedings be permitted on a larger scale again"; after all, "particularly in matters of eugenics . . . a regular and uninterrupted administration of justice [was] important."[35]

· 14 ·

The Euthanasia Program

The policies of the Hereditary Health Courts found their logical continuation in the euphemistically named "Program T4" for euthanasia. Although responsibility for this mass murder of the physically and mentally handicapped and "asocial types" lay primarily with the medical profession, the legal profession was associated with it in a variety of ways. The idea of killing people who represented mere "ballast" to society was not an invention of the Nazis. In 1920, as has already been mentioned, Karl Binding, one of the most prominent figures in criminal law in imperial Germany, had written in cooperation with the psychiatrist Alfred Hoche a plea entitled *Sanction for Destroying Lives Not Worth Living*. In the early days of the Third Reich, no consistent policy on such matters existed as yet. A report by the Official Commission on Criminal Law issued by minister of justice Franz Gürtner in 1935 contained the bald pronouncement: "Sanction for the destruction of so-called life not worth living is out of the question."[1] On the other hand, Nazi party circles were demanding that the government go beyond the half-hearted measures of the Law for the Prevention of Hereditary Diseases. In 1934 the Bavarian state commissioner for health called for the "eradication of psychopaths, imbeciles, and other inferior individuals,"[2] and in 1937 a candidate for the degree of Doctor of Laws wrote in his dissertation:

> Only a racially superior person has a right to exist within the community. An individual who is useless or even harmful to the community by virtue of his inferiority should be removed from it . . . Whether society is ready to accept the removal of inferior beings through killing must remain an open question . . . This important task should not be impeded, however, by petty quarrels over jurisdiction that would paralyze its effectiveness . . . because the boundary between measures of criminal law and those of racial health might in some circumstances become blurred.[3]

At the start of the war, these ideas were put into practice. Inmates of state hospitals were transferred to camouflaged institutions and then murdered by the "Charitable Association for Patient Transport, Inc.," with injections or in gas chambers.[4] Yet even though fictitious names and forged medical records were used, the systematic destruction of "life not worth living" could not be kept secret for long. As the first criminal charges were filed by relatives, the chief public prosecutors of the various states reported to the Reich Ministry of Justice that the population was becoming alarmed. On November 28, 1940, the chief public prosecutor in Munich wrote about a rumor then being circulated, to the effect "that now lists were being drawn up in old-age homes, too,"[5] and the president of the Bamberg Court of Appeals reported on January 2, 1941: "The fact that the incurably mentally ill are being liquidated has now leaked out here as well, and has caused considerable consternation."[6] Minister of justice Gürtner, who no longer opposed the program himself, did intervene again and call for the establishment of a legal basis on which the mass murder could be carried out in a "constitutionally correct" manner. Like other critics of the programs' illegality, however, he was referred to a paper in which Hitler "assigned responsibility to *Reichsleiter* Bouhler [a high official in the Nazi party] and Dr. Brandt . . . to broaden the authority of certain physicians (yet to be named) to enable them to carry out mercy killings on patients who, in the most critical appraisal of their condition and in the best human estimate, were incurably ill."[7]

Complaints and criminal charges continued to flow in nonetheless. The bishop of Münster, Count Galen, pressed charges in one case;[8] in another, a judge from the Mark Brandenburg issued an injunction prohibiting removal of the wards of his court from local hospitals and initiated criminal proceedings against Philipp Bouhler. In Wels in Upper Austria, a public prosecutor even opened an investigation into physicians' activities at the Hartheim extermination center.[9] On the other hand, courts on a few occasions interpreted criticism of the murder program as "malicious attacks" on the government. In order to avoid "mishaps" in the future, Franz Schlegelberger, the department undersecretary who was acting as minister of justice (after Gürtner's death on January 29, 1941), called one of the highest-level conferences of jurists ever to take place in the Third Reich. Present at "Air Force House" in Berlin on April 23–24, 1941, were Schlegelberger's fellow undersecretary Roland Freisler, Supreme Court president Erwin Bumke, People's Court president Dr. Thierack, the chief public prosecutors attached to both these courts, numerous high officials from the Ministry of Justice, the presidents of all thirty-four Courts of Appeals, and all thirty-four chief public prosecutors of "Great Germany."[10]

The first point on the agenda was "Program T4," and Schlegelberger acquainted the participants "with all the decisions of the Führer," so that "judges and public prosecutors would not cause grave damage to the legal system and the government by opposing measures which they believed sincerely but mistakenly to be illegal, and would not place themselves in opposition to the will of the Führer through no fault of their own." After reports by Viktor Brack, a medical officer, and Professor Werner Heyde on the program for the killings, Schlegelberger explained that since "a legally valid decree from the Führer [existed] for these measures, there could be no further reservations about carrying out the euthanasia project." Curt Rothenberger, president of the Hamburg Court of Appeals and later undersecretary in the Ministry of Justice, was alone in finding a legal regulation of the matter still necessary. The rest of the country's legal elite had no reservations. The instructions that all criminal charges filed in connection with the euthanasia program should be referred to the Ministry of Justice and should be classified as matters outside the jurisdiction of the lower courts were received in silence by the judges and public prosecutors, who had all appeared at the meeting in their Nazi party uniforms. No questions were raised about how such a directive was to be reconciled with the principle that all crimes were to be prosecuted, with the laws on murder, and with the prohibitions against perversion of justice and aiding and abetting crimes.

In August 1942, after more than 70,000 people had been murdered, the program was officially ended, but approximately 100,000 more fell victim to "unofficial" euthanasia actions which continued after this date.[11] The experienced "euthanasia personnel" were later assigned chiefly to the death camps in Poland.[12]

· 15 ·

"Defenders of the Law": The Supreme Court as a Court of Appeals

The possibilities available to defendants to appeal verdicts of guilty were drastically reduced during the Third Reich. At the same time, entirely new possibilities were created enabling public prosecutors to have even valid decisions reversed: these possibilities were offered by the plea of nullity and the extraordinary appeal. The plea of nullity, a petition to a review panel of the Supreme Court to set aside the decision and refer the matter back to the original court, at least bore a resemblance to traditional rights of appeal, but the new "extraordinary appeal" was lodged "on behalf of the Führer" by the chief public prosecutor of the Reich and, if granted, automatically rendered the previous verdict void. The new trial then took place before the Special Panel of the Supreme Court ("the Führer's Tribunal"). Decisions in such cases were regarded as establishing important principles. All files on extraordinary appeals bore a stamp marking them as "of particular historical value"; they were stored with appropriate care and have thus been preserved in their entirety. They provide unique documentation of the murderous cooperation among the officials of the Reich Ministry of Justice, public prosecutors at the national level, and the Special Panel of the Supreme Court.

Extraordinary appeals were lodged a total of twenty-one times, but only one was made on the defendant's behalf. This was in the case of the police officer Wilhelm Klinzmann (see Chapter 19), a case that ended not with a verdict but with cancellation by the Ministry of Justice. In two cases the Special Panel reduced slightly the sentences handed down by the court of first instance; in four cases it increased them drastically; and in fourteen it altered prison sentences to the death penalty.

However, it was not so much the relatively rare extraordinary appeals as the pleas of nullity—entered in the thousands, especially against decisions of the Special Courts—that show how willing the Supreme Court was to defer to the regime's wishes. The aim of this kind of appeal was expressed in intentionally vague wording as the correction of "unjust decisions," and it created the possibility of overturning every valid judgment. Once a plea of nullity had been entered, the Supreme Court had three choices: it could reject the plea, or grant it and refer the case back to the original court or to another court of its own choosing, or grant it and decide the case itself. The cases in which the Supreme Court failed to accede to the wishes of public prosecutors were extremely rare. In only one case out of twelve was the plea that had been entered against a lower court's decision (which was always legally binding) rejected. Of the 437 pleas dealt with by the Third Criminal Panel alone (all six Criminal Panels were empowered to hear them), only one fourth had been entered on the defendant's behalf; three fourths were pleas for a harsher sentence.[2]

From 1939 on, when defendants were found guilty by the Special Courts, they were punished according to the fundamental principle that a person who broke the law was always an enemy of the community, but that the penalty for his actions must "be incomparably more severe if he continues his asocial behavior while his entire nation is engaged in a bitter struggle to defend itself against the enemy of the fatherland."[3] The Supreme Court had no intention of closing its ears to such reasoning. In carrying out their function of review of the Special Courts' decisions—for which no right of appeal was supposed to exist—the justices did not seize the opportunity to give the vague regulations more precise legal contours, much less limit their broad range of application, as might have been expected. Instead, they adopted the extreme interpretations developed by the Special Courts and occasionally urged them to implement even harsher practices.

During the German occupation of Prague, for example, two Czech citizens, the brothers Karl and Wenzel H., had stolen some used ration coupons for clothing and sold them. For this petty crime they were sentenced by the Prague Special Court on November 7, 1941, to eight and ten years in a penitentiary, respectively. Wolfgang Immerwahr Fränkel, a county court judge, lodged a plea of nullity on behalf of the chief public prosecutor of the Reich. The Supreme Court thereupon set aside the decision and returned the case to Prague with the instruction: "Should the Special Court once again conclude that the preconditions for applying paragraph 4 of the Decree on Asocial Elements are present, then it must here consider whether a sentence of death should not be passed as the most severe of the possible penalties." In fact, the paragraph 4 referred to provided only for a penitentiary sentence in most cases, the death sentence being reserved for a "particularly reprehensible act." The Special Court got the message, however, and after renewed proceedings sentenced the two brothers to death.[4]

As a rule, once it had granted the plea of nullity, the Supreme Court would refer a case back to the lower court. This practice was in accord with its status as a court of review, whose function was solely to reexamine decisions for possible errors of law. However, since most of the time no errors of law were involved in the granting of the plea of nullity and the decisions were simply characterized as "unjust" in general, the Supreme Court usually returned such cases to the lower courts, along with its thoughts on what a "just" decision would be.

The Supreme Court handed down a decision of this kind itself for the first time in 1942. By this time, it had become common practice in German cities to send inmates of concentration camps and penal institutions to search for survivors after air raids. A prisoner named Friedrich C., who was serving an eleven-year penitentiary sentence for robbery, had used one such rescue assignment to steal a coat that he intended to wear in an escape attempt he was planning. For this petty theft the Bremen Special Court gave him a further penitentiary sentence of five years, to be followed by preventive detention. A plea of nullity was raised against this lawful decision by the chief public prosecutor of the Reich—prepared once again by Judge Fränkel—asking for the death penalty, and on April 14 he was able to report to the Ministry of Justice that "the Supreme Court in a decision of April 13 of this year set aside the decision of the Special Court of January 28 of this year and sentenced the defendant to death in accordance with my petition . . . This decision is notable because the Supreme Court itself imposed the death sentence here for the first time in proceedings that had been initiated by a plea of nullity."[5]

A decision by the Supreme Court on its own in such cases continued to be the exception, however. Normally it limited itself to setting out certain doctrines and interpretations of National Socialist laws for the Special Courts as well, a practice that led only too often to drastic tightening of sentencing rules that were already harsh. Since the start of the war, for instance, a decree entitled "Extraordinary Measures Related to Broadcasting" had made it a crime punishable by a penitentiary sentence to listen to foreign radio stations. The act of passing on foreign news which was likely to "threaten the capacity of the German people to resist" was even a capital crime. Such "broadcasting criminals" fell under the jurisdiction of the Special Courts; in order to prosecute them, a petition from the Gestapo was required.[6] However, the decree allowed the courts a certain measure of leeway in judging the circumstances of the offenses and above all in imposing the sentence.

In one such case, a Special Court acquitted a landowner who had informed one of his hired hands on March 27, 1941, that the government of Yugoslavia had been overthrown after joining the so-called Triple Pact (signed by Italy, Japan, and Germany) on March 25 in Vienna. This piece of news was broadcast throughout the Reich itself during the evening hours of March 27, but the defendant had heard it shortly before on a Swiss radio station. The Special Court was of the opinion that the report was not likely to threaten the capacity of the German people to resist, since it was not only accurate, but broadcast only a few hours later in Germany as well and was not unexpected, as the internal political difficulties of the Yugoslavian government had been well known when the pact was signed. The Fourth Criminal Panel of the Supreme Court nevertheless reversed this acquittal and demanded a penitentiary sentence. The justices determined that for the defendant to be found guilty it was not necessary for "damage to have occurred or for there to have been a particularly negative effect or even for resistance to have in fact been weakened. The likelihood or threat referred to in the decree is inherently present in all news which . . . in its content can be detrimental to the German people in their vital struggle . . . The time and form for making unfavorable news known must be left to the authorities. The fact that the news is later made known by German sources . . . does not render an act which has already been committed exempt from punishment." [7]

That in this case legal arguments could be made for acquittal with just as much propriety as for conviction is already documented by the decision of the Special Court. The determination amounting almost to frenzy with which the Special Court punished minor offenses emerges even more clearly from another case where the wording of the decree clearly pointed to the acquittal. The defendant had been in the habit of listening to foreign radio broadcasts before the war, although what interested him was not so much news and political commentaries as the music on the Swiss station in Beromünster and the Dutch station in Hilversum. After this music lover had been acquitted by a Special Court, the Fourth Criminal Panel of the Supreme Court overturned this decision on August 17, 1940, and declared foreign music programs to be subversive as well: "Although the preamble to the decree states, 'Every word broadcast to this country by the enemy is obviously untrue and designed to cause damage to the German people,' this is intended merely to stress the primary means by which foreign radio strives to harm the German people . . . [The decree] prohibits listening to any foreign station. Therefore, the prohibition also extends to music programs broadcast by stations in enemy or neutral countries." [8]

The wording of the Decree on Asocial Elements was also vague enough to leave some questions open. Paragraph 4 stated that perpetrators of certain specified crimes "against life, limb, or property" were to be regarded as "asocial elements," but it was unclear what constituted the "other criminal acts" mentioned there. According to the wording itself, even a simple insult or traffic violation could have been "another criminal act." Given the fact that the offenses covered by the decree were punishable by death, however, the context suggested that only serious crimes were meant. It would thus have been easy enough to avoid invoking the decree in trifling matters. To send someone to a penitentiary or even to the gallows who had exploited wartime conditions to commit "a public nuisance" or to drive "with excessive speed in villages and towns"[9] was clearly not the intention of even the Council of Ministers for the Defense of the Reich, which was the body that had issued the decree.

To start with, the courts did in fact interpret the phrase "other criminal acts" to mean only major offenses, but then a process of continual expansion of the scope of the Decree on Asocial Elements set in. Finally the Supreme Court included under the act even such petty offenses as were often prosecuted only if an injured party came forward to complain.

In a case heard by the County Court of Seigen, a man was accused of making indecent proposals in letters to a married woman whose husband had been drafted into the army. After the woman had filed charges, the court not only found him guilty of insulting behavior—for which he normally would have had to pay a small fine—but also found that in so doing he had "exploited the unusual circumstances caused by the war." This made him an "asocial element," and he was sentenced to death. Previously, the Third Criminal Senate of the Supreme Court had always insisted that for a crime to be punished under the decree, one had to prove both that it had been committed by exploiting wartime conditions and that the accused corresponded to the type of "asocial element" whose "particularly reprehensible" behavior would be considered genuinely deserving of a penitentiary or death sentence "in healthy popular opinion."[10] In this case, however, the Supreme Court showed no hesitation in affirming the death sentence. The justices were of the opinion that the aim of the decree, "the apprehension of every last asocial element," required the application of "paragraph 4 to all criminal offenses," including such bagatelles as insulting behavior.[11]

A short time later the Second Criminal Panel extended the scope of the decree even further, to include "crimes of omission." A defendant who had no previous criminal record had been drinking, and while intoxicated had been a passenger in a car involved in an accident; the owner, who had been driving, had fled. The Berlin Special Court had proceeded on the assumption that leaving the scene of the accident had been an attempt to exploit the wartime circumstance of the blackout. It also found the passenger guilty of failure to assist, because he had not prevented the driver from leaving the scene. In addition, the court interpreted this omission as a "crime against life and limb" that also exploited the blackout. The Supreme Court affirmed this conclusion, and had no particular difficulty in coming up with the necessary evidence that the perpetrator was truly an "asocial element": "The fact that the accused has no previous record and is not a criminal personality in light of his previous life does not necessarily prevent him . . . from appearing as an asocial element, given the crime he has now committed." The decree, the court stated, was applicable even to a person who "otherwise is not a criminal personality," since commission of the crime itself proved "that the perpetrator, even though without a previous criminal record, has displayed in his crime an attitude toward the national community in wartime that shows him to be its enemy." [12]

In its use of the Decree on Violent Criminals, the Supreme Court led the way for other courts by offering "creative" interpretations going far beyond the limits of this already extremely harsh regulation. The decree made the death sentence mandatory if during an attempted rape, highway robbery, bank robbery, or other violent crime someone had used a "weapon to shoot, strike, or stab or an equally dangerous means of injury or had threatened life or limb of another person with such a weapon." The penalty was the same for a criminal who "commits an assault or defends himself with a weapon" against pursuers. [13] The Special Courts had already found any number of things to be a weapon or equally dangerous means of injury, including a bell and a "shoe-covered foot." [14] Apparently, however, they lacked the imagination necessary to add the mere hands of the perpetrator—without the aid of an object of any kind—to this category. It took the Supreme Court to hit upon the idea that "the use of one's own physical strength" was as dangerous a means of injury as a revolver. It applied the decree to a case of robbery in which the victim had been seized by the throat, since it was "not to be assumed" that the lawmakers in specifying weapons and equally dangerous means of injury "had only those means in mind which are located outside the body of the attacker"; "such a narrow interpretation of the word 'means' would run counter to the purpose of the regulation." [15]

This Supreme Court decision was published in several different places and gave a signal to the Special Courts that all offenses in which violence played any kind of role should be punished under the Decree on Violent

Criminals. In effect, this meant imposing the death penalty. This sealed the fate of countless defendants.

One such individual was a twenty-two-year-old Jewish bargeman named Josef C. As soon as the Supreme Court's decision was published, the presiding judge of the Hamburg Special Court invoked his rights and urged the Sixth Criminal Chamber of the County Court, which was responsible for "racial sexual offenses," to hand Josef C.'s case over to him. Since, according to the new decision of the Supreme Court, the charge on which the case was based was now to be classified as a "violent crime," jurisdiction belonged no longer to the ordinary criminal courts but to the Special Court.

Late on the evening of August 27, 1939, Josef C. had gone ashore from his river barge with coworkers to visit a dance hall. There he met Frau J., a young woman who was doing a good deal of drinking in the company of some friends and relatives. The two of them left the dance hall at several points in the course of the night to pursue their flirtation in private, but were interrupted each time. When the party broke up at dawn, the bargemen accompanied the other group part of the way home. After the two groups separated, the woman called Josef C. back one more time. They embraced; Josef C. pulled the woman into a ditch; and there they had sexual intercourse. Afterward she went home, and that would have been the end of the matter, had Josef C. not bragged about his exploits. His boasting led to a denunciation and charges of "dishonoring the race."

After Josef C. had spent more than a year in jail awaiting his trial, his case was brought before the panel responsible for "racial" crimes. In her testimony, Frau J. gave very inconsistent answers to the question of whether Josef C. had used force. At one point, she spoke of his having "choked her slightly." The act had been committed three months before the Decree on Violent Criminals took effect, but paragraph 5 of the decree explicitly permitted prosecution of crimes committed prior to its promulgation. In a report to the Ministry of Justice, the public prosecutor noted: "I regretted at the time the charges were made that we had no harsher provisions at our disposal to use on C., since it is a very nasty case of dishonor to the race. However, at that time I was following the interpretation of the Decree on Violent Criminals put forward by the Special Court here and assuming that the perpetrator's own physical strength could not be regarded as 'the equally dangerous means' referred to in paragraph 1. In the meantime the Supreme Court has taken the opposite point of view. This means that the Decree on Violent Criminals can be applied . . . It seems to me possible that C. will be sentenced to death."

In a brief hearing before the criminal panel of the County Court, the petition to have the case transferred to the Special Court was granted. A three-day trial took place in which much remained contradictory and un-clarified in the testimony of the chief witnesses for the prosecution. Never-theless, this tribunal, referring to the epoch-making decision of the Su-preme Court, sentenced Josef C. to death as a violent criminal. The sentence was to be carried out immediately. An appeal for clemency that went into the doubtful argument of whether someone's bare hands were actually a "weapon" was rejected on June 25, 1940, and the execution set for the next morning. Fate seemed to be taking a turn in Josef C.'s favor when the County Court granted his last-minute petition for a reopening of the case; the court noted the existence of "considerable doubt as to whether the choking in the present case [could] be regarded as use of means equally dangerous as a weapon to shoot, strike, or stab." The post-ponement was a brief one, however, for in the early morning hours of June 26 the Hanseatic Court of Appeals reversed the order of the County Court, and at 9:03 A.M. the same day Josef C. was executed.[16]

The pernicious influence of the Supreme Court on lower courts was not limited to extraordinary appeals and pleas of nullity, however; it was felt in the way it carried out its chief function as a court of review. Its decisions on review in matters of the Race Laws are not unique. In other areas as well, the justices identified themselves with the aims of the regime. In one case, the court granted precedence to the Service Code of the SA, placing it over the Criminal Code, although this Service Code was in fact merely an internal set of regulations for the party organization without any gen-eral legal validity.

In a garrison town in northern Germany, relations between an SA naval unit stationed there and the local SA commander had been strained for a long time. On June 30, 1934, the commander, accompanied by a squad of his SA men, burst into a dance party being held by the naval unit; he demanded that the party be ended at once and insulted the officer in charge. After he had left the room, there was a brief scuffle outside with some of the sailors. The commander, flanked by ten of his own men, drew his "dagger of honor" and stabbed one of the attackers. The wound was fatal. Since it was not a case of self-defense, the jury at the County Court of Verden/Aller found the SA commander guilty of manslaughter. Al-though Article 8 of the SA Service Code did permit a superior attacked by someone under his command to make use of a weapon, the court found that this article could not grant any further rights than those contained in Criminal Code's provisions on self-defense. The Supreme Court then reversed this decision and interpreted the law on self-defense in terms of the SA Service Code: in the opinion of the high court, the accused was "not only authorized . . . but indeed entitled and obliged to defend the prestige and the interests of the power of command embodied by and vested in him." The fatal stabbing was thus "lawful."[17]

Arbitrary Decisions in Everyday Life

The readiness of the courts to bow to the wishes of their political masters was not limited to criminal cases and the discriminatory Race Laws: in all areas of the law and in all kinds of courts, genuine or presumed opponents of the regime were deprived of their legal rights. Following are a few examples documenting the widespread injustice.

On March 5, 1934, in a civil suit, the Prussian Supreme Court in Berlin granted the petition to have a Jewish judge removed from a case. The judge had already been demoted and transferred to a County Court. The court found in favor of the petitioner, because he was "a high-ranking National Socialist" and had been an "anti-Semite for a long time."[1]

The Supreme Labor Court of the Reich upheld the right of an employer to fire an employee without notice because a local Nazi party leader had filed a—demonstrably false—negative report on the employee, who had thus come under suspicion of being "an enemy of the state." The court referred to its "established" doctrine "that unfounded criticism, even unfounded suspicion on the part of the authorities can carry such weight that it alone can be significant grounds for dismissal."[2]

The Hamburg Court of Appeals in 1936 posed the question "whether a legal obligation is present to continue an existing contract between two persons if the welfare of the community requires that it be terminated." The court found that the nonterminable contract between a newspaper and an unpopular editor could be terminated after the Nazi official in charge of "coordinating" the press had demanded that the paper get rid of the editor. Even though the demand had been made "primarily . . . for reasons of partisan politics," the judges wrote, nevertheless "the legal and economic consequences" of not firing him made it binding for the court.[3]

The Hamburg County Court took custody of children away from Jehovah's Witnesses and had them placed in children's homes, because the religious education they were receiving "endangered the children's intellectual and spiritual welfare in the extreme."[4] The Petty Court of Berlin-Lichterfelde found that "the danger posed to children by a Communist or atheistic upbringing warrants their removal from their parents,"[5] while the Petty Court of Wilster put into a state home all children whose fathers had not sent them to join the Hitler Youth, since "anyone keeping his children out of the Hitler Youth . . . is abusing his parental authority."[6] Even if children so much as refused to give the "Hitler salute" at school, the courts sometimes considered this sufficient grounds for taking children away from their parents.[7]

On a number of occasions the courts simply ignored the law, either equating the interests of the Nazi party with the law of the land, or, even worse, giving its regulations priority. This happened, for example, when the Prussian Administrative Court of Appeals refused a driver's license to a known opponent of Nazism;[8] when the Supreme Court found a man guilty of "fraud" for wearing a false Nazi party badge, although he had gained no financial advantage from it and the court itself recognized that this was essential for proof that fraud had indeed been committed;[9] when the Supreme Court found a person guilty of "damaging the people's welfare," although in fact what had been damaged was merely a subsidiary organization of the Nazi party;[10] and when the Supreme Court found that financial irregularities in the lower ranks of the Nazi party amounted to "grave misuse of public office for embezzlement."[11]

Even though the courts were playing an active role in supporting the injustices occurring every day, they nonetheless went to great lengths to defend their reputation. The slightest reference to the high-handed breaches of law that were constantly occurring could result in criminal charges, even if the speaker refrained from all direct criticism. In one case, when a pastor concluded his sermon by asking the congregation to pray for a member of the church who "has been detained since February 2, 1937, although the charges against him have been dropped," the Supreme Court reacted quite strongly to his use of the word "although." The pastor was found guilty of a "breach of the public peace" (under paragraph 130a of the Criminal Code), since "in the manner of connecting the two phrases the implied criticism that L. should have been released but nevertheless was unjustifiably still detained" could have created the impression among his listeners "that the actions of the state had no basis in law but were instead despotic and arbitrary."[12]

· 17 ·

The People's Court

The creation of the People's Court (*Volksgerichtshof*) is usually ascribed today to the Nazis' dissatisfaction with the outcome of the Reichstag fire trial. This view, which also tends to create the impression that the trial, adjudicated by the Supreme Court, had been a model of correct legal procedure, is based on pure speculation, however, since Hitler had announced his plans long before: it was before the Supreme Court, in fact, when serving as a witness in a trial of the three army officers from Ulm, that he had declared heads would roll when his party succeeded in establishing its own tribunal. The dimensions of the reckoning he had in mind were revealed in *Mein Kampf* as early as 1924. There he stated categorically "that one day a German national tribunal must condemn and execute several tens of thousands of the criminals who organized and are responsible for the November treason and everything connected with it." [1] In 1928, during a debate on the legal system in the Reichstag, deputy Wilhelm Frick (later minister of the interior) became specific in his threats, saying that "in the coming Third Reich" the Nazis would make Ernst Heilmann, a Social Democratic politician (and party whip in the Prussian Chamber of Deputies), "the first to be hanged by a German state tribunal . . . in a fully lawful manner." [2]

This tribunal was finally created under the name of the "People's Court" by a law passed on April 24, 1934. [3] To begin with, it was given jurisdiction over those criminal cases which had previously come directly before the Supreme Court: treason, high treason, attacks on the president of the Reich, major cases of destruction of military property, and assassination or attempted assassination of members of the national or state governments. With this stroke, the Nazi rulers realized their old dream of a revolutionary tribunal. However, during the opening ceremonies on July 14, 1934, the regime tried to avoid giving the impression that what was being created was a special Nazi institution. The newspaper *Der Völkische Beobachter* denied "malicious reports in the foreign press" claiming it was to be a summary court of justice,[4] and Reich minister of justice Franz Gürtner concluded his speech with the appeal, "Discharge your duties as independent judges, bound only to the law and accountable to God and your conscience."[5]

The court was composed of three panels with five members each, only two of whom were required to have professional qualifications as judges; legally the tribunal had the status of a Special Court. Its first president and presiding judge of the first panel was the former presiding judge of the Berlin Special Court, Dr. Fritz Rehn; the chief prosecutor, Paul Jorns, had been the prosecutor in charge of cases of treason during the Weimar Republic and was one of the most scandalous figures in the legal system of that era. Jorns was assisted by Heinrich Parrisius and Wilhelm Eichler. At the beginning a total of about eighty people were employed in capacities associated with the tribunal, a figure which gave it a status clearly below that of the Supreme Court, and indeed in the early days the highly touted new institution was somewhat neglected by the judicial bureaucracy. When President Rehn died only two months after taking office, the post remained empty until the reorganization of the court system referred to as "nationalization" had been completed and administrative responsibility for all courts transferred from the states to the Reich. Dedicated Nazis in the legal profession objected to this disadvantageous treatment, among them Roland Freisler, then an undersecretary in the Ministry of Justice. Freisler observed that "such a high court, political in the noble sense of the word in that it guards the security of the nation," should be "a permanent achievement of National Socialist leadership," and he demanded that "the court [be] organized and expanded so that its outward appearance matches its role."[6] The aim envisaged in its creation should be realized quickly as possible. The first anniversary of the court's founding was celebrated in an article by Wilhelm Weiss, a high-ranking officer in the SA who was also deputy editor of the party paper *Der Völkische Beobachter* and himself a member of the court. Weiss wrote that it was the task of this "highest national tribunal" to demonstrate that the National Socialist state regarded treason as "the most reprehensible form of attack on the national community and is consequently determined to punish this crime with the severest possible penalties."[7]

Finally, in 1936, the prestige of the People's Court was increased. Its status was changed from that of a special or extraordinary court to a regular one,[8] and the new president, Otto Thierack, was considered to have the appropriate high standing, since he had previously been provisional minister of justice in the state of Saxony and was vice-president of the Supreme Court. As a visible sign of their promotion, a special decree of the Führer's granted the tribunal's judges the right to wear the symbolic red robes previously reserved for justices of the Supreme Court. Of course, none of this changed the nature of their political task, namely "to exterminate the enemies of the Third Reich, especially Communists and Social Democrats, to the last man."[9] On the contrary, now they felt able to drop all pretense and speak openly in public addresses and ideological articles. On August 7, 1937, on the occasion of Friedrich Parey's installation as a new senior prosecutor at the People's Court, minister of justice Gürtner referred to its personnel as a "task force for combatting and defeating all attacks on the external and internal security of the Reich,"[10] and the *National Socialist Legal Mirror,* the official publication of the Nazi party's Office for Legal Affairs, wrote: "In our view, the People's Court must play the role in the domestic political life of our nation that the army plays in foreign affairs, for its goal is to guarantee the security of the government on the home front: here its tasks are similar to those of the state police."[11] In 1939 the vice-president of the court, Karl Engert, demanded that its members must be politicians first and judges second,[12] while senior prosecutor Heinrich Parrisius declared that the purpose of the People's Court was not to dispense impartial justice "but to annihilate the enemies of National Socialism."[13]

The court's rise in status was not reflected only in the prestigious reputation of its new leaders. It also began to acquire a whole series of new assignments beyond its original jurisdiction over cases of treason and high treason (which it even had to share with the Courts of Appeals). These new responsibilities included prosecution of persons who failed to report cases of treason and high treason, cases of economic sabotage, and above all, crimes under martial law, such as evading military service, being absent without leave, undermining morale, and engaging in espionage. The larger "volume of business" also required more personnel. In the period between 1939 and 1944 alone, the number of judges—either permanent members of the People's Court or assigned there from elsewhere—rose from 17 to 34, while the number of those serving without pay rose from 95 to 173. Those who served without pay were "specialists" from the armed forces and various branches of the Nazi party who had received special political training; their presence was intended to emphasize the political character of the tribunal. They were appointed by the chancellor on the recommendation of the minister of justice. In 1944 they consisted of 40 army officers, 13 high officials of the Nazi party, 32 officers from the SA, the SS, Hitler Youth, and the National Socialist Drivers' Corps, 10 leaders of the Work Corps (*Arbeitsdienst*), and 28 "others," mostly leading figures from politics or the civil service.[14] The number of cases brought before the court increased constantly, and so did the length of sentences the court imposed (see Table 1).[15]

In its early years (1934 to 1936), the People's Court imposed the death penalty only 23 times. During its final and bloodiest phase, however, the tribunal probably sentenced a further 2,000 people to death. (The exact figure is unknown, since official statistics are available only through the middle of 1944 and do not include the results of the mass trials after the attempt on Hitler's life on July 20, 1944.)

The striking increase in death sentences in 1942—twelve times as many as in the previous year—is due above all to the intensification of the war. However, another major factor was certainly the change in court leadership. In 1942 the government finally decided, after much hesitation, to make a tactical change in the figures on its chess board: the post of minister of justice, which had been filled provisionally by undersecretary Franz Schlegelberger following Gürtner's death in January 1941, was given to the president of the People's Court, Otto Thierack, while undersecretary Roland Freisler moved over from the ministry to become the new president of the court.

Today it has become popular to contrast the vicious and bloodthirsty Freisler era with the "constitutional" Thierack period, and a glance at the statistics may tend to confirm such distinctions. It should be remembered, however, that before his appointment Freisler had not been considered a hardliner (as undersecretary in the Ministry of Justice he had been too

Table 1. Sentences imposed by the People's Court, 1937–1944.

Year	Number of defendants	Number receiving the death penalty	Number sent to penitentiary		Number sent to prison	Number of acquitted
			More than 10 years	Less than 10 years		
1937	618	32	107	216	99	52
1938	614	17	85	202	105	54
1939	470	36	70	189	131	40
1940	1,091	53	119	649	188	80
1941	1,237	102	261	654	143	70
1942	2,572	1,192	442	596	183	107
1943	3,338	1,662	290	886	259	181
1944	4,379	2,097	129	1,260	331	489
Total	14,319	5,191	1,503	4,652	1,439	1,073

"legal minded" for leading Nazis), while Thierack can hardly be described as a proponent of strictly constitutional ideas. It is true that the decisions of the People's Court under Thierack's leadership were more thorough and better argued, and had more of an appearance of legality; for example, the decision in the case of the writer Ernst Niekisch and his codefendants Joseph Drexel and Karl Tröger, who were accused of "preparations for high treason," runs to a full 147 pages in the reprinted version.[16] Nevertheless, Thierack gave ample proof during his term of office that he was a jurist after the Führer's own heart, someone who knew how to get around the letter of the law to produce the wanted results.

His crowning achievement was the trial of Alois Eliáš. Following the occupation of "rump Czechoslovakia" and the establishment of the German "Protectorate of Bohemia and Moravia," Eliáš had been named head of the protectorate government by the grace of the Germans. ["Rump Czechoslovakia" refers to the territory remaining after division of the county by the Munich treaty of 1938—*Translator.*] After the occupation of France in 1940, however, documents of the exiled Czech government fell into German hands—documents that supposedly contained evidence about contacts between Eliáš and Czech politicians in exile. The "Reich protector" at the time, Konstantin von Neurath, was able temporarily to prevent Eliáš' removal from office and arrest. [The "Protectorate of Bohemia and Moravia" was headed in theory by an "autonomous" Czech government but in fact by the "protector," who was named by Hitler.—*Translator.*] However, immediately after Neurath's replacement by Reinhard Heydrich, the head of the Reich Security Office, Eliáš was taken into custody and handed over to the People's Court for sentencing. In order to have Eliáš sentenced as quickly as possible after the arrest, Heydrich and Thierack made the following legal and political deal: the charges would not be raised by the public prosecutors attached to the court, as the constitution prescribed, but instead by the SS. As part of a hastily arranged secret scheme, the entire First Panel of the People's Court was flown to Prague on September 30, 1941, and before the Office of Public Prosecutions or the Ministry of Justice had time to protest, proceedings were opened in the headquarters of the SS Security Services there, formerly the teller area of the Petschek Bank. Although evidence to back up the prosecution was scanty—there was no proof for the major charges against Eliáš—the People's Court, after a four-hour trial, sentenced him to death for "supporting the enemy." On the evening of October 1, Heydrich was able to send a telegram to the head of the party chancellery, Martin Bormann, reporting the satisfactory outcome: "In spite of various attempts by the Ministry of Justice and Undersecretary Schlegelberger to hinder us, we succeeded in holding a trial and reaching a verdict only three days after the arrest, thanks to the outstanding cooperation and political acumen of President Thierack."[17] It is probable that the willingness of the career-minded judge to participate in this sort of unscrupulous scheme tipped the scales in favor of his nomination for the long-vacant post of Minister of Justice.

Thierack's successor as president, Dr. Roland Freisler, had been a member of the Nazi party since 1923. Before the Nazis seized power, he had practiced law in Kassel and served on the city council there. There were rumors that he had become a Communist temporarily, while a prisoner of war in Russia during the First World War. He was never able to get rid of this stigma; Hitler is quoted in his *Table Conversations* as saying in 1942 that Freisler was "a Bolshevik in his whole manner."[18] It is a fact, however, that he was a tireless champion of the "National Socialist legal order." As president of the People's Court and presiding judge of its First Panel, he now had an opportunity to show how to put this kind of "justice" into operation. He took over all the important trials himself and for a while assigned cases to the different panels as it suited him, although this was not official procedure. Even after the Ministry of Justice had intervened to stop this illegal practice, his panel retained sole responsibility for "attacks on the Führer" and "criminal acts connected with intelligence gathering and management of the economy."[19] Goebbels noted in his diary on September 23, 1943: "Freisler, as president of the People's Court, [has] become a bird of an altogether different feather. He is once again the radical National Socialist he used to be in the Prussian Chamber of Deputies. Just as he did too little as undersecretary in the Ministry of Justice, today as president of the People's Court he is doing too much."[20]

Still, Freisler's leadership was not necessary in order to establish the People's Court as a supreme summary tribunal for the suppression of every hint of opposition to the regime; this development had occurred with the outbreak of war. What gave the court virtual carte blanche was paragraph 5 of the Decree on Martial Law ("undermining morale"), which provided for the death penalty if someone "publicly attempts to paralyze or undermine the will of the German or an allied nation to defend itself." The death penalty was the rule for this crime, but for less serious cases any milder form of punishment—in theory even a one-day prison sentence—could have been imposed. As the war went on, this decree gradually came to replace completely the 1934 Law against Treacherous Attacks on the State and Party and paragraph 90f of the Criminal Code ("malicious propaganda"); the former had made it a punishable offense to utter disparaging remarks about the country's leaders, but neither one provided for the death penalty. Franz Vollmer, a senior official in the Ministry of Justice, included in his summary of judicial decisions for 1943–1944 a whole catalogue of remarks which now ranked as capital crimes: "Not to be tolerated and as a general principle deserving of the death penalty . . . are remarks of the following kind: the war is lost; Germany or the Führer started the war frivolously or to no purpose, and ought to lose it; the Nazi party should or would resign and clear the way for peace negotiations, as the Italians have done; a military dictatorship ought to be established and would be able to make peace; people ought to work more slowly, so as to bring an end to the war; the spread of Bolshevism would not be so bad as the propaganda makes out, and would harm only leading Nazis; the British or Americans would stop the Bolsheviks at the German border; verbal propaganda or letters to the front urging soldiers to throw away their guns or point them at their own officers; saying that the Führer is sick, incapable, a butcher of men, and so on."[21]

The fact that such remarks were always punishable by death—regardless of whether they were made in public or to family members or close friends—was due to a peculiar interpretation of the term "public" that had become accepted not only by the People's Court but by the two other highest courts as well. The Supreme Court found that an opinion expressed by an individual to two drinking companions in a tavern was "public,"[22] and the Supreme Court-Martial (*Reichskriegsgericht*) regularly affirmed that a remark was to be considered "public" even when made to only a small number of people, if the possibility existed that this remark could be passed on—and, as the court stressed, this possibility could never be entirely excluded. The wording of the Decree on Martial Law itself allowed only one interpretation of the term "public"; however, in the eyes of the court this "would not have fit the intention and purpose of . . . the decree."[23]

It is not surprising that the standard interpretation of the Decree on Martial Law used by the Supreme Court and the Supreme Court-Martial was also taken over by the People's Court. But whereas the other two courts at least tried shamefacedly to cover up their broad interpretation by linking it to certain conditions such as a "limited public sphere" for a remark or "the possibility of [its] being passed on," the People's Court dispensed with such ceremony and all reference to limits. In the opinion concerning a dealer in machine parts named Fritz Gröbe, whom it sentenced to death for making disparaging remarks about Goebbels and Göring, the court observed, "When [Gröbe] claims that he did not speak in public, this claim is false, because it is the aim of National Socialism for the entire German people to concern itself with politics and because every political remark must be regarded as a public statement in principle . . . A criminal cannot claim confidentiality."[24]

Generally speaking, the finer points of law did not play much of a role in the day-to-day work of the People's Court, nor did the court spend much time mulling over the precise meaning of words. Instead it fell right into line with the wishes of propaganda minister Goebbels, who had specifically warned its judges in a speech on July 22, 1942, that their decisions should "be based less on law than on the fundamental idea that lawbreakers are to be eliminated from the community of the *Volk*."[25] Thus, for example, it summarily equated the terms "giving aid and comfort to the enemy" and "undermining morale." The relevant paragraph of the Criminal Code (paragraph 91b) did state that the perpetrator of the former crime "undertakes during a war to give assistance to an enemy power . . . or to put the army of the Reich at a disadvantage"—that is, it referred specifically to the military situation. However, once it was argued that in a state of "total war" even the slightest psychological advantage or disadvantage could be decisive, then any doubt expressed to a single person about the victorious outcome of the war could be interpreted as "giving aid and comfort to the enemy."

Such an interpretation was made in the following instance, even though the individual addressed retained an unshakable belief in the final victory. While on a concert tour, the Dutch pianist Karlrobert Kreiten stayed in Berlin with an long-time friend of his mother's who was an ardent National Socialist. During a meal at her house, where only the two of them were present, he made some derogatory remarks about the regime. In order to provoke her, he called Hitler "brutal, sick, and insane" and predicted that the war and the Nazi era would soon be over. For this he was accused of "giving aid and comfort to the enemy" and "undermining morale" and tried before the People's Court. The court condemned him to death on September 3, 1943, on the following grounds: "Whoever acts as Kreiten did is doing . . . precisely as our enemies would wish. He becomes their henchman in their war of nerves against the steadfastness of our people (paragraph 91b of the Criminal Code)." Even the presence of obvious contradictions in its own reasoning did not appear to bother the court; the main thing was to arrive at a death sentence one way or another. In addition to finding him guilty of aiding the enemy as cited above, the court justified its condemnation of him for "undermining morale" by observing that no "aid to the enemy" could in fact be given, since the German population could be relied on to react appropriately:

[Kreiten's] action is a scurrilous attack on the confidence of a member of the German nation. He thereby publicly attacked our ability to defend ourselves manfully in our fateful struggle (paragraph 5 of the Decree on Martial Law). Publicly, because everyone must reckon with the fact that German citizens who hears something like this . . . will report it to the authorities of the state or the party. And publicly, because our National Socialist Reich wishes every citizen to concern himself with politics and because every political remark represents a part of the fundamental political thought of our nation.

Karlrobert Kreiten was executed during the night of September 7–8, 1943.[26]

Such an interpretation of the decree was going too far even for some leaders of the regime. In a letter to Freisler of September 11, 1943, minister of justice Thierack criticized the decision, saying that it "robbed of all meaning the concept of 'public' in paragraph 5 of the Decree on Martial Law."[27]

While the People's Court was blithely sweeping aside all traditional legal forms, however, the Reich Office of Public Prosecutions was carrying out its bureaucratic duties with great exactitude. It is hard to imagine a greater contrast to the above than the painstaking detail of the itemized bills sent out to relatives of prisoners to cover the cost of their executions (see Table 2).[28]

The People's Court played its most important role in the legal "resolution" of the failed attempt to assassinate Hitler on July 20, 1944. The bomb planted by Count Stauffenberg had gone off, but the dictator survived the explosion. Stauffenberg and three other officers were shot "according to martial law" that same evening, and then the regime ordered a wave of arrests followed by torture, show trials, and numerous further executions. Thousands of relatives and friends of those under suspicion were arrested on the basis of "guilt by association" and sent to concentration camps. Hitler himself—as "supreme head of the judicial system"—determined the kind of trial the conspirators would be given: "This time I will make short work of them. These criminals will not be brought before a Court-Martial; they will come before the People's Court. They will not be allowed to speak at all, and the sentence must be carried out immediately, within two hours of its pronouncement. They will hang at once, without the slightest pity."[29]

In response to the suggestion that the leaders of the revolt be executed after "summary proceedings," Hitler is supposed to have remarked, "Freisler will take care of it; he is our Vishinsky."[30] He was referring to the chief prosecutor at the Moscow show trials of 1936–1938 and alluding once again to the rumors of Freisler's "Bolshevist" past. Legally the People's

Court had no jurisdiction over the officers involved in the coup; paragraph 3 of the Military Criminal Code stated that even those "criminal acts committed by members of the armed forces which [are] not military crimes or misdemeanors" must be dealt with by military courts. A hastily created "Court of Honor" presided over by the field marshal and general Gerd von Rundstedt expelled the conspirators from the army, however, so that the way was cleared to the People's Court.[31]

The first trial involving the attempted coup of July 20 took place on August 7–8, 1944. The defendants were the generals von Witzleben,

Table 2. Sample of itemized bill sent to prisoners' relatives.

Reich Office of Public Prosecutions
  at the People's Court
Transaction number: 3 J 297/44

Bill
in the criminal proceedings against _____
for undermining morale

Quantity	Item of expenditure and no. of relevant regulation	To be paid	
		Marks	Pfennigs
1	2	3	4
	Death-sentence fee	300	—
	Mailing costs, according to paragraph 72 of the Law on Court Costs	2	70
	Fee for attorney, Mr. _____	81	60
	Pretrial detention costs, according to paragraph 72 of the Law on Court Costs: from 12/20/43 to 3/28/44 = 100 days, at 1.50 marks per day	150	—
	Posttrial imprisonment: from 3/29/44 to 5/18/44 = 50 days, at 1.50 marks per day	75	—
	Cost of carrying out sentence	158	18
	Cost of stamps for mailing bill	—	12
		767	60

Hoeppner, Stieff, and von Hase and the younger officers von Hagen, Klausing, Bernardis, and Count Yorck von Wartenburg, who were all friends of Colonel Stauffenberg and had worked closely with him. They received brutal treatment at the hands of the Gestapo before the trial, and in addition they were forced to appear in court in as bad a light as possible: poorly fed, in ill-fitting clothes, and unshaven. Their belts and suspenders had been taken away, so that Field Marshal von Witzleben was compelled to hold up his oversized trousers during cross-examination. Cynically Freisler snapped at him, "You dirty old man, why are you always fiddling with your pants?" [32]

As presiding judge, Freisler reduced all the other participants in the trial—the accused, their court-appointed defense attorneys, the prosecutors, and even his colleagues on the panel—to mere extras. He berated, vilified, and mocked the conspirators, shouting at the Catholic priest Alfred Delp, for example, who had been arrested for membership in the "Kreisau Circle," "You wretch, you little pip-squeak of a parson—and someone like you dares to try to kill our beloved Führer. A rat is what you are. You should be stepped on, squashed flat." [33]

The trial of the conspirators was filmed secretly with a camera hidden in the courtroom. Originally the film material had been intended for propaganda purposes, but it turned out to be completely unsuitable. It was declared "top secret" but preserved; today it has been assembled in a powerful and shocking documentary showing a legal system that lacks all trace of justice. Even at the time, Freisler's conduct of the trial, so lacking in propaganda appeal, did not meet with undivided approval from his colleagues on the bench, and certainly not from the Ministry of Justice. In a report on the trials submitted to Martin Bormann, chief of the party chancellery and Hitler's secretary, the minister of justice commented:

> [Freisler] would not let Leuschner and von Hassell finish their sentences. He shouted them down repeatedly. That made quite a bad impression. Otherwise there is no objection to the way the trial was handled politically. Unfortunately he treated Leuschner like an idiot and Goerdeler like a half-wit, and referred to the accused as pip-squeaks. This seriously undermined the gravity of the proceedings. Lengthy and repeated speeches made by the presiding judge solely for propaganda effect are repellently out of place. Once again, the gravity and dignity of the court suffered. The presiding judge totally lacks the kind of ice-cold authority and control such a trial requires. [34]

The tribunal pronounced the predictable death sentences upon the resistance fighters on August 8, and the sentences were carried out the same day. In accord with Hitler's instructions that "they should hang like slaughtered cattle," the condemned men were strung up at the Plötzensee Prison on meat hooks.[35]

How little the tribunal deserved its status as a "regular court" is illustrated by a minor incident that occurred during the trial: in the proceedings against Count Moltke and other members of the "Kreisau Circle," it was at one point necessary to consult the Criminal Code, but no copy of the text of the law could be found in the entire courtroom.[36]

Even before the People's Court was finished with all the men and women who had participated in this resistance movement (some of them were executed in summary proceedings only a few days before Germany surrendered to the Allies), it was faced with a wave of new trials. After the conspirators themselves had been dealt with, it was the turn of the "Bravos," as they were referred to in People's Court jargon, and they were dealt with swiftly. Merely expressing approval of the assassination attempt or regret that it had failed earned a person the death sentence, because the court regularly construed such an opinion as *post hoc* participation in the coup. The tone of a decision handed down on November 6, 1944, in the case of Ehrengard Frank-Schultz, the landlady of the arrested conspirator Lieutenant Wendelstein, shows how little importance the court attached to legal distinctions. At the same time, it offers a prime example of Freisler's harangues:

> Mrs. Frank-Schultz told a Red Cross nurse she was sorry that the attempt to murder our Führer failed, and had the audacity to claim that a few years of Anglo-Saxon rule would be preferable to "the current reign of terror." She therefore made common cause with the traitors of the twentieth of July. Through this, she has become dishonored forever. She will be punished with death . . . Whoever acts in this fashion must disappear from our midst. If any sentence other than the death penalty were to be passed here, our soldiers at the front would ask with legitimate doubt whether the festering boil of the twentieth of July had really been lanced completely, so that we may go on, strong and healthy, to prevail in the struggle. Because Mrs. Frank-Schultz has been found guilty, she will also bear the costs.[37]

Roland Freisler was killed in an air raid on February 3, 1945. As the eulogy in the journal of the Nazi Federation of Guardians of the Law put it, the German legal system had lost "one of the outstanding champions of our legal reform," who had pursued without faltering his goal "of eliminating outmoded liberalism from legal thinking." "With fanatic determination" Freisler had used his high office to lead "from his front-line position an uncompromising attack on enemies of the state and traitors."[38]

As accurate as this characterization is, the brutality of the "Freisler court" cannot be explained solely by the personality of the presiding judge. Too often today Freisler is portrayed as the incarnation of all the crimes committed in the name of the law during the Third Reich, and the commentators almost never fail to mention that he had once been a Communist. But his time in office coincided with a general rise in brutality in the workings of the courts, as is demonstrated by the sharp increase in death sentences passed by the regular criminal courts, the Special Courts, and the Courts-Martial, as well as in the far harsher decisions handed down by the higher courts, up to and including the Supreme Court. Judge Freisler was more a symptom of the state terror than a cause, and he was merely one of the most fitting representatives of Nazi justice. Something else that is too often forgotten nowadays is Freisler's reputation as a brilliant legal thinker. Hundreds of articles, speeches, and memoranda show him to have been a hard-working, intelligent, and well-read leader in shaping the National Socialist legal system,[39] an expert whom law professors were fond of citing. The historian Michael Freund considers it symptomatic "that the Germans [chose] not a servile subordinate" but rather "a highly gifted jurist to preside over their revolutionary tribunal": "Even for mechanized mass murder, they demanded high marks on the bar exam."[40]

· 18 ·

Summary Courts of the "Inner Front": Jurisdiction of the Special Courts

"Irregular" courts of special jurisdiction were not invented by the National Socialists. It had been common practice in Germany in the politically turbulent years after the First World War to establish such courts, but they were shut down again after a short time.[1] On March 21, 1933, when the new regime issued its decree on the formation of Special Courts,[2] it was in fact authorized to do so by an ordinance dating from the republican era, granting the government powers to determine the courts' personnel, procedures, and jurisdiction.[3]

To start with, a Special Court was created in each of the twenty-six Court of Appeals districts, with jurisdiction over violations of the Reichstag Fire Decree and the Decree to Protect the Government of the National Socialist Revolution from Treacherous Attacks, passed after the Reichstag fire. Three professional judges were assigned to each court, usually transferred from the County Courts, and the procedures established satisfied the wishes of most conservatives for a drastic reduction in the rights of defendants and a stronger position for the prosecution. The court was required neither to conduct a pretrial investigation nor to open the trial with a determination that the charges brought by the prosecution were in fact justified. Judges were required to sign all orders for arrest presented by prosecutors; defense attorneys had no right to demand proof of charges, and the court could determine the extent of evidence to be considered entirely as it saw fit. Defendants had no right to appeal verdicts, which became enforceable at once. The speedy trials made possible by these regulations met the wishes that had often been voiced for "eliminating formalism" in criminal proceedings.[4] They also corresponded to the ideal of the "good criminal trial," which, in the words of Supreme Court judge Otto Schwarz, "fulfills the aim of punishing a crime . . . by letting the penalty follow upon the criminal act with the greatest possible thoroughness and speed, and at the lowest cost."[5] The aims of the Nazi leadership with regard to the legal system were in large measure realized when the Special Courts were created. The presence of three judges on the bench ensured that they would keep an eye on each other, and at the same time circumvented the inconvenient participation of laymen. The fact that defendants had no recourse and that a sentence took effect immediately freed the judges from the necessity of making sure that procedures were followed carefully and that their decisions would stand up under review. This made the work of the courts simpler in two ways: there were no appeals proceedings, and the trials that did take place could be shorter.

Furthermore, the methods developed by Nazi jurists, in particular the doctrine of "criminal types" and "teleological interpretation," allowed the courts to dispense with fine distinctions about how the law defined a particular crime and whether the act committed actually fulfilled these requirements. And finally the brief and usually very general wording of the decrees on those crimes falling under the jurisdiction of the Special Courts in particular gave the judges even more freedom. Occasionally the laws in question set no limits at all on sentencing, so that every conceivable penalty, from one night in prison to death, was permissible. Thus, all in all, the decisions of the Special Courts tended to match the expectations put forward by the Reich minister of justice in one of his notorious "Letters to the Bench": "A member of the *Volk* does not expect judges to provide detailed and learned commentaries on the law, nor is he interested in the numerous minor points which they have taken into consideration in reaching their opinion. He would like to be told, in a few words understandable to the general public, the decisive reason for his being right or wrong."[6]

The advantages of the Special Courts were so striking that soon after their creation, demands were raised for extending their jurisdiction to cover a broader range of crimes. Apart from the new offense of "insulting the Nazi party," however, they received no new jurisdiction for the time being. Clearly the regime wished to profit as long as possible from the legitimation provided by the regular courts.

The situation began to change as the country prepared for war. The onset of war was planned to coincide with a major offensive against "the enemy within," for according to the myth of the "stab in the back" which the Nazis in particular helped to keep alive, the unfortunate end of the First World War had been caused by "the collapse of the home front," and Hitler had always held the legal system partly responsible. The National

Socialists in the legal bureaucracy were happy to subscribe to this assignment of guilt. According to undersecretary Roland Freisler, there had been no "administration of justice worthy of the name" at all in the years 1914 to 1918. To prevent something similar from occurring again, plans were laid to turn the courts into an "effective army corps on the inner front" right from the start of the new war.[7] The decree entitled "Measures on the Constitution of Courts and Legal Procedures," issued September 1, 1939, and usually referred to as the "Simplification Decree,"[8] did away with all lay participation on the bench of public courts, making them more flexible and at the same time freeing urgently needed "defense personnel." Lay magistrates in petty courts were replaced by a single professional judge. In the County Courts—where criminal trials took place before a panel of three judges and six lay magistrates or before a panel of judges and a jury, depending on the gravity of the charge—three judges now presided alone, after the model of the Special Courts. Simultaneously, the means of legal recourse for defendants to challenge verdicts were limited still further.

A series of other new decrees increased the possible sentences for certain offenses: prison was changed to penitentiary; for serious crimes the death penalty was introduced and occasionally—as in the case of the Decree on Violent Criminals—made mandatory. Virtually all regulations passed or revised after 1938 gave jurisdiction to the Special Courts. The crime of "intentionally tuning in to foreign radio broadcasts" was to be prosecuted before a Special Court, as were the offenses listed in the Decree on Asocial Elements, those in the Decree on Violent Criminals, certain economic crimes, and "gangsterism." As Wilhelm Crohne, a department head at the Ministry of Justice, put it, the population should see the Special Courts as "the swiftest and most effective means of eliminating gangster elements from the community at one stroke, either permanently or temporarily."[9]

The new criminal laws, written with the Special Courts in mind, contained drastically harsher provisions; couched in "terse, clear, and martial language," they did not go into "detailed analyses of the elements of an offense" or waste much time on fine legal distinctions. A typical example of the wording of regulations under martial law is the "Decree for Safeguarding the Metal Collection of the German People," issued on March 29, 1940:

> The Council of Ministers for the Defense of the Reich hereby decrees:
> The collection of metal is a sacrifice demanded of the German people in the struggle for survival which has been forced upon them.
> Whoever reaps a profit from collected metal or metal designated for col-

lection by the authorities or otherwise prevents such metal from being used for the designated purpose is guilty of causing harm to the Great German liberation struggle and will be punished by death.

This decree takes effect as soon as it is proclaimed over the radio. Its validity extends to incorporated Eastern areas.[11]

A large number of "economic" offenses, most of them of a minor nature, such as the illegal slaughtering of animals, the hoarding of goods, and fraud involving food or rationing, were raised from the status of petty offenses to capital crimes. Relatively minor violations of the Decree on the War Economy,[12] the Decree on Continued Use of Motor Vehicles, and the Regulations for Consumption of Vital Commercial Products[13] had draconian penalties attached to them.

The fundamental offense underlying all wartime criminal statutes was a failure to see what was required in a "total war": "Whoever stands on the sidelines while others risk life and limb for the glory of Germany and the liberty of future generations is a parasite. He incurs the contempt of the nation and the punishment he deserves from our courts."[14] The key statute in the practice of the Special Courts after 1939 was thus the Decree on Asocial Elements. In addition to the mandatory death penalty for looting or arson, it provided penitentiary or death sentences for offenses which took advantage of the blackout as well as for the thoroughly unspecific offense of "exploiting the unusual conditions imposed by the war [to commit] any other crime."

If the courts had ever undertaken a strictly legal interpretation of the decree, they would have had to consider in all such cases whether the perpetrator would have committed the act even without the presence of particular wartime conditions such as an understaffed police force, poorer lighting at night, or less traffic in the streets. In fact, no court ever pondered such subtle questions. As a rule, the courts used the Decree on Asocial Elements as a basis for imposing generally harsher sentences, and since the focusing of all government efforts on the war led to budget cuts even for crime prevention, in the last analysis wartime conditions favored every sort of crime—if only because the quality of available paper declined. For example, Hugo Göhring, a railroad worker and father of seven children, who had to support his family on a salary of 260 marks per month and a dependents' allowance of 50 marks per month, had over a long period been in the habit of removing objects of low value from the damaged packages he had to load and unload: brushes and combs, articles of clothing, and food. Since he had a previous record of petty thefts, he was tried as a "dangerous habitual criminal" before the Weimar Special Court. In its decision of October 13, 1944, the court observed: "The accused cannot be regarded as a dangerous habitual criminal." It nevertheless sentenced him to death as an "asocial element," because he had "exploited the unusual conditions imposed by the war" to commit his crimes. In peacetime, Göhring's thefts would not have been possible, for "even packing materials are of considerably lower quality today than in peacetime." The court conceded explicitly that he was not "an asocial element on the basis of his personality . . . but the deed itself brands him as one . . . He has deserted the inner front and, in a despicable manner, has thought only of himself and not of the community." [15]

As a general rule, the Special Courts attached less importance to precise interpretation of the law than to defamatory distinctions between "criminal types." A semiofficial commentary on developments since the outbreak of the war, published in 1940 and written by the press secretary of the Ministry of Justice, divided the clientele of the Special Courts into five groups: "(1) political and military enemies of the state, (2) economic parasites, (3) asocial elements, (4) destructive outsiders, (5) parasites in daily life." [16] Offices of Public Prosecution were granted the right to include anyone else in this group if they found such a step necessary; they could prosecute through the Special Courts not only those crimes for which they had specific jurisdiction but also all other crimes and offenses, if the prosecutors believed that "swift sentencing by a Special Court [was] called for in view of the seriousness or depravity of the deed, public reaction to it, or the danger it posed to public order and safety." [17] Simultaneously, the relevant Decree on Jurisdiction provided for even speedier proceedings: "All trials before a Special Court must take place at once and without granting of delays if the perpetrator is caught in the act or is otherwise plainly guilty. In other cases, the defendant is granted a stay of twenty-four hours before proceedings are opened."

As a result of expanded jurisdiction and these streamlined procedures, the Special Courts "advanced to the front lines in defending the state against serious crime [and] became the very core of criminal justice." [18] The increased "volume of business" made a considerably higher number of such courts necessary; one Special Court in each Court of Appeals district could not keep up with the work. At first, the number of judges assigned to the existing courts was doubled or tripled. In 1940 the number of courts was raised to fifty-five, and still several panels were required for each one. In Berlin alone, where at the beginning only one Special Court had been established for the entire jurisdiction of the Prussian Supreme Court, there were later no less than nine. [19] Nonetheless, even these numerous newly created courts had a constant backlog of cases. Prosecutors made generous use of their right to bring all cases of ordinary criminality before the irregular courts, because—as the Reich Ministry of Justice observed—they obviously had "more faith in the Special Courts" than in the regular ones.[20] For this reason, the percentage of cases they dealt with in relation to the total was continually on the rise. In Hamburg, for example, from 1936 to 1939 only one out of every six criminal trials took place before the Special Court; by 1943 the proportion was already two thirds.[21] Although the large number of cases dealt with was due partly to the increased number of such courts, it resulted in large measure as well from the speed with which the courts reached their decisions. In official language, the term "summary courts of the inner front" came into common usage, a reference not only to the short work that was made of trials there but also to the brutally harsh sentences passed. As high-ranking bureaucrats noted with satisfaction, they were "not very timid about long penitentiary sentences or the death penalty."[22]

This kind of dispensation of justice was the result not only of the wartime laws but also of a particular personnel policy. Insofar as possible, judges assigned to the Special Courts were young people who had received their training only during the Third Reich. These same young men were needed at the front, however, and fears arose within the Ministry of Justice that in view of the large number of judges required, it would "not be possible to avoid a certain watering-down of the original concept of the Special Courts." These fears proved to be unfounded. The president of the Hamburg County Court was able to report in 1943 that prosecution before the Special Courts had lost none of its effectiveness as a deterrent to crime, "because it is well known that particularly good and energetic judges are assigned to them and that one cannot reckon with unwarranted leniency."[23]

The full extent of these "energetic" judges' ruthlessness is illustrated by the case of Georg Hopfe, an office messenger who had been wounded in the war. On March 24, 1944, Hopfe and a friend who happened to be on home leave went on a pub crawl through Weimar; somewhere along the way, they were joined by a laborer named Fritz Nauland. After they had each drunk about six beers and had started for home, there was an air raid. When they saw a burning building that had been hit by bombs and several soldiers and rescue crewmen standing around waiting for the fire trucks to arrive, they decided to pitch in and do something at once. Nauland broke down the door, and the three men helped to save some of the building's contents. In the course of this effort, Hopfe helped himself to an open bottle of perfume from a collection of them and later put a knockwurst in his coat pocket. Nauland took two bars of soap. For this, Hopfe was summoned before the Weimar Special Court on April 11 as an "asocial element." A medical expert testified that the office messenger was "feeble-minded to a slight degree," and he freely admitted everything, since he considered the charges trivial: he and his friends had saved objects of much greater value by their courageous intervention, and he testified that he had only taken the knockwurst because he had not had anything to eat all evening. These circumstances did not in the least exonerate the accused in the eyes of the court, for "the value of the objects stolen is irrelevant." It was just as irrelevant that he had not broken into an evacuated house in order to loot it—this alone would have been sufficient to constitute the crime of looting—but rather to rescue the property of the absent owners; the court found him guilty of looting "according to the intent of the law and healthy public opinion." The "vile attitude evinced by the deed" and the "baseness of his character" revealed Hopfe to the court as an enemy of the people who deserved the death penalty: "Whoever commits such a despicable crime places himself outside the bounds of society." Fritz Nauland had already been condemned to death by the same court earlier on account of the two bars of soap.[24]

The Nazi leaders had dreamed of a judicial system in which the harshest of sentences could be imposed after a minimum of formalities, and with the Special Courts this wish was fulfilled. In their daily practice, the judges of these courts carried out their task of "intimidating the general public through psychological terror" to the complete satisfaction of the country's leaders.

"Heralds of German Legal Culture": Special Courts in Eastern Europe

The Special Courts, important as they were in the "Old Reich," had far more significance in the occupied territories. [The term "Old Reich" refers to the territory of Germany before the annexation of Austria and subsequent conquests—*Translator.*] There they served not only to combat the "enemy within" and the "member of the *Volk* forgetful of his duty," but also contributed to the suppression of national resistance and stabilization of German rule.

In Poland, particularly in the "incorporated" or annexed regions, the courts were given specific additional tasks in the campaigns against Polish nationalism and against all that was un-German and "alien."[26] Special Courts and the rule of German criminal law were established in occupied Polish territory during the very first days of the war. Criminal justice in this territory was based entirely on these summary courts, and several were set up immediately in each of the County Court districts. The districts of Danzig (Gdansk) and Posen (Poznan) even had five apiece.

The Special Courts were supposed to base their decisions on German law, but they were not so particular when the defendants were Poles; at such times, they tended to depart from the statutes through very broad interpretations and "appropriate further development" of the laws. On October 8, 1939, the Führer had issued a decree declaring that "existing law" continued to be valid in occupied territory so long as it did not run counter to "the meaning of incorporation." Using this decree as formal justification for their actions, the courts generally fell back on "the general intent" of German laws only when the exact wording of the laws "permitted criminal penalties either not at all or not to an appropriate degree." In a report entitled "Application and Further Development of German Criminal Law in Incorporated Eastern Regions," Public Prosecutor Thiemann in Posen noted, not without pride, that the courts there had "passed countless sentences for armed breach of the peace. In many cases, they found in favor of the death penalty."[27] His praise was in reference to the legal system's response to attacks by Poles on ethnic Germans, the "September Crimes" exploited so successfully by German propaganda. Even though "Task Force IV" of the SS Security Service had carried out large-scale reprisals in Bromberg (Bydgoszcz) and boasted in their daily report of September 13, 1939, that following their "mopping-up operation . . . no more perpetrators remain to be tried,"[28] the Special Courts, with the aid of a legal trick, nevertheless condemned hundreds more Polish nationalists to death for "armed breach of the peace."

In most cases, the accused had not been armed at all. Still, the courts invented a link between their demonstrations and events that had taken place in entirely different locations at entirely different times. They simply dispensed with the formal necessity for "physical participation in certain acts by the perpetrator," and construed a "psychological support" for events even in cases where the accused had usually not even been aware of those events. One defendant accused of having been part of an "unlawful violent assembly" was in this manner charged with "deliberate and intentional cooperation with armed elements," an offense that counted as "aggravated armed breach of the peace" under the Reichstag Fire Decree and was punishable by death. As Prosecutor Thiemann was pleased to point out, such a construction of the law showed that the Special Courts "were not formalist in their thinking," for only in this way could many Poles be prosecuted "with success according to the intent and mission of the law."[29]

Excessive use was made of the Decree on Asocial Elements in Poland as well. The "peculiar total situation existing in the incorporated Polish regions" and "the extraordinarily high degree of Polish criminality that, on account of the war, has not been stopped" were considered to constitute "extraordinary circumstances" under the meaning of the decree. Thus, it became possible to treat any sort of crime as "exploitation of wartime conditions," and judges were able to impose the death sentence whenever they liked.[30]

Although the use of such deadly interpretations of the law had enabled the courts to create in effect a special penal code going far beyond the ordinary German Criminal Code, special regulations were issued for the incorporated eastern regions as well. As a rule, they stipulated the death penalty for all offenses committed against members of the German army or police, and against German citizens "because of their membership in the German nation." In addition, damage to German institutions and "incitement to disobey German regulations" were made capital crimes.[31]

The coexistence of German and Polish criminal law was finally ended by the Council of Ministers for the Defense of the Reich, chaired by the Reich marshal, Hermann Göring. On December 4, 1941, the council issued the "Decree on Criminal Justice Regarding Poles and Jews in Incorporated Eastern Territories."[32] Its substance had been dictated by Hitler's notion "that there can be only one master for the Poles, and that is the Germans."[33] Section 1 established that Poles and Jews were obligated, as a general duty, to obey all German directives: "Poles and Jews in the incorporated eastern territories must act in accordance with German laws and the regulations concerning them issued by the German authorities. They must abstain from all acts detrimental to the sovereignty of the German Reich and the reputation of the German nation."

Just as the criminal code for Germans was based on a general obligation to act in good faith, the criminal laws for Poles and Jews were founded on a duty to be obedient, and every case was to be judged on this premise. As a general principle, Jews and Poles were to be sentenced to death for all violations of the above-mentioned decree, and only in "less severe cases" could exceptions be made to this rule. The individual offenses listed in it were in fact sweeping generalizations, especially Section 1, paragraph 3, which was praised by Roland Freisler as a "wonderful regulation": Poles and Jews "will be punished by death, and in less severe cases with imprisonment, if they demonstrate an anti-German attitude through malicious or inflammatory acts—in particular by making anti-German remarks, or by destroying or damaging facilities or installations of the German authorities—or if they otherwise act so as to lower or cause harm to the prestige or welfare of the German Reich or the German people." As typical instances in which this regulation could be applied, Freisler mentioned "wearing . . . a badge or other indication that falsely suggests . . . membership in the German ethnic community, or engaging in sexual intercourse . . . with a German woman."[34] By this means, any action whatsoever could be treated as a capital crime.

The readiness of the courts to perceive harm done to "German prestige" was experienced, for example, by a Polish housemaid named Rosalie Kulesa. Mrs. Kulesa was employed in the household of a German forester in Surowe, in the district of Zichenau. On October 8, 1942, her employer sent her to do some shopping at a dry-goods store in the town of Mischinitz, eighteen kilometers away. The German shopkeeper, Meta Baschek, had temporarily closed the store in order to rearrange some displays. Rosalie Kulesa saw that the door was open, knocked, and entered the store when someone called, "Come in." Three women were engaged in moving goods around. When asked what she wanted, Mrs. Kulesa explained her errand in Polish and was told that they had no time for her. Mrs. Baschek took no notice of a document from the German forester explaining that the goods were being purchased on his behalf, but instead took the customer's shopping basket and put it down outside the door, and then began to push the woman out, shouting in German, "Go, go!" In the course of the pushing and shoving, Rosalie Kulesa's handbag—later described by the court as "of slightly less than medium size and made of a substance similar to cardboard"—hit the German woman in the face. Whether this happened by accident or design remained an open question.

When she was brought before the Zichenau Special Court on charges of "damaging the prestige of the German people," Mrs. Kulesa objected that she had not purposely flung her handbag in Meta Baschek's face; on the contrary, Mrs. Baschek had hit her on the head; and furthermore, Mrs. Kulesa had not even been aware that the proprietor of the store was German. Naturally the court believed not her but the German witness, and it employed a trick to give the latter's testimony even more weight: the court had the witness testify under oath (although injured parties are not normally asked to take an oath), whereas the Polish defendant was not permitted to do so. The court found her claim that she did not realize she was dealing with a German "unconvincing," since she ought to have recognized that Mrs. Baschek's self-confident demeanor was "clearly and beyond doubt the manner of a German." On January 11, 1943, Rosalie Kulesa was sentenced to death, for "the security and authority of every German in this region require that acts of violence committed by Poles against Germans be punished in the severest manner." Although no one denied that the scuffle had been started by the German woman, the court refused to treat the slight blow inflicted with the handbag as a "less serious case" which would have resulted merely in imprisonment. The judges claimed in their decision, just as if they had had no other choice, that "the death penalty, the only sentence permitted under the law, . . . had to be imposed on the accused."[35]

The slightest signs of insubordination on the part of Polish workers were regarded by the courts as threats to German rule, and every expression of Polish national pride was treated as a crime. Another case involved Leonhard Kinal and Therese Ginter, both employed during the war on a farm run by Germans. The farmer's wife gave them frequent beatings, allegedly because they were poor workers. After one such episode, Kinal said to the woman, "Things haven't gone so far that we will dance to your singing. It will change—Poland still exists." (This was a veiled reference to the outlawed national anthem, "Poland Is Not Yet Lost.") Another time, he had even dared to defend himself and to hit back. Both Leonhard Kinal and Therese Ginter were thereupon tried before the Posen Special Court, which judged their actions on the basis of the special regulations mentioned above, even though these regulations had not been in force at the time of the events in question: "Both of the accused were to be sentenced according to Section 1, paragraph 3 on the Decree on Criminal Justice Regarding Poles and Jews (issued December 4, 1941), which was here applied retroactively in an agreement reached with the prosecutors. Both of the accused evinced an anti-German attitude through malicious and inflammatory actions, in particular through anti-German remarks, and caused harm to the welfare of the people through the sum of their behavior . . . [by] being repeatedly unwilling to work, lazy, and refractory, by performing their work badly or sometimes not at all, and even by using physical force against their German employers." Since Therese Ginter had once saved the lives of her employer's entire family, she was sentenced to "only" six years in a penal camp (concentration camp); the court sentenced Leonhard Kinal to death.[36]

In addition to actively supporting the political oppression of the Polish population, the German courts were required, as one of their main tasks, to safeguard the ongoing economic plundering of the country. Polish farmers who were unwilling to deliver all their produce to the occupying forces incurred the sanctions of the Decree on the War Economy; every private use of their own produce was treated as an act of anti-German sabotage. In a whole series of trials, the Zichenau Special Court, for example, sentenced Polish farmers to death for "illegal slaughtering," even if the case involved a single pig. The decision in the case of a man by the name of Wladislaus Fortas spelled out the reasons: "The case involves a pig weighing seventy kilograms. Illegal slaughtering endangers the just distribution of meat products among the German population, and also jeopardizes the export of agricultural surpluses from this territory to the Old Reich." [37] On February 18, 1943, fourteen Polish farmers faced such charges before the same court. Two were acquitted for lack of evidence, nine were sent to penal camps, and three were sentenced to death. [38]

In the territory under the "General Government" headed by the "Reich legal director," Hans Frank, the Special Courts were given an even freer hand. The special criminal regulations regarding Poles applied here, too, but in addition the governor general had issued a number of decrees establishing other capital crimes. Since this region was becoming a "staging area" for hundreds of thousands of deported Jews from all over Europe prior to their extermination in the death camps, a decree had been issued on April 19, 1941, creating official ghettos for all Jews. (This decree preceded the "Wannsee Conference," where the "final solution to the Jewish question" was decided upon.) Any Jew who left one of these ghettos without authorization was considered to have committed a capital crime. Once the first death camps of Belcec, Sobibor, and Treblinka had been put into operation in the spring of 1942, the Jewish population in Poland was swept by wave upon wave of deportations. [39] In the fall of 1944, when a new major deportation action was imminent, a Jewish tanner named Eisenberg from Szydlowiec thought he would be spared because his skills were still needed. However, he feared for the safety of his two daughters (aged six and seven), and asked Bazyli Antoniak, a Ukrainian, to hide them for a few weeks. Antoniak took the girls to relatives of his who lived three hundred kilometers away in the district of Lemberg (Lvov), where he gave out the story that they were Polish children. After the authorities learned of the matter, the girls were sent to one of the death camps, and Antoniak and his wife were tried before the Special Court of Radom. Bazyli Antoniak was sentenced to death and his wife Zofia-Antonina, to three years in a penitentiary; they were accused of "harboring criminals" (or aiding and abetting such), as well as "aiding and abetting unauthorized departure from a Jewish housing district." [40] In its eagerness to punish the crime, the court apparently failed to notice that in the latter case the "principals" were six and seven years old—that is, minors who could not be charged. Thus, no crime had in fact been committed which it would have been possible to "abet."

The criminal regulations for Poles provided for only two kinds of sanctions: penal camps (meaning concentration camps) and the death sentence. The law existing in Germany dividing criminal acts into three categories—petty offenses, misdemeanors, and felonies—and the distinction between greater and lesser offenses did not apply to Poles and Jews. In addition, it was the intent of the decree to dispense with the distinctions between attempting and committing a crime, and those between inciting, aiding and abetting, and acting as an accomplice; such was the explanation of Fritz Grau, an official in the Ministry of Justice and one of the decree's authors. Every criminal act, even the most trivial, represented a violation of the general obligation of Poles and Jews to obey German directives and was thus treated as a felony.[41] The courts soon stopped providing detailed legal arguments in their decisions and developed simple phrases such as "The accused is found guilty as a Pole of . . ." or "The accused is found guilty as a Pole and as a dangerous habitual criminal."[42]

The Ministry of Justice disapproved of this diction, but the wording was precisely suited to its purpose. The wartime laws and decrees, already extremely severe to begin with, became brutal instruments of oppression in Poland through their broad and undifferentiated application. One instance is a decree of the Führer issued on December 23, 1941: the Decree to Protect the Collection of Winter Clothing for the Front. It provided the death penalty for anyone misusing the collection for personal profit.[43] The decree did specify that the crime had to be committed with intent, however; in other words, the perpetrators had to be aware that the articles in question were part of the collection. The Special Courts in Poland were not so particular on this point either, as shown by the following case.

A twenty-three-year-old Polish waitress named Anna Zegarska, described by her German employer as "completely trustworthy, clean, and hardworking," was given a second-hand fur jacket in January 1942 by a friend in the German army. The soldier had taken the jacket from the stores of the winter collection, a fact of which Anna Zegarska knew nothing—as the court itself later acknowledged. She was unaware of the existence of both the winter collections and the drastic penalties in the decree concerning them. When she heard about them ten days after receiving the present, she became concerned about where the fur might have come from and packed up the jacket again in order to give it back. Before she could return it, however, she was arrested, tried before the Special Court of Thorn (Torun), and sentenced to death for "violating the criminal regulations concerning Poles in connection with the Führer's Decree to Protect the Collection of Winter Clothing for the Front."[44]

The decision in the case, reached by three trained jurists, consists of several pages of legal argumentation of the most outrageous kind. In the opinion of the court, it was not necessary for the defendant to have "knowingly" removed an article of clothing from the winter donations in order for her to be found guilty of violating the decree; "on general principles" it sufficed for there to have been "a limited intent to commit the deed." This statement in itself was entirely false, but in this case the defendant, who had not known anything about the collection when she received the jacket, did not have even this "limited intent." At most she had only a "subsequent intent" at a later time, something that was not punishable under German law even then. However, the judges at the Special Courts did not trouble themselves with such fine points of law in trials involving Polish defendants.

Trials of people accused of violating the criminal regulations for Poles were conducted in an even more streamlined manner than Special Court proceedings in the "Old Reich." Defendants had no possibility of appeal whatsoever, and every sentence could be carried out at once. Poles and Jews could not claim possible bias on the part of a German judge and request that a different judge hear their case. Arrest and preliminary detention could take place at any time, even without demonstration of cause. Poles and Jews were not permitted to testify under oath, a circumstance which consistently gave their testimony less weight than that of their German adversaries. Most important, however, prosecutors and judges were given a free hand to conduct trials as they liked, so long as they were "based on German criminal procedures"; they could depart from the normal course wherever it was "conducive to swift and vigorous dispatch of the case." The general clause granting the courts freedom from all restrictions in conducting trials was given particular approval by the bench. The president of the Court of Appeals in Posen, for example, sent a letter to all the County Courts in his jurisdiction praising the opportunity this measure opened up "to develop a swift procedure . . . unhampered by formalities."[45]

The trials actually conducted by these "heralds of German legal culture"—as German judges of the Special Courts in the occupied eastern territories liked to call themselves—were all too often a mockery of proper criminal proceedings. Occasionally defendants sat in the dock in chains. They were permitted to answer only "yes" or "no" to questions put by the court. Although many of the accused did not understand German, it was the only language spoken. Defendants were not allowed to put questions to witnesses, and witnesses' testimony was not translated for them. Judges frequently reacted with tirades and threats when defendants disputed the charges against them. Decisions spoke of Poles as an "inferior race" and contained references to "murderous Polish rabble" and "Polish banditry."[46] Numerous decisions document the carelessness of the courts in hearing witnesses and admitting evidence.

A Polish carpenter named Ignatz Kazmierczak, father of two children, was even condemned by the (hearsay) "testimony" of a dog. Section 4, paragraph 2 of the Decree on Criminal Justice Regarding Poles and Jews prescribed the death penalty (and in less severe cases imprisonment) for persons in incorporated territories who "intentionally damaged facilities of the German authorities or objects used by them in their work or in the public interest." When a German police dog was stabbed and wounded in early August 1940 by a person or persons unknown (there were no witnesses to the act), the public prosecutors in Posen investigated the incident and charged Ignatz Kazmierczak with "intentional damage to official property." In its decision of December 4, 1941, the Posen Special Court summarized the evidence against him as follows: "The witnesses themselves did not actually see who injured the dog, but the guilt of the accused is established by the following facts. When the accused was arrested on August 4, 1940, the witness Knippel brought along his injured dog. On seeing the dog, the accused became alarmed, began to tremble violently, and threw up his arms in fright. The dog, for his part, immediately became enraged and set upon the accused. The defendant's behavior proves that he is the one who stabbed the dog, and what is more the dog recognized the accused at once as his enemy." On the basis of this evidence, Ignatz Kazmierczak was condemned to death.[47]

In other occupied countries no special regulations such as those for the incorporated regions of Poland or the territory of the "Government General" existed, but the Special Courts nevertheless functioned there as brutal suppressors of every form of national resistance. Only a few months before the war ended, for example, the Special Court of Prague sentenced to death a sixty-three-year-old Catholic priest named Karl Kratina, who had been accused of making "malicious remarks." Kratina had said an illegal Mass for the soul of a Czech condemned to death and executed by the Special Court; he had also preached on several occasions against violence and godlessness and had told a church sexton that Jews were being tortured in Theresienstadt. Among close friends, the priest had also told political jokes, such as that Germany could not win the war because it had "the CSR" against it. ("CSR" was the abbreviation for "Czechoslovak Republic.") When his hearers shook their heads in disbelief, he spelled it out for them: "Churchill–Stalin–Roosevelt." Since the death penalty was by no means mandatory, the Special Court said in its judgment of December 6, 1944, regarding its choice of penalty: "Spreaders of political calumnies, who as clergyman find it proper to poison wells and stab the German Reich in the back when it is engaged in a war being waged ultimately to guarantee freedom of religion, deserve no other fate than to be eliminated from their national community." Kratina was guillotined on January 16, 1945.[48]

Although strictly speaking, the Decree on Criminal Justice Regarding Poles and Jews applied only in occupied Polish territory, it was used with almost as much brutality in the heart of Germany against Poles performing forced labor in the "Old Reich" as in remote regions of Poland. Here, too, the courts were inventive in their legal constructions when it was a matter of keeping the approximately ten million foreign workers in check.

A farmer's son named Walerian Wrobel, fifteen years old, was one of the approximately two million Polish workers in the "Old Reich." After his family's farm had been razed and his parents presumably killed, he "volunteered" for labor in Germany. Assigned to farm labor in Bremen-Lesum, he soon began to suffer under the harsh working conditions, bad treatment, and isolation (since he spoke not a single word of German) and above all from homesickness. He ran away and started to walk the nine hundred kilometers back to Poland, but was quickly seized, warned, and sent back to his post. Then he hit upon the idea of setting fire to a shed, thinking that as a "punishment" he would be sent home. He carried out this plan a few days after his sixteenth birthday. The fire was discovered and extinguished before any serious damage occurred, and the boy himself helped put it out. Far from being sent home, however, Walerian Wrobel was charged "as an asocial element and Pole" under the Decree on Asocial Elements in combination with the Decree on Criminal Justice Regarding Poles and Jews.

The first decree declared that grave or aggravated arson was a capital crime if it "undermine[d] the resistance of the German people." For arson to be considered "aggravated," however, the fire had to be set in a human dwelling, and since the building in question was a shed, the charge could only be simple arson. Nonetheless, the Special Court concluded from the boy's assumption that he would be sent home after the deed that he must also have reckoned with "the house catching fire as well." "Therefore," the court found, Wrobel had "intentionally set fire to a building serving as a human dwelling." One could hardly claim that the resistance of the German people had been undermined by this small fire, but in its decision of July 8, 1942, the court determined that this resistance was "damaged under the meaning of the act, even if the resistance was merely threatened." Before the death penalty could be imposed, the court still had to overcome the problem of the boy's age: the law on minors forbade such a penalty. Yet even this presented no serious obstacle to the Bremen Special Court: "The accused is still a minor under the meaning of the statute on prosecution of minors, since he had just passed his sixteenth birthday when he committed the act. This statute does not apply to him as a Pole, however. The provisions of the statute on prosecution of minors are intended solely for young Germans, providing educational measures to make them respectable members of the community." On August 25, 1942, Walerian Wrobel, though hardly past childhood, was executed.[49]

Administration of "justice" in this manner was aided by the extremely harsh laws, but in the end did not depend on them alone. The system was capable of producing similar results even in cases outside the jurisdiction of the Special Courts.

In one such case two young Greeks, Nikolaus Kondojianis (nineteen years old) and Andreas Dadopulos (twenty), had been seized in their hometown of Patras in February 1944 and sent to perform forced labor in the Reich. They were housed in the foreigners' barracks at the labor camp in Steyr, Austria, at the coldest time of year, half starving and completely inadequately clothed. On February 29 the young men found two old pairs of trousers in the rubble of a bombed-out house, and two pistol holsters in the street. Dadopulos took the things, planning to use the leather of the holsters to repair their worn-out shoes as best he could. When Dr. Pichler-Drexler, the senior public prosecutor of Linz, learned of the incident, he decided to make an example of the two foreign "asocial elements." He drew up charges on the same day and on the next morning drove the forty kilometers to Steyr, along with presiding judge Dr. Eypeltauer and the other members of the Linz Special Court, in order to hold the trial on the spot. The court recognized neither the youth nor the distress of the defendants as extenuating circumstances, nor the fact that no one else had any interest in the abandoned articles. It did, however, consider that the Greeks' crime was aggravated by their abuse of the "hospitality" they were enjoying in the German Reich. It found Andreas Dadopulos guilty of theft and Nikolaus Kondojianis guilty as his accomplice, although there was no evidence at all to indicate that Kondojianis had participated in the act. Both were condemned to death as "asocial elements."

The sentence was effective immediately, but there was no executioner to be found in either Steyr or Linz. For the sentence to be carried out, the prisoners would have had to be transferred to Vienna or Munich, a delay which would have given them an opportunity to enter a plea for clemency. Therefore, on the evening of March 1 the prosecutor general of Austria, a man named Löderer, telephoned the Ministry of Justice in Berlin for special permission to contravene paragraph 13 of the Criminal Code (which prescribed beheading for condemned prisoners) and to have the men shot by the Linz police. Minister Thierack gave his approval on March 2, and the same day a hastily assembled police firing squad executed the two Greeks. Along with them was executed a French laborer named Mario

Berry, father of four under-age children: the Linz Special Court had sentenced him to death for stealing two articles of clothing and some bread.[50]

"Night and Fog" Justice

Soon after the German war machine had rolled over half of Europe, resistance movements began to organize in the occupied countries. Their activities ranged from small acts of defiance (as in Alsace-Lorraine and Luxemburg, where the mere wearing of a beret was considered evidence of an anti-German attitude) to sabotage and raids on occupying troops. The German army was not prepared for continuous guerrilla warfare behind the front, and in the long run the resistance movements came to pose a serious threat. The Armed Forces High Command therefore demanded that the "most rigorous means" be used, so as "to stamp [them] out in the shortest possible time." An order from General Field Marshal Keitel issued July 23, 1941, stated that, given the extent of the occupied territories, the available security forces would be sufficient only "if every act of resistance is punished not by prosecuting the perpetrators through the courts, but by waging an army campaign of terror designed to crush within the population every inclination to resist."[51] High Command Secret Order 002060/41, issued September 16, 1941, provided details: "In such cases, suitable retribution for the life of one German soldier must generally be reckoned to consist of the deaths of fifty to a hundred Communists. The manner in which the executions are carried out must heighten the effect of intimidation."[52]

The final step in this development was a decree of Hitler's signed by Keitel which specified that "crimes committed by non-German civilians against the Reich or the forces of occupation and posing a threat to their security and effectiveness" were to be punished as a rule by the death sentence. Judgment should be passed on such crimes in the perpetrators' home country only if it was probable that death sentences would actually be imposed and swiftly executed. In all other cases, the criminals should be deported to Germany and all information about their whereabouts withheld. The head of the High Command of the Armed Forces, whose duty it was to determine how the Führer's decree would be carried out, ordered on December 12 that persons accused of acts posing a threat to the security of occupying troops were either to be executed within a week or deported to Germany with the utmost secrecy, and without being given any opportunity to inform their relatives.[53]

Although the decree applied expressly to all occupied territories, it was enforced mainly in countries to the west of Germany, above all in Belgium.

It was generally referred to as the "Night and Fog Decree" (or "Night and Fog Order")—an appropriate name, since in German the common phrase "by night and fog" (*bei Nacht und Nebel*) suggests clandestine and illicit action, as well as the fact that kidnapped prisoners were supposed to vanish without a trace. In official correspondence, they were always referred to as "NN prisoners": the abbreviation stood both for prisoners under the *Nacht und Nebel* decree and for the Latin phrase *non nominatur* ("not named"), because their identity was not to be disclosed. On February 6, 1942, the Reich Ministry of Justice sent out a memorandum establishing jurisdiction and procedures in "NN" cases. If the accused came from occupied France, the Special Court in Cologne had jurisdiction; if from Belgium and the Netherlands, the Special Court in Dortmund was responsible. Norwegians were to be tried by the Special Court in Kiel, and all others by the Special Court in Berlin. The acting minister of justice, Franz Schlegelberger, reserved the right to assign jurisdiction himself "in special cases."[54] Every indictment was to be submitted to him; defendants could not choose their own defense attorneys; foreign evidence, and foreign witnesses in particular, could be admitted only with special permission from the Ministry of Justice, and no information about the proceedings was to be provided in response to inquiries.

A further memorandum—that is to say, a purely internal bureaucratic measure—also extended jurisdiction in NN trials to the People's Court. Since the courts had to cope with such a large number of cases, the ministry directed that proceedings be held directly in the prison camps, where prisoners were crowded together by the hundreds or even thousands. The Essen Special Court convened regularly three times a week in the guards' mess room at the Esterwegen camp, and sentenced precisely 1,578 prisoners there in the months of March and April 1944. Even the People's Court traveled several times to Esterwegen and Papenburg, to condemn the more prominent members of the Belgian resistance: politicians, clergymen, professors, physicians, and university students. On one day alone (September 1, 1943), the court sentenced thirty NN defendants there, all of them to death. The sentences were carried out at once.[55]

To make completely sure that no information about the fate of the foreign prisoners reached the outside world under any circumstances, the sentences were entered neither in the official statistics of the Reich nor in the ordinary criminal records. Relatives were not notified of executions or of deaths from other causes—and thousands died as a result of the inhuman conditions in the camps. On March 6, 1943, the Ministry of Justice directed that "last letters written by condemned NN prisoners . . . are not to be forwarded, nor are any others." The usual practice of informing the press of executions and of posting notices in public places was omitted. Graves of NN prisoners could "not be inscribed with the names of the deceased."[56] The survey of April 1944 intended for internal use at the Department of Justice is incomplete, but it names 8,639 NN prisoners who had been deported to Germany and brought before Special Courts and the People's Court. The trials were conducted in assembly-line fashion—often defendants did not learn what the charges against them were until the main trial; defense attorneys were seldom admitted to court, and due process formalities were ignored altogether. Even so, the courts could hardly keep up with the demand. Of the 8,639 NN prisoners mentioned in the April survey, only 1,739 had been sentenced. Even as the courts were hopelessly overburdened, prisons were overcrowded. The Bebrach prison near Bamberg, for example, was designed to hold a maximum of 595 inmates but contained 1,600 NN prisoners after 1944, and in the peat-bog camp of Esterwegen 1,800 foreign resistance fighters had been housed together in one block.[57] Atrocious as conditions were for all "peat-bog soldiers" (as German prisoners in the Emsland camps were called), a British military court later found that the lot of the NN prisoners was "the worst in the whole of the Emsland."[58] As a result of their total isolation and the uncertainty of their fate, they were subjected to unbearable psychological pressures. And since NN prisoners were not sent out to perform heavy physical labor in the peat bogs like the others, but were occupied only with "lighter" tasks such as the sorting of scrap metal and other materials to keep their presence a secret, they were forced to subsist on only eight hundred calories a day. In the Esterwegen camp alone, sixty-seven of them died within a short time from undernourishment and brutal treatment. This occurred in spite of the fact that it was officially not even a concentration camp but a prison facility under the supervision of the Ministry of Justice.

In the fall of 1944, all NN trials were broken off no matter what stage they had reached, and responsibility for all foreign prisoners transferred to the Gestapo. The Gestapo then distributed them among the various concentration and death camps. Prisoners in the district of Berlin were sent to Oranienburg; those from Belgium, Holland, and France at the Emsland camps were dispersed to Dachau, Gross-Rosen, and Auschwitz; others went to Mauthausen, Flossenbürg, and Buchenwald; and most of the women were sent to Ravensbrück. According to a directive from the Reich Ministry of Justice, issued January 21, 1944, the few NN prisoners who had been acquitted were to be handed over to the Gestapo in any case.[59] No one was ever released after serving a sentence, since the prison sentences (if they were passed at all) were so harsh that none had elapsed by the time the NN cases were turned over to the Gestapo.

It is still not known today how many victims were claimed by the clandestine NN operations of the Special Courts, how many prisoners were sent to concentration camps without trial, and how many were transferred there when the Ministry of Justice ceased to be responsible for them. The victims were never heard from again, and all traces of them were obliterated.

19

"Correcting" Decisions:
The Judicial System and the Police

Ruthless prosecution of the regime's political opponents had to a large degree become, for the judicial system of the Third Reich, a question of its own survival. Hitler was not the only one who considered jurists "complete fools" incapable of recognizing what measures the state had to take.[1] Once the Gestapo was established as a new system of power, a system that was not subject to control by the courts, the latter, during the twelve years of Nazi rule, were forced to relinquish more and more of their authority to the constantly expanding influence of this apparatus. Eduard Kern, a professor of criminal law, had already written in his 1933 book *The Independence of the Judiciary and Its Limits:* "In principle, the liberal state prescribed that all decisions concerning the freedom of the individual and the authority to punish should be made by an independent judiciary. Both principles have been abandoned to a large extent today. Since the [Reichstag Fire] Decree of February 28, 1933, decisions concerning an individual's freedom tend to be made by the police, chiefly in the form of preventive detention, a curtailment of liberty without legal prerequisites or time limits, on grounds not subject to verification by a judge."[2] The National Socialists did not bother to bring formal charges against the majority of their political enemies, but simply took them into this "preventive detention," meaning that they dispatched them to one of the many concentration camps.

Furthermore, persons acquitted by the courts were often simply taken into preventive detention, sometimes even rearrested in the courtroom itself and shipped to concentration camps. Thus, all the defendants found not guilty in the Reichstag fire trial were nonetheless taken directly from the Supreme Court building to a camp.[3] This practice naturally tended to diminish the authority of the courts, a result that even leading Nazis found hard to accept if they were jurists. The acting "law leader of the reich" (a

Nazi party official) wrote to the Minister of Justice to express his "serious concern about the status of due process in Germany," noting critically that the refusal to grant access to counsel in cases of preventive detention was incompatible with "the National Socialist conception" of due process" and offended "the northern races' natural regard for law."[4] Reich minister of justice Gürtner, too, demanded from the Secret State Police Bureau a clear separation between the powers of the judicial system and the police, but he was rebuffed by the Gestapo's chief counsel, SS general Dr. Werner Best. Best insisted that "the imposition of preventive detention [was] also possible when there is evidence that a crime has been committed."[5] In other words, it was all right for the police to be in competition with the courts. The Ministry of Justice was well aware of what happened to defendants who fell into the hands of the Gestapo, regardless of whether they had previously been acquitted or found guilty by the courts. Several times in their status reports to the ministry, the chief public prosecutors of the various states pointed out the Gestapo's habit of shooting prisoners who were "attempting to escape."

Thus, on January 27, 1942, the chief public prosecutor attached to the Prussian Supreme Court in Berlin complained about the shooting of four people who had been given prison sentences, "although . . . the sentences imposed were in my opinion not too lenient." He vented some of his anger in the remark that "it is hardly a secret to the general public that prisoners killed 'while resisting' are shot for other reasons."[6]

For a while, the Ministry of Justice even kept a file of known cases in which the police had shot or hanged suspected criminals without a court sentence. There were eighteen such cases between September 1939 and January 1940 alone.[7] Two of these victims, Paul Latacz and Erwin Jacobs, had made an amateurish attempt to rob a bank in the Berlin district of Teltow. After the attempt had failed, they fled and were hit by a taxicab. During their trial, they were lying seriously injured and incapable of leaving their beds in a prison infirmary. The Berlin Special Court even had to convene at the infirmary for this reason.[8] Immediately following their sentencing to ten years in a penitentiary, Latacz and Jacobs tried (according to the version in the Nazi newspaper *Der Völkische Beobachter*) "to offer physical resistance. The two criminals were shot at once."[9]

Even at the People's Court, the Gestapo occasionally tried to rearrest acquitted defendants before they could leave the courtroom. In one such instance a former Communist, a woman accused of high treason for allegedly participating in illegal meetings of Communists and Social Democrats, was acquitted by the Second Panel of the People's Court for lack of evidence. When two Gestapo officers present in the courtroom tried to take her into preventive detention immediately after the decision had been announced, the presiding judge and another member of the panel protested vigorously, explaining that it was not permissible "to take into preventing detention persons who had been acquitted by the court." After all, the People's Court had "been created by the Führer and [was] therefore, as the highest court of the German Reich, completely sovereign"; it would be "an impossible state of affairs" if decisions of this court were open to "criticism by an administrative body." [10] Hereupon the police officers withdrew without making the arrest, but two days later the woman was nevertheless seized again and sent to a concentration camp. In January 1939 Otto Thierack, then president of the People's Court, wrote to the Ministry of Justice to say that "all judges on the panel, including those acting in an honorary capacity," found it "intolerable" that preventive detention was being imposed on people they had acquitted. [11] It should be pointed out, however, that not long afterward Thierack himself stated that it would be wrong to grant "every little hanger-on the honor of a trial before the People's Court"; it would be better if such people "were brought to reason by a spell in a concentration camp." [12]

The outrage expressed on occasion was directed not so much against the injustice of rearresting people who had been acquitted as against the affront that such an obvious "correction" of a court's decision posed to the judicial system. On January 24, 1939, the Reich minister of justice instructed the presidents of the Courts of Appeals to make certain that the Gestapo at least waited until defendants were outside the courtroom before making an arrest. [13] Otherwise the ministry did what it could to support the practice. As early as May 1933, the minister of justice had directed that the names of all prisoners serving sentences for political crimes were to be given to the political police four weeks before their release, so that the police could check to see whether "preventive detention [was] required." [14] Such instructions were repeated regularly; in 1936 the minister even gave instructions that the pending release of political prisoners should be reported not only to the Gestapo but also to the Security Service of the SS. [15] The word "political" was to be understood in the broadest sense. On July 2, 1937, the Ministry of Justice included members of the German branch of Jehovah's Witnesses on the list of prisoners to be reported; on March 8, 1938, it included all persons who had been convicted of sexual offenses under the race laws. The Ministry of the Interior also instructed that "professional criminals" and "asocial elements" being released should, as a rule, be checked to see whether they ought not to be sent to concentration camps.

Frequently, if charges were withdrawn against people being held in prison awaiting trial, the legal system would itself hand them over to the Gestapo. The basis for this practice was either local agreements between judicial officers and the political police or simply the "good will" between them, which the Reich minister of justice had enjoined the Offices of Public Prosecution and the courts to foster. In a memorandum dated May 28, 1937, he directed every Court of Appeals to appoint one prosecutor to serve as "officer for political defense," who was to maintain contact with the local Gestapo "for the purpose of discussing state police problems." As a rule, the chief public prosecutor of the district took over this important task personally. The Ministry of Justice itself appointed one of its officials, Dr. Günther Joël, to serve as liaison to the Reich Central Office of Security.[16]

These measures obviously worked well. The chief public prosecutor for Dresden, for example, reported to the Ministry on the agreements reached with the president of the State Police in Saxony, praising the "close and positive cooperation" between the Office of Public Prosecutions and the Gestapo in cases of political crime. On July 29, 1940, the chief public prosecutor of the Reich at the People's Court could report to the minister:

> In agreement with the president of the People's Court, I shall basically hand over the persons concerned to the Secret State Police if an acquittal or a stay of proceedings is ordered, or if the sentence is declared to have been served through the detention itself, unless the Secret State Police give express orders to the contrary. If there is an acquittal because innocence has been proved, I shall inform the Secret State Police before the transfer takes place and ask them whether this is then really necessary. On the other hand, should the Secret State Police declare the penalty of arrest to be necessary, I shall arrange for the transfer.[17]

Of course, people kept in preventive detention had no possibility whatsoever of lodging an appeal against police measures. However, according to the rule of law which still existed in theory at least, public prosecutors were duty bound to investigate every criminal act of which they became aware, even if it had been committed by other officials of the state. In the aftermath of the "Röhm putsch," a retroactive law had been passed declaring that murder of political opponents constituted "defense of the state" and was therefore "legal,"[18] and a generous amnesty had covered these excesses. However, there was absolutely no basis in law for the continuing brutal terror in the Gestapo prisons and concentration camps, although within the camps special regulations prevailed according to which SS guards were supposed to shoot prisoners for the slightest infringement of the rules, especially for any attempt to escape.

"Shot while trying to escape" became the standard phrase to account for all deaths of camp inmates. The chief public prosecutor in Berlin objected that duty regulations could not exonerate manslaughter, for "as they do not have the force of law, they cannot set aside the illegality of the action." Yet since the murders in the camps were clearly known to and tolerated by those in high places, prosecutors as a rule contented themselves, when they learned of such deaths, with drawing up reports to their superiors rather than criminal charges.[19]

The judicial system also quickly learned to live with the fact that defendants appeared in court bearing signs of torture or testified that confessions had been extracted from them by force. In the beginning, these cases caused judges acute embarrassment, and the minister of justice was unable to accept such police interference in the operations of the courts. A committee of top legal advisers from the Ministery of Justice and the Gestapo found a practical solution, however: they legalized the terror, to such an extent that they even established a "standard club" to be used in beatings, so that torture would at least be regularized. The minutes of the meeting expose more clearly than almost any other document the judicial system's tactics and contempt for human life during the Third Reich:

Confidential!

To: Chief Public Prosecutor in Düsseldorf
Subject: Mistreatment of Political Prisoners

Meeting at the Reich Ministry of Justice on June 4, 1937
My last report was June 1, 1937—16 A.R. 26/37

The conference with the Secret State Police took place as announced on June 4 in Berlin (Reich Ministry of Justice). Present were:

1. Dr. Crohne, Reich Ministry of Justice Berlin
2. Senior Public Prosecutor von Haake, Reich Ministry of Justice Berlin
3. Senior Public Prosecutor Dr. Joël, Reich Ministry of Justice Berlin
4. Dr. Best, Gestapo Berlin
5. Möller, Gestapo Berlin
6. Chief Public Prosecutor Dr. Jung, Berlin
7. Chief Public Prosecutor Dr. Semler, Hamm
8. The undersigned

Dr. Crohne opened the meeting with some remarks on the need for a confidential discussion on ways and means of eliminating difficulties that had occurred . . . By way of introduction, Senior Prosecutor von Haake explained the following:

It has been recognized by government leaders at the highest levels that more rigorous interrogations are necessary and indispensable. In such cases, it would be nonsensical to prosecute the officers carrying out the interrogation for exceeding their authority. However, public prosecutors must carry out the letter of the law and have no possibility of choosing to prosecute or not as they may judge fit . . . At present, we thus have a situation which cannot continue: a deficient sense of what is right on the part of judicial officers; an undignified position for police officers, who try to help matters by foolish denials. The purpose of this meeting is to discuss the possibility of relevant limits. There followed a discussion of individual questions:

Question 1: For which offenses are more rigorous interrogations permissible?

There was general agreement that, in principle, interrogations of this kind may be undertaken in cases where charges involve the immediate interests of the state. These are chiefly treason and high treason. Representatives of the Gestapo expressed the opinion that a more rigorous interrogation could also be considered in cases of Jehovah's Witnesses, explosives, and sabotage. However, they refrained from taking an official position on the matter until they could confer further with the Reich leader of the SS. It was unanimously agreed that charges under paragraph 175 of the Criminal Code [that is, charges of homosexuality] should not be considered as grounds. A more rigorous interrogation is, as a general principle, never permissible in the case of foreigners. In cases of this nature, the files should be studied to get a picture of the situation, not only by the local state police authorities but also at Gestapo headquarters in Berlin, by an officer specially assigned to such duty.

Question 2: Nature of corporal punishment?

As a general principle, in more rigorous interrogations only blows with a club on the buttocks are permissible, up to the number 25. The number is to be determined in advance by the Gestapo (see Question 3). Beginning with the tenth blow, a physician must be present. A standard club will be designated, to eliminate all irregularities.

Question 3: Who may order a more rigorous interrogation?

As a general principle, only Gestapo Headquarters in Berlin. Local state police stations must obtain permission in advance from Berlin. Without permission, a more rigorous interrogation may not be conducted.

Question 4: Who administers corporal punishment?

In no case may the official conducting the interrogation also administer corporal punishment. An officer must be selected for this duty by local state police units.

Question 5: What assurance exists that innocent persons will not be interrogated with the more rigorous measures?

This question is considered to be answered by the measures named under Question 3.

Question 6: How are judicial officers to deal technically with cases
a) in which permissible corporal punishment has been inflicted under the terms stated above?

If an office of public prosecution receives a complaint, it contacts the state police and confirms that permission was granted (by the Gestapo Berlin). If said permission can be presented, no charges are pressed. Only a formal announcement: "Investigation has shown that a criminal act was not committed."

b) in which corporal punishment has been inflicted not permissible under the terms stated above?

If it transpires that permission was not obtained, commence investigation immediately and report at once to the Central Office of Public Prosecutions.

c) in which corporal punishment was inflicted with doubtful permissibility under the terms state above (borderline cases)?

Case to be handed over at once with a report to the Central Office of Public Prosecutions. During the discussion, opinion was unanimously expressed (including by representatives of the Gestapo) that the method of applying more rigorous interrogations used hitherto must not be continued. Cases still pending should be clarified by the criminal justice authorities with greater speed. An effort to establish contact between the Gestapo and the Reich Ministry of Justice about these cases has been undertaken. Decision expected momentarily.

The Gestapo will receive a copy of the results of the discussion from the Ministry, whereupon it is to act on them immediately (see Question 1) and issue instructions to state police stations. The Ministry of Justice will for its part then issue instructions to public prosecutors.

(Signed)_____[20]

This agreement covered only the official campaign of terror against those accused of "political" crimes. Torture of "normal" defendants remained a punishable offense according to the principle established by Gestapo chief counsel Werner Best: "So long as the police force carries out the will of the country's leadership, it acts legally, but if the will of the leadership is disregarded, then it is no longer a case of the actions of the police force, but becomes a case of one member of the force exceeding his authority"— an offense which prosecutors were to investigate.[21]

All the same, the case of Police Captain Wilhelm Klinzmann shows that there was a "solution" even in such sensitive cases. After several barns had burned down in the district of Seehausen / Altmark, Klinzmann had arrested a farm laborer named Robert Blödling. He forced a confession out of him by brutal means, and on the basis of it the laborer was sentenced to death. When word leaked out about how the confession had been obtained, Klinzmann was brought before the County Court of Stendal for infliction of bodily injury while in office, and was given a prison sentence.

The Supreme Court rejected his appeal as "obviously without foundation," and the sentence was then supposed to take effect.

On December 17, 1941, however, acting minister of justice Franz Schlegelberger authorized the Reich chief prosecutor to "enter an extraordinary appeal" in the matter. On December 23, Reich chief prosecutor Brettle noted in the file: "Yesterday I discussed . . . the criminal charges against Police Captain Wilhelm Klinzmann with Undersecretary Freisler in Berlin. The purpose of lodging the extraordinary appeal is to nullify the County Court's decision, so that the Reich Minister of Justice can then cancel the proceedings." A way was found to avoid a trial before the Special Panel of the Supreme Court that heard cases involving extraordinary appeals, so that the judges could be spared the painful alternative of either withdrawing their own rejection of the appeal or taking a stand against a wish of the Führer. On December 24, 1941, Schlegelberger canceled "the proceedings pending before the Supreme Court after lodging of the extraordinary appeal, by the authority granted [him] by the Führer."[22] The new procedure of "cancellation," created on February 16, 1934, gave the government a means to end every current investigation or trial independently of judicial decisions.[23] Once the extraordinary appeal had erased his previous conviction, Klinzmann was free and was not even considered to have a criminal record.

The Reich Ministry of Justice had always tried to maintain at least the appearance of observing legal formalities (in contrast to the methods of the police) and also to protect an area in which the courts had exclusive jurisdiction. This area continued to shrink, however. The alleged reason for the ministry's willingness to yield territory was to prevent all powers of criminal justice from passing into the hands of the police or SS. Abolishing the court system completely would hardly have been a practical possibility in any event, for administrative and political reasons. Far worse than complete transfer of power to the SS or police, because it was gradual and less spectacular, was the tactic of giving the SS ever more say in such matters little by little and relinquishing piece by piece what finally amounted to considerable powers in the administration of criminal justice.

On September 18, 1942, the Ministry of Justice conceded to the SS the right to correct "overly lenient" judicial decisions. At a conference in Himmler's field headquarters, at which (in addition to the SS chief) the new minister of justice Thierack, his undersecretary Rothenburger, and the SS officers Streckenbach and Bender were present, the subject of "compensating for too lenient criminal sentences through special police treatment" was discussed, and it was agreed that henceforth the minister would decide "whether special police treatment should be given." In case of disagreement between Thierack and Himmler, "the opinion of party chief Martin Bormann" was to be sought.

The second subject of this conference was "the delivery of asocial elements from penal institutions to the head of the SS for elimination through hard labor." The further agreement reached on this point was noted in the minutes of the Ministry of Justice: "To be handed over without exception are all Jews, gypsies, Russians, and Ukrainians in preventive detention; Poles sentenced to more than three years and Czechs and Germans sentenced to more than eight years are to be handed over on the decision of the Reich minister of justice. To begin with, the most depraved asocial elements among the latter should be handed over. The Führer is to be informed of these measures by party chief Bormann."[24]

In practice, the agreement was more than fulfilled. At a meeting at the Ministry of Justice on October 9, 1942, it was agreed that all Jews, gypsies, Russians, Ukrainians, and persons of other nationalities and ethnic origins in preventive detention were to be handed over to the SS without exception. To carry out the corresponding order, a committee consisting of Mr. Marx and Dr. Hupperschwiller from the Ministry of Justice, senior public prosecutor Meyer, first public prosecutor Gündner, and the director of the Reich Central Office of the Nazi party (Herr Giese) made a tour of penitentiaries and selected the prisoners to be handed over, according to whether—on the basis of the committee's own criteria—they were "asocial" or not.[25] On October 13, Minister of Justice Thierack wrote to Martin Bormann at the Führer's headquarters to announce that "criminal prosecution of Poles, Russians, Jews, and gypsies" would henceforth be left entirely to Himmler. Thierack assumed thereby "that the judicial system could contribute but little to the liquidation of members of these groups"; "without doubt the courts pass most severe sentences upon such persons, but that itself is not sufficient. It also makes no sense to keep such persons alive in German prisons and penitentiaries for years . . . On the other hand, I believe that by handing over such persons to the police, who can then initiate measures free from criminal legal sanctions, much better results can be achieved."[26]

After this assurance had been made known to the relevant Gestapo and police departments, and to Offices of Public Prosecution in a number of secret guidelines, memoranda, and decrees, the Minister of Justice decided on July 1, 1943, to give it the full status of law. Paragraph 1 of the Thirteenth Decree on Administration of the Citizenship Law now stated succinctly: "Criminal acts committed by Jews will be prosecuted by the police. The Decree on Criminal Justice Regarding Poles and Jews no longer applies to Jews."[27]

20

The Legal Officers' Corps: Military Courts in the Second World War

As previously noted, Hitler always blamed Germany's catastrophic defeat in the 1914–1918 war on the "failure" of the judicial system, and of the military courts in particular. Above all, in his opinion, Germany later paid a terrible price for "virtually eliminating the death penalty, which amounted to abolishing the Articles of War."[1] Hitler was not alone in taking this view, for it was widely shared by conservative members of the armed forces and the legal profession. General Ludendorff, for example, saw "a grave threat to the discipline and effectiveness" of the army in the "mild sentences" received by soldiers who showed cowardice under fire, went absent without leave, or refused to obey orders. It was considered especially disturbing that only 150 death sentences had been passed during all of World War I, and of those only 48 had actually been carried out. During the same period, British military courts had handed down more than 3,000 death sentences and carried out 346 of them.[2]

Since no special military jurisdiction had existed during the Weimar Republic, the army, the legal profession, and the Nazi party agreed that the Third Reich must install new and vigorous military courts as soon as possible. The legal framework for doing so was created by the Law on Reintroducing Military Jurisdiction, passed on May 12, 1933.[3] A more inclusive law that would have replaced the much amended Military Criminal Code of 1872 was discussed but never realized. The old law was now amended again several times, to "simplify" it and above all to increase its severity. "Concepts were eradicated" that no longer "corresponded to the necessities of modern warfare."[4]

A whole new dimension was added to military law by a series of wartime decrees based on the idea of total mobilization of the country's people: the decrees virtually abolished any distinction between members of the armed forces and civilians. In particular, the Decree on Extraordinary Criminal Regulations in Wartime and Special Emergencies (passed on August 17, 1939), which prescribed the death penalty in cases of espionage, armed insurgency, and undermining morale, proved to be a trap for thousands of soldiers and civilians when it was broadly construed. Since the chief of the High Command of the Armed Forces could amend and expand it according to the exigencies of the military situation, it provided military authorities with the unprecedented power to issue criminal regulations applying to civilians. These wartime decrees not only blurred the boundary between military and civilian criminal law; they also matched the Nazis' notion of total control in the extent to which they went beyond all the traditional methods for prosecuting crimes. As Heinrich Dietz, the War Ministry's expert on military law, made clear as early as 1933, the intent was there from the beginning to make sure that the *Volk* was "united in one blood, one sacrifice, and one fate," and that "the state, the people, and the armed forces are one."[5]

The number of military judges organized in the "Legal Officers' Corps" grew steadily throughout the war. In December 1939, there were 290 courts with 463 judges; four years later, there were 687 courts with 1,133 judges, and they used their new powers ruthlessly. By mid-1944, which is as far as the available statistics go, they had passed 11,664 death sentences. The numbers rose sharply after the "turning point" of the Battle of Stalingrad, and almost doubled with each succeeding year: in 1940–41 there were 447; in 1941–42 there were 1,673; in 1942–43 there were 2,769; in 1943–44 there were 4,118.[6] It is virtually certain that in the "struggle for final victory," the most brutal phase of the Third Reich, the number doubled yet again. Manfred Messerschmidt, head of West Germany's Army Institute for Military History, studied the figures for a single month of the year 1945 and found that five times as many death sentences were passed as during the entire First World War.[7] The research of another military historian, Otto Hennicke, has revealed that German military courts passed 3,500 additional death sentences against civilians assigned to duties with the army in occupied territories and against foreign soldiers attached to units of the German army, as well as 6,000 death sentences against prisoners of war and members of resistance groups.[8] One must therefore assume a total of approximately 33,000 death sentences passed by Nazi military courts. Just as appalling as this total number is the percentage of them actually carried out. Whereas during the First World War two thirds of all the men condemned to death were shown mercy, during the Second World War 89 percent of them were executed.[9]

The degree to which the military courts were politicized is evident from the grounds on which the sentences were passed. The statistics for the

1,640 death sentences handed down between January 1940 and March 1943 by judges of the army courts alone show that 1,299 were for desertion and 216 for undermining morale—that is, a political or ideological aspect played a role in about 75 percent of them. Of course, it was possible to regard almost any criminal act from an ideological point of view; the number of wartime decrees with increased penalties enabled the courts to evaluate an action under a variety of headings and to impose any desired punishment, from mild disciplinary measures to the death sentence. Nazi ideology turned every offense into a breach of loyalty to the Führer and to "the national community engaged in a life-and-death struggle." Deserters became "inferior elements . . . spreading demoralization at the front," and those who committed simple theft were "asocial elements undermining army morale."[10] One military judge named Klein, for example, recommended that stealing from packages sent to the front, which amounted to simple theft if not mere pilfering of food, should be prosecuted either under paragraph 4 of the Decree on Asocial Elements as "exploitation of wartime circumstances to commit a crime" or under paragraph 5a of the Decree on Extraordinary Criminal Regulations ("a criminal act in violation of discipline among the troops"). Both regulations provided for the possibility of the death sentence.

On January 16, 1942, the court attached to the garrison of Greater Paris condemned a corporal to death for stealing eight pairs of woolen socks and a silk scarf. Since he had taken the articles from a collection rather than regular army supplies, the court found him guilty under the Decree to Protect the Collection of Winter Clothing for the Front, although it was clear that the regulation was designed to protect the clothes while they were being collected and not while they were being distributed among the soldiers. Furthermore, the judges ignored the passage stating that the death penalty was to be reserved for major violations of the decree. The decision merely stated that the accused had been aware that the articles could have been assembled "only [through] the willingness of the German people to make sacrifices." There could be no explanation for his crime except a "fundamentally asocial attitude" and an "inferior character." The soldier had a poor discipline record and had been convicted of a previous theft; in addition, as the court specifically emphasized in its decision, he had drawn attention to himself in his unit through "insolent behavior." The combination of these factors led the court to find in favor of the death sentence.[11]

If a defendant was given a relatively mild sentence, the reviewing opinion of a judge at one of the Military Courts of Appeals would often increase its severity up to and including the death penalty. In one instance, the court of the army garrison in Vienna had sentenced Anton Melzheimer, a corporal in the naval artillery, to "only" ten years in a penitentiary for desertion. Since Melzheimer was serving in a unit not on active duty at the time, the court was of the opinion that no particularly harsh punishment was required to "maintain discipline among the troops"; furthermore, the same loyalty to the Führer and the nation could not be expected of him as of a full-blooded member of the *Volk,* since he was part Jewish and should never have been drafted at all. After the commander-in-chief of the Western Naval Command had set aside the verdict and after a second trial had resulted in a sentence of "only" fifteen years, Admiral Dönitz as the navy's supreme legal authority set aside the second verdict, because he considered the death penalty absolutely "necessary." When yet another trial, this time before the Navy Court in Berlin, ended once again with a sentence of fifteen years in a penitentiary, the verdict was set aside for a third time; the leadership of the navy was not fighting for a principle. The chief of the navy's Legal Department, Joachim Rudolphi, found it absurd that the defendant's Jewishness was regarded as an extenuating circumstance. He wanted to prevent at all costs "that the Jewish defendant receives better treatment than one of German blood." On July 20, 1944, the fourth trial, held once again before the Navy Court, finally resulted in the desired death sentence. It was carried out the following day.[12]

It was not always the case, however, that superiors intervened in order to have a sentence made harsher. Even the worst crimes could be overlooked if they furthered the aims of "total war." On December 29, 1942, the Field Court-Martial of the Seventh Air Force Division in Smolensk had condemned to death Hans Georg L., a highly decorated first lieutenant (Trophy of Honor for Outstanding Achievements in the Air War, German Gold Cross). L. had had three soldiers in his company shot in the back for stealing food and cigarettes and reported to his superiors that their deaths had been the result of enemy action. However, he had previously announced in a company order, "I will not have these traitors to their comrades charged in a court, so that they can sit out the war behind the lines while our best men bleed to death up here." Instead, he would see to it that they and their like were "destroyed root and branch." At the request of L.'s superior officers, Hitler—who had declared "matters pertaining to officers" his personal preserve—commuted the sentence to imprisonment in a fortress. In addition, the sentence was suspended and L. given an opportunity to prove himself on especially dangerous stretches of the front lines. The war hero "redeemed" himself at Monte Cassino. The "Hermann Göring" tank and paratroop division then requested that L. be allowed to go unpunished and be given a special promotion, since he had shown outstanding leadership qualities and was a devoted soldier and National Socialist. Thereupon the three-fold killer was indeed promoted and awarded the Knight's Cross.[13]

In view of the fact that the military courts were contributing their share to the enormous losses of soldiers—the number of condemned men added up to several divisions, after all—even commanders whose severity and ruthlessness were proverbial sometimes had to restrain the military judges and reduce the penalties.

One such instance involved Anton Reschny, a seventeen-year-old called up as part of the last mobilization effort in August 1944. After an air raid in Vienna, while voluntarily helping to clear out some houses that were structurally unsafe, he had taken an empty coin purse and two watches, one of which he immediately gave away. Only a week after he was drafted, when he had not yet even been instructed in the duties of a soldier, Reschny was brought up before the Court-Martial of the 177th Division. The charge was theft under exploitation of wartime conditions, a violation of the Decree on Asocial Elements. The maximum sentence under the decree was the death penalty, although according to the law on criminal prosecution of minors the maximum sentence for a seventeen-year-old was ten years' imprisonment. The presiding judge was Erich Schwinge, an officer in the reserves and in civilian life a professor of criminal law and author of the most widely used commentary on military criminal law. Judge Schwinge ignored the recommendation of the prosecutor and sentenced Reschny for "looting" according to the Military Criminal Code, which in contrast to the juvenile court code had no provisions for milder sentencing of minors. Schwinge had written in his commentary that "the practical significance of this regulation" lay in the fact that "the young soldier who has committed a military crime is denied the advantage of the law in the juvenile courts, chiefly for reasons of deterrence."[14] In general, Schwinge emphasized the "special significance of deterrence" in his commentary.[15]

Even military law punished looting with a prison sentence or with the milder penalty of imprisonment in a fortress; for particularly serious cases the maximum penalty was a life sentence in a penitentiary, and only the worst of the particularly serious cases were supposed to be punished by death. Reschny's act was actually less a case of looting than a case of petty larceny by a finder, but in spite of this and the obviously slight nature of the theft, the court condemned him to death. "Otherwise," the decision ran, "it is not possible to keep such elements in check." However, this verdict appeared too harsh for the supreme legal authority in Reschny's case, the commander of the Army Reserves, so Heinrich Himmler himself commuted the sentence to fifteen years in a penitentiary, and Anton Reschny survived.[16]

The more hopeless the military situation became, the more verdicts of guilty for "undermining morale" piled up. Paragraph 5 of the Decree on Extraordinary Criminal Regulations in Wartime provided the death penalty for anyone who "publicly solicits or encourages a refusal to carry out duties in the German or an allied army, or otherwise publicly attempts to paralyze or undermine the will of the German or an allied people to defend themselves with arms." Less serious cases of "undermining morale" were punishable by prison or penitentiary sentences.

The second part of this regulation came to be used in an almost inflationary manner as the war went on, so that the courts regarded any anti-Fascist remark or disparaging word about a Nazi leader as detrimental to the war effort. In effect, they were using the law to protect the stability of the National Socialist regime. An order of November 1, 1944, to the air force stated: "It goes without saying that anyone who expresses doubt concerning the Führer, criticizes him or his measures, spreads derogatory information about him, or defames him is without honor and deserves to die . . . Whoever expresses doubt concerning the final victory and thereby weakens others' resolve has also forfeited his life."[17] And this was in late 1944!

In one case a machinist named Arthur Weinert, in the presence of fellow soldiers, made the following comment about a photograph showing Hitler standing behind a fence: "Thank God they've put that madman behind bars. We've got him to thank for this war—he was the one who wanted it." A Navy Court thereupon gave him a ten-year penitentiary sentence, but the supreme commander of the Northern District set the verdict aside. He was of the opinion that the death penalty was called for, since the remark's meaning was obvious and it could not be regarded as "a slip of the tongue while under the influence of alcohol." A second trial resulted in a death sentence that was confirmed by Admiral Dönitz, who ordered it executed on May 4, 1945 (only four days before the capitulation).[18]

The "total war" increasingly blurred all distinctions between the troops in the field and the civilian population, and—as enemy troops penetrated ever deeper into German territory—between the actual front and the "home front" as well. The result was the virtual disappearance of all difference between military and civilian criminal justice. Punishing "underminers of morale" could not alter the fact that the war was a lost cause, however, and in spite of all the "bitter end" propaganda, more and more Germans were coming to doubt the existence of the Führer's "miracle weapons" that were supposed to bring "final victory." Since the system could hardly keep up with the sheer numbers of skeptics, minister of justice Otto Thierack promulgated a new decree on February 15, 1945: the "Decree for the Establishment of Summary Courts in Areas of the Reich Threatened by the Enemy."[19] These courts consisted of a presiding judge assisted by a party political officer and a military officer, and were "responsible for all criminal acts endangering the effectiveness or determination of Germany to fight." The judges were restricted to verdicts of the death sentence, acquittal, or transferral of the case to a regular court; in practice, however, only death and acquittal were real alternatives, since the judges usually realized that the advance of Allied troops made a transfer equivalent to acquittal.

The closer the end of the war came, with the Allied armies deep inside the Reich and more and more Germans convinced of the impossibility of victory, the greater the frenzy of these new courts to intimidate the exhausted population. Whoever surrendered to Allied troops, hung a white sheet out of a window, or attempted to convince others of the futility of further resistance was caught in their machinery, charged with undermining morale, and executed without pity.

In 1945, a week before Easter, American tank troops had passed through the town of Lohr in Franconia, and the local population regarded the war as over. Shortly thereafter two Nazi party officials turned up, however, with instructions to organize a last-ditch defense effort and to establish a Summary Court. Judge Koob of the local Petty Court was placed in charge. Employed at the Lohr hospital at that time was a certain Dr. Brand, who while a party member was also a morphine addict with a loose tongue at times. When a nurse asked him what should be done with patients if enemy troops arrived, he replied that he would personally go out to meet the Americans with a white flag. On the evening of Easter Saturday, he was heard telling people in a restaurant that the Nazi party district leader had given him instructions to hand Lohr over to the Americans. Called on the carpet by Judge Koob, he repeated his claim in the same terms. He was arrested that very night, and Koob informed the district leader. The party official thereupon named two persons to form a Summary Court with Judge Koob and appointed a lieutenant in the reserves as prosecutor, although he had no authorization, and neither the assisting judges nor the prosecutor fulfilled the minimal requirements of the decree. The "court" convened at once, with the clearly intoxicated district leader as sole witness. He denied giving Dr. Brand any instructions, and after a ten-minute trial the physician was sentenced to death for "aiding and abetting the enemy and undermining morale." Koob had neglected to inform his assistants about the possibility of transferring the case, so they did not know there was a further alternative beyond the death penalty or acquittal. Without confirmation by the proper authority, the Reich commissar for defense, the verdict was carried out by a firing squad on the afternoon of Easter Sunday. It was the last opportunity, since American troops had already begun shelling the town and captured it on Easter Monday.[20]

It was difficult to bring this legal machinery to a halt once it had been set in motion, and the judges were obviously so caught up in the Nazi obsession with extermination that they could not imagine a return to other legal categories after the regime's collapse.

On May 4, 1945, a capitulation proclamation was signed in Lüneburg for the German troops in Holland, Denmark, and the North German regions of Friesland, Bremen, and Schleswig-Holstein. The cease-fire included the German torpedo-boats in the harbor of Svendborg, Denmark. At dawn on May 6, four sailors named Wehrmann, Schilling, Gail, and Schwalenberg, who had decided to desert, left their posts and set out for home on foot. They were soon seized, however, and charged with "an aggravated case of desertion in the field." A Summary Court under a presiding staff judge named Holzwig sentenced them to death—five days after the partial capitulation and one day after the unconditional surrender of the entire German Reich had gone into effect. On May 10, the sentences were carried out by a firing squad and the bodies thrown into the sea.[21]

It was not the only execution to take place at such a late date. After receiving the May 8 order of the High Command of the Armed Forces to cease all hostilities, the commander of the Mountain Artillery Regiment stationed in Norway had issued the order to his units, "We will fight Bolsheviks even after midnight." This order met with resistance in the Fourth Company of the regiment, where the noncommissioned officers and men were fearful of being shot as irregulars if they obeyed it. They decided to cross the border to the safety of nearby Sweden, but only forty-eight of the sixty soldiers made it there. The other twelve were caught and brought before a Court-Martial on charges of mutiny and desertion. On May 10 the court, presided over by a senior field judge named Spies, gave six of them long penitentiary sentences and sentenced the soldiers Rudolf Zatsch, Josef Wenzl, Leopold Wickenhauser, and Helmut Feyertag to death. The decision stated, "The accused acted . . . with the intention of permanently deserting their duty to serve in the army . . . A man who decides to abandon his comrades when they are still courageously holding out and to abandon his German fatherland in its darkest hour and time of greatest need has earned, on general principles and without further justification, the sentence of death." The divisional commander, Colonel

Remold, gave the verdicts his emphatic approval, and they were confirmed by General Field Marshal Jodl in Narvik over the telephone. The sentences were carried out two days after the war had come to a complete end. The minutes of the execution noted, "The command 'Fire!' was given at 10:16. The condemned men died instantly." Even as late as May 18, the same court sentenced to death in absentia nine of the men who had fled to Sweden. The decision in their case concluded with the statement: "The harshest punishment should be meted out to the guilty parties, particularly at the present time, when unity is all." And once again, Colonel Remold urged his superiors "to confirm the sentence and to issue an order for execution in case they were apprehended."[22]

Unfortunately, the Allies failed to put an immediate stop to the German system of military justice and its machinations. They did in general abolish the military courts, but allowed the Field Courts-Martial to continue operating after the capitulation, in order to ensure discipline during the demobilization. Officially, these courts were now authorized to impose only sentences of up to two years in prison and required approval from the Allied military government for anything exceeding that. In fact, however, they continued to operate along the old lines. Corporal Kurt Petzold learned this to his sorrow. Confident that the end of the Nazi era had arrived, he refused to carry out an order from his battery commander, saying, "Those days are gone for good. I'm a free man. You're finished, you Nazi pigs. This war was your fault. I'm going to tell the British what Nazi pigs you are—then my day will come."

Petzold was mistaken: "his day" had not yet arrived. Instead, on May 29, 1945, he was sentenced by a military court under the navy staff judge Dr. Hans Karl Filbinger, to six months in prison for refusing to obey orders and "provoking displeasure," as the crime of "undermining morale" had been called before the Nazi era. The decision criticized the accused for "exhibiting defiant and undisciplined conduct . . . since May 1, although he is a former leader in the Hitler Youth." In addition, by removing the swastikas from the insignia on his cap and uniform jacket, he "demonstrated his intention to rebel against discipline and order. His remarks reveal how far morale has degenerated."[23]

21

Resistance from the Bench

Roland Freisler was certainly exaggerating when he announced triumphantly in 1935, "The German judicial system can take pride in being the first branch of government in the Third Reich to carry out in its personnel policies, throughout the Reich and at all levels of the civil service, the principle that the movement, the people, and the state are one."[1] Not every judge conformed with this description or with the ideal expressed by Curt Rothenberger, Freisler's successor as undersecretary at the Ministry of Justice: "The apolitical, neutral judge of the liberal multiparty state, who stands on the sidelines, must become a National Socialist with sure instincts and a feeling for the great political aims of the movement. Politics, philosophy, and justice are one and the same."[2]

Refusals to cooperate did occur in the judiciary. After the war, Hubert Schorn, a retired County Court judge, filled a whole book with accounts of judges' resistance and went so far as to claim that "the overwhelming majority" of judges had opposed the system. Schorn added, however, that a judge had "no alternative but to apply the unjust laws, and risked . . . his own life if he objected."[3] Fritz Hartung, a judge of the postwar Supreme Court in West Germany who for many years had served under presiding judge and Supreme Court president Erwin Bumke on the Third Criminal Panel of the previous Supreme Court (among other things, he had helped shape its interpretation of the Race Laws), likewise later claimed that if judges had made any other decisions, they would have risked their lives.[4]

Two prominent judges were in fact executed for resistance during the Third Reich. Dr. Karl Sack, a general staff judge, was arrested on September 8, 1944, and murdered on February 4, 1945, in the Flossenbürg concentration camp. Dr. Johann von Dohnanyi, a Supreme Court judge, was killed in the camp at Sachsenhausen, presumably on April 8, 1945.[5] Both men paid with their lives for their participation in the plot against Hitler. Their honorable conduct and resistance could have served as an example to the rest of the judiciary. It is a matter of record, however, that neither judge was persecuted for professional conduct. On the contrary, both of them had had highly successful careers in the Third Reich. Dohnanyi, born in 1902, had been temporarily assigned to the Ministry of Justice as a very young man; after a few other assignments, he was appointed to a regular post there on June 1, 1933, and promoted on March 1, 1934. In 1938, having just turned thirty-six, he became the youngest member of the Supreme Court,[6] where the average age at the time of appointment was fifty-three. After three years on the Third Criminal Panel under presiding judge Bumke, Dohnanyi left the court. He had clearly become an opponent of the regime before this, and for a long time had been keeping a record of "crimes committed by party leaders." In 1941, Admiral Walter Wilhelm Canaris recruited him for the intelligence service, where he played a key role in the circle around Canaris and Hans Oster. He was arrested on April 5, 1943, for (among other things) illegal currency transactions, since he had been helping Jews transfer their assets to Switzerland. Not until after his arrest did investigators turn up private records that documented his extensive work for the resistance movement.[7]

Judge Sack was named to the Supreme Military Court Panel for Treason and High Treason in 1938; he was assigned to the Army High Command in 1942, and made a general staff judge in 1944. Sack may have been one of "the noblest and most courageous figures in the resistance movement," as the historian Gerhard Ritter said,[8] but the accuracy of Schorn's claim that he influenced "the judges working under him . . . to maintain the rule of law with his own spirit of benevolence"[9] is best tested against the decisions handed down by the Supreme Court-Martial.

The numerous other "martyrs of the judiciary" cited by Schorn were either attorneys or Jewish judges whom the Nazis removed from office and then murdered.

All the same, there is one documented case of resistance in which a judge opposed the system in the course of carrying out his professional duties. He was Dr. Lothar Kreyssig, a judge at the Court of Guardianship in the town of Brandenburg, on the Havel River. Kreyssig, who was appointed to the County Court in 1928, had always been considered a good judge by his superiors, until the president of his district Court of Appeals noted in his file that "since the spring of 1934 his conduct has given grounds for complaint, in that he has drawn considerable attention to himself as a member of the Lutheran Confessional Church." For a time, he was even president of the Confessional Church Synod in Saxony. After

Kreyssig had committed numerous minor acts of insubordination, such as departing early from a ceremony in his court when a bust of Hitler was being unveiled, and protesting publicly against the suspension of three judges after passage of the Law for Restoration of the Professional Civil Service, the head of the Nazi party in Saxony lodged a demand for his dismissal with the Reich Ministry of Justice in March 1936. During the summer of 1937, Kreyssig received a formal warning from the president of the Prussian Supreme Court, under whose jurisdiction his court now fell, because he had "violated regulations of the press laws" by distributing leaflets for the Confessional Church. A formal investigation was begun, with the aim of removing him from the bench, after he referred to Nazi church policies as "injustice . . . masquerading in the form of law." When he publicly protested the arrest of the prominent theologian Martin Niemöller in June 1938, a criminal investigation was even opened on suspicion of "misuse of the pulpit" (paragraph 130a of the Criminal Code) and infringement of the 1934 Law against Treacherous Attacks on the State and Party.

At his own request, Kreyssig was reassigned to the Petty Court in Brandenburg, where he also functioned as a judge for the Court of Guardianship. When he learned that inmates were being secretly removed from the mental hospital in Brandenburg-Görden and killed, he sent a letter about these occurrences to the president of the Prussian Supreme Court, asking for "clarification and advice." One passage of the letter ran, " 'Whatever benefits the people is lawful': in the name of this terrible doctrine, which has yet to be contradicted by those whom it behooves to protect the law in Germany, entire areas of communal life have been placed beyond the reach of the law—the concentration camps, for example, and now institutions for the mentally ill as well." [10] This earned Kreyssig a summons to appear at the Reich Ministry of Justice, where undersecretary Roland Freisler personally listened to his complaints but failed to change his thinking on the matter. Kreyssig then issued injunctions to several hospitals in his capacity as judge of the Court of Guardianship, prohibiting them from transferring wards of his court without his permission. In addition, he brought criminal charges against Nazi party leader Phillipp Bouhler before the public prosecutor in Potsdam, since Freisler had named Bouhler to him as the man responsible for the euthanasia program "T4."

Once again, the stubborn judge was summoned to the Ministry of Justice, where this time minister Franz Gürtner himself tried to persuade him that the program had been an "order of the Führer" and was therefore lawful. Gürtner also pointed out that if Kreyssig "did not recognize the will of the Führer as the fount of law," then he could no longer be tolerated as a judge. Soon thereafter, Kreyssig wrote Gürtner that since his conscience would not allow him to withdraw the injunctions against the hospitals, he was requesting permission to retire ahead of schedule. Kreyssig was granted temporary permission to retire on December 10, 1940; this was finally confirmed on March 4, 1942, and included full pension rights. In April the criminal investigation against him was closed, and from then on the Third Reich left the courageous judge in peace.[11]

Kreyssig's case is extremely revealing. It shows that if a judge refused to accept the injustices of the system, the worst he had to fear was early retirement. Judge Hermanns was another example of a man who took early retirement. An "old comrade" who had joined the Nazi party on February 1, 1932, and quickly risen to the position of presiding judge at a County Court, he gradually withdrew his support from the dictatorship and finally sent a 130-page report to the Reich Ministry of Justice in 1943, documenting many cases in which local party and government officials had broken the law and overstepped the bounds of their authority.[12]

However, most of the instances of "resistance" cited by Schorn tend to read as follows: "County Court Judge Husanger was rejected for membership in the National Socialist party as a previous member of the Center party and was transferred to Bochum. He was unable to return to Cologne until 1946."[13] It is difficult to discern any real act of resistance in many of the case histories recounted in Schorn's book, especially in those of the more prominent judges. Schorn mentions by name Paul Vogt, presiding judge of one of the Supreme Court panels, Supreme Court judges Niethammer and Schäfer, Supreme Court judge and later president of the West German Supreme Court Hermann Weinkauff, and attorney Carl Kirchner, later a judge of the West German Supreme Court, as "examples of men who will go down in history, among many that have remained unknown, as courageous defenders of law and justice."[14] For anyone familiar with the role these men played in the history of the Supreme Court of the Third Reich, such extravagant praise reads like satire. Vogt, who had been a member of the Nazi party since 1932, led the investigation of the "Cheka" case, the largest trial of Communist party members during the Weimar Republic, and the scandalously one-sided investigation into the Reichstag fire, when he was responsible for keeping the defendants in chains illegally for months. Later, as presiding judge of the Second Criminal Panel of the Supreme Court, he was responsible for the worst excesses committed in the name of the Race Laws. Niethammer was a leading commentator on criminal law and a shaper of National Socialist legal practice. Weinkauff joined the Nazi party in 1933 and later received a decoration for loyal service.[16] Kirchner, head of one of the departments at the Reich Office of Public Prosecutions, showed great zeal in writing pleas of nullity, which regularly aimed at increasing sentences to the death penalty, since, in his words, "the protection of the community of the *Volk* requires that the accused be eliminated."[17] His department entered twice as many pleas of this kind as all the other departments combined.[18]

No matter how hard one searches for stout-hearted men among the judges of the Third Reich, for judges who refused to serve the regime from the bench, there remains a grand total of one: Dr. Lothar Kreyssig, judge of the Court of Guardianship in Brandenburg on the Havel. Other, less striking cases of judicial resistance to Nazi terror must surely have occurred now and then, and remain to be discovered. Yet they are far from representative of German judges, the overwhelming majority of whom shared responsibility for the terror.

The degree to which the judiciary became a smoothly functioning part of the National Socialists' system of intimidation—today they prefer to say they became "enmeshed" or "entangled"—becomes clearer when one looks at the number of death sentences passed. There are no exact statistics, but Martin Hirsch, a retired judge of the Federal Constitutional Court, has estimated that the courts handed down "at least 40,000 to 50,000 death sentences," not counting the verdicts in the summary proceedings of the military and the police, and that approximately 80 percent of these were carried out.[19] A more recent publication from the Ministry of Justice of the Federal Republic mentions the figure 32,000,[20] while the *Brown Book* published in the German Democratic Republic sets it as high as 80,000.[21] In his book *The People's Court in the National Socialist State,* Walter Wagner, a former federal prosecutor general, reports that 1,807 executions were carried out in the Brandenburg Penitentiary alone, 1,785 in the Plötzensee prison, and 1,184 in Vienna.[22] Figures from the "Department of Military Losses" of the High Command document 11,500 death sentences passed by Courts-Martial up to the middle of 1944, 90 percent of which were carried out.[23] The "lower" estimates of how many people were condemned by the judicial system are all based on official publications of the Third Reich, which cease in mid-1944 and are also very incomplete. They contain neither the "NN" prisoners nor the enormous numbers of death sentences passed in occupied territories. Since it was the courts in the eastern regions that made the greatest use of the death penalty, and since the brutal suppression of all opposition within Germany itself was just entering its bloodiest phase in the summer of 1944, an estimate of 80,000 victims probably comes closest to the truth.

Comparisons with figures from Germany's two Fascist allies, Italy and

Japan, reveal that this brutality was unparalleled. In both countries, mass arrests of political opponents did occur, and there were also irregular courts, harsher laws to protect the governments, and internment camps. However, the Special Tribunal established in Fascist Italy in 1926, which in personnel and procedures more closely resembled a military court, handed down only twenty-nine death sentences and seven sentences of life imprisonment in 5,319 trials. In Japan, 6,000 persons were arrested after passage of the "Peace Laws" of 1925, but charges were pressed against fewer than 10 percent of them. And even though Japan instituted the death penalty in 1928 for crimes against the state, the German spy Richard Sorge and his Japanese informer Hozumi Ozaki remained the only two people sentenced to death by civilian courts in that country.[24] The jurists of the Third Reich had no peers anywhere in the world.

· III ·

The Aftermath

22

Collapse and Reconstruction

The unconditional surrender of the Great German Reich not only brought an end to institutionalized terror; it brought an end to the entire judicial system. In Proclamation 1, the commander-in-chief of the Allied forces ordered that "all German courts . . . within the occupied territory are closed until further notice."[1] Jurisdiction was withdrawn from the People's Court, the Special Courts, the SS Police Courts, and all the other forms of special criminal justice. Their functions were taken over to a large extent by the Allied troops themselves, and the authorities even considered closing all German courts for ten years and replacing them with a "colonial" system, so that a new generation of judges could be educated in the meantime.[2]

Most German jurists were bewildered by so much "mistrust" toward the judges of the Third Reich.[3] They patched up their partly bombed-out offices as best they could and clung to the illusion that the previous hierarchy and allocation of functions would go on much as before. As one report of 1945 put it, "They carried on through the fiction that business would continue as usual."[4] Even though the highest court in the land had also been closed "until further notice," various public prosecutors continued to send inquiries addressed to "The Supreme Court, Leipzig" well into 1946, seeking information about the files "sent for review of the plea of nullity entered."[5] Clearly, they wanted to finish up the legal terror of the Nazi Special Courts in a proper manner, which included making upward adjustments to the original sentences.

The Allies were unable to agree on a radical solution to the problem. By June 1945, the German Petty Courts and County Courts were already back in operation, and the first presiding judges were appointed to the Courts of Appeals in the fall.[6] Nonetheless, the intent was thoroughly to eliminate Nazis from the judicial system in the Western zones of occupation. Thus, the Control Commission's Law 4 of November 30, 1945, stated: "To effect the reorganization of the judicial system, all former members of the Nazi party who have been more than nominal participants in its activities and all other persons who directly followed the punitive practices of the Hitler regime must be dismissed from appointments as judges and prosecutors and will not be admitted to these appointments."[7]

It soon became evident, however, that such draconian de-Nazification measures would keep the German courts closed for good. In Westphalia, for example, 93 percent of court personnel had been members of either the Nazi party or one of its subsidiary organizations.[8] In the district of the Bamberg Court of Appeals, 302 out of 309 jurists had been in the party, and at the Petty Court in Schweinfurt the figure was a solid 100 percent.[9] In the American enclave of Bremen in the British Zone, the Americans found a grand total of two judges who could be considered to have an untainted record. One solution was to call back judges who had retired prior to 1933, and to employ attorneys on the bench part time. It soon became clear that these measures would not solve the problem. The British decided to treat all jurists who had joined the Nazi party after 1937 as having a clean slate, including former army judges who for a long time had not been allowed to join. When these steps also failed to produce a sufficient number of acceptable judges, they came up with the "piggy-back method": For every untainted judge, one with a bad record could also be employed. Even this restriction was lifted in June 1946, and every jurist could be considered for the bench who had been through de-Nazification.[10]

When the judges from the Weimar Republic were sent into retirement for the second time, their places were quickly taken by the bulk of Special Court judges and former SA members, who by this time had gone through the very liberal de-Nazification procedures. The de-Nazification commissions of the British Zone and the similar tribunals of the American Zone had begun with strong measures, but were soon classifying virtually everyone in either Category 4 ("followers") or Category 5 ("exonerated"). Other Allied authorities viewed with concern the "returning stream of Nazis to the German judiciary and judicial system" that resulted.[11] By 1948, 30 percent of the presiding judges and 80 to 90 percent of the assisting judges at the County Courts in the British Zone were former party members.[12] The other western zones presented a similar picture.

A report from the American commissioner for the State of Bavaria to the high commissioner, John McCloy, entitled "Some Aspects of Re-Nazification in Bavaria," reveals that in 1949, 752 of 924 judges and public prosecutors were former Nazis, or 81 percent. According to the study, "the return of party members to positions of power and influence [is] proof of how little has changed."[13] For example in the district of Lower Bavaria/Upper Palatinate between November 1948 and March 1949, when government agencies were being reopened and new staff was being hired, it had been impossible to find jobs for fifty-eight former government employees who had not been Nazis. But during the same period, in the same district, sixty-nine former Nazi party members had been reemployed in some sector of public service.

In his book *De-Nazification: A Chapter of Postwar German History*, the historian Justus Fürstenau has described the conflict of that time as one between the political parties of the center and the right, who were pressing for the rehiring of former National Socialists, and the Social Democrats and Communists on the left, who wanted to see preference given to anti-Fascists and the unincriminated. "The old conflict arose once again," Fürstenau writes, "between the bourgeois parties' orientation toward the rule of law and the . . . political considerations of the parties on the left."[14] The "rule of law" carried the day everywhere. A stream of civil servants was pouring from the previously German-occupied territories and the Soviet zone of occupation to the east, and from Alsace-Lorraine and other occupied regions to the west, into the three western zones, which taken together did not cover even half the area of the old "Greater German Reich," and all of these people were seeking employment. This resettling led to a concentration of (former) Nazis such as even the Third Reich had not known. Some government agencies had more party members working at them in 1948–1949 than they had had under Hitler.[15]

In order to create more room for ex-Nazi civil servants in the now overfilled agencies, the "outsiders" hired with limited contracts after 1945 were let go, especially the numerous people given preference by the De-Nazification Tribunals—people who had usually been victims of Nazi persecution and opponents of Fascism. Although they had often been promised further employment in government service, they had no legal claim to it. There was a general sense of relief at being rid of the unpopular "de-Nazifiers." Only a minority of them found other work quickly; two thirds remained dependent for a long time on welfare and unemployment benefits.[16] The exclusion of these outsiders, who could have provided a counterweight in the government agencies of the postwar period, accelerated the process of re-Nazification that was to have a profound effect on the development of democracy in West Germany. The few experienced public servants without an incriminating past, who were needed so urgently, were now considered to have "incriminated" themselves by supporting de-Nazification; in the early years of the Federal Republic, this was a far worse stigma than having been a National Socialist.

The ex-Nazis had no real legal right to employment either, but legal scholars—many of them seriously incriminated themselves—simply claimed they did. In the late forties, jurists were heatedly arguing the question of whether the German Reich had ceased to exist or whether it had continued after the unconditional surrender—a discussion which at first could seem somewhat macabre. Hans Kelsen, a professor of constitutional law who had been dismissed by the Nazis and who was now living in exile, argued in several publications, against the majority of his German colleagues, that there could be "no continuity between the defeated Nazi state and the new, democratic Germany" in a legal sense: "the democratic Germany that will join international organizations should be a society with no legal ties to Nazi Germany."[17] For this opinion, Kelsen was "expatriated" for a second time in the early fifties. In 1954, a West German professor of constitutional law reported that scholars had "defended the continuing existence of the German state with a kind of moral unanimity," and as if to demonstrate to what extent the old ways of thinking had survived, he continued, "Teachers of constitutional law who were not in Germany . . . cannot be counted in the question of moral unanimity."[18]

The seemingly absurd debate about the cessation or continued existence of the German Reich was not just an academic exercise, however. It had quite genuine relevance to the question of whether civil servants of the Reich still had a claim to their old status. At issue was whether these people had had their connections with the civil service permanently severed when the Allied forces of occupation had dismissed them, or whether they had merely been temporarily suspended. The reformers in the military government had always assumed that dismissal of incriminated German officials meant permanent loss of office and of all claims to benefits such as pensions. In the beginning, the German authorities shared this view. A directive from the State Ministry of Baden-Württemberg of December 5, 1946, stated: "Officials removed from office by the military government, by order of the military government or otherwise, are to be regarded . . . as dismissed, with the consequent loss of all their rights as civil servants."[19]

In the debates of the Parliamentary Council, which was meeting to draft a new German constitution, the delegates—many of whom were high-level civil servants themselves in various ministries—could not agree on a policy for civil servants with an incriminating Nazi past. The first version prepared by the drafting committee had included the statement: "Any person who was a civil servant or government employee on May 8, 1945, cannot claim a right to reemployment on these grounds."[20] In the final debate, however, the council decided to postpone a solution to the problem, and Article 131 of the Basic Law (*Grundgesetz*), as it was eventually passed, directed future lawmakers "to regulate by federal law . . . the rights of persons employed in the civil service as of May 8, 1945, including refugees and those expelled from their homes, who ceased to be employed there for reasons other than those covered by the civil service or salary laws and who until now have either not found employment at all or not at the former level."

When the Bundestag (Federal Parliament) met to discuss such a law, no mention at all was made of the reasons why the judges and civil servants had been dismissed. Instead, members of parties across the entire political spectrum spoke of the need to help these "admirable people"[21] who had "spent a lifetime in public service,"[22] so that "the group affected by Article 131 can feel they are recognized as valuable members of the state."[23] References were also made to the "reestablishment of a constitutional state," a task for which "the contribution of their knowledge, experience, and manpower" was needed.[24]

The statute referred to colloquially as "the 131 Law" was passed on May 11, 1951, effective retroactively as of April 1. In effect, it gave a foundation in law to the reintegration of Nazi officials in the civil service, a process that was by then almost complete in any case.[25] After an amendment was added in August 1953, the statute gave all public servants of the National Socialist state a legal claim to reemployment, and also the right to claim back pay for the time they had not been able to work.[26] The sole exceptions were agents of the Gestapo and civil servants who had been classed as "major offenders" in de-Nazification proceedings. In addition, the law required that at least 20 percent of employees in all departments of public administration be former Nazis; departments failing to meet this requirement would be fined an amount equal to the salaries thus "saved." These new legal claims and the quota system now meant that old party members had to be given first priority in hiring, and thus more than 90 percent of the Nazi officials dismissed after 1945 found their way back into public service. Since public funds were so limited and the civil service bureaucracy so overstaffed (by 1949 the German administrative regions, or *Länder*, were virtually bankrupt), for all practical purposes former membership in the Nazi party became a requirement for joining the civil service.

At the same time, Article 132 of the Basic Law empowered the government to dismiss the whole class of "outsiders" mentioned above or, if they had been appointed for life after 1945, to place them "in retirement, on waiting lists, or in a position with lower pay." These "outsiders" were all those appointed to the judiciary or the civil service after the war who had not been eligible for promotion during the Third Reich. Since, in the Nazi era, political reliability and "racial purity" had been prerequisites for admission to both administrative training and universities, those who had been unable to complete their careers had all been political or "racial" undesirables. The effect of Article 131 (with its corresponding law) and Article 132 was thus just the same as if the Nazi "Law for Restoration of the Professional Civil Service" of 1933 had been reintroduced.

Nevertheless, passage of the 131 Law met with opposition from many members of the legal profession, because it did not provide a claim to reemployment for all Nazis without exception. A test case of the law came before the Federal Constitutional Court in the form of a suit by thirty-four former Gestapo officials. Contrary to the widely held opinion that the German Reich had not ceased to exist on May 8, 1945, and that civil servants therefore remained in office (a view also expressed in the government's position paper on the law), the Federal Constitutional Court stated clearly on December 17, 1953: "All connection between civil servants and the state ceased on May 8, 1945."[27] German jurists reacted with almost unanimous protest. The Federal Supreme Court decided not to heed the decision, which had the force of law—the only time in the history of the Federal Republic that such a judges' mutiny has occurred.[28] In contrast to the Federal Constitutional Court, the Federal Supreme Court was made up almost entirely of judges who had served on the bench during the Third Reich. The Grand Civil Panel of the Supreme Court under presiding judge Hermann Weinkauff dismissed the injustices committed by National Socialist judges and officials that had been painstakingly compiled and cited by the Federal Constitutional Court, calling them mere "window dressing" with only a negligible effect on these people's actual work: "The great majority of German officials . . . remained loyal above all to the state and its legitimate tasks, . . . despite infamous and unlawful pressure." The personal oath of loyalty each had sworn to Hitler had applied not to each official personally, but to the official as the "supreme authority of the state."[29]

On February 19, 1957, in a second decision related to the 131 Law,[30] the Federal Constitutional Court dealt with the further view commonly held by jurists that, all in all, the everyday practices of the legal system during the Third Reich had followed the traditional rule of law. To back up its argument about "window dressing," the Federal Supreme Court had cited the leading legal scholars of postwar Germany, but unfortunately, and embarrassingly, most of them were identical to those of Nazi Germany. In response, the Constitutional Court quoted, not without relish, what these same authors had written earlier; it concluded that it could see no reason "to take their recent comments more seriously than their earlier ones."[31] Drawing up a complete list of all forms of jurisdiction and administration, the Constitutional Court demonstrated to the Supreme Court judges how the law had been administered in such a way that all fields, even those that seemed unpolitical on the surface, had shared responsibility for the injustices of the Nazi dictatorship.

The two decisions of the Federal Constitutional Court based on the 131 Law represent crowning achievements of the German legal system in a democratic and republican spirit. They are also the most serious attempts undertaken until now to free the system from the shadows of the past. Yet neither the rest of the judiciary nor the legislative branch of the government was willing to follow the lead of the Federal Constitutional Court in dealing with this chapter of history. They continued to gloss over and cover up the truth, and to show favor to former officials of the dictatorship. In June 1961, the Bundestag passed a law extending considerably the scope of the already controversial 131 Law.[32] During the debate, the Free Democrats had proposed to add the following sentences to the bill: "Former career officers and noncommissioned officers of SS military units in service before May 8, 1945, can be granted pensions upon application. Proof must be furnished that they served only in functions such as those of the regular army."[33] The majority of legislators were unwilling to include this provision in the law explicitly, but the federal government did assure the former officers that they would proceed in this way all the same, and that the minister of finance had already budgeted the necessary funds.[34]

Putting such a regulation into practice then required clarification of what counted as "service similar to that in the regular army." The Federal Social Court in Kassel established the following principle: "Anyone who saw service during the Second World War as a member of an SS combat unit (*Waffen-SS*) of a kind that, had these units not existed, would have been performed by soldiers in the regular army, is to be considered, as a rule at least, to have performed service similar to that in the regular army." With this clarification, the court recognized even the guard duty of the Second SS Death's Head Regiment at Dachau as "service similar to that in the regular army."[35]

· 23 ·

Restoration in the Legal System

There could be no real question of recalling to active service those who had been leaders of the legal profession during the Nazi era. If they were still living, however, the new German government granted them pensions corresponding to their former high offices. Thus, for example, the jurists who at Nuremberg in 1947 had been tried by the Americans, found guilty, and removed from office received pension payments covering even the time they had spent in prison. After April 1, 1951, the chief prosecutor at the People's Court, Ernst Lautz, received a federal state chief prosecutor's monthly pension of 1,342 marks; this amount was reduced to 762 marks only in the 1960s.[1] Franz Schlegelberger (who had received the sum of 100,000 reichmarks from Hitler on his retirement in 1942), was paid a monthly pension of 2,894 marks, in addition to 160,000 marks in back pension—at a time when a skilled worker was earning about 400 marks per month. His successor as undersecretary at the Ministry of Justice, Curt Rothenberger, received 2,073 marks per month.[2] Only those few jurists with "political" posts were forced into retirement with a pension, however. Less prominent Nazi judges at high and even the highest levels were rehired within the judicial system, usually in a similar position, and often with a promotion or two.

Attempts were made quite openly to maintain continuity with the judicial system of the Third Reich. At the opening ceremonies of the Supreme Court of the British Zone, the court was coyly referred to as a "little *Reichsgericht*," and much was made of the coincidence that its first (and only) presiding judge, the former president of the Berlin Bar Association, Ernst Wolff, was a grandson of Eduard von Simson, the first president of the *Reichsgericht*.[3] Despite this, the Supreme Court of the British Zone distinguished itself from the other courts of the time by not adhering to the calamitous tradition of the *Reichsgericht* in either personnel or approach to the law. The slim volume of the court's decisions is a document of a rare sort in German legal history. Unbroken continuity with the tradition of the *Reichsgericht* was achieved only with the creation of the Federal Supreme Court in Karlsruhe. At the dedication ceremony on October 8, 1950, Thomas Dehler, then federal minister of justice, invoked "the memory of the great achievements of the *Reichsgericht*" and exclaimed, "My wish is that the spirit of that court may also pervade the work of the Federal Supreme Court."[4] In a *Festschrift* published on the occasion of the opening of the court, Georg Petersen, an official in the Federal Ministry of Justice, stated that one of the present government's chief aims was "to name to the Federal Supreme Court former members of the *Reichsgericht* familiar with its tradition," since "in addition to the visible tradition of the *Reichsgericht* there exists an invisible tradition, which can be gleaned from collections of its decisions, no matter how complete, only indirectly or not at all."[5]

The ministry's goal was soon achieved. Only four years later the Federal Supreme Court celebrated the seventy-fifth anniversary of the founding of the *Reichsgericht* as if it were its own jubilee, and the president of the court, Hermann Weinkauff, himself a member of the *Reichsgericht* from 1935 to 1945, declared with pride that the Federal Supreme Court had "taken over the heritage of the *Reichsgericht*."[6] Walter Strauss, then undersecretary in the Ministry of Justice, even addressed the gathering of Supreme Court justices with these words: "You are not celebrating today the seventy-fifth anniversary of a bygone court, although it would most assuredly deserve such a celebration. No, you are commemorating the founding of your own court seventy-five years ago . . . On October 1, 1950, the *Reichsgericht* [was] reopened." And he continued: "Just as our Federal Republic [was] established not as a new nation" but rather as "the immediate lawful continuation of the German Reich . . . , so we see the Federal Supreme Court not only as the lawful continuation of the *Reichsgericht* but as identical with it." By contrast, the five years from 1945 to 1950 (those years, that is to say, which were marked by hopes for a new and democratic beginning and by attempts by the Allied powers and democratically minded Germans to break with the disastrous traditions of German justice) were for Strauss "merely a tragic interval for the law."[7]

The Ministry of Justice had of course always attached great importance to tradition and continuity. Even in the Weimar period, the Reich Office of Justice (*Reichsjustizamt*), as the ministry was formerly called, had been a stronghold of reaction. Curt Joël had seen to that. Joël, the "steward of German law" who served as undersecretary to the constantly changing ministers of justice (there were twelve between 1920 and 1931 alone) and who was briefly minister himself in the second Brüning cabinet, played a key role in the development of the legal system of that era. During the Third Reich, Joël, a conservative German Nationalist by conviction, suffered from his Jewish background, which he had always regarded as a blemish himself. His friends in high places were able to save him from the fate of most German Jews, however, although not from a great deal of humiliation. He survived the Nazi era in relatively privileged circumstances in Berlin.

Joël's successor as senior civil servant in the Ministry of Justice in 1931 was Franz Schlegelberger, who continued as undersecretary during the Third Reich and even became acting minister of justice in 1941–1942. At the Nuremberg jurists' trial, he was given a life penitentiary sentence, but he was released in 1950. Under Schlegelberger and Freisler (the associate undersecretary), a senior prosecutor by the name of Günther Joël began making a name for himself. He joined the Nazi party on May 1, 1933, and was considered reliable enough to be assigned to the Central Office of Prosecutions in the Reich Ministry of Justice, the department responsible for tidying up the party's legal affairs. In 1937, Minister Gürtner appointed him to serve as the ministry's liaison with the SS, its Security Service, and the Gestapo; in 1941 he was promoted within the civil service; and in 1943 he was made prosecutor general in Hamm and an officer in the SS. It was Günther Joël who masterminded the arrest and trial of Czech leader Alois Eliáš in such a way that the Ministry of Justice was kept out of it, and he later became a key figure in the "night and fog" (or "NN") program.[8] For these activities, he was sentenced at Nuremberg in 1947 to ten years in a penitentiary, but was then granted amnesty and released in January 1951. Thereupon he was allowed to work undisturbed in the legal department of a large corporation.[9]

In 1947 another Günther Joël, son of the former undersecretary and minister Curt Joël, entered the civil service and swiftly rose to become head of the Department of Trade and Finance Law in the Federal Ministry of Justice in 1950. The two Günther Joëls, one an official of the Ministry of Justice in the Third Reich and the other in the Federal Republic, are often confused with each other, but are in fact not related and certainly not identical. The second Günther Joël, son of Curt Joël, was an attorney in private practice in Berlin during the Third Reich and managed, by virtue of his connections to prominent figures in the legal profession, to intervene repeatedly on behalf of his Jewish father.

The first postwar undersecretary at the Federal Ministry of Justice was Walter Strauss, who was appointed in 1949 and remained in office for thirteen years under five successive ministers. Strauss had been expelled from the civil service in 1935 for "racial reasons," and managed to support himself during the Third Reich through "various forms of nongovernment legal activity."[10] After the war he helped found the Christian Democratic party, served as an undersecretary in the government of the State of Hesse, and was a member of the Parliamentary Council. In 1949, Liberal party member Thomas Dehler brought him to the Federal Ministry of Justice. In 1962 Walter Strauss became involved in the "*Spiegel* affair." [The "*Spiegel* affair" of 1962 involved charges, later proved unfounded, that the news magazine *Spiegel* had betrayed military secrets. The intimidating police-state tactics accompanying the editors' arrests and false statements by cabinet officials triggered widespread protest and a major government crisis in Bonn.—*Translator.*] Serving as department heads under him, in addition to Günther Joël, were Walter Roemer, in charge of the Department of Public Law and former first prosecutor at the Munich Special Court,[11] and Josef Schafheutle, in charge of the Department of Criminal Law and Criminal Procedure. As a civil servant at the Reich Ministry of Justice in 1933, Schafheutle had helped to draw up the special Nazi criminal laws for dealing with political offenders,[12] and along with Gürtner, Freisler, Thierack, and Lautz had drafted the laws governing criminal trials during the Third Reich. It was the same Schafheutle who was then placed in charge of the criminal laws of the new Federal Republic, and he clearly left his mark on them. Working under Schafheutle in his department, with special responsibility for political crimes, was Ernst Kanter, who had formerly been a judge on the Second Panel of the Supreme Court-Martial of the Reich, and after 1943 was "judge advocate general" and the highest-ranking judge with the High Command of the German Army in Denmark. Death sentences for at least 103 members of the Danish resistance movement had passed through his hands. At the Federal Ministry of Justice after the war, one of Kanter's responsibilities was coordinating the work of the General Commission on Criminal Law, and ironically it was he who was assigned to review the charges raised by the German Democratic Republic against former Nazi judges.[13] In 1958 Kanter was named presiding judge of the Third Criminal Panel of the Federal Supreme Court, responsible for political crimes, but in 1959 he was forced into early retirement by public protests.

He was replaced at the Ministry of Justice by Eduard Dreher. From Dreher's time in office as first prosecutor at the Innsbruck Special Court, several cases are documented in which he made a concerted effort to push through the death penalty for trivial offenses.[14] At the ministry, he was promoted to house expert on criminal law, and drafted all the intentional and "unintentional" amnesty laws. Since he was also "general adviser" to the General Commission on Criminal Law and author of the most widely used commentary on the Criminal Code, in which he provided the correct interpretation to go along with "his" laws, Dreher became the most influential man in the development of postwar criminal law.

Many other figures from the Third Reich found employment at the Federal Ministry of Justice, among them Franz Massfeller, who had written a commentary on the Nuremberg Race Laws and had represented the Reich Ministry of Justice at the Wannsee Conference on the "final solution" of the Jewish question,[15] and Heinrich Ebersberg, personal assistant to Otto Thierack when he was the Nazis' minister of justice. When he was placed on trial for his earlier activities at the Reich Ministry of Justice, Ebersberg testified that he had "been called to the Federal Ministry of Justice in 1954 by undersecretary Dr. Walter Strauss on the recommendation of the son of the former minister of justice, [Curt] Joël."[16] Ebersberg was promoted to his former rank at the ministry the same year.[17]

Although the Günther Joël who was an official in the Reich Ministry and found guilty at Nuremberg did not (despite what many people claim) later become an even higher official in the Federal Ministry, the confusingly identical names put one on the right track. The organization of the postwar judicial system in Germany and its relationship to that of the Nazi era cannot be explained simply as a matter of identity, but neither is it explained by cases of discontinuity in personnel, which are not so numerous. The history of the Ministry of Justice is symptomatic of the development of the German judicial system, and the startling "exchange of roles" by the two Günther Joëls warns one that a closer look is necessary to recognize the lines of tradition.

Just as judges from the higher ranks of the courts and the legal bureaucracy moved into the West German judicial system, so did many of the others from the Special and Military Courts, judges from the People's Court and judges from the Race Law trials. Wolfgang Möhl, author of the indictment against Ignatz Kazmierczak, became senior prosecutor at the Court of Appeals in Munich, and the judge in this scandalous trial, Dr. Kowalski, rose to the position of County Court judge in Essen. Fritz Sperrhake, prosecutor in the case of the railroad employee Hugo Göhring, became a County Court judge in Tübingen.[18] County Court judge Blankenburg, who had signed the death sentence of the office messenger Georg Hopfe, sat on the bench in Lower Saxony after 1945, and an investigation into his earlier activities was closed. Judge Muhs, who had presided over the Special Court in Radom and condemned the Ukrainian Bazyli Antoniak to death for "harboring criminals," served on the bench at the Court of Appeals in Hamm until his retirement in 1958. Mrs. Kulesa's two judges at the Zichenau Special Court, Judge Weiss and Judge Breustedt, became, respectively, judge at the Oldenburg County Court and prosecutor in Giessen. Dr. Jungmann, the prosecutor in the proceedings against Leonard Kinal and Therese Ginter at the Posen Special Court, served as a prosecutor in Essen after the war, while assisting judge Johann Peter Hucklenbroich rose to become a senior member of the County Court in Wuppertal in the 1960s. The presiding judge at that trial, Karl Bömmels, even became presiding judge of a panel at the Zweibrücken Court of Appeals. Judge Strödter, who signed the death sentences for Nikolaus Kondoianis and Andreas Dadopulos, became a Petty Court judge in Wetzlar. And all the judges of the Special Court that condemned Karl Kratina to death found later employment in the postwar judicial system. The presiding judge, Dr. Bellmann, became a senior judge at the Hannover County Court, and his assistants Dr. Dannegger and Dr. von Zeynek served, respectively, as Petty Court judge in Wiedenbrück and County Court judge in Nuremberg.[19]

Nor did the careers of the judges at the Bremen Special Court, which sent young Walerian Wrobel to the scaffold, suffer on account of their previous activities. County Court judge Warneken retired as scheduled after the war; judges Heumann and Landwehr were classified as "not incriminated" in de-Nazification hearings and subsequently returned to the bench.[20] The prosecutor at that trial, Dr. Hartger, who also successfully pleaded for the death penalty in the cases of the four sailors Wehrmann, Schilling, Gail, and Schwalenberg after the war had ended, became a senior public prosecutor after the war, a position which enabled him to drop the proceedings that had been opened against Petty Court judge Kolhoff on May 23, 1960. Kolhoff, as a Special Court judge at Zichenau, had sentenced a number of Poles to death for obtaining meat through illegal slaughtering.[21]

The presiding judge at the Military Court in Vienna that sentenced the seventeen-year-old soldier Anton Reschny to death so that his fate could serve as an example to others was Professor Erich Schwinge, who received a chair again at the University of Marburg Law School in 1946. Schwinge even served for a time as rector of the university, and in 1977 published a study entitled *Military Justice in the National Socialist Era*, in which he glossed over and defended the role of the military courts.[22]

Dr. Hans Puvogel, author of a dissertation containing a plea for the "removal of inferior beings through killing," was named minister of justice in the state of Lower Saxony in 1976. When a judge drew public attention to the dissertation, disciplinary proceedings were opened not against Puvogel but against the judge! He was officially reprimanded, for by publishing the information he was guilty of failing to show the proper respect to his superior. And navy judge Hans Karl Filbinger, for whom the removal of Nazi emblems from a uniform three weeks after the end of the war showed "to what great degree morale had degenerated," could even become premier of the state of Baden-Württemberg. Field judge Wilhelm Spies, who ordered death sentences carried out on May 10, 1945, and even handed down further death sentences as late as May 18 (fortunately in the prisoners' absence), later served as a senior judge at the Braunschweig County Court; his superior officer, Colonel Remold, rose to the rank of chief of the Mobile Police Force in Bavaria.[23]

For the authors of the most widely used "scholarly" commentaries on the Law for the Protection of the Blood, participation in the crimes of the Third Reich from their desks also proved no hindrance to a postwar career. Judge Boschan returned to his Petty Court in Hildesheim; County Court judge Franz Massfeller received a call to the Federal Ministry of Justice in Bonn as has already been mentioned, and Dr. Friedrich Knost, who headed the section for Racial Identity (which handled proofs of "Aryan blood") at the Reich Race Office of the SS, became president of the Administrative District of Lower Saxony in Braunschweig.[24] An even more stridently racist commentary existed, so "sterling in quality" that Roland Freisler, in his review of it, said it should not "be missing from the bookshelves of any guardian of the law."[25] Its authors, too, found places in the postwar civil service. Dr. Wilhelm Stuckart, formerly undersecretary in the Reich Ministry of the Interior, where he was in charge of all "Jewish questions," was classified as a "follower" in his de-Nazification hearing and became city treasurer in Helmstedt in 1949, and later managing director of the Institute for Promotion of the Economy in Lower Saxony.[26] Stuckart's coauthor Hans Globke also began his postwar career as a city treasurer in Aachen. The post led him to the Federal Chancellery in 1949, where he quickly rose to become undersecretary and the most influential civil servant in the new republic.[27]

Seventeen of the judges who had handed down decisions in Race Law trials in Hamburg were still living after the war; of these seventeen, eleven found new positions in the judicial system.[28]

Even membership in the People's Court did not pose an obstacle to employment in the higher ranks of the postwar system: the prosecutors Karl-Hermann Bellwinkel, Dr. Bruchhaus, Dr. Heinz-Günther Lell, Kurt Jaager, Dr. Konrad Höher, Helmut Scherf, and Karl Spahr all served as public prosecutors again after 1945 (and as a rule were promoted to the rank of first prosecutor or senior prosecutor).[29] Occasionally, service in association with this "instrument of National Socialist terror" (as the Federal Supreme Court once called the tribunal)[30] was the starting point for an outstanding career. Alfred Münich, made a judge there in 1937, and Helmut Jaeger, first prosecutor at the People's Court, became, respectively, presiding judge of a panel and prosecutor at the Munich Court of Appeals after 1945, and Franz Schlüter, prosecutor and officer in charge of executions there, became presiding judge of a panel at the Federal Patent Court in Munich.[31]

In appointing Nazi jurists to new positions after the war, those responsible often showed a lack of tact. Günther Schultz, who as a member of the Sixth Criminal Panel of the Hamburg County Court in 1940–1941 had participated in Race Law decisions, was made a Court of Appeals judge in Hamm after the war. Then he of all people was named presiding judge of a board in Hamburg to hear the cases of war victims claiming damages; here he decided claims filed by the survivors of his own earlier trials, and by the relatives of those he had sentenced to death.[32] As a prosecutor at the Kattowitz (Katowice) Special Court during the war, Karl-Heinz Ottersbach successfully recommended a large number of death sentences; afterward he became public prosecutor for political crimes at the County Court of Lüneburg, where he again acquired a dubious reputation. At least once, Ottersbach told Communist defendants during their trial: "I see going to prison between 1933 and 1945 didn't teach you a thing."[33]

On December 1, 1958, a "Central Office of State Administrations for the Prosecution of National Socialist Crimes" was created in Ludwigsburg for the purpose of coordinating the various investigations underway. Named to head it was Erwin Schüle, who had joined the SA in 1933 and the Nazi party in 1935.[34] It hardly came as a surprise that Schüle, who as head of the Central Office must have known the true extent of Nazi crimes better than anyone else, recommended in 1964 that a statute of limitations be imposed in May 1965, and that no murders from the Nazi era be prosecuted after that time.[35] Finally, in late 1965, he was replaced by a man of integrity, the senior prosecutor Adalbert Rückerl. Schüle's departure from Ludwigsburg was sweetened for him by promotion to the post of prosecutor general in Stuttgart.

Wolfgang Immerwahr Fränkel, during the war a department head at the Reich Office of Public Prosecutions, was responsible for a large number of pleas of nullity entered against "overly lenient decisions": the president of the Stuttgart Court of Appeals, Richard Schmid, once referred to him as a "fanatic on the death penalty."[36] On March 21, 1962, Fränkel was appointed prosecutor general of the Federal Republic. An investigation into his past was closed by the Karlsruhe Court of Appeals on September

3, 1964, with the remarkable argument that no evidence existed to prove that Fränkel, by now the highest-ranking prosecutor in the country, had ever "even doubted the validity of the regulations named . . . during the war, let alone recognized their invalidity."[37] After Fränkel's past, which he had artfully concealed, became known to the public, it still took months to force his resignation, and he has continued to receive a full pension to this day.

On September 8, 1961, the Law on Judges was amended to give all judges and public prosecutors who had "participated in the administration of criminal law from September 1, 1939, to May 9, 1945," the opportunity to resign from office by June 30, 1962, with no reduction in pension. Only 149 former jurists of the National Socialist era took advantage of it, however.[38] Most of them chose to remain in office even after this date, and several continued to exercise influence on the legal order of the young democracy from high positions.

In the spring of 1971 a major case involving physicians from the euthanasia program came up for review before the Second Criminal Panel of the Federal Supreme Court under presiding judge Paulheinz Baldus. The prosecutor representing the victims, Professor Friedrich Karl Kaul, requested that Judge Baldus excuse himself from the case. In his motion, Kaul referred to testimony at the trial of a former SS officer at Auschwitz named Oswald Kaduk, who had been sentenced to life imprisonment. Kaduk testified that he had received his orders from the Führer's chancellery from "a certain Baldus, now a presiding judge in Karlsruhe." In 1939, Baldus had in fact moved from the Department of Criminal Justice at the Reich Ministry of Justice to the Reich chancellery, where he became a member of the legal staff.[39] During the war he served as a field judge.[40] No decision was ever made on the motion for recusation. Instead, Judge Baldus broke off the proceedings and left the bench; he was due to retire shortly, in any case.

Before this, however, Baldus had managed to leave his mark on legal developments in the Federal Republic. As presiding judge of the Disciplinary Court at the Federal Supreme Court (the Panel for Disciplinary Proceedings against Judges and Prosecutors), he had served as the country's highest-ranking guardian of professional standards. And as presiding judge in the trial of members of the "Society for German-Soviet Friendship," he had put himself in the forefront of the prosecution of Communists. On July 28, 1955, Baldus' panel charged officers of this organization with "participation in an association guilty of treason toward the constitution," with "membership in a secret society," and with "participation in a criminal association." The panel found the crime aggravated by the fact that the society—which had not been made illegal in most *Länder*—had "held a meeting of the steering committee while the trial was taking place in Karlsruhe and issued public statements."[41] Another decision handed down by Judge Baldus has had an effect on other cases up to the present: it involves the peculiar definition of "force" in connection with charges of unlawful duress developed by the Second Criminal Panel under Baldus' leadership in the notorious "Laepple decision" of August 1969.[42] Klaus Laepple, then president of the Association of Students at the University of Cologne and a member of the Christian Democratic Students' Circle, had led a protest with other students against fare increases in the city's public transportation system. They had staged a sit-in on the streetcar tracks and had succeeded in blocking several trains. In a first trial, they were acquitted by the County Court of Cologne. However, the Second Criminal Panel set aside the verdict, warning the lower court that "recognizing a right to demonstrate to the extent accepted by the Criminal Chamber [of the County Court] would be equivalent to legalizing terror committed by militant minorities." Baldus himself remarked during the proceedings, "The panel has no intention . . . of creating a special legal status for university students."[43] Since that time, the classic forms of non-violent protest have counted as the use of force in West Germany.

In 1975, some formerly prominent National Socialist jurists even had an opportunity to decide what sort of political past was acceptable for a servant of a free and constitutional state and what sort branded him as an "enemy of the constitution." On February 6, 1975, when the Second Criminal Panel of the Federal Supreme Administrative Court had to reach a final decision on the question of whether members of the German Communist party could join the civil service, judgment was passed on the teacher Anne Lenhart by federal judges Edmund de Chapeaurouge and Rudolf Weber-Lortsch. Chapeaurouge had served on the bench in Race Law trials in Hamburg, and the decision in the case of Leon Abel ("an inferior human being") bears his signature.[44] Weber-Lortsch, who became a high-ranking officer in the SA in 1933, was acting chief of police in Kattowitz, Königshütte (Kro-dewska Huta), and Sosnowiec in occupied Poland, and later became an SS and police officer in the "Reich Territory of the Ukraine," where mass murders of Jews and Ukrainians were carried out by special army and commando units. From 1942 on, Lortsch served as head of the Legal and Administrative Office of the Senior Officer of the SS and Police Forces in Norway. On November 25, 1942, his office was able to report that under its direction 700 Norwegian Jews had been "transferred to Auschwitz."[45] The decision which finally barred the Communist teacher from permanent employment in the school system criticized her for joining the German Communist party when she was aware "that the federal government considers the goals of this political party opposed to the constitution." [46] The decision convicting Abel of "dishonor to the race" had used similar language in reproaching him for not avoiding a woman "of German blood," even though the attitude of the Reich government had been known to him for three years: "It represents an extraordinary piece of effrontery on the part of the accused to have dared, at this date . . . ," and so on. [47] The two cases exhibit some differences, but the language of servile obedience to the wishes of the government remains the same.

Three months after the Lenhart decision was handed down by the Federal Supreme Administrative Court, the Federal Constitutional Court passed its "Decision on Radicals." [48] It was written by judge (and law professor) Willi Geiger, who while serving as a prosecutor at the Bamberg Special Court had successfully pleaded for at least five death sentences. [49] And in his dissertation, "The Legal Position of Newspaper Editors" Geiger had placed journalists on the same level as civil servants—namely, "raised to noble champions of a duty to the public." He deduced that no one could be tolerated in this occupation who had "proved himself to be an enemy to the *Volk* or the state in his professional or political activities," particularly if these consisted of "working for the Marxist press." Geiger took his claim that editors must "be of Aryan descent as a matter of principle" directly from the platform of the Nazi party. [50] Nevertheless, he saw no reason to plead partiality and remove himself from a case involving civil servants' loyaly to the constitution in a free and democratic state, but instead seized the opportunity to express once more his undemocratic and authoritarian view of the civil service: "The duty of political loyalty— loyalty to the constitution and the state—demands more than assumption of an attitude which while formally correct is otherwise characterized by indifference, coolness, and inner distance toward the state and the constitution." What was required of the civil servant was that he "feel at home in the state which is he to serve—now and at all times." [51]

24

Coming to Terms with the Past

Virtually no professional group emerged from the Nazi era with so good a conscience as that of the jurists. They began by denying categorically that German judges had participated at all in the injustices of the Hitler dictatorship. Hubert Schorn, for example, whose book *Judges in the Third Reich* is one long justification yet still a standard work today, ascribes all guilt to the lawmakers; he sees the fact that jurists followed the existing legislation as a result of their "positivistic training." Of course it is true that legal positivism, with its demand that judges be strictly bound to the law, had been the unchallenged doctrine of the authoritarian state under the kaiser. During the fourteen years of the Weimar Republic, however, the judicial system and legal scholars had assumed a position of decided coolness toward the democratic government. Only a minority of legal theorists had implored the judiciary to obey the laws of the democracy. Gustav Radbruch, for example, the legal philosopher who served briefly as Social Democratic minister of justice in the early twenties, issued a warning in 1925 that if the courts were permitted to decide themselves whether they wanted to apply a law or not, then the constitution would soon be nothing more than a "piece of cloth the jurists will fight over like dogs, until nothing but a torn, dirty, and insignificant rag remains."[1] The profession proved deaf to such appeals, however. The courts of the Weimar Republic rarely announced that a particular law could not be applied or was unconstitutional, but with a great deal of hair splitting and "interpretations" that had little to do with its actual wording, they could achieve the same effect. Apart from a small minority of supporters of the republic, no one in the German legal profession endorsed positivism any longer. Carl Schmitt accordingly observed in 1932 that "the era of legal positivism has come to an end,"[2] and professor of constitutional law Ernst Forsthoff avowed in his credo of 1933, *The Total State:* "Under no circumstances can the state of today draw any sustenance from positivistic thinking, which is of necessity individualistic and lacking in authority."[3]

Placing the judiciary under a strict obligation to follow the letter of the law would have been an impediment to the "legal order" of the Nazi regime and would have limited its power; for this reason, judges were required to declare their loyalty to the Führer rather than to the law itself. Any appeal to the letter of the law was dismissed as "moral and legal thinking typical of Jewish liberals."[4] No less an authority than the Grand Criminal Panel of the Supreme Court presided over by President Bumke exhorted German judges to recall that "the judiciary . . . can fulfill the task imposed on it by the Third Reich only if it does not remain glued to the letter of the law, but rather penetrates to its innermost spirit; the judiciary must do its part to see that the goals of the lawmakers are achieved."[5]

Although it was clear to every jurist during the Nazi era, and especially afterward, that National Socialist legal doctrines were the exact opposite of legal positivism, the claim that judges and prosecutors were merely following the laws and that, after all, this was how they had been trained by their democratic professors during the Weimar Republic became a blanket excuse for the whole profession. This justification of their behavior even found its way into several works of postwar literature. Rolf Hochhuth satirizes the attitude in his play *Die Juristen* (The Jurists), when he has a formerly ruthless navy judge deliver the following speech full of pathos:

> *You should see me as jurists,*
> *To reach a just conclusion.*
> *You must admit that I never,*
> *No, never violated the creed*
> *Of that great anti-Fascist and cabinet minister*
> *Of the Weimar Republic, Gustav Radbruch,*
> *At whose feet I sat in Heidelberg in 1932.*
> (He lectures with one finger raised:)
> *"We despise the clergyman who preaches a sermon*
> *Opposed to his own convictions,*
> *But we admire the judge who ignores the promptings*
> *Of his own sense of justice and remains*
> *True to the law . . ."*[6]

It is not at all clear who invented this legend of jurists' loyalty to the letter of the law during the Nazi period, a legend which came to be turned so elegantly and effectively against democrats who served on German law school faculties during the Weimar era, such as Gustav Radbruch, Gerhard Anschütz, and Hans Kelsen—all men who lost their jobs in 1933. Professor Hermann Jahrreiss used the argument in his defense of the accused at the Nuremberg jurists' trial. He explained the "German legal system" by citing Gerhard Anschütz, one of the "outstanding jurists of the Weimar Republic," who taught the view "that laws passed in a proper procedure could not be questioned by the courts or administrators either on constitutional or on ethical grounds." According to this doctrine, there were allegedly no legal obstacles in Hitler's path: "He was *legibus solutus*, free from all laws."[7]

In any case, this explanation for the downfall of the rule of law under National Socialism soon became established. Hubert Schorn, a retired County Court judge, saw the "positivistic miseducation" of jurists as responsible,[8] while Hermann Weinkauff, retired judge of the *Reichsgericht* and first president of the Federal Supreme Court, numbered arbitrary decisions by judges and legal murder by the courts among the "disastrous consequences of legal positivism."[9] Christian Friedrich Menger, a professor of constitutional law, believed that the "bitter experiences of those years [were necessary] for us to overcome this erroneous doctrine."[10] Eberhard Schmidt, a military judge in the reserves and a professor of criminal law, objected to attempts to disparage the "devotion to the law" displayed by judges of the Nazi era, even finding it "inappropriate to speak today, *ex post facto,* of a positivistic 'miseducation' of the judiciary prior to 1945. Even Radbruch himself wrote in 1932 . . . that the unconditional loyalty to the law arising from a positivistic orientation contributed to an earnest and self-denying stand on professional ethics."[11]

Even leading Nazi jurists began subscribing to this theory. Carl Schmitt, who had proclaimed the death of positivism in 1932, cleverly seized the opportunity to reinterpret his own plea against parliamentary democracy as a "warning" and "cry of alarm" about the "doctrine of positivism reigning at that time."[12] Given the general trend toward twisting and misrepresenting the facts, a few more outrageous claims did not seem to matter much. Hans Welzel, one of the leading ideologists on criminal law under the Hitler dictatorship, made use of the favorite Radbruch quotation ("We despise the clergyman . . .") to exclaim: "Written thus in 1932! We must not forget that German jurists entered the Third Reich trained in these doctrines! The Third Reich truly took . . . the doctrine of positivism at its word!"[13] Actually, Welzel should have known better, since he himself had pleaded in 1935 for a view of law in which "concrete ways of ordering life [must] be seen as part of the great unity . . . in the community of the *Volk,* with the requirements demanded by the concrete historical situation, which in the legal field find their most visible outcome in the expression of the Führer's will—that is, in the law."[14] Even Günther Küchenhoff, who was one of the most radical Nazi professors and in 1934 had seen "the ultimate fount of law in the vital rhythm of the community of the *Volk*, where all are united in one fate,"[15] claimed in 1953 that "positivism, which sees the ultimate fount of law in the state," had served "totalitarian tendencies," and was not above mentioning Gustav Radbruch and Roland Freisler in the same breath.[16]

A conscious lie or unconscious repression of the truth? Since the fairy tale of positivism whitewashed the entire profession, it was seized upon most gladly by those who should have been held responsible for the crimes they had committed during the Nazi era, and the courts readily accepted their self-justification.

The Kassel County Court, for example, even used the argument of positivism to acquit the judges who had condemned the engineer Werner Holländer to a penalty not mentioned in the law by means of their "creative interpretation," and had sent him to the scaffold: "Even before the Hitler regime came to power, German courts adhered both in theory and practice to the belief that judges had an unconditional obligation to the law . . . If one takes into consideration that the defendants Hassenkamp and Kessler were trained in legal positivistic thinking and were perhaps "convinced" National Socialists, . . . the possibility cannot be excluded that they had a positive conviction that their decision corresponded to the law."[17]

The fact that those engaged in such attempts to whitewash the past soon became entangled in massive contradictions did not seem to bother anyone. Anyone daring enough to point out these contradictions and to uncover the fatal history of the judicial system and legal scholarship in the 1950s and 1960s would have been risking his future career. Thus, Hubert Schorn, as has already been pointed out, was able to claim without fear of contradiction that devotion to the law and "positivistic miseducation" had led jurists to commit all their legal crimes. In the same paragraph he was able to state that in the Third Reich, "many judges recognized the conflict between the law and justice [and] accordingly acted in violation of the law";[18] indeed, "the vast majority" of judges offered resistance to the regime. After a short description of the Nazi dictatorship, which tended to make it appear far more harmless than it actually was, Schorn even waxed lyrical: "But in this darkness there shines one bright light—the clear and unambiguous commitment of the judges at the old *Reichsgericht* and the majority of the German judiciary to the fundamental truths, those absolute and inviolable norms of divine and natural law that served as guidelines in their daily work and in their quiet devotion to duty."[19]

These falsehoods and distortions of history were intended to exculpate an entire profession and to discredit the reputation of the democrats on law school faculties, but they had a further advantage as well. So long as no one knew for certain whether or not the new democratic government in West Germany would introduce basic social reforms, a fundamentally obedient stance was rejected in advance, as a precautionary measure. Had not the Third Reich demonstrated where unconditional loyalty to the law could lead? As a result of their "bitter experience" with judges "blinded by positivism," the judicial system and legal scholars of the postwar period began to propound an orientation toward Christian natural law. They proclaimed that above all the laws of a democratic government there existed an "ultimate legal order," or, in the words of Federal Supreme Court president Hermann Weinkauff, "an area of objective legal obligation, corresponding to a preexisting value order and binding in an absolute sense." It was only from this source that laws "derived their inner binding force" or, as might also occur, "were stripped of their legal validity." [20] German courts now claimed the right to measure all laws by this "suprapositive" standard; even the constitution was not to be spared such examination and review by the severely incriminated courts. The Federal Supreme Court itself was of the opinion that the question of "whether constitutional norms can be reconciled with the higher norms of the constitution or supralegal justice [must] be open to review as a matter of principle." [21]

Adherents of this "ultimate legal order" freely admitted that the criteria by which to judge it "lie beyond the realm of scholarly proof and certainly beyond what is evident in terms of formal logic"; such criteria could be grasped only with "a feeling of inner certainty," through the "sincere exertion of reason and conscience by a legally minded and experienced judge of such matters, with a relatively large degree of reliable intuition." [22] This doctrine enabled the judicial system once again, as in the days of the Weimar Republic, to declare whatever did not suit it to be invalid. And indeed, "God-given standards of justice" and the "ultimate legal order" were invoked with striking frequency when cases involved the "legitimately acquired rights" of former Nazi officials. [23]

The president of the Federal Supreme Court devoted his considerable energies to opposing any return to clarity of norms and to predictability in the law, lamenting the "scientific character of our legal order." [24] The country's highest-ranking judge wished to see the "coordination" of the German people maintained, although under a different banner. The foundations of every democratic system, a "pluralistic society" and the "pluralism of ideologies" were to him "matters in which the thing itself is as dangerous as the term is repellent." [25] Above all, however, the corps of officers of the courts should remain ideologically coordinated; Weinkauff called emphatically for "closed ranks in the judiciary—indeed, [for] a truly united profession."[26] The method he propagated for reaching just decisions, based on an "organic" and "intrinsic approach" to and an "instinctive grasp" of the law, is not unlike the methods of the previous era, and neither are the values such a method strove to uphold. Merely by switching the labels, large segments of the conservative world view, formerly classed as part of the "way of life of the *Volk*," could not be presented as "Christian natural law." Common to both was a view of society as something static, an attitude that aimed at preserving traditional values from democratic developments through appeals to a status quo preordained in nature.

The degree to which some clung to the values underlying the Third Reich while offering superficial verbal disclaimers is revealed by their attitudes on the relationship of the sexes and the legal status they were willing to grant to women. According to National Socialist doctrine, women were characterized by "thought and will linked to the moral sphere and therefore rooted in the realm of the ideal: . . . their lively and warm sensibility, their closeness to the earth and to nature, their sense for nurture and preservation, their spiritual creativity."[27] "Women's emancipation," on the other hand, was, in Hitler's own phrase, "merely a word invented by the Jewish intellect, and its content bears the stamp of the same spirit."[28] The official Nazi party view of woman's nature had been formulated by Gertrud Baumgart, a leader of the BDM, or German Girls' Federation (the girls' organization within the Hitler Youth):

> The essence of a woman is determined by nature. Motherhood is her fate, her life work; every historical development must come to a stop when confronted with this unalterable biological fact. A woman will contribute to the tasks of the man. Her spiritual, her intellectual abilities will develop and grow; in some individual women they will even emerge as dominant, but motherhood remains the ultimate foundation of her nature, to which she is indissolubly tied. Life and warmth radiate into her being from this core, just as the sacred fire of the hearth, whose guardian she is, warms and enlivens the house, whose center she forms.[29]

Because of "bitter experiences under the state-controlled injustice of the National Socialist period," the Federal Supreme Court supposedly acquired a new orientation and, in the words of its president, moved "increasingly toward a view based on natural law."[30] In 1954, in a report on equal rights for both sexes, the First Civil Panel of the court demonstrated exactly how much this view had changed:

> The two sexes are fundamentally different . . . not only in the biological and sexual sphere itself, but also in their relationship to one another and to children in the familial order, as determined by their own natures and the Crea-

tion ... The man begets children; the woman conceives, gives birth, and nourishes them, and raises them to maturity. The man provides for the stability, development, and future of his family, with a particular orientation toward the outside world; he represents it outside the home. In this sense he is its "head." The woman, with a primary orientation toward the inner sphere, devotes herself to the internal order and internal arrangements of the family. The law cannot brush aside these fundamental differences in a doctrinaire manner, when it examines the question of equality between the sexes in the context of the family.[31]

Given such a large degree of continuity in thinking, it is not surprising that almost no one wished for a radically new orientation in postwar legislation. The resistance by German judges and legal scholars to de-Nazification of the statute books was as stubborn as it had been to de-Nazification of the system's personnel. After the capitulation, when the Allies began to cleanse the German legal order of "typically Fascist perversions of justice," their first step had been to rescind the Enabling Act, the Race Laws, the Nazi Law for Protection of the State, and numerous special laws. In the case of other statutes that were not so obviously Fascist in content, however, the Allies encountered massive resistance from virtually the entire legal profession. Calling upon the same fluency with which, prior to May 8, 1945, they had celebrated every measure violating the rule of law as a hallmark of true National Socialism, jurists now argued that these regulations were not "typically National Socialist" in spirit.

The very first law proclaimed by the military government set in motion a most unfortunate chain of development. It forbade the "interpretation and application of German law according to National Socialist principles," as well as further use of court decisions and legal constructions "that expound or apply National Socialist aims or doctrines."[32] The problem was that, on close inspection, there was little that appeared to be "typically National Socialist." Jurists were willing to concede after the war that the Race Laws and decisions based on them belonged to Nazism, but they wanted to see many other "achievements" of the Third Reich preserved. They wanted to save the Criminal Procedure Reform Act of 1935, the major court reforms of 1938, the Law on Dangerous Habitual Criminals, and even the Decree on Further Accommodation of the Criminal Justice System to the Demands of Total War, issued December 13, 1944[33]—now referred to somewhat shamefacedly as the "Fourth Simplification Decree." Some were also demanding the preservation of a whole series of newly defined crimes and legal constructions, since although these regulations might indeed be authoritarian, pre-Enlightenment in spirit, and opposed to liberal constitutionalism, they were not "typically National Socialist."

As early as 1946, a commission made up of German jurists from all the zones of occupation agreed that certain key points of the Nazi Criminal Code should be preserved, such as preventive detention and emphasis on the personality of the perpetrator, as set forth in the murder statute (paragraph 211); they noted that similar statutes had existed in other countries and thus could not be regarded "as typically National Socialist for that reason alone."[34] Legal scholars, with an overwhelmingly conservative orientation, were agreed that "fundamental reforms" were "not desirable, at least not at the present time."[35] One scholar of criminal law, whose past was certainly not incriminating, has summed up this period as follows: "After 1945 vigorous attempts were made to introduce English and American legal principles, but it was necessary to oppose them to maintain a sensible continuity of law"![36] After different laws had been in force temporarily in the various Western zones of occupation, uniformity was to be achieved "by reverting to old and tested regulations"—that is to say, to laws passed during the Third Reich. The draft of a Law on Uniformity prepared by the West German federal government contained the warning that "premature changes [will] have a disastrous effect and will damage the prestige of the German legal tradition."[37]

In anti-Fascist resistance circles, plans had been drafted for de-Nazification and for the democratic reconstruction of the legal system after the war. Among other things, they envisioned a sweeping reform of the cours so as to bring about more lay participation and to abolish life tenure for judges. The "Kreisau Circle" even came up with a plan to recruit judges from the ranks of practicing attorneys, following the British model.[36] These plans did not figure at all in most discussions among jurists during the postwar years, however, and did not have the slightest chance of becoming reality.

The Nazis had greeted many decisions of the *Reichsgericht* from the 1920s and early 1930s as heralds of their own legal order—with some justification—and although its decisions from the years 1933 to 1945 were still fresh in everyone's mind, by 1950 jurists had begun to cite "the principles developed in the sound tradition of the *Reichsgericht*."[39] Professor Emil Niethammer, who in 1937, as a member of the highest German court, had emphasized its role "as a pacesetter in criminal justice according to current law and in the future,"[40] wrote one of the very first legal articles to be published after the war, entitled "The Enduring Effectiveness of *Reichsgericht* Decisions." In it he stressed the fact that "all the decisions" of this court "were based on humanity, truth, and justice," and that its work could continue to be accepted "without limitations." As if anticipating a reaction of disbelief among his audience, he added explicitly, "This is fundamentally true for all its decisions."[41]

The extent to which legal norms from the Third Reich were carried over to the Federal Republic was enormous. The usual procedure was merely to delete the most offensive phrases and to present the remainder as a "democratic" or "liberal" law. In this manner, for instance, the "German Civil Service Law of January 26, 1937, edited and adapted for the current situation by Dr. Walter Jellinek" and published in November 1945, became the model for all laws pertaining to civil servants in the Federal Republic. Jellinek, a respected and unincriminated professor of constitutional law at the University of Heidelberg, simply took a red pen and a copy of the 1937 law, which the Nazis themselves had regarded as a cornerstone of their platforms, and crossed out the phrases giving the Nazi party a voice in appointments to the civil service, establishing discrimination on the basis of race, and requiring an oath of loyalty to the Führer. He pronounced the result to be a "piece of legislation in the very best German legal tradition."[42] The required "loyalty to the Führer" was replaced by the phrase "loyalty to the constitution," and the prerequisite for appointment, namely that the civil servant "can be relied upon to support the National Socialist state unconditionally," was changed to "can be relied upon at all times to support the liberal democratic order as established by the constitution."

In another case, the occupying forces did not explicitly revoke the Law for the Prevention of Hereditary Diseases that had led to the sterilization of approximately 350,000 people. At the Nuremberg jurists' trial, in an attempt to exculpate the defendants, it was referred to as "something reasonable people could discuss."[43] In theory, the law had continued in force after the war (since it was "not National Socialist" in character), but there was no institution available to enforce it after the dissolution of the Hereditary Health Courts. It was primarily the medical profession that began pressing for the government to reintroduce measures for forced sterilization, in view of the country's many "juvenile delinquents," but concern for the health of the German people also motivated some jurists. In 1951, for example, legal administrators in the city of Hamburg asked that "the question of whether and when sterilization is permissible be decided anew by the country's legislatures, whereby sufficient attention should be paid to the principles established by the science of eugenics and to practical experience gathered even before 1933."[44]

The Nazi law was not officially revoked until 1974,[45] and it took until 1979 for the Bundestag to reach the conclusion that forced sterilization was irreconcilable with "the concept of human dignity." Not until February 7, 1986, however, did a German court—in this case the Petty Court of Kiel—determine for the first time that the Law on Hereditary Diseases "violated the constitution and therefore was invalid after the war, according to Article 123, paragraph 1GG."[46]

There were also long debates in the postwar period on other provisions of the Criminal Code that had an ideological slant, such as paragraph 175 on homosexuality, as rewritten by the Nazis. In a decision of January 22, 1947, the Hamburg Court of Appeals conceded that earlier *Reichsgericht* decisions in this area were "obviously influenced by National Socialist tendencies," but nonetheless the drastically increased penalties introduced during the Third Reich were in the eyes of the court "justified on objective grounds and can thus not be regarded as part of National Socialist doctrine, so that in principle no objection exists to using the new version."[47] The Braunschweig Court of Appeals also insisted that the framers of the 1935 law "reverted to older doctrines not based on National Socialism when they altered and expanded paragraph 175."[48] The Oldenburg Court of Appeals pointed out to the lower courts in its district that paragraph 175 *et seq.* had been made more severe during the Third Reich and that only after 1935 had it become a crime even to attempt this "serious and unnatural form of fornication"—prior to 1935, a mere attempt had not been punishable. When the court concluded that the new and more severe penalties could therefore not be imposed, it was harshly criticized. Hermann Steidle, president of the Stuttgart Court of Appeals, wrote a note on the decision pointing out "that even after the downfall of National Socialism a well-founded need exists, not only in Oldenburg but also elsewhere, to punish attempts to commit an offense that qualifies as fornication. Satisfaction of this need should not be made impossible unless there are compelling reasons."[50] It did not appear to disturb Judge Steidle unduly that section 8 of "General Instructions to Judges, Number 1," a law binding for all courts, forbade sentencing according to regulations that had been increased in severity after January 30, 1933.[51] The usual way to get around this provision was to declare the Nazi version of the statute to be not an "increase in severity" but rather a "new law." The courts could then continue to use it so long as it did not number among the laws that had been specifically revoked, since it was then considered not to be based on "National Socialist principles." In effect, this gave the courts the power to decide arbitrarily which laws continued in force and which did not; whenever they found that a legal norm created during the Third Reich was "justified on objective grounds," they argued that it contained no "National Socialist principles."

The Hamburg Court of Appeals also wanted to preserve a law which had classed abortion as a felony.[52] Members of the court were willing to dispense only with the interpretation of the Third Reich courts that had usually increased the penalties still further. Their decision on this matter contained the following noteworthy principle: "The laws passed during the National Socialist era are . . . to be interpreted strictly as they are worded."[53] On January 10, 1947, the Braunschweig Court of Appeals even found that a 1939 decision of the Grand Panel of the *Reichsgericht* which referred to the "healthy opinion of the *Volk*"[54] was "still convincing today. It is not rooted in National Socialist doctrines."[55]

That the de-Nazification of the legal order was merely superficial is well illustrated by paragraph 240 of the Criminal Code (on "unlawful duress"), which is still applied today in cases of nonviolent protest. Until 1943 this paragraph read, "Whoever illegally prevents another person from carrying out his normal activities or constrains his freedom of movement by the use of force or through threats to commit a crime or misdemeanor will incur a prison sentence of up to one year or a fine."[56] According to prevailing opinion at the time, this meant that unlawful duress had occurred only if the perpetrator intimidated others with physical violence or threats of a serious crime.[57] On May 29, 1943, the definition of this offense was broadened in several respects: "Whoever illegally compels another person to commit an act or prevents him from carrying out his normal activities or constrains his freedom of movement by the use of force or through threats to do him significant harm is guilty of unlawful duress and will be punished with a prison sentence or a fine, and in especially serious cases with a penitentiary sentence (up to fifteen years) or a prison sentence of not less than six months. The act is illegal if the use of force or threat to inflict harm for achieving the desired purpose runs counter to the healthy opinion of the *Volk*."[58] This wording made it impossible to distinguish precisely between legal and illegal actions; judges were free to decide on the basis of National Socialist principles whether an instance of duress was unlawful. The fifteen-fold increase in the maximum penalty also matched the Nazis' fondness for barbarically harsh sanctions.

However, German legal scholars and judges of the postwar period agreed that the wording of the 1943 law contained no "National Socialist principles,"[59] and courts continued to apply the Nazi paragraph without scruples even though the "General Instructions to Judges, Number 1" of the military government expressly prohibited the use of penalties increased under Nazi rule. When legislative power passed back into German hands, the 1943 version of the law was included in the Criminal Code; the only change made was the replacement of the offensive phrase "runs counter to the healthy opinion of the *Volk*" by the words "is to be regarded as reprehensible." Thus, the intentionally vague definition of the offense permitting sweeping interpretation was retained, and the higher maximum sentences remained as well.[60]

Developments were similar in almost all other cases where maximum sentences had been increased by the Nazis. The definition of extortion had also been altered in 1943 and, like the crime of unlawful duress, had been worded in terms of the "healthy opinion of the *Volk*,"[61] but in June 1946 the Stuttgart Court of Appeals determined that "the prohibition against punishing actions on the basis of the 'healthy opinion of the *Volk*' does not mean that the full range of sentences set in paragraph 253 as amended may not be applied." After all, the court noted, the regulation had not been "specifically revoked."[62] Although it was indeed true that the law had not been revoked, the catalogue of laws revoked by the Allies in 1945 had never been intended as complete or final; other regulations reflecting Nazi tendencies were also to be considered as invalid.[63] Nonetheless, as a rule the German judicial system regarded the list as exclusive. In one of its first acts, the newly constituted Federal Supreme Court even issued a strict prohibition to lower courts barring them from treating any laws as invalid except those specifically mentioned by the Allied powers.[64]

Reluctantly, the courts occasionally recognized that the prohibition against adopting Nazi sentencing standards tied their hands—"for the time being," as they always stressed. When the limitations imposed by the Allied military governments ceased to apply, judges were at long last free to return to the framework for sentencing created in the Nazi era. Paragraphs 175, 175a, and 175b of the Criminal Code (the paragraphs on homosexuality) remained partly in force until 1969; to a certain extent, they are still valid today. Paragraph 218 (on abortion) continued in force in the wording of the Third Reich until 1976. The maximum sentence for unlawful duress was reduced in 1969, but it is still three times as severe as it was prior to 1933. Generally speaking, one can say that the increased penalties for most crimes have been retained up to the present day, and the maximum sentences for many of them are still two to three times as severe as they were under the Reich Criminal Code of 1871.[65] Dr. Fritz Hartung, a former member of both the Federal Supreme Court and the *Reichsgericht*, was thus able to comment approvingly in 1971: "In the field of law, particularly criminal law, the National Socialist regime . . . brought advances of a fundamental kind . . . , improvements which have been maintained until the present day, so that criminal law has become unimaginable without them."[66]

25

The Opposition Goes on Trial Again

In its efforts to preserve "valuable" statutes from the Third Reich, the Bundestag did not even balk at passing laws which had been revoked immediately after the war as "typical of National Socialism." One of the Allies' very first de-Nazification measures was abrogation of the lushly proliferating criminal statutes of 1934,[1] designed to protect the regime and to suppress political opposition.[2] The fundamental underlying aim of the architects of these laws, minister of justice Franz Gürtner and his undersecretary Roland Freisler, had been to "shift the field of battle forward"[3]— that is, to prosecute as treason not only criminal or violent acts but any action expressing opposition to the regime, even if the action as such did not violate the law.

Less than six months after the Bundestag had been created, the elected government presented a draft of a "First Law to Amend the Criminal Code," which contained large sections of the National Socialists' laws on political crimes—laws that had been abolished in 1945–1946. The Federal Ministry of Justice presented a document in support of these measures in which, for simplicity's sake, it actually quoted Gürtner and Freisler: "The modern state cannot rely for protection on the classic definitions of high treason. It [requires] new statutes that . . . advance its line of defense."[4] The echoes of Nazi legal thinking were no accident: the bill on the protection of the republic had been written by none other than Dr. Josef Schafheutle, now an official of the Federal Ministry of Justice, and, as a former official of the Reich Ministry, a participant in the formulation of the political criminal statutes of the Third Reich.[5] The aims of the government's bill became clear when it was debated on the floor of the Bundestag. Eduard Wahl of the Christian Democrats reported for the Legal Committee that the "new" regulations made it possible to prosecute acts which were "more or less harmless in and of themselves." It was the intention with which they were committed that made them criminal: "This intention reflecting hostility to the state is . . . the technical legal means by which enemies of the state can be distinguished from the loyal opposition."[6] When the objection was raised that this reinstated the Nazi statutes making a person's attitude a criminal offense, a speaker for the Federal Democratic party replied, "Yes, indeed, . . . we are in a certain sense reintroducing a law that makes opinion a crime; however, we do not intend to punish the opinion, but only the act arising from this opinion."[7] The act could of course be any of a multitude of acts not criminal as such; it was only the opinion behind them that made them into crimes. With this stroke the Bundestag had, in the laconic words of Gustav Heinemann, then minister of the interior and later president of the republic, "brought back to life" the definition of treason "created [by] the Third Reich in 1934, when it altered the criminal norms of 1871."[8]

Even though the "Law on the Defense of the State" from the Weimar period had been aimed at leftists, and the Social Democrats' expert on legal affairs, Otto Heinrich Greve, attacked the "parallel developments in the judicial system after 1918 and 1945,"[9] some legislators persisted in claiming that the enemies against whom the state should mount its defenses lay on the right-wing end of the political spectrum. The opposition Social Democratic party presented an alternative to the government's bill, a bill on "Enemies of Democracy,"[10] intended to combat "ideological remnants from the era of National Socialism" and "reactionary, National Socialist, neo-Fascist, and generally antidemocratic endeavors." Given the judiciary of the 1950s, however, any campaign in this direction was an illusion. Social Democrats in the Bundestag recognized that the political views of judges "in office today whom we have inherited from the past" (Georg-August Zinn)[11] were "not sufficient guarantee that the laws of a democratic government [would be] enforced" (Greve).[12] It must have been clear to them even at that point that, given the statutes of yesteryear on political crimes, the judges of yesteryear would prosecute only the familiar "enemies of the state" on the left.

Court decisions based on the federal Law on the Defense of the State as it was finally passed indeed exceeded many people's worst fears. Since opinions and intentions are neither measurable nor verifiable categories, the "political" Criminal Panel of the Federal Supreme Court came to require less and less proof for "an intention endangering the state," and found citizens guilty of "endangering the state" who had merely protested against rearmament or favored "free elections on German reunification"— only because the Communist government of the German Democratic Republic had also endorsed the latter aim. The courts limited themselves to reviewing the question of whether "the perpetrator" had "consciously acted in accord with the aims of an unconstitutional movement." The motives that might have prompted him to do so were "legally without significance," since—in the opinion of the Federal Supreme Court—"anyone who does not share the unconstitutional aims of the Socialist Unity party [the East German Communist party] but nevertheless consciously participates in their activities to undermine our government acts with an intent hostile to the constitution." According to the court's "new yet old" interpretation, "aims and actions" were to be regarded as "directed against the constitution" even if they were limited to "maintaining modes of thought which embrace a concept of the state hostile to liberal democracy." [13] In their campaign against Communists, the West German courts then proceeded to characterize strikes as "force" under the meaning of the laws on treason. It also characterized the East German Sports Federation (which had chapters in West Germany as well) as "a camouflage organization of the Communist party," and possession of East German newspapers after a visit to relatives in the East as a "violation of the statutes outlawing the Communist party." [14]

At the County Court of Lüneburg, which showed particular vigor in its dealings with Communists, prosecutors viewed an offense as "aggravated . . . by the fact that the accused has a record of previous convictions on the same charge." What they meant was that the defendant had twice been convicted (in 1933 and 1940) of "undermining army morale"! By contrast, the same court treated as extenuating circumstances "model leadership as a soldier in the Second World War," because "military service as such demonstrates possession of the qualities of patriotism and self-sacrifice," regardless of "the goals at which the political leadership aimed through such service." [15]

Using such "interpretations of the law," the judicial system of the 1950s and 1960s opened investigations on 125,000 Communists and other critics of Chancellor Adenauer's policies, mainly opponents of German rearmament. "Only" 7,000 of these investigations led to verdicts of guilty, but even the opening of an investigation could have serious consequences for those involved. Werner Maihofer, a professor of criminal law and later federal minister of the interior, has reported how easy it was to become the subject of an investigation: when a law student writing a doctoral dissertation under Maihofer's supervision once requested information about the number of Communists who had been investigated, his reply came in the form of an announcement that an investigation had been opened on him. [17]

As was the case during the Third Reich, prosecution of an enemy of the state was not reserved for the criminal justice system. Conviction for an offense related to the Communist party regularly carried with it the loss of one's job, and sometimes not even a conviction was necessary: labor courts were known to treat pretrial detention as "unauthorized absence from the workplace"[18] and to uphold the employer's right to dismiss the employee. On occasion the mere opening of an investigation, even if it was later closed or the person involved was acquitted, was recognized as grounds for dismissal.[19] Convicted Communists had their driver's licenses revoked, since they were not "suitable persons to be in charge of a motor vehicle."[20] Communist pupils in high schools were denied their diplomas, and university students were refused admittance to final exams. Communists were not permitted to be foster parents or to work as traveling salesmen, since they did not possess "the necessary solidity of character" for selling on the road. The wife of a convicted Communist was refused a permit to operate a boarding house, because her husband (!) did not offer "a proper guarantee for the orderly management of a public establishment to the satisfaction of the legal authorities and the police." Even though he was employed elsewhere, he might have had "sufficient opportunity to exercise a decisive influence on the planned establishment and to provide shelter for persons of his ilk."[21]

The zeal with which courts devoted themselves to prosecuting Communists prompted even the highest-ranking prosecutor for political crimes, federal prosecutor general Max Güde, to draw political parallels in 1961: "The political justice of today operates on the same basis—a lack of backbone—that explains the Special Courts of the Third Reich."[22]

26

Law Schools

Although the military governments of the Allied powers in the western zones made a thorough search for old Nazis in the schools and bureaucracy (at least at the beginning), it was apparent that they could not quite bring themselves to do the same in the field of higher education. They had too much respect for the traditions of the German universities and their intellectual leaders. Certain particularly prominent Nazis on university faculties were suspended in the early days, and the military governments tended to name men who had not been Nazis but who had kept their professorships during the Third Reich as rectors—a position roughly equivalent to that of a university president in the United States. The victorious nations were apparently unable to imagine that German scholarship might have become corrupted through and through. Nonetheless, German university faculties stubbornly opposed any interference in their affairs. They argued that a repetition of the developments after 1933 could be avoided only by reducing government influence on higher education and increasing the universities' autonomy; in this way they managed to achieve a quiet restoration of the old status. Just as faculties had willingly opened the universities to Nazi doctrines, they now blocked all attempts to allow a democratic government an equal degree of influence. Their impassioned defense of German universities' traditional independence, which had once contributed so much to their renown, now served to disguise the fact that the Nazis had dismissed almost one third of all professors, including the majority of German Nobel laureates.[1] By 1939, roughly 45 percent of university professors had been appointed during the Third Reich; at law schools the figure was 60 percent.[2] About half of all faculty members thus owed their careers to the Nazi regime, while the other, thoroughly conservative half had been opportunists or at the very best had never openly opposed the dictatorship.

As soon as the universities reopened, these faculties began to concern themselves with the fate of their colleagues who had been victims of dismissal—not those who had been persecuted by the Nazis, however, but rather those suspended by the Allies. At the first conference of university rectors in the British zone of occupation in the fall of 1945, a question posed by the "reeducation officer" about procedures for recalling colleagues who had been driven out by the Nazis was received with embarrassed silence. And when the rectors of universities in the American zone assembled in Heidelberg in November 1945, motions were presented to block all attempts to make the universities more democratic and to give the students a voice in decisions, while demands were heard for the reinstatement of Nazi professors suspended by the Americans. No one spoke up in favor of recalling their former colleagues now living in exile.

In the British zone, universities at least yielded to pressure from the military government to grant victims of Nazi persecution "in all appropriate cases full restitution of their character as faculty members at German universities." That was as far as they were willing to go, however, for their practical concern was devoted mainly to colleagues in need for other reasons. The rectors' conference approved a recommendation that "the universities here represented establish a fund for needy professors and their families from the East, as well as other cases of need." And indeed a "solidarity fund" was created: professors contributed 5 percent of their salary to colleagues who were streaming into West Germany from the Soviet zone of occupation and from the former occupied territories further to the East, and of course for the "other cases of need," as the victims of Nazi persecution were euphemistically named.

By 1953 a total of 409 dismissed full professors had not been rehired. Of these, 67 had died, 70 had reached retirement age and been granted full pensions, and 89 more had taken early retirement. Ninety-five had been granted financial settlements under the "131 Law," and 43 were employed in other professions or in foreign countries. There remained a total of 183 former professors entitled to return to their chairs under the 131 Law.[3] However, the universities' official autonomy, which was generally respected, permitted the faculties to make appointments as they wished as time went on. Their policies tended to favor recall for professors who had been suspended by the Allies immediately after the war, while those in exile were allowed to remain there. Only 17 percent of the full professors dismissed by the Nazis were ever recalled to their former positions.[4] Younger men who had completed their preparation for academic careers at foreign universities during the Third Reich had no chance whatever to be hired in Germany, especially in traditional faculties such as law schools. Neither Wolfgang Abendroth nor Franz Ludwig Neumann succeeded in obtaining law professorships; they had to make do with appointments in political science departments. On the other hand, Ernst Forsthoff, Georg Dahm, Walter Hamel, Ernst Rudolf Huber, Günther Küchenhoff, Karl Larenz, Theodor Maunz, Herbert Krüger, Hans-Peter Ipsen, Ulrich Scheuner, Werner Weber, Arnold Köttgen, Hans-Carl Nipperdey, Heinrich Henkel, Friedrich Schaffstein, Erich Schwinge, and all the others who had participated in shaping the National Socialist legal system returned to their chairs and continued to dominate German legal thinking in the 1950s just as they had in the 1930s and 1940s. Their commentaries on laws, so important in the daily practice of the profession, continued to appear, as if nothing had happened, in new editions prepared by the old authors.[5]

Law professors continued to teach the same doctrines they had during the Nazi era; only their terminology had been de-Nazified. Walter Hamel, for example, the Third Reich's leading authority on police law, had always set great store by "the nature of a political state that has been freed from the chains of liberalism." Once National Socialism had "incorporated the free citizen into the *Volk* and the state," he observed, "the freedom of the individual exists only as a function of his service to *Volk* and state."[6] In 1957, Hamel—now reinstated as a law professor (in Marburg) and undaunted by the downfall of the Fascist dictatorship and the establishment of a liberal constitution—continued to proclaim: "A legal person in the German view is not identical with the individual as defined by the French Revolution. He does not have the freedom to do anything that does not harm another person or infringe upon that other person's rights. He has the responsibility to serve others and social values; values of the community have priority . . . limiting an individual's autonomy and imposing communal obligations." Using terminology only slightly different from that which he had used twenty years previously, Hamel had once again managed to transform basic individual rights into obligations. He then concluded that such fundamental rights were "intended not to grant a status of special privilege to the rights of individuals, but rather to link together the sociological forces existing in the state so as to form a community with a harmonious structure . . . The purpose of fundamental rights is to constitute the unity of the state, indeed the unity of the *Volk*."[7]

Hans Welzel, a professor of criminal law, had once developed a "doctrine of final causes" whose elimination of rational criteria from criminal law fit well with the general picture of the Third Reich, although it failed to prevail against more radical theories at the time. His theories came into their own in the 1950s, however. Welzel continued to teach that criminal law had "a positive moral force"; it just happened that the "lasting values" the law was supposed to protect had not lasted so well after all. Prior to 1945, they had been "loyalty to the *Volk,* the Reich, and its leadership, obedience to state authority, and readiness to defend it with arms,"[8] whereas afterward they had become "respect for the life, health, freedom, and property of others."[9]

Even the keystone of Nazi legal reforms, the admission of analogy (used to the disadvantage of defendants), was rehabilitated by legal scholars after the war. Walter Sax, who dominated academic discussions on West German criminal procedure in the 1950s and 1960s, published his dissertation in 1953. It was entitled *The Prohibition of Analogy in Criminal Law* and asked whether "the path taken by National Socialist lawmakers when they revised paragraph 2 of the Criminal Code (admission of analogy) [was] not the right one after all, even though it set false accents and was laden with unnecessary political bombast." The only reason Sax considered it to have been a "mistake" was the fact that it was "superfluous, since the principle of teleological interpretation alone contains all the possibilities needed to provide a modern solution to the problem of analogy."[10] With the aid of the same method of interpretation that had enabled judges in the Weimar Republic to sabotage democratic laws and to render Nazi laws in the Third Reich even harsher, Sax achieved the same result, namely, the "extension of [overly] restrictive phrasing to include cases not covered by the wording of the law itself." In plain language, this meant a decision opposed to the law's text. Sax even managed to use this method—later embraced explicitly by both the Federal Supreme Court and the Federal Constitutional Court—to turn Article 103 of the West German constitution into its opposite. Article 103 specifically prohibited use of legal analogy against a defendant, but Sax demonstrated that in fact it did no such thing: "Since, in the last analysis, no obstacle exists even in the case of criminal law to full application of teleological interpretations, analogy is admissible in criminal law, as well as in cases where it serves to justify or to increase a sentence. No 'prohibition against analogy' exists."[11]

Sax's arguments used virtually the same wording as Friedrich Schaffstein's 1933 text *Political Theory of Criminal Law.* Sax assured conservatives, who had become somewhat alarmed in the face of so much dynamism, that the goal of this "unfolding of the objective element of meaning," this "dynamic view of the law," was merely to protect the conservative canon of values from democracy: "The dynamic interpretation of the law as described herein presents no obstacles to practice of a healthy legal conservatism, which stresses the continuity of law as part of its function in preserving order. On the contrary, it alone offers a secure foundation . . . for a conservative legal stance in the genuine and positive sense."[12]

27

Punishing Nazi Criminals

Even before the war ended, the Americans, British, and Russians agreed in the "Moscow Declaration" of October 30, 1943, that after Germany's defeat "those German officers and men and members of the Nazi party who have been responsible for or have taken a consenting part in the above atrocities, massacres and executions will be sent back to the countries in which their abominable deeds were done in order that they may be judged and punished." The most important war criminals were to receive sentences "by joint decision" of the Allied governments. The statement vowed that the three Allied powers would "pursue them to the uttermost ends of the earth" and would "deliver them to their accusers in order that justice may be done."[1] Immediately following the capitulation of Germany, the Allies began preparations for trying the chief war criminals in Nuremberg; and in the liberated countries of the Soviet Union, Poland, Czechoslovakia, Yugoslavia, Greece, Norway, Denmark, Holland, Belgium, Luxemburg, and Italy, the Nazi criminals who could be seized were also placed on trial. Many of them had gone underground using false names, however, mainly in the three western zones of occupied Germany.

Here the reconstituted German criminal justice system likewise took up prosecution of former Nazis, but only in cases involving crimes by Germans against Germans. Occasionally their decisions caused storms of controversy. One of the first crimes to be prosecuted after the courts were reorganized was one of the most memorable murder cases of the Weimar era, the assassination of Matthias Erzberger, a member of the Center party and former Reich minister of finance who had signed the surrender of 1918. One of the two assassins, the former naval officer Heinrich Tillessen, had fled abroad and returned to Germany shortly before Hitler seized power. On March 21, 1933, the "day of Potsdam," he was granted amnesty for an act committed "in the national revolutionary struggle of the

German people."[2] The County Court of Offenburg, where Tillessen was tried after the war, regarded this amnesty as legally valid and dropped the charges against him on September 10, 1946; this step was justified in a twenty-one-page document that also praised Tillessen's "patriotic motives" and defended his action as stemming from "overzealous patriotism" and a conviction that Germany must be "rescued."[3] It was understandable that this decision was received with outrage at the time, but some of the reactions were also hypocritical. The prosecutors, who were French, were finally moved to nullify the court's decision by reports from three legal experts, all of whom declared the amnesty granted Tillessen to be invalid. These three experts, however, were none other than Theodor Maunz (who had become a professor of constitutional law at Freiburg), and the professors of criminal law Eduard Kern (University of Tübingen) and Eduard Kohlrausch (University of East Berlin), all of whom had played leading roles in the Nazi legal system and had themselves created the theoretical foundations for the amnesties granted to numerous "patriotic" assassins.

Tillessen's case was not the only judicial scandal of that time. On December 23, 1946, the County Court of Lübeck sentenced a journalist named Garbe to five months in prison because, after being sentenced to death by a military court in Stralsund on December 29, 1943, he had succeeded in knocking down a police officer and escaping. Garbe had gone underground for a while, but when he resurfaced after the war, believing that he would no longer be prosecuted, he was arrested in Lübeck and charged with "resisting state authority" and even with "attempted manslaughter." The court derived Garbe's alleged intention not only to flee but also to kill the police officer solely from the fact that he had been an opponent of National Socialism; his political opinions alone made him capable of manslaughter in its eyes. The Kiel Court of Appeals upheld this decision on March 26, 1947, stating that "the actions of an officer of the court attempting to carry out a decision are always legal . . . Therefore, a defendant who has received a sentence must allow it to be carried out when it becomes effective."[4] In other words, Garbe was sent to prison after the war for not allowing the Nazis to execute him.

Verdicts of this sort led to heated public discussions, and critics spoke of a "crisis" in the criminal justice system, but often without pausing to reflect on the nature of the system during the Third Reich. Soon after the Federal Republic was founded, the Allies withdrew from the prosecution of Nazi crimes, leaving them entirely up to the new government. West Germany thus also became responsible for crimes committed by Germans against foreign nationals in other countries.[5] Since the Federal constitution, which went into effect on May 24, 1949, prohibits extradition of

German citizens to foreign countries, the Nazi criminals who had gone underground within its territory could be prosecuted only by West German courts.

Intentional and "Unintentional" Amnesties

One of the first laws passed by the new Bundestag granted a general amnesty for all crimes committed during the Nazi era with a maximum penalty of one year in prison or less. And in order to smooth the way into the new German state for the large numbers of Nazis who were living there under assumed names, the Bundestag also granted amnesty to anyone who had "disguised his identity for political reasons" by forging documents or giving false information.[6]

After the victors had dealt with the leaders and various groups of the Nazi regime in the major Nuremberg War Crimes Trial and eleven succeeding trials, and de-Nazification had come to an end (more or less broken off rather than fully completed), many Germans in influential positions in the new state still felt that enough retribution had been demanded. Even a Social Democrat in the Bundestag, Hans Merten, was of the opinion that it must be "clear even to a layman that the trials . . . did not serve to further justice, but were political trials with a law created ad hoc. They served the exercise of political power and political force." In consequence, Merten recommended, "We must put an end to this legal discrimination against Germans, put an end to trials dictated by a desire for revenge and retaliation."[7] And when the "Himmerode Conference" of former high-ranking World War II officers was held, under the leadership of former *Wehrmacht* general and later West German army general Hans Speidel, the conference participants, in order to prepare a German "contribution to Western defense," passed a resolution calling for "pardons for war criminals and an end to the defamation of German soldiers, [as] a prerequisite for any military contribution."[8] At that time, the term "war crimes" was used to cover all crimes committed by the Nazis, including the mass murder of Jews and other atrocities committed in the concentration camps. But even this euphemism (for atrocities unrelated to the war itself) was too negative for Hans Ewers, the Deutsche Partei ("German party") member of the Bundestag: he asked that the word "war criminals" be avoided in general, since "for the most part they are not criminals, after all."[9] It becomes understandable, given such a climate of public opinion, that the criminal justice system made no attempt to deal with any of the major Nazi murder campaigns. By the early 1950s, officials would react only when a member of the public brought charges, usually in connection with Nazi crimes from the prewar period. When the numbers of these cases dropped, public prosecutors undertook no further initiatives. In 1949 there were 1,523 convictions for such cases; in 1950 the figure was still high, at 908; but by 1954 there were only 44, and in 1955 the grand total was 21.[10]

In 1954 the Bundestag passed a new amnesty law covering all crimes that had maximum sentences of up to three years and that had been committed "under the influence of the unusual circumstances of the collapse between October 1, 1944, and July 31, 1945, while carrying out an official or legal duty, particularly an order." Renewed appeals were made for those in hiding to come forward, and the government continued to grant amnesty for "disguising one's identity for political reasons." Penalties imposed by de-Nazification boards immediately after the war were erased from the criminal records.[11]

In the meantime, the Western Allies appeared to have caught a "pardoning fever," as Robert Kempner, one of the prosecutors at the Nuremberg trials later put it,[12] and were also granting amnesty to almost all the Nazi criminals they had previously sentenced. Of the thirteen men condemned to death at the "special service units trial" in April 1948, for example, only three were executed; the sentences of the others were commuted to imprisonment in a penitentiary. Most of them had already been paroled by 1953, and the last one was released in 1958.[13]

"Pardoning fever" proved to be catching. When West Germany acquired full sovereign status, the Bundestag passed a "First Law on Ending the Occupation,"[14] which did away with all Allied laws that in their turn had done away with Nazi laws and that had punished crimes against humanity. And just as if it were an incidental matter, section 5, paragraph 1 of this law again altered the statute of limitations that had been suspended by the Allies: it now declared that no prosecution of crimes committed during the Third Reich would be possible after December 31, 1956, with the exception of murder and manslaughter.

In 1960 the West German parliament, without much debate, declared a statute of limitations on all homicides from the Nazi era except for murder. The Social Democrats waited until the end of March of that year to put forward a proposal that the period from May 8, 1945, to December 15, 1949, not be counted.[15] Late as it was, this proposal would have given prosecutors at least another four and a half years, but it was voted down. The prosecutor general of Hesse at that time, Fritz Bauer, found it understandable that after such parliamentary decisions, public prosecutors and the courts believed "it was appropriate to conclude that in the view of the legislative and executive branches of the government, the legal part of the task of dealing with the past had been completed."[16] In 1960 Walter Menzel, a Social Democratic delegate, reported to the Bundestag that the states of West Germany, "beginning in about 1950 and increasingly after 1952," had been half-hearted in their investigations into Nazi crimes because they believed, according to the Federal Ministry of Justice, that a "kind of public trend" existed "not to attach so much importance to prosecuting those offenses any more."[17]

It was not until 1964, when the Auschwitz trial in Frankfurt caused a considerable public stir, twenty years after the fall of the Third Reich, that the spectacular debates commenced in the Bundestag about extending the statute of limitations. They began with a request to the minister of justice to provide information about the extent to which Nazi criminals had been prosecuted previously. The minister and the government in power he spoke for were of the opinion "that it would violate the constitution to extend the statute of limitations for crimes committed before May 9, 1945." In his report, he then attempted to prove that violent crimes "had been vigorously prosecuted by the German judicial system" and that an extension was unnecessary, among other reasons because judges had already handed down orders interrupting the term of limitations for the crimes of the most prominent Nazis. As an example, the report cited the case of "Adolf Hitler, period of limitations interrupted through summoning of witnesses before the Petty Court of Neuss on February 8, 1965, at the request of the Petty Court of Berlin."[18]

Despite this report, the Bundestag voted on April 13, 1965, "not to count" the time between May 8, 1945, and December 31, 1949, in the period of limitations.[19] In essence, this amounted to approval of the Social Democratic proposal that had been defeated in 1960. However, the law expressly excluded those crimes which already fell under the statute of limitations, so that in fact it applied only to murder. The solution of the problem had thus merely been postponed for four years, and in 1969 the question of how to treat unexpiated Nazi crimes arose again. A second major debate in the Bundestag on the statute of limitations led to an extension of the limit for murder from twenty to thirty years, and the crime of genocide (paragraph 220a of the Criminal Code) was made subject to no limitation at all.[20] Also, according to the ninth "Law to Alter Criminal Statutes," the limit on acts of manslaughter and accessory to murder now became twenty years (formerly fifteen). Neither of these new provisions was relevant for Nazi crimes, however. Paragraph 220a was not added to the Criminal Code until 1954;[21] it describes precisely the type of murders committed by the Nazis, but like all criminal statutes it could not be applied retroactively. And so far as manslaughter was concerned, instances committed prior to May 8, 1945, had already fallen under the then-existing statute of limitations in 1960.

In addition to these "official" regulations concerning limitations on prosecution, there existed several other, little-known ones that—supposedly without anyone's really having intended it—provided for limitations or other obstacles to prosecution of crimes committed during the Third Reich. Along with the "general treaty" signed by the Federal Republic and the three Western powers occupying West Germany, a minor treaty regulating some aspects of the transfer of power went into effect on May 26, 1952; this was known as the "Treaty on Questions Arising from the War and Occupation."[22] An inconspicuous clause of this agreement prohibited German courts from prosecuting crimes for which "investigations [had been] brought to a final conclusion by the criminal justice officials of the nation or nations in question."[23] Clearly the victors wished to prevent German courts from revoking their verdicts. The actual effect, however, was to ensure that the many Nazi criminals who had received only mild sentences from the Allied powers were at liberty for good.

This regulation, as interpreted by the Federal Supreme Court, applied to the 1,314 men found guilty in absentia by French military courts of murdering 80,000 French Jews and executing 29,000 hostages and other civilians.[24] The treaty on the transfer of power brought these criminals a three-fold advantage. Verdicts passed in absentia were not recognized in the Federal Republic. The Federal constitution prohibited extradition of German nationals (Article 16, paragraph 2), and the treaty now made it illegal to try them in West Germany. As a result, they got off scot-free.

France thus began to press for an addition to the treaty that would at least make it possible to prosecute those who had been sentenced in absentia. This provision was agreed to by the French and West German governments on February 2, 1971,[25] but the Bundestag postponed its ratification year after year. At that time, the chairman of the parliamentary Foreign Relations Committee, and thus the person in charge of this matter, was a Federal Democratic delegate named Ernst Achenbach. Between 1940 and 1943, Achenbach had been assigned to the German Embassy in Paris and had been responsible, among other things, for deportations of Jews.[26] When the Bundestag finally ratified the amendment to the treaty in 1975, the higher chamber of the legislature, the Bundesrat or Federal Council, agreed only on the matter of murder.[27] All other offenses, including manslaughter, remained closed to prosecution.

Another "unofficial" amnesty turned out to have even more far-reaching consequences. It was clear that a further amendment to existing laws would be necessary if all murders committed during the Third Reich were not to fall under the statute of limitations on December 31, 1969. Before the inevitable debate on an extension even began in the Bundestag, however, an "error" contained in another law put virtually all of these killings beyond the reach of prosecution.

When the "Law Accompanying Introduction of the Law on Illegal Activities" went into effect on October 1, 1968, its Article 1, number 6 contained a hidden depth charge. This apparently insignificant piece of legislation, which had been unanimously adopted by the Bundestag after very little debate, added a new paragraph to the Criminal Code. The new paragraph 50, section 2 read: "If particular qualities, relationships, or circumstances which establish the criminal quality of the actor (particularly those of a personal nature) are lacking in the case of an accomplice to said crime, then his sentence is to be reduced and reckoned according to the rules governing an attempt at such a crime."[28] Before this law took effect, the relevant paragraph 49, section 2 of the Criminal Code on accomplices to crimes had established that sentences were to "be based on the law applying to the act which he has knowingly helped to commit." An accomplice's sentence could be reduced, but reduction was not mandatory. The maximum penalty remained the same as for commission of the crime itself. In the case of murder, the penalty was life imprisonment, and thus, prior to alteration of the Criminal Code, the statutory limit for prosecution of an accomplice to murder was twenty years, reckoned from December 31, 1949. Now, however, the newly added paragraph 50, section 2 required that the sentence of an accomplice to murder with no ascertainable personal motives that would classify his act as murder had to be reduced—in this case, from a maximum life sentence to a maximum of fifteen years. But since all offenses with a maximum sentence of fifteen years' imprisonment had already fallen under the statute of limitations on May 8, 1960, the net effect was to exclude from prosecution, retroactively and with one stroke, the crimes of all Nazi accomplices to murder. And according to established construction of the courts, only Hitler, Himmler, and the top echelon of Nazis were murderers; everyone else was an accomplice.

During a later parliamentary debate on the statute of limitations, Richard Jaeger, the minister of justice who had presented this "back-door amnesty" to the Bundestag, expressed surprise at the result: "What is astounding here is the fact that no one—not the otherwise so outstanding department of criminal justice at the Federal Ministry, not the eleven state Ministries of Justice with their experts who are hardly what you would call incompetent either, not the federal prosecutor general with his staff, and not even the members of the Federal Supreme Court, who were all asked for their opinion on this bill—pointed out the problem of its effect on the statute of limitations."[29] Yet this revision of the Criminal Code had been approved long before by the General Commission on Criminal Law, a body created by minister of justice Thomas Dehler in the 1950s which had performed the task assigned to it by drafting an extremely reactionary penal code. The secretary of this commission was Dr. Eduard Dreher, the criminal law expert of the "otherwise so outstanding department of criminal justice at the Federal Ministry of Justice," and former prosecutor at the Innsbruck Special Court. In view of the extensive and thorough debate of the General Commission (the arguments in support of paragraph 50, section 2 alone fill two closely printed pages in their report), it is difficult to believe later protestations that "in preparing the Law Accompanying Introduction of the Law on Criminal Activities, the consequences of paragraph 50 for the statute of limitations, and in particular for the offense of accomplice to murder, were obviously overlooked."[30] They are made even more unconvincing by the fact that just as the Bundestag was beginning once again to debate the highly charged topic of statutory limits, Dreher had the paragraph inserted into the Criminal Code by means of the inconspicuous Law on Criminal Activities, whereas all the other alterations to the general section of the code recommended by the General Commission were not discussed or voted on in the Bundestag until a year later and did not go into effect until five years after that.[31]

The consequences of this legislative "error" became evident on May 20, 1969, when the Fifth Criminal Panel of the Federal Supreme Court made a ruling of fundamental significance in the first trial of what had originally been planned as a major series in connection with the activities of the Reich Central Security Office. The judges ruled that the new passage of the Criminal Code placed beyond the reach of prosecution all the atrocities that had been conceived and planned there. Overturning the Kassel County Court's conviction of an official in charge of Jewish affairs at the Krakow Police Department, the court observed:

> As the first trial established, . . . [the accused] knew that the victims were being killed purely out of racial prejudice. He did not share this base motive, however, but was merely obeying orders as a police officer and member of the SS, although he had come to realize that the orders were criminal. According to the new version of paragraph 50, section 2 of the Criminal Code, acting as an accomplice to murder in this manner . . . may now be punished only with a penitentiary sentence of three to fifteen years. Paragraph 67, section 1 of the Criminal Code further specifies that this offense may not be prosecuted after the statutory limit of fifteen years has elapsed. This period

had already expired when the first court action concerning the accused in connection with these events took place . . . The charges against him are therefore dropped.[32]

This decision brought to a halt the largest series of trials against Nazi criminals ever planned in the Federal Republic, just as they were getting underway. Eleven public prosecutors and twenty-three police officers had sifted through 150,000 files and divided the material into three main categories: participation in the "final solution," leadership of special military units, and participation in mass executions. The names of 2,700 witnesses had been collected and preparations completed for eighteen trials involving 300 defendants.[33]

With its decision to stop the trial, the Federal Supreme Court gave a clear signal to other courts. Soon thereafter, the Berlin County Court also dropped charges against seven high-ranking officials of the Reich Central Security Office. Those who remained as candidates for charges of murder committed "of their own will" with personal motives—such as Dr. Werner Best (organizer of the special SS units for Poland), Otto Bovensiepen (chief of the largest Gestapo office in Berlin and responsible for the deportation of 35,000 Jews from the city), and Bruno Streckenbach (chief of staff at the Reich Central Security Office and the man who planned the special units for all of Russia)[34]—submitted medical certificates to the courts attesting that they were unfit to stand trial.

Another aspect of the new version of paragraph 50 was that it covered only those cases in which "personal characteristics and traits" qualified a homicide for consideration as murder. However, another section of the Criminal Code (paragraph 211) dating from September 4, 1941, and still in force today defines murder not only in terms of the perpetrator's attitude (such as "base motives") but also in terms of the crime itself, which may qualify as murder if it was committed "with malicious intent" or "with means dangerous to the public at large."[35] If the homicide in question was of this nature—something far easier to prove than the perpetrator's hidden motives in any case—then he could still be convicted as an "accomplice to murder." Thus, Article 1 of the Law Accompanying Introduction of the Law on Illegal Activities produced the absurd result that the planners and strategists of the mass murders were granted amnesty, while those at the bottom of the chain of command who had actually done their dirty work for them could still be prosecuted. This led Joachim Kügler, one of the prosecutors in the Auschwitz trial held in Frankfurt, to make the bitter remark, "The Bundestag, and in its wake the Federal Supreme Court, have handed over to the courts and criminal justice system only the small fry of the extermination campaigns. It appears as if the Supreme Court were protecting some of the murderers."[36]

The two great debates on the statute of limitations, held in the Bundestag in 1969 and 1979, were carried on in an atmosphere of solemnity and high moral purpose; the legislators were proud enough of themselves to have the debates printed up afterward in an elaborate three-volume edition.[37] In view of the "unintentional" amnesty the lawmakers had approved only a short time before, however, the debates were actually little more than shadow-boxing. The bills passed on August 4, 1969, and July 16, 1979, to extend the statutory limits for murder and genocide[38] amounted to a deception, although perhaps unconscious, of the general public. The paragraph on genocide had not been added to the Criminal Code until 1954 and thus was not applicable to Nazi crimes in any case, something obviously not understood by most people in Germany or outside it. What the Bundestag had actually done was to decide that there would be no statute of limitations for all future cases of genocide, but that there would be one for the mass murders by the Nazis. Nor would the killers of the Third Reich be much affected by extending the limits for murder. According to the courts' standard construction of the law, there had been only a handful of "real perpetrators" in any event, and all of them were already dead. Even as the legislature was still debating, the crimes of those who had acted as accomplices to their inconceivable atrocities passed irrevocably beyond the reach of criminal justice.

Murderers and Their Accomplices

Some criminal trials took place all the same, but if the courts could not close their eyes completely to the terrible crimes being exhibited to them, they still did not want to hold anyone accountable. Judges' reluctance to call anyone at all a "murderer" produced some decidedly odd results. The Hannover County Court, for example, found a former Nazi who had personally killed several people guilty as an "accomplice to murder"—that is, someone who had provided assistance to the actual perpetrator. It then sentenced his superior officer, who had given the orders and should the logically have been held responsible, for having "incited to murder."[39] Since there was no one else between them in the chain, these crimes remained "murders" without a "murderer." On November 15, 1951, the Mönchengladbach County Court also found someone who had given an order to kill guilty of "inciting to murder" but acquitted the man who had carried it out, since he had acted under duress.[40] However, if the order had in fact subjected the subordinate to such extreme duress, his superior should have been sentenced as the perpetrator in at least an indirect sense.

Seeing as it was impossible to use such stratagems for most Nazi crimes, in the mid-1950s the courts developed another construction that allowed them to offer the public a few "actual" criminals of the period. Since that time, virtually every decision related to crimes of the Third Reich has begun with a paragraph on the "chief perpetrators."

Two members of the wartime summary court, Walter Huppenkothen and Dr. Otto Thorbeck, were tried before the County Court of Augsburg in connection with the murders of members of the resistance—Bonhoeffer, Canaris, Gehre, von Dohnanyi, Oster, and Dr. Sack—in the concentration camps of Flossenbürg and Sachsenhausen. In its decision of October 15, 1955, the court observed, "The leaders of the National Socialist regime, Hitler, Himmler, and Kaltenbrunner . . . caused the execution of the above-named men from base motives . . . Their behavior had sunk to the lowest level of irresponsible human action . . . In this connection the defendant Huppenkothen is guilty on six counts of aiding and abetting, and the defendant Dr. Thorbeck is guilty on five counts of the same."[41]

The decision at the County Court of Ulm in a jury trial of participants in SS special units in eastern Europe, dated August 29, 1958, described in detail the brutal murder of 4,000 people near the Lithuanian border and concluded:

> The originators of the measures calling for "special treatment of potential enemies," meaning the annihilation of all Communists in the eastern territories and all Jews without regard to age or sex, have been identified by the court as Hitler, Himmler, Heydrich, and their immediate circle. Together they hatched the murderous plot, developed the organizational and technical means for its realization through the Reich Central Security Office, and had it carried out by the special units and the death camp personnel, all of whom were following orders. The court must therefore analyze the role played by the originators of these deeds before it can turn to that played by the defendants.

The judges then proceeded to find that the ten defendants had had the same awareness of wrongdoing as the "chief perpetrators," and had committed their crimes not under the duress of military orders but rather of their own free will. Nonetheless, they had not been "personally motivated to commit the murders"; instead, they had "in every case acted with the intention of contributing to and supporting the deeds of the chief perpetrators." Thereupon they were all given short penitentiary sentences as accomplices (averaging two days for each proven murder).[42]

In another trial, high-ranking civil servants at the Reich Ministry of

Justice were accused of ordering the transfer of thousands of inmates from prisons to the Gestapo or to concentration camps, where, as the Wiesbaden County Court established, they were "hanged, shot, bludgeoned, or beaten until death occurred." The trial ended with a decision that found Hitler, Himmler, and minister of justice Thierack guilty "as indirect perpetrators of the murders of at least 573 prisoners sent to concentration camps." The ministry officials who had ordered them handed over were found to be "unwitting tools" who had not understood what they were doing, and were acquitted. Supposedly the evidence had not shown "that while they were engaged in this activity, they knew of or considered as possible the intended or already effected killings of the prisoners." It was admittedly true that the Ministry's correspondence had frequently referred to the prisoners' "annihilation," but in the view of the Wiesbaden County Court, their "awareness that the word 'annihilation' was being used did not in and of itself . . . represent a sufficient basis to conclude that the defendants knew or suspected the killings were taking place."[43]

In March 1957 the Stuttgart County Court reached the following decision in the case of Dr. Günther Venediger, Gestapo chief in Danzig (Gdansk), who was accused of personally murdering four English prisoners of war: "With reference to the killing of these four officers in Danzig, the perpetrator was the former Führer and chancellor of the Reich, Adolf Hitler. In so doing, he acted in violation of the law and with intent." Thus, Venediger had been merely an accomplice to these deeds. Still, the court was clearly unwilling to sentence him even as an accomplice to murder (maximum sentence: life imprisonment), and so it applied to "chief perpetrator" Adolf Hitler the doctrine that "in case of doubt," one decided "in favor of the accused": "It cannot be proven with sufficient certainty that Hitler had an even limited premeditation or malicious intent" (that is, when he gave orders to shoot prisoners "attempting to escape"). This conclusion allowed the court to ascribe "base motives" to Hitler and still eliminate the quality of "malicious intent" necessary for homicide to be murder. The crime had been carried out with malicious intent by the accomplice Venediger, to be sure, but it was no longer possible to prove that the "chief perpetrator" had had such in mind. Therefore, after first acquitting Venediger twice (both acquittals were overturned by the Federal Supreme Court), the court finally found Venediger guilty of "aiding and abetting manslaughter" and imposed a two-year penitentiary sentence.[44]

Just as high Nazi party officials had been classified as "followers" in the early de-Nazification hearings and all responsibility ascribed to those leaders who were already dead, so now in an analogous manner the courts began to construe their actions consistently as those of mere "accomplices." Their decisions usually cited the "Bathtub Case" heard by the *Reichsgericht* in 1940: a young woman who had given in to her sister's pleadings and drowned the sister's newborn baby was found guilty not of manslaughter but only of aiding and abetting infanticide. The court had based its verdict solely on a highly subjective interpretation of the attitude of the perpetrator, for which no objective corroboration could possibly be presented.[45] This construction had been developed as much as ten years earlier, as a means to allow politically motivated assassins to get off lightly.[46] The principle as defined then stated that a person must have "personal motives" to be considered responsible for a homicide. Anyone carrying out the wishes of a third party was merely an "accomplice." From the very beginning, the postwar West German Federal Supreme Court rejected this doctrine; as late as 1956 it stated a principle flatly contradicting the Bathtub Case: "Whoever personally effects the killing of another is to be regarded as a perpetrator on principle, even if he does so under the influence and in the presence of a third party and solely in that party's interest."[47] It should be noted, however, that the decision from which this sentence is taken involved not a Nazi crime but an "ordinary" case of domestic murder. At the same time, the high court did everything in its power to support the "accomplice" construction of lower courts in Nazi trials by regularly upholding such decisions but omitting to include them in official collections. For a long time, in other words, the Federal Supreme Court applied two entirely different interpretations of the murder laws, one for Nazi atrocities and the other for ordinary crimes. But in 1962, just as the major case of Auschwitz guards appeared to signal a flood of further Nazi trials, the spectacular defection of a Soviet agent offered an opportunity to shift over to the "subjective" interpretation. A KGB agent named Stachinski had killed two Ukrainian politicians living in exile in Munich; he had used a sophisticated poison dart pistol and had acted "on the highest Soviet authority." [The KGB, or "Committee for State Security," is the Soviet secret police.—*Translator.*] According to the Supreme Court's own principle that anyone who effects the killing of another is a perpetrator, Stachinski should have been found guilty of either manslaughter or murder. The constellation of circumstances was ideal for allowing the court to state a principle concerning perpetration of murder ordered by a government, since the court could do so without risking accusations of protecting Nazis. However, the purpose of the arguments presented by the high court in its decision on the Soviet agent was too obvious to be missed. They were perfectly tailored to fit Nazi trials, even though it might not have appeared so on first glance:

The particular circumstances of crimes ordered by the state in no way exonerate the participants from legal responsibility. Every national community may and must require its citizens unconditionally to abstain from crime, including those committed through misuse of official authority . . . This principle also applies to cases where the regime itself is criminal. In certain circumstances, government orders to commit a crime may provide grounds for milder sentencing. If, however, someone yields easily to murderous propaganda, silences his conscience, and makes others' criminal aims the basis of his own convictions or actions, and if someone ensures that in his own area of influence or official responsibility such orders are carried out without reserve, or in some other way displays agreement or zeal in carrying them out or exploits state-ordered terror for his own purposes, then such a person may not later claim to have been merely the accomplice of his superiors . . . Such a person is regularly to be regarded as a perpetrator.

Following the obligatory condemnation of participation in state crimes, the Supreme Court executed a 180-degree turn and offered a loophole to all those Nazis who might later be accused of grave offenses, particularly killings they had committed personally and directly:

The legal situation can, however, present a different appearance in the case of persons who do not approve of such criminal orders and find them repugnant but who carry them out nonetheless as a result of human weakness, because they are not strong enough to resist the superior force of state authority and give in to it, because they cannot summon the courage to resist or the intelligence to be able to evade the order, or because they attempt for a time to use political slogans to salve their conscience and to justify their own actions to themselves. There is no sufficient reason in law to equate such persons and their form of participation, a priori and without exception, with the true authors of such crimes, with an unscrupulous criminal acting on his own convictions, or the person who willingly receives such orders and makes such convictions his own.

Thus, the court was able to conclude, in the end, that the perpetrator in this case was Alexander Sheliepin, then head of the KGB, while Stachinski, who had actually committed the murders, had merely acted as his accomplice. The "decisive" factor in distinguishing between perpetrator and accomplice was precisely this "personal attitude toward the crime," so that "a person, though his act itself fulfills all the requirements for murder, may still be merely an accomplice."[48]

Once this principle had been determined, lower courts no longer needed to produce long-winded justifications for deciding that a Nazi defendant had been only an accomplice; they could simply cite the Stachinski decision, and this in turn allowed the Federal Supreme Court to make references to its own "established and long-standing doctrine." In November 1964, a case appealed by public prosecutors came before the Federal Supreme Court: the acquittal of a defendant accused of murdering Jews. Alois Häfele, a former SS officer who had participated in the killing of more than 89,000 people in the Kulmhof (Chelmo) death camp, had helped to organize the camp, had supervised the cleaning and maintenance of the gas vans, and had personally pushed the victims into them. He had stripped the dead of their valuables for personal profit and had received 800 marks and special leave from Heinrich Himmler as a reward. For all this, the Bonn County Court had classified him as a mere "accomplice without the intentions of a perpetrator."[49] On November 25, 1964, the Federal Supreme Court rejected the appeal of the Office of Public Prosecutions and referred to its own "distinction between perpetration of a crime and the act of aiding and abetting as established in the Stachinski case." "A decisive influence on the course of action, . . . the high rank of the accused, . . . [and] his extremely active participation in carrying out the murder program" all presented no obstacle to classing him as only an accomplice in the Holocaust, since "this participation was not based on his own motives but was instead limited to the forms established by the criminal leadership."[50] The Supreme Court even succeeded in classing as an accomplice Karl Wolff, an SS general who had functioned as Himmler's personal liaison officer at Hitler's headquarters and had shared responsibility for the murder of millions. Even though the court itself was convinced that Wolff "viewed Himmler's instructions to kill Jews as necessary and correct and approved his aims in carrying out this allegedly 'historic mission,'" it took the view that the decisive factor "for distinguishing between a perpetrator and an accomplice . . . [is] his personal attitude toward the crime," and supposedly there was no proof that the SS general had acted on his own convictions "when he requisitioned and scheduled the trains" that transported the victims to the death camps. The court assumed that Wolff had merely "wanted to help Himmler carry out his task" (!) and "lent his occasional support to Himmler's criminal motives from his subordinate [!] position."[51]

Murder and Manslaughter

Once the Bundestag had declared a statute of limitations on all cases of manslaughter from the time of the Third Reich, the classification of a crime as murder or manslaughter acquired great significance. A murderer is defined by paragraph 211 of the Criminal Code (in the revised version of 1941) as "someone who kills . . . a person for the pleasure of killing . . . or otherwise from base motives, with malicious intent or by means dangerous to the public at large." If courts accepted one or more of these criteria in the case of a Nazi criminal, they had to sentence him; but if they rejected them all, then he could not be sent to prison. Thus, although judges could not deny what had occurred, it was within their power to interpret it in such a way that the perpetrator would escape prison, because of the statute of limitations. As questionable as the various criteria of the murder paragraph may seem, still there were times when one of them was quite obviously fulfilled, and this forced the courts into an extremely tortuous line of reasoning. For example, in the case of Dr. Kurt Borm, SS *Obersturmführer*, euthanasia practitioner, and member of Hitler's personal staff, the Frankfurt County Court found that he had killed 6,652 people "basely" and "maliciously," but it acquitted the mass murderer all the same.

The accepted interpretation of the phrase "with malicious intent" (*heimtückisch*) in the murder laws has always been that the killer exploited a situation in which the victim was unsuspecting and defenseless. If ever there were unsuspecting and defenseless victims, then certainly they were the mentally and physically handicapped patients sent by Borm into "shower rooms" where they were poisoned with carbon monoxide gas. (In official correspondence, this procedure was always referred to under the code word "disinfection.") Nonetheless, the court accepted Borm's claim that he himself had not recognized any malicious intent in his actions.

At his trial, he consistently spoke only of "release" and "mercy killings." On March 20, 1974, the Federal Supreme Court upheld the acquittal, since allegedly it could not be disproved that the SS officer had regarded these mass murders "chiefly as an act of humanitarianism." In the court's view, even Borm's deception of the victims' relatives—to whom he wrote under an alias, giving false information about the cause of death—could be seen as a humanitarian act, intended "not to burden their consciences by asking for their consent to killings they either desired or to which they were indifferent."[53] The small slip in this sentence betrays more about the judges' views on right and wrong than a dozen decisions of principle, since they actually seem to assume that the murders of the asylum inmates would have been lawful had their relatives consented to them.

The Supreme Court's decision merely confirmed, at the highest level, the opinion already widespread in the criminal justice system that the physicians of the euthanasia program had been led to murder countless people by "considerations of an ethical nature." In 1949, for example, a trial took place involving the staff of the Grafeneck "asylum," where about 10,000 victims were first "disinfected" and then disposed of by burning. On July 5, the Tübingen County Court found that the determining factor in the behavior of psychiatrist Dr. Valentin Faltlhauser had been "pity, one of the noblest motives for human action."[54] And on October 24, 1951, the Cologne County Court acquitted the neurologist Dr. Leu because he had been moved to participate in the euthanasia program "out of idealism." He had, in the words of the court, "seen in the inmates of the asylum creatures still human and deserving of pity," as was proven "by the concern he showed in procuring the coffins necessary to bury" them.[55]

Some sophisticated reasoning was also required on the part of the Kiel County Court to reach a verdict of "not guilty" in the case of former Secret Police commissar Heinz Gerhard Riedel. Riedel was accused of having ordered the murder of seven partisans "cruelly and with malicious intent" as leader of Secret Police Field Group 570. The evidence had established that Riedel, acting on his own initiative rather than orders, had locked the partisans in a van, led a hose from the exhaust pipe into its interior, and killed them with the fumes. On June 14, 1974, the court acquitted him, since in its eyes he had acted neither cruelly nor with malicious intent. The information that suffocation was not a cruel form of death had been provided by the expert testimony of a professor at the Kiel University Medical School. Professor Steigleder stated that the victims must have lost consciousness within minutes after the fumes began to enter the van, although it was true that they would have first felt dizziness, nausea, and cramps. This did not suffice, however, for the court to assume the presence of "cruelty." Nor, in its opinion, was there any question of "malicious intent": the victims could not have been unsuspecting, for they ought to have known that the Germans were using gas vans.[56]

The French historian Alfred Grosser has pointed out that a list of the absurd arguments used in trials of Nazi criminals would be endless: "Sometimes murder and systematic torture are excusable because the defendant acted in a frenzy of anti-Semitism, and the guilt lies with those who trained him to think this way. At other times the fact that he acted in cold blood mitigates his guilt, precisely because he did not act in a frenzy but was merely obeying orders from above."[57]

Sentencing

When, as did happen, Nazi criminals were actually found guilty, the courts often imposed sentences that, in the words of Fritz Bauer, former prosecutor general of Hesse, came "close to making a mockery of the victims' suffering."[58] In the early 1960s, the German Coordinating Committee of the Christian-Jewish Society said it had been observing "with increasing concern for some time that mass murders and violent crimes from the National Socialist era (concentration camps, ghettos, special extermination units, and so forth) . . . were being treated by judges and juries differently from other murder cases." The Nazi criminals would "receive minimum sentences for 'aiding and abetting murder,' sentences that in the eyes of the public reduce participation in mass murder to an offense about as serious as grand larceny, or regularly receiving stolen goods."[59] One or two days in prison per proven murder was quite common in these trials, and this was by no means due solely to the astronomical numbers of victims.

On occasion, judges made use of paragraph 47 of the Military Criminal Code, which was in effect at the time the deeds were committed, although not when the trials were held. Section 2 of this paragraph ran: "If the guilt of the subordinate is small, then a sentence may be dispensed with." Indeed, this law applied only to the armed forces and not to the police, but if the police duty in question was considered equivalent to "service in the war," then courts treated it as military service.[60] Sometimes even participation in the mass murders in the eastern territories was regarded as "service in the war." In the Chelmo trial mentioned above, for instance, the Bonn County Court determined on March 30, 1963, that paragraph 47 might be invoked even in those cases "involving the mass annihilations of innocent Jews that had nothing to do with the conduct of the war and were carried out in secrecy." The judges conceded that the defendant Mehring had participated "in the murder of at least 26,000 people," but argued—using paragraph 47—that the "discrepancy" between his guilt and the minimum sentence of three years would be "so crass" that imposing it "would represent an indefensible hardship." They therefore acquitted him of murder.[61] When the prosecution appealed the verdict, the Federal Supreme Court set it aside and instructed the Bonn County Court that it had been mistaken in its reckoning of the penalty: the minimum sentence was not three years, but only nine months.[62] In a new trial, the County Court then reached a decision, on July 27, 1965, that even this greatly reduced sentence "would stand in such disproportion to the guilt of the accused that it would constitute an unjust and indefensible hardship. If the legal minimum penalty would lead to such a situation of hardship, . . . then no penalty should be imposed at all."[63]

In another case, Wilhelm Stryzio, a former member of the SA who had gone to the apartment of a Jewish man on the *Reichskristallnacht* in 1938 and stabbed him to death, was also let off lightly. A jury at the County

Court of Paderborn considered his crime to be mitigated by the fact that he had been "roused to a frenzy" by his commanding officers in the SA and had thus acted in a highly emotional state. Stryzio was sentenced to five years in prison.[64] In the case of Emanuel Schäfer, an SS officer and chief of the Security Police in Berlin, the Cologne County Court in 1953 recognized as extenuating the circumstances that one of the people he had murdered "had great hatred for Germany," and that another was a Communist: "Patriotic considerations were uppermost in the mind of the accused; this was his whole nature."[65]

The courts regularly counted time served in prison abroad, as well as in internment or prisoner-of-war camps, toward the total sentence. If a defendant made the—unverifiable—claim that he had been interrogated about his crimes while a prisoner, then the courts assumed he was telling the truth and that the internment or imprisonment had occurred in connection with the same crime for which he was then being tried.[66] The Federal Supreme Court took great care to ensure that this practice was closely followed. When in one case a jury sentenced a former officer in the Security Police to seven years in prison for his participation in mass murders, they took into account the fact that he had already spent four and a half years in a camp as a prisoner of war: "Without this period of detention the sentence would have been considerably more severe." Since the jury had not subtracted this time formally from the sentence pronounced, however, the Federal Supreme Court reduced the already reduced sentence again by this amount.[67] Formally reckoning the time served as a prisoner of war as if it were a prison sentence brought with it the great advantage that a prisoner was eligible for parole much sooner. Normally a prisoner was eligible after serving two thirds of his sentence, and in this case the former police officer had to serve all of two months before he was released.

Courts also tended to be extremely lenient in the sentences they were willing to impose and in sparing defendants the "side effects" of acquiring a criminal record. In the case of Martin Fellenz, for example, the prosecutor asked for a life sentence for his participation in the murder of 40,000 people. However, in 1963 the County Court of Flensburg sentenced him to only four years in a penitentiary, and counted three years and eleven months of it as already served in pretrial detention. The court stated explicitly that Fellenz was not deprived of his rights of honor as a citizen.[68]

Even those few former Nazis who received life sentences were not excluded from such leniency. As a rule, life sentences were commuted to fixed terms (a maximum of fifteen years). Then other forms of detention or imprisonment were subtracted, and finally a prisoner could apply for parole after serving two thirds of the total. It was standard procedure to grant these petitions.[69] In a comprehensive study entitled *The Trials and Sentences of National Socialist Criminals,* written in 1979, Ulrich-Dieter Oppitz formulates his conclusion with great restraint: "It is clear that the courts strive to exhaust the legal possibilities for keeping sentences low, reckoning periods of internment or other forms of imprisonment generously in the total, and making sure that periods of the sentence actually served are not disproportionately long.[70]

"Unfit to Stand Trial"

Many defendants were found guilty and sentenced after trials that received a great deal of publicity. It then turned out, however, that they did not actually have to go to prison, or were released after a short time, with little or no publicity. The reason given in such cases was usually ill health. Thus, for example, Robert Mulka, the chief defendant in the Auschwitz trial, was given a fourteen-year sentence by a jury in Frankfurt but was freed again only a year after the trial, for medical reasons.[71]

Such "biological amnesty," as it came to be called, was granted even—or, it might be more accurate to say, especially—to the most prominent criminals. First decades would elapse before they were brought to trial; then more and more Nazi defendants began pleading poor health. In many documents reporting that defendants were "unfit to stand trial," the courts' relief is evident. Judges readily accepted physicians' findings and dropped charges.

The SS *Obergruppenführer* Bruno Streckenbach had headed Section 1 of the Reich Central Security Office, where he was in charge of planning the mass murders in Poland and the Soviet Union. The Russians had sentenced him to twenty-five years of hard labor. He was deported to West Germany in 1955, but the authorities there did not begin investigating him until 1957. The investigation was closed after only a short time, but then reopened in 1961 in response to international protest. Streckenbach was arrested, but was released from prison after only four months, on medical advice. The Office of Public Prosecutions opened yet another investigation, in the course of which a single prosecutor took depositions from more than a hundred witnesses and filled 30,000 sheets of paper with information.[72] The pretrial investigation lasted from 1970 to 1973, and when the indictment was ready—filling 512 pages and accusing him of causing the deaths of at least one million people—[73] Streckenbach, now seventy-two years old, called in sick. He was suffering from coronary insufficiency and poor circulation, not unusual ailments at his age. A physician at a Hamburg hospital certified that his fitness to stand trial was therefore "limited," meaning that the proceedings would have to be interrupted several times a day to let him rest. The Seventh Grand Criminal Panel of the Hamburg County Court then found that a trial in this form would be irreconcilable with the defendant's human dignity, and proceedings were ended for good on April 30, 1974.[74]

In another case, SS *Obersturmbannführer* Helmut Bischoff was found fit to stand trial. Nonetheless, the Hamm Court of Appeals stopped the proceedings just before the verdict, and did so out of caution, since, in its own words, "there appears urgent reason to assume that if the trial were to proceed, . . . the charge that the accused was guilty of murder would of necessity be presented in a form likely to cause the excessively high blood pressure mentioned in the prognosis submitted to the court by the expert Dr. de Boor."[75]

On August 6, 1976, the Nuremberg County Court found two more defendants unfit to stand trial; they were Karl Josef Ferber and Heinz Hugo Hoffmann, the two assisting judges in the trial of Leo Katzenberger for "dishonoring the race." (The presiding judge, Oswald Rothaug, had been tried and sentenced in the Nuremberg jurists' trials of 1948.) The fact that one of the defendants was still actively running a law firm did not pose any major obstacle to declaring his health too poor for him to stand trial, since, in the court's words, "Dr. Hoffmann is unfit to stand trial not because of physical infirmity but rather because he suffers from intellectual and emotional disturbances. The intent of the accused to continue . . . to devote himself to the practice of law does not contradict the finding that he is unfit to stand trial, for it is only the organic degeneration of his brain caused by aging that renders the accused unfit to withstand a lengthy, intellectually complex, and emotionally draining trial."[76]

· 28 ·

The Deserving and the Undeserving: Reparations for the Criminals and Their Victims

Most of the people found guilty of Nazi crimes had been civil servants during the Third Reich, since the worst atrocities had been ordered by the government. A conviction on criminal charges has unpleasant consequences for a civil servant; in the case of Nazi criminals, according to paragraph 31 of the Criminal Code (now paragraph 45), a conviction carrying with it a penitentiary sentence automatically resulted in "disqualification for office." Those still active in the civil service were dismissed and lost all rights to a pension, while pension payments immediately ceased for civil servants already in retirement. This rule did not apply, however, to convictions handed down by "non-German" courts. In effect, that is to say, someone found guilty of murder by a court in another country had a legal right to reemployment in the German civil service, and in some circumstances even to back pay. The Nuremberg war crimes trials of Nazi leaders and related trials were counted as "non-German" convictions.

Nevertheless, a solution was also found for officials with convictions from German courts: since 1924, persons who leave the civil service have been able to transfer their previous pension insurance payments to a pension fund for non–civil service government employees.[1] Paragraph 141 of the old Civil Service Law prohibited such a transfer in the case of a criminal conviction, but on July 14, 1953, when this law was revised and passed as the Federal Civil Service Law (in essence, merely a de-Nazified version of the old one), this limiting clause was dropped. When a general reform of pension regulations took place in 1957, the transfer of money paid into pension funds was expressly permitted, regardless of the reasons for departure or dismissal from the civil service.[2] According to the new law, the government was not only permitted but even required to grant retroactive insurance to officials who had been denied their civil service pensions by court decisions[3] and furthermore the "131 Law," which had been designed to deprive Nazi officials of their pensions, at the same time contained the provision that they must receive a retroactive pension insurance transfer. As a result, such persons suffered not the slightest inconvenience, even if they had been convicted of murders numbering in the thousands. For those in the middle or upper echelons of the civil service, this transfer was even advantageous, because the pension as calculated according to the new law was not only higher than their original one but also tax free. The Federal Social Court established a principle of "value-free social insurance"[4] guaranteeing the right to a pension transfer even in cases where an official had been found guilty of the worst crimes against humanity or the rule of law. The Federal Administrative Court specifically upheld this principle in a case involving the pension of no less a person than Dietrich Klagges, a former minister of the interior in the state of Lower Saxony and later its premier, who had acquired German citizenship only in 1932 when Hitler appointed him to a government post.[5]

The courts were even generous in filling "gaps" in the careers of former Nazis that would have led to reduced pensions. In one case, the Federal Social Court reckoned as "equivalent" to a period of employment for pension purposes the time a career Nazi party official had spent in prison after sentencing by a French military court.[6]

The "value-free" principle in recognizing pension rights turned out to apply only to Nazi criminals, however. According to the laws first passed after the war, victims of Nazi laws or crimes first had to prove that they were not "unworthy of reparations" before a pension or payments were granted. One man who had received a two-year penitentiary sentence for "dishonoring the race" was refused a reparation payment in Hamburg because he had joined the SA in 1933.[7] The heirs of a Jewish businessman sentenced for a "racial sexual offense" were also told that he had been found "unworthy." Their application was rejected by the Reparations Office in Hamburg on the grounds that their relative, who died in 1943, had "committed adultery over a period of many years. [At that time] he could have incurred criminal penalties for it." The lawsuit over the family's application for reparations was ended only by a settlement reached at the County Court.[8]

Another application for reparations was filed by a man who had spent seven months in prison in 1940, when he was sixteen years old, because of his fondness for jazz; at that time, he was also under investigation for possible racial sexual offenses. His application was rejected by the Hamburg Reparations Office on the following grounds: "German citizens of German blood who were deprived of their liberty for racial sexual offenses cannot qualify for reparations on this basis alone; they must clearly demonstrate that they were sentenced for a racial sexual offense because of their political convictions or beliefs." But when the young man in this case was able to demonstrate that he had indeed been arrested for opposing National Socialism, because he had spoken out against Nazi policies to fellow students at his school, this still did not help his cause. The authorities remained convinced that since the petitioner had not been born until 1924, "he could . . . certainly not express sensible opinions relating to political matters. On the contrary, . . . his fondness for outlandish music proved clearly that he had not reached a degree of maturity which would permit one to speak of reasoned judgment." It took a four-year court battle before the jazz lover was granted his reparations payment.[9]

As a general rule, readiness to make reparations to people who had been persecuted by the Nazi regime or to their relatives stood in striking contrast to the generosity shown its officials. The Federal Reparations Law of 1953, for instance, did not even cover all the different types of victims, but only those who had suffered discrimination or injury "because of their opposition to National Socialism or because of their race, creed, or ideology."[10] The wording of the law thus excluded large groups or victims from the very start, including the 350,000 people who had undergone forced sterilization and the families of all those murdered in the course of the euthanasia program. Applications for reparation payments filed by the former group were regularly turned down "because sterilization was not a form of persecution but was performed purely for medical reasons," and because "the Law for Prevention of Hereditary Diseases was not unconstitutional as such."[11]

Other groups of those persecuted, tortured, or murdered by the Nazis were left empty-handed by the courts' and bureaucracies' extremely narrow interpretation of the law. In the case of the gypsies (Sinti and Roma tribes), for example, although they were actually sent to concentration camps and murdered for racial reasons, the official explanation given during the Third Reich was "prevention of crime." Since gypsies were regarded as members of the "Indo-Germanic race," their deportation had to be justified on the grounds that they were allegedly "work shy" and "asocial." Courts and officials in postwar West Germany willingly seized on this terminology, and as a result Sinti and Roma who had suffered persecution before March 1, 1943, had no legal claim to reparation payments. Courts continued to uphold this view, even though the 1936 commentary on the Race Laws by Stuckart and Globke clearly stated that "as a rule, in Europe only Jews and gypsies [are] of alien blood," and even though on December 8, 1938, Heinrich Himmler, in a memorandum to the SS and police, had given instructions that it was time "to deal with the gypsy question in connection with the nature of the race."[12] Even as late as 1956, the Federal Supreme Court determined that "in spite of the occurrence of racial considerations, the measures taken were based not on race as such but rather on the gypsies' asocial characteristics."[13]

Minor acts of resistance to the regime during the Third Reich also gained neither recognition nor reparation after the war, since the courts did not recognize them as "opposition to National Socialism" and therefore refused to consider the often brutal sanctions imposed as "Nazi coercion." A typical case was that of Erna Brehm, a housemaid in the town of Calw. At the age of seventeen she had fallen in love with a young Polish auto mechanic named Marian Gawronsky, one of the more than ten million "foreign workers" brought into the "Old Reich" to replace the men at the front. When word of their love affair leaked out, the police arrested Erna Brehm and shaved her head in the middle of the market square as a public humiliation. The Stuttgart Special Court then sent her to prison for eight months for violating the ban on "associating with prisoners of war." After serving her sentence she was not released, but was sent to the Ravensbrück concentration camp; according to the order for preventive detention dated February 6, 1942, and signed by Reinhard Heydrich, her behavior endangered "the future and security of the *Volk* and the state." The young woman was not equal to the barbaric conditions at the camp, and after two years during which she wasted away to mere skin and bones and caught tuberculosis in both lungs, she was returned to her parents with the notification that she was "unfit for further internment." Erna Brehm never recovered from this treatment; in 1947 she still weighed only about eighty pounds and suffered from the delusion that any government official she encountered was plotting her death.

Erna Brehm's application for a disability pension was rejected, and her appeal against this decision was rejected by the Calw Petty Court on August 9, 1951, in a decision which also ordered her to pay all court costs. The decision was recorded on a six-year-old (and illegal) form from the Nazi era under the heading "In the Name of the German People" (instead of "In the Name of the People"), and its tone also echoed Heydrich's detention order. The grounds given for rejecting the application offer a profound glimpse into the workings of German criminal "justice." Erna Brehm was imprisoned on political grounds; supposedly she had posed a threat to "the future and security of the *Volk* and the state," and while in the concentration camp she was forced to wear the red badge identifying political prisoners. After the war, however, the court refused in her case to recognize the "opposition to National Socialism" required by the Reparations Law. "Her youth alone," the court found, argued against the assumption "that her contact with the Pole [was] based on firm political convictions that were opposed to National Socialism." It thus assumed that Erna Brehm had been prosecuted not for "political reasons but rather for entirely personal ones." The fact that the Third Reich itself had treated her actions as a political offense was supposedly irrelevant. To the question whether the prohibition against contact with foreigners might have been an example of Nazi injustice with possibly racist motives, the court responded that this law had been not a "purely Nazi law but rather a requirement for national security. The order for preventive detention also argues along these lines . . . Thus, the order for preventive detention is based on security considerations of a general nature and not on an intention to persecute the plaintiff for her politics." Erna Brehm died on August 19, 1951, at the age of twenty-seven. Her parents' suit for reparations, which they continued after her death, was rejected by the Tübingen County Court.[14]

Acts of resistance categorized as "purely personal" were not the only sort to be refused recognition and reparation; in many cases, the judicial system also refused to grant petitions for reparations even if they admitted that the petitioners had acted from political motives.

In one such case, a Social Democrat named Georg Bock had protested against the invasion of Poland by tearing up his draft notice and refusing to report to the army. For this, he was sentenced to three and a half years in prison by a Court-Martial in late 1939. After serving two years of this sentence in the fortress of Torgau, he was drafted into a prisoners' battalion and sent to work on fortifications at the Russian front. There Bock refused to lay minefields, because he was unwilling to have anything to do with lethal weapons. For this continued defiance, he was given a second prison sentence of a year and a half.

Bock's later suit for reparations for the time he had spent in prison reached the Federal Supreme Court, where it was rejected on the grounds that his actions had indeed been politically motivated, but that resistance to the Third Reich could "be regarded as rightful, and accordingly a government action punishing this resistance be regarded as injustice in the legal sense, . . . only if the chances of success for this act of resistance were such as to make it a serious and practical attempt to eliminate existing unjust conditions." Bock's refusal to lay minefields did not qualify as such at all; the court could "not even determine whether this refusal was in any way likely to bring about or hasten the military defeat of the National Socialist regime." Even if his actions had been likely to do this, however, Bock would still not have deserved reparation, for according to the decision, "by his actions he caused possible danger to the lives of German soldiers or failed to provide a means of protecting them from danger."[15] The Supreme Court judges reached their decision on July 14, 1961. How they envisioned a contribution to the "military defeat of the National Socialist regime" that did not offer "possible danger to the lives of German soldiers" was a matter they failed to explain.

Yet even "more effective" forms of political resistance to the Nazi dictatorship were not recognized. This was made possible by a special clause in the Reparations Law which the courts strengthened through broad interpretation. Before the federal law was passed on September 18, 1953, reparations had been paid in the various German states on the basis of legislation initiated by the occupying powers. When the Federal Republic was founded, France, Great Britain, and the United States signed a treaty with the new government entitled "Regulation of Questions Arising from the War and Occupation," which was the basis of the Federal Reparations Law.[16] It guaranteed to all those persecuted by the Nazis the same legal status they had formerly had in the American zone of occupation. The new German government agreed to pay reparations "without discriminating against any persecuted group or class of persons." Nevertheless, the federal law then passed did not recognize a claim to reparations from persons who had "provided support for the National Socialist or another form of dictatorship" or who "opposed the basic principles of freedom and democracy."[17] This political clause had a model in an older law: the Nazis had also made pension and disability payments dependent upon political good behavior. In 1936 the national insurance regulations were altered so that no payments would be made "if the claimant [had] actively opposed the government after January 30, 1933."[18]

In the case of paragraph 6, section 1, number 2 of the West German Reparations Law, the wording was aimed not so much at Nazis as at Communists. Many Communists lost their pensions and were refused reparations payments; if they had already been paid, the government demanded the money back. A suit connected to this breach of the treaty reached the Federal Supreme Court. On October 19, 1955, the court handed down a decision stating that an international treaty created obligations only among the signatories and granted no rights to individual citizens of the participating nations. The decision as to whether such a treaty would actually be respected within a given country must be left to its lawmakers.[19] The Federal Constitutional Court also failed to find any valid objections to the violation of the treaty.[20]

The anti-Communist mood of the 1950s and 1960s led the courts to make strategic use of the political clause in the Reparations Law. For example, Heinz Renner, a delegate to the Bundestag, was ordered to pay back the sum of 27,000 marks he had received after the war, although he was never convicted of an offense.[21] In another instance, distributing a mere seven copies of the East German Communist party organ *Die Wahrheit* (Truth) sufficed for the Federal Supreme Court to find that the distributor "lost his claim to reparations . . . as a result of this propaganda activity," since the newspaper's contents clearly aimed at "bringing discredit upon the political, social, and economic order in the Federal Republic and West Berlin and upon its leaders, and thus at paving the way for the elimination of this order and its replacement by the dictatorship existing in the so-called German Democratic Republic."[22] Even opposition political leaflets proved to the Federal Supreme Court "that the authors' sole aim was to defame the political leaders, to undermine popular confidence in them, to stir up the population against them, and thus . . . to make a violent overthrow of the government possible." Distributors of such leaflets lost their rights to reparation payments.[23] Membership in either the Association of Victims of the Nazi Regime or the Free German Federation of Trade Unions was automatic grounds for loss of reparation rights, and as late as 1970 the Federal Supreme Court refused to recognize such rights in one case because, among other reasons, the victim of persecution had hung a red flag out of his window on the first of May.[24]

The courts continued to refuse reparation payments even to opponents of Nazism who had long since given up their Communist affiliations and sympathies. One example is Ernst Niekisch, author of the books *Hitler, ein deutsches Verhängnis* (Hitler, Germany's Doom) and *Das Reich der niederen Dämonen* (The Realm of Base Demons), who has been called "the last great Prussian" by men of such widely differing views as Fabian von Schlabrendorff, Sebastian Haffner, and Bernt Englemann. Niekisch was arrested in 1937, and given a life penitentiary sentence by the People's Court in 1939. In April 1945, after eight years' imprisonment, he was liberated from the Brandenburg Penitentiary by the Red Army; he was half-starved, crippled, and nearly blind, but amazingly still in full possession of his mental powers. He was offered a professorship at Humboldt University in East Berlin in 1948, and elected to the East German legislature in 1949. But Niekisch, who had begun publishing a journal with the revealing title *Widerstand* (Resistance) in 1926, proved no more of a yes-man in the new Germany than he had been in the old. His critical comments on social developments soon embroiled him in conflict with the East German regime; he moved his residence to West Berlin and finally lost his university chair in 1954. Niekisch's application for a disability pension on the basis of the permanent damage to his health sustained in Nazi prisons was denied by the West Berlin authorities, who argued that he had "provided support for a dictatorship." This was the beginning of a wearying and protracted court battle that went all the way to the Supreme Court: in 1953 the Berlin County Court rejected his suit against the decision, and in 1955 the Federal Supreme Court found against him on appeal. After the Reparations Law was amended, Niekisch filed suit again, but on March 23, 1960, the suit was rejected by the Berlin County Court, since Niekisch had opposed "free and democratic order within the meaning of the constitution after May 23, 1949." The Federal Supreme Court rejected the second appeal. Niekisch thereupon lodged appeals with the West German Federal Constitutional Court and the European Human Rights Commission. The Constitutional Court proposed a compromise settlement, but the Berlin authorities refused to agree to it and did not change their stance until 1964. Finally, after a twelve-year struggle, Niekisch—crippled, blind, seventy-three years old—was granted a pension, but no German court had been willing officially to rehabilitate the "last great Prussian."[25] The writer Alfred Kantorowicz commented, "the case of Ernst Niekisch has become an embarrassment and a permanent stain on Berlin's record, above all in those parts of the world we are accustomed to call free."[26]

Kantorowicz, holder of doctorates in both civil and canon law and a literary scholar, had good cause to know. During the war he himself was placed in a French internment camp by the government of Marshal Pétain. Later he edited the journal *Ost und West* (East and West) for several years, and became a professor of German literature and director of the Heinrich Mann Archives in East Germany. After the revolt in Hungary was suppressed, the "professor, writer, Jew, Communist, ex-Communist, and Spanish freedom fighter" (to use his own description) gave up his tenured position and fled to the Federal Republic. Kantorowicz, too, was denied reparations by the authorities, this time in Bavaria, because he had "supported crimes against humanity." Finally, in 1961, the city of Hamburg granted him a minimal pension of 500 marks per month, which was never increased. Kantorowicz died in 1979 in acute poverty.[27]

The salaries and pensions of Nazi criminals, who for the most part were government officials after all, rose over the years to ten times their original level, but the reparation payments for their victims were never adjusted. Even today the reparation for a year in a concentration camp is a single payment of 1,800 marks.

The reparation policy had a method in it: if someone without a political affiliation became involved in a conflict with the Third Reich, then his act of resistance was classified as "merely humanitarian," and he received no reparations for time spent in prison or camps or for resulting damage to his health. The most clearly politically motivated resistance had come above all from Communists, but unless they renounced their ideology immediately after the war, they were accused of supporting "another dictatorship" and were also refused payments. If someone had contributed to the rebuilding of Germany in the Soviet zone of occupation, either because he placed more confidence in a socialist system or because he feared that his outspokenly anti-Nazi sympathies would prevent him from finding a job in the West, then he was automatically regarded as a supporter of dictatorship. Even if they had tried, Niekisch and Kantorowicz would never have succeeded in becoming professors at a West German university. However, once they had clearly placed their opposition to the East German regime on record and had given up all claim to their pensions there, West German judges and officials who had supported an incomparably more brutal dictatorship to the very last minute refused them reparations, and this with the argument that they had not withdrawn their support from a totalitarian government in time.

The unfair pension and reparations system ensured high payments to perpetrators of Nazi crimes, even to murderers whose original loss of office and pension rights resulted from criminal convictions, and even if they remained incorrigible Nazis. If their victims remained true to their convictions, on the other hand, the tainted officials withdrew their far smaller reparations payments, although these were supposed to be merely compensation for previously sustained injuries to health.

29

Jurists on Trial

"Case 3"

Even as the German judicial system was being recreated in the old mold and the identical personnel was attempting to forge links with the past, the most comprehensive investigation of Nazi jurists ever undertaken was proceeding in Nuremberg. The third in the series of trials organized by the Americans in the wake of the main War Crimes Trial, known as "Case 3" or the "Altstoetter trial," was devoted to the jurists of the Third Reich. But just as in the other Nuremberg trials—the physicians' trial, the trial of Field Marshal Milch, the Pohl, Krupp, Flick, and I. G. Farben trials, the Reich Central Security Office trial, the special units, Wilhelmstrasse, and Armed Forces High Command trials—the main emphasis was placed on crimes committed against foreigners. The Americans had no particular interest in prosecuting crimes committed by Germans against other Germans, and this would also have gone beyond the international law justification of the proceedings. As in the eleven other trials, the charges leveled against the jurists concerned war crimes, organized crime, and crimes against humanity.

The sixteen defendants, "the embodiment of what passed for justice in the Third Reich" in the eyes of their accusers, stood in the dock as representatives of the entire system. Its highest leaders could no longer be prosecuted, in any event. Reich minister of justice Gürtner had died in 1941. His successor, Otto Thierack, had committed suicide in 1946 in a British prison camp. Erwin Bumke, president of the *Reichsgericht,* had taken his own life as the U.S. Army was entering the city of Leipzig, and Roland Freisler had been killed in an air raid in March 1945. The highest official on trial was thus Franz Schlegelberger, former undersecretary in the Reich Ministry of Justice and acting minister; he was flanked by Thierack's two undersecretaries, Curt Rothenberger and Ernst Klemm. The other defendants included several more high-ranking officials from the Ministry of Justice: Ernst Lautz, prosecutor general at the People's Court; the senior public prosecutors Paul Barnickel and Oswald Rothaug (the latter, for a time, had been presiding judge of the Nuremberg Special Court and had sentenced Leo Katzenberger among others); the vice-president of the Nuremberg Special Court, Karl Engert; the presiding judge of one of its panels, Günther Nebelung; and two presiding judges of other Special Courts.

Although the evidence produced represented only a sample of the workings of the Nazi legal system, what it brought to light was damning. It was probably for this reason that the proceedings received so little public notice and were virtually ignored by professional law journals, and not, as prosecutor Telford Taylor surmised, because those who were most incriminated could not be put on trial.[2] In a certain sense, it was a fortunate accident of history that Schlegelberger and his cohorts were in the dock instead of the most prominent Nazi jurists, namely Freisler, Thierack, and Bumke. Precisely because the men on trial were not fanatic National Socialists, the ordinary workings of the judicial system during the Third Reich were exposed to view, and it became clear to what extent the largely conservative legal profession and its symbolic figurehead, Undersecretary Schlegelberger, had been profoundly involved in the reign of terror.

The main charges against the jurists were "judicial murder and other atrocities which they committed by destroying law and justice in Germany, and by then utilizing the empty forms of legal process for persecution, enslavement, and extermination on a vast scale."[3]

Schlegelberger, expressly recognized by the court as a "tragic figure," based his defense on the claim that he had remained at his post to prevent the worst from happening, and that only for this reason had he committed all the acts of which he stood accused. In the last analysis, however, this argument could be used not only by him and all the other jurists on trial to exonerate themselves, but also by every jurist, physician, official, and soldier who had any share in the crimes of the Third Reich. Even Hans Frank, the former governor general of Poland who was sentenced to death in the main war crimes trial, had fallen back on this line of defense, which in the end would have left Hitler as the sole culprit.

The court gave this hypothesis very careful and thorough study:

> Schlegelberger presented an interesting defense . . . He feared that if he were to resign, a worse man would take his place. As the event proved, there is much truth in this also. Under Thierack the police did usurp the functions of the administration of justice and murdered untold thousands of Jews and

political prisoners. Upon analysis this plausible claim of the defense squares neither with the truth, logic, or the circumstances.

The evidence conclusively shows that in order to maintain the Ministry of Justice in the good graces of Hitler and to prevent its utter defeat by Himmler's police, Schlegelberger and the other defendants who joined in this claim of justification took over the dirty work which the leaders of the State demanded, and employed the Ministry of Justice as a means for destroying the Jewish and Polish populations, terrorizing the inhabitants of occupied countries, and wiping out political opposition at home. That their program of racial extermination under the guise of law failed to attain the proportions which were reached by the pogroms, deportations, and mass murders by the police is cold comfort to the survivors of the "judicial" process, and constitutes a poor excuse before this Tribunal. The prostitution of a judicial system for the accomplishment of criminal aims involves an element of evil to the State which is not found in frank atrocities which do not sully judicial robes.[4]

During the trial, 138 witnesses were heard and 2,093 pieces of evidence examined. The court devoted a great deal of time to discussion of the Criminal Regulations for Poles, the "Night and Fog Decree," the transfer of inmates from the prison system to the SS for "extermination through work," the death sentence passed on Leo Katzenberger by the defendant Rothaug, and various death sentences passed by Special Courts on Poles doing forced labor in Germany and on juveniles in Poland.[5]

From the overwhelming mass of evidence, the court finally drew this conclusion: "Defendants are charged with crimes of such immensity that mere specific instances of criminality appear insignificant by comparison. The charge, in brief, is that of conscious participation in a nationwide government-organized system of cruelty and injustice, in violation of the laws of war and of humanity, and perpetrated in the name of law by the authority of the Ministry of Justice, and through the instrumentality of the courts. The dagger of the assassin was concealed beneath the robe of the jurist."[6] What was most shocking to the court, however, was not the various appalling crimes themselves (the previous trials had exposed the outrages of the Third Reich with sufficient clarity) but the fact that they had been committed under the cloak of legality.

The court gave the two undersecretaries Schlegelberger and Klemm, and the Special Court judges Rothaug and Oeschey, life sentences in a penitentiary; four of the other defendants were acquitted, and the rest received prison sentences of five or six years. Although the Nuremberg trial could deal only with a limited number of examples—in the short time available, the prosecution could barely scratch the surface of Nazi crimes committed through the legal system—it has remained until today the most concerted effort to shed light on the role of the judiciary under the National Socialist dictatorship. Still, it had little effect on the German legal profession, which tended to dismiss the Nuremberg trials as pure "retribution" on the part of the victors.[7] And the American and West German authorities themselves soon began undoing the results of the trial. To begin with, the life sentences were commuted to twenty years, and by 1951 all the defendants were at liberty again except for Rothaug, who was not released until 1956. Even Schlegelberger, who had been released "provisionally" for health reasons in 1950, was free for good by January 1951.[8]

Trials in other countries occupied by Germany during the war produced quite similar results. In 1948–1949 in Luxembourg, for example, a group of former judges and prosecutors at the German Special Court there were tried as representatives of what had been done by the Nazi judicial system in the occupied Grand Duchy. At the end of the trial, the Special Court's presiding judge, Adolf Raderschall, was sentenced to death in absentia; prosecutor Leon Drach received a penitentiary sentence of fifteen years, and prosecutor Josef Wienecke a sentence of ten years. Wienecke had to be sentenced in absentia as well, since he had used a prison leave to flee to West Germany, after giving his "word of honor" to return. Dr. Otto Bauknecht, another judge at the Special Court during the German occupation, was sentenced to four years in prison. In 1954, however, the last member of this group was pardoned and deported to West Germany "out of humanitarian considerations which were totally foreign to him in practicing his own profession."[9] All the defendants at this Luxembourg trial were able to reenter the German judicial system as civil servants. Wienecke became a public prosecutor in Koblenz in 1953, and was promoted to the rank of first prosecutor soon thereafter. Leon Drach was promoted to senior prosecutor not long after he was rehired. Raderschall, who had been sentenced to death, was appointed a petty court judge. In 1956 Otto Bauknecht was named presiding judge at the County Court of Bad Kreuznach, and later became head of the board of examiners in law for the state of Rheinland-Pfalz; this is to say that in spite of his criminal conviction at the Luxembourg trial, he was placed in charge of the education of the next generation of lawyers.[10] In yet another case, Dr. Kurt Bellmann, known as "the hanging judge of Prague," rose to the position of senior judge at the Hannover County Court after his deportation to the Federal Republic, although he had been given a life sentence in Czechoslovakia.[11]

It goes without saying that a criminal conviction in the Russian zone of Germany presented no obstacle to a career in the West. In June 1948 Dr. Erich Anger, who as a former prosecutor at the Leipzig County Court had successfully pleaded for the death penalty in a number of cases, was sentenced in Dresden to twelve years in a penitentiary for crimes against humanity. After serving his sentence, he moved to the West and became first prosecutor in the city of Essen.[12]

German Jurists Deal with Their Own Past

Before the mass of prosecutions of Nazi criminals came to an abrupt halt in the 1950s, German postwar judges had managed to sentence 5,288 people.[13] Members of their own profession were not among them, however, although there was no lack of damning opinions from even the highest places concerning the role played by the legal profession from 1933 to 1945. The decision in the Nuremberg jurists' trial referred to "progressive perversion of the legal system" and to trials "devoid of every fundamental element of justice," while the Supreme Court of the British zone of occupation used phrases such as "Nazi control of the courts"[14] and measures "that resembled . . . judicial decisions only in their outer form, but in reality [were] administrative acts of annihilation."[15] After studying all the branches of the system—the finance, disciplinary, and administrative courts, civil and criminal proceedings, and military courts—the West German Federal Constitutional Court concluded, "It becomes evident everywhere that judges considered it their duty to interpret and apply regulations to correspond with National Socialist aims—meaning above and beyond what the letter of the law demanded."[16] Even the Federal Supreme Court determined that the proceedings of the People's Court had had "nothing to do with the administration of justice" and had amounted to "exploitation of judicial formalities for the purpose of illegal killing": "It is precisely in this manner that such an administration of justice reveals its true nature as an instrument of terror."[17]

These forthright words from the highest German criminal court stood not in the sentence of a colleague from the bench, but in that of a woman who had denounced several people to the Nazi authorities. In 1956 the Federal Supreme Court upheld her conviction with the argument that the People's Court had not been a real court at all, and the woman should have known that. Numerous other decisions from the years 1947–1950 were based on the assumption that informers were delivering those they betrayed to a judicial system "which dealt mercilessly with political opponents at that time, as the population was well aware."[19] It was "coldly calculated and executed persecution . . . that ought to be impossible in every civilized country"; in other words, the people denounced were being handed over to "the executioner."[20] In 1948 a laborer named Max Willi Reiche, who had turned in a man he had seen writing anti-Nazi slogans, received a fifteen-year penitentiary sentence from the Berlin County Court, and in 1949 the Düsseldorf County Court imposed a life sentence on Hans Wienhusen, a Gestapo informer who had denounced his employer to the People's Court.[21] In both cases, the court had considered imposing the death penalty.[22]

From the early 1950s on, however, trials of informers tended to end in acquittal. A machinist named Fritz Hoffmann was tried for informing on his brother; Hoffmann had testified against him at the People's Court, saying, "People like him must be eliminated." In Duisburg in September 1950, Hoffmann was given a two-year prison sentence for "crimes against humanity," but after the Federal Supreme Court set the verdict aside, the Duisburg County Court acquitted him in 1953, because—as the opinion now ran—Hoffmann could supposedly not have known that his brother would receive only a show trial: "In large circles of the German population these breaches of law, particularly in the practice of the People's Court, were as unknown as the concentration camp atrocities and the murders of Jews." Even the fact that the defendant had demanded his brother's "elimination" was considered irrelevant, since "the expression 'eliminate' did not necessarily . . . have the meaning of 'kill,' but could have been intended in the sense of 'put away,' 'remove,' or 'render harmless' by means of a prison sentence." The same argument was used by the Essen County Court to acquit the city's former mayor, Just Dillgardt, on March 9, 1953.[23]

A former department head in the Reich Ministry of Propaganda, a certain Dr. Froehlich, was charged before the Hamburg County Court with having denounced a man in 1943 (who had then been promptly sentenced to death by the People's Court). Froehlich himself was acquitted on May 8, 1964. After previous decisions in which it was assumed that a tool-and-die maker, a seamstress, a laborer, a man on welfare, a man with a small repair shop, and a warehouse workman (the latter described as "intellectually not a very flexible man") should all have been capable of recognizing the unjust nature of proceedings at the People's Court, the County Court now turned around and claimed in the case of Dr. Froehlich (whose doctorate was in law) "that, given his perspective at that time as a trained lawyer and ardent National Socialist, the defendant could have been of the opinion that a court of the Third Reich would not act improperly and would commit neither perversion of justice nor manslaughter." His acquittal was upheld by the Federal Supreme Court on April 27, 1965.[24]

Once the People's Court had been classified as an "instrument of terror," it would have been only consistent to make the public prosecutors and judges who had wielded it accountable. When the question was one of charging those who had not merely aided and abetted crimes but had personally been practitioners of terror, however, it suddenly became clear to the courts—with the Federal Supreme Court in the vanguard—"what unusual difficulties in points of both fact and law are encountered in prosecuting National Socialist judicial crimes."[25]

At the time of the Nuremberg jurists' trial, when the German criminal justice system had not even begun to think of bringing charges against judges for their actions in the Third Reich, an academic discussion got underway concerning the extent of their legal accountability. Ironically, it was none other than Gustav Radbruch, a professor of criminal law whom the Nazis had driven from his university, whose musings on the accountability of judges presented a golden opportunity for self-justification to former Nazis. Radbruch wrote, "If a judge is to be considered guilty of homicide, it must be determined at the same time that he is guilty of a perversion of justice." An instance of perversion of justice was a criminal offense only if a judge performed it "consciously" and against his own better knowledge—that is, with "direct intent."[26] To prevent the possibility that even the most fanatic Nazi judge would claim he had been blind to politics and had considered everything happening in the Third Reich to be perfectly legal, however, Radbruch had added a proviso that "such blindness with regard to justice" did not automatically "preclude the notion of intent." Radbruch did not want his doctrine to lead to a general amnesty and asked, "Were the German people, including the perpetrators, so thoroughly deluded that the idea . . . really never occurred to any of them that even though the Führer's orders had the status of laws, they were in fact criminal?"[27] The majority of legal scholars and officials enthusiastically adopted this view—that a judge could be found guilty of murder, manslaughter, or false imprisonment only if it could be proved that he had knowingly broken the law. At the same time, they chose to ignore the limits Radbruch had imposed on his own claim.

Many Nazi criminals profited from the notion developed during these years that an "insufficient awareness of injustice" in connection with an act rendered its perpetrator innocent in the eyes of the law. As it turned out, the professional group to benefit most from this concept were precisely those who were supposed to embody an "awareness of justice" for the whole country. "There is no one today who can make head or tail of the split personality common among lawyers," wrote Fritz Bauer, prosecutor general of Hesse, in 1962. "In the de-Nazification files we read that they were opposed, to the last man. But then the minute prosecutors and judges are to be called to account for an excessive number of death sentences, they claim to have persecuted and killed with the clearest conscience, so that according to prevailing opinion we cannot accuse them of perversion of justice and manslaughter."[28]

The Kassel County Court, for example, did not believe that "conscious perversion of justice" could be proven on the part of the former Special Court judges there, who had sentenced the engineer Werner Holländer to death as a "dangerous habitual criminal" for carrying on a love affair. The County Court argued on behalf of Judge Kessler, author of the Holländer opinion and "probably the ablest jurist in Kassel," that his thinking was "imbued with the spirit of the saying 'Whatever benefits the people is just,' and he may have believed it was just retribution and in the interest of the Volk to find Holländer guilty and have him executed." Indeed, the court continued, Kessler may even have believed that this murderous perversion of justice represented "a high level of judicial achievement." The court cited, in the defendant's favor, the argument that in 1943 the former judges of the Special Court "were ardent, even fanatic Nazis," although this argument would have been used against other criminals of the era. Because of the judges' fanaticism, "the possibility of blindness to injustice, based on political delusions, . . . cannot be excluded." The verdict was therefore "not guilty."[29]

Similar verdicts were passed in the cases of the navy judge Holzwig and his commanding officer Petersen, who had sentenced sailors to death after the capitulation. The Federal Supreme Court set aside a previous conviction with the argument that even after May 8, 1945, the death penalty could be imposed "according to the sentencing guidelines for desertion established by the Führer as commander-in-chief of the army on April 14, 1941," "if it was 'essential' for 'maintaining discipline among the troops.'"[30] The Hamburg County Court thereupon acquitted the defendants on February 27, 1953, since even after the collapse of the Nazi dictatorship "no reason [existed] to regard these guidelines, taken as a whole, as unjust or excessively harsh or invalid." In the case of the sailors who had attempted to return home as quickly as possible after the cessation of hostilities, the Court-Martial at that time had merely "correctly affirmed the existence, in legal terms, of an aggravated case of desertion according to Article 1, paragraph 2 of the guidelines." The court was unwilling to recognize "unlawful action" on the part of the fanatic Nazi judge; "the fact that he was an active National Socialist" did not in any way suffice to justify such a conclusion, "since he could have been such for thoroughly understandable and laudable reasons."[31]

The Federal Supreme Court even specifically recognized the right of SS general Max Simon to act as a judge in the very last hours of the war, when he had confirmed summary court verdicts that made a mockery of all genuine legal proceedings with the remark, "Hang the fellows!"[32] A jury at the Ansbach County Court then acquitted him, since although Simon had allowed himself "to be used as a tool by the National Socialist leaders to suppress their ideological opponents," it "could not be proven that he knowingly became an accomplice in their perversion of justice, and the emphasis here is to be placed on 'knowingly.'"

Also acquitted were Karl Brumshagen, the presiding judge of a summary court, and *Gauleiter* Florian, who had ordered Düsseldorf chief of police Jürgens shot at the last minute before Allied troops crossed the Rhine. The Federal Supreme Court saw no "conscious violation of [the defendant's] fundamental rights" in the various procedural errors of the summary trial; the judge "was of the opinion that the case represented a treasonable offense and therefore [had] no awareness that his own action could be considered a perversion of justice."[34]

In handing down decisions relating to their colleagues from the Third Reich, judges used phrases like these repeatedly, until they became part of their stock in trade. It did not stop there, however: after a series of acquittals, prosecutors and courts began using them in their orders to close an investigation on a case before it even came to trial. On September 3, 1964, the Karlsruhe Court of Appeals, for example, dropped charges against Wolfgang Fränkel, the federal prosecutor general who had entered pleas of nullity and altered the prosecution's recommendation to the death penalty in at least fifty cases during the Third Reich. The court saw no "possibility of proving that the accused had ever so much as doubted the validity of the regulations in question . . . during the war, much less recognized their invalidity."[35]

Although no other Nazis were allowed to get away with it, the excuse that they had thought their actions were perfectly legal and just at the time was supposed to exonerate the Third Reich's "guardians of the law." Another case decided by the Federal Supreme Court in 1960 shows that such interpretations were by no means universally applied, however. Among the many citizens of East Germany who arrived in the West via Berlin before the Berlin Wall was built was Ernst Oehme, former presiding judge of the Sixth Criminal Panel of the Magdeburg County Court. In this capacity, in accordance with Article 6, paragraph 2 of the East German constitution, he had given a number of Jehovah's Witnesses penitentiary sentences ranging from three and a half to ten years for "espionage, pacifist propaganda, and urging a boycott"; under socialism just as under National Socialism, Jehovah's Witnesses refused to perform military service. Once in the West, the former judge was charged with perversion of justice, but was acquitted by the County Court of West Berlin on the grounds that as presiding judge of a panel concerned with political crimes, he had been subject to pressure and not an "independent judge." However, the Federal Supreme Court set this acquittal aside, arguing, "The legal order requires from every civil servant with the power to make decisions in cases of law—including those duty-bound to follow the instructions of their superiors—that he proceed on the basis of what is just and lawful, regardless of any instructions he might receive to the contrary." The high court conceded that the sentences passed by Judge Oehme "were correct from his perspective at the time as judge in the Soviet zone of occupation," but they constituted perversion of justice all the same: "Even if his sentence contains no intended perversion of justice, a judge commits it nonetheless if he knowingly imposes a sentence which by its nature and severity stands in egregious disproportion to the crime itself and to the guilt of the perpetrator." Judge Oehme had used the same defense that had always been accepted in the case of Nazi judges, and the Supreme Court could no more disprove his claim that he had considered his sentences appropriate than it could in the case of the acquitted Nazis. Here, however, the judges found that such a defense did "not automatically" exclude an intention to pervert justice. After all, they noted, the accused "was fully trained in the law, and he can be expected to have a sense of whether a sentence stands in egregious disproportion to the crime and the guilt of the perpetrator." [36]

If the Supreme Court judges truly believed that penitentiary sentences stood "in egregious disproportion" to the conscientious objection of the Jehovah's Witnesses, then they ought to have found the death sentences passed on members of the sect by the People's Court and the Special Courts even crasser instances of the same injustice. Let us look at a case involving a reparations claim for a Jehovah's Witness that came before the Federal Supreme Court four years later. A member of the sect had been sentenced to death during the Third Reich for refusal to perform military service (although this sentence was later commuted to ten years in a penitentiary). When his relatives petitioned for reparations, however, the judges of the Fourth Civil Panel could "not take the view that what happened to him [was] an example of National Socialist injustice." The Supreme Court rejected their suit, since "nowhere in previous decisions has doubt been cast on the lawful nature of the regulation in question," meaning the regulation prescribing the death penalty for conscientious objectors. [37]

In spite of this last case, it did seem as if the surprising about-face made by the Supreme Court in its interpretation of the statute on perversion of justice had paved the way for dealing with some of the worst excesses of the Nazi legal system. One opportunity to escape the shadow of the past was offered by the case of Hans-Joachim Rehse, who, after Roland Freisler, was the most incriminated judge at the People's Court. There was evidence connecting him with at least 230 death sentences. He had joined the court in 1939 as an investigative judge and had been named to the First Panel under Freisler in 1941, a position he continued to hold until the end of the war. The Office of Public Prosecutions in Munich opened an investigation into his activities in 1962, but charges were dropped on the usual grounds that no intent to commit homicide could be proved. Then, however, after the publication of *Priester vor Hitlers Tribunalen* (Priests before Hitler's Tribunals),[38] which documented the treatment of Catholic clergy during the Third Reich and which cited fifteen death sentences with Rehse's signature, prosecutors in Berlin opened another investigation and brought charges of murder and attempted murder for the most outrageous instances of perversion of justice. The indictment was based mainly on cases where the concept of "public" contained in the special wartime criminal regulations had been so interpreted that even remarks made in the most intimate circle of family or friends were considered "public."

On July 3, 1967, the Berlin County Court found the former hanging judge guilty on three counts of aiding and abetting murder and four counts of aiding and abetting attempted murder, and sentenced him to five years in a penitentiary. The decision followed the standard interpretation for Nazi crimes and found that the actual perpetrator was Freisler, since he had exercised "a dominant influence" on the other members of the First Panel. It was found that Judge Rehse had merely suppressed "all criticism of Freisler and accepted his authority." But the court was not willing to accept "blindness owing to Nazi propaganda" as a defense, because there was a difference as to whether a judge made an error in assessment of the case or in interpretation of the law in a single instance, "or whether he was deluded into attempting to pursue illegal aims over a long period of time." In an obvious reference to the Supreme Court's Oehme decision, the County Court found that Rehse was "fully trained in the law and could have been expected to preserve a sense of fitting punishment. If he had consulted his conscience sufficiently, he would have had to recognize the illegality of his actions." The court clearly took some pleasure in pointing out that, if one were to exclude the presence of intent to pervert the law on grounds of "political blindness owing to Nazi propaganda," then one could just as well acquit Roland Freisler himself, for the claim that he was deluded would apply to him better than anyone else.[39]

Both the prosecution and the defendant appealed the verdict, and on

April 30, 1968, the Fifth Criminal Senate of the Federal Supreme Court handed down a decision in the case. It devoted particular attention to the question whether an assisting judge on a panel should be regarded as an accessory or merely an abettor in the perversion of justice committed by the presiding judge. In contrast to its usual practice in Nazi trials, the Supreme Court cited paragraph 1 of the Law on the Constitution of Courts (which was also in force during the Third Reich, although only on paper) and assumed that the judge had been not an abettor but a coconspirator. The argumentation—which virtually invited misunderstanding—ran that, on votes, a People's Court judge had been "independent even according to the law prevailing at the time, with equal rights, accountable only to the law and his own conscience," and that he had been obliged "to act solely on the basis of his own convictions." At first glance, this looked like a rehabilitation of the People's Court as an actual court of justice, but its real intent was to recognize Rehse's status as a judge. For if he were regarded not as an abettor of Freisler's murders but as an independent perpetrator, then for a conviction the prosecution would have to prove that Rehse personally had the intent to kill from base motives. (The offenses of manslaughter and perversion of justice had long since fallen under the statute of limitations.) Furthermore, although the Berlin County Court had explained in detail in the first decision how it understood the concept of "blindness to justice," the Federal Supreme Court claimed to see "obscurities and contradictions." Blindness to justice and political delusion, "in the usual sense of the words," did not seem in its eyes "reconcilable with intent to pervert the law." The case was returned to the County Court with the undisguised recommendation to find for acquittal.[40]

A new jury in Berlin in the court of the young judge Ernst-Jürgen Oske thereupon reached a decision acquitting not only Rehse, but in effect the entire People's Court and the entire Nazi judicial system. One People's Court case had played a central role in Rehse's second trial—the case of Max Josef Metzger, a Catholic priest. Interestingly enough, the Federal Supreme Court had dealt with this case before in another context. Metzger had been denounced to the People's Court by a Gestapo agent named Dagmar Irmgart in 1943. In its 1956 decision on the charges brought against Irmgart, the highest West German court found that the legal interpretation used by the People's Court to sentence Father Metzger to death was not justice, but "merely an exploitation of judicial forms to commit homicide." Such an approach, the decision continued, served "solely to annihilate political opposition and eroded the inviolable core of the law. It is here that this kind of 'administration of justice' reveals its true nature as an instrument of terror. The conviction of Father Metzger and the passing of sentence upon him were therefore premeditated illegal homicide under the cloak of criminal justice."[41]

If, after reading these sentences, one turns to the arguments used in acquitting Rehse fifteen years later, it is difficult to believe that they are describing the same People's Court. The Berlin County Court stated, for instance, that it "could not determine that the defendant at that time, Father Metzger, was prevented from defending himself in a manner that deprived him of his legal rights." The extreme interpretation of the law regarding the giving of "aid and comfort to the enemy," namely that any remark critical of the Nazi regime benefitted the other side, "remained within the bounds of reasonable interpretation . . . It corresponds to the nature of modern warfare." On the whole, the Berlin court found, laws in Nazi Germany reflected "the right of every nation to provide for its own security, in times of danger threatening from without, by passing rigorous wartime regulations." The court took the view that "Metzger's actions objectively fulfilled the criteria for giving aid and comfort to the enemy." This last conclusion was one that not even the People's Court had reached in 1943, for the decision there stated that "Metzger's actions [were] so abominable that it does not matter whether they are technically found to constitute high treason, aid and comfort to the enemy, or defeatism: none of this is relevant, since every member of the *Volk* is aware that such desertion from our front-line battle is a monstrous crime, a betrayal of our nation in its life-or-death struggle, and that such a betrayal deserves punishment by death." The Berlin County Court remained convinced, in spite of such diction, that the argumentation of the People's Court remained "within the bounds of rational deliberation," and the Berlin judges also found nothing to object to in the view of the People's Court that a conversation between two people was "public": "an extension of the notion 'in public' in this manner" seemed "problematic" in their eyes, "but acceptable in terms of Federal Supreme Court decisions." They concluded, "In the majority of cases [decided by Judge Rehse] the evidence submitted, regarded in light of the criteria established by the Federal Supreme Court, failed to establish a violation of established principles in determining the severity of the sentence."[42] The most scandalous part of the Berlin decision consisted of Judge Oske's comments on the character of the People's Court: "The Federal Supreme Court has established . . . that the People's Court was an independent court subject solely to the law under the meaning of paragraph 1 of the Law on the Constitution of Courts." In actual fact, the Supreme Court had never made this claim; it had preferred, in 1968, to avoid any comment on "whatever actual circumstances may have obtained" there, and had merely stressed that it would have been Rehse's duty "to act solely upon his own convictions."[43] However, in its efforts to acquit Third Reich judges of responsibility to the last man, the Supreme Court had virtually invited such a misunderstanding of its intentions.

The prosecution appealed the decision of the Berlin court, but before a new trial could take place the defendant died. Judge Oske's general pardon for the People's Court as a whole has remained uncontradicted as the last word from West German courts on the Nazi judicial system.

There was one man who still refused to give up. He was attorney Robert M. W. Kempner, a prosecutor at the main Nuremberg war crimes trial in 1945–1946, who had repeatedly initiated investigations into the activities of Nazi jurists, including Joachim Rehse. At Kempner's urging, Gerhard Meyer, the Social Democrat senator for justice in the West Berlin government, made a last attempt to bring to justice the 67 surviving judges and prosecutors from the 570 members of the People's Court. Investigations recommenced, but in 1983 Meyer's successor, Christian Democrat Rupert Scholz, requested the public to be patient, since the inquiry was proving to be "extraordinarily difficult, extensive, and protracted." Still and all, after four years' work, prosecutors had managed to question two of the alleged perpetrators![44] When the inquiry began, most of those under investigation were in their eighties, and in the course of the next seven years half of them died. The Berlin Office of Public Prosecutions finally put an end to the macabre farce by closing the case on September 26, 1986.

The judicial system of the Third Reich remains an open chapter. The People's Court was the chief symbol of a system without justice and no doubt its most openly brutal institution, but it was only a part of that system. If its judges had been tried and found guilty, then it would have been impossible to acquit the numerous others who had handed down sentences on the Race Laws elsewhere or had presided at the Special and Military Courts. Conviction of a single judge of the Third Reich would have started an avalanche that would inevitably have engulfed the majority of postwar West German judges. Only with difficulty could it have been prevented from reaching the judges of the Federal Supreme Court, the Federal Administrative Court, and even the Federal Constitutional Court. As the journalist Jörg Friedrich observed bitingly, "Judge Rehse of the People's Court could not have committed murder, for this would have meant that the West German judicial system had been established by murderers in the hundreds."[45]

30

Injustice Confirmed

All too often, Nazi jurists could be acquitted only at the cost of declaring that the brutal laws and show trials of the Third Reich had been "legally perfectly sound." The acts of injustice had to be minimized and the victims of terror convicted for a second time, so to speak.

In one instance of this, the Wiesbaden County Court found in March 24, 1952, that the instructions issued by the Reich Ministry of Justice for transferring convicted Jewish, Russian, and Ukrainian criminals to the SS for "elimination through work" were not unlawful. The fact that all Jewish prisoners were included in this regulation, regardless of the length of their sentences, was considered by the court to be "unjust, certainly, but the tension between the legal norm [meaning the illegal secret agreement between the minister of justice and the chief of the SS] and what would have been just had not yet reached an intolerable level." And so the Wiesbaden judges arrived at the conclusion that "depriving the Jewish prisoners of their liberty was therefore not objectively in violation of the law."[1]

In another case, the Kiel County Court found that the death sentence passed by a Court-Martial on a U-boat captain named Kusch for anti-Nazi remarks was on the mild side, since several phrases left a door open for granting him clemency. Kusch had expressed the opinion that there was no such thing as "world Jewry" and that Hitler was "an insane Utopian" who had sought an opportunity to start the war. On September 25, 1950, the court found these "demoralizing remarks" "reprehensible and irresponsible." After the father of the executed man informed the County Court that toward the end of the war, his son had found it irresponsible on the part of the authorities "to send . . . innocent men to the bottom of the sea for no good reason," the judges in Kiel could no longer contain themselves: "Even if the full circumstances were not known to the Court-

Martial at the time, this evidence proves that the judges made no mistake whatsoever in their assessment of the crime."[2]

In the Franconian village of Brettheim, Mayor Leonhard Wolfmeyer and local Nazi party chief Leonhard Gackstatter, who were acting as judges of a summary court, refused to sign a death sentence only a few hours before American troops took the town; they pleaded on behalf of the accused. For this humanitarian act, they were immediately executed themselves. On July 23, 1960, the Ansbach County Court pronounced their action to have been "a violation of duty," since "by encouraging the previous perpetrator, Wolfmeyer and Gackstatter undertook to paralyze and undermine the will of the villagers, and consequently of the German people, to defend themselves." It had been perfectly correct to make them pay with their lives.[3]

In the trial of the judges of the Kassel Special Court who had condemned Werner Holländer to death for violating the Race Laws, the Kassel County Court found on March 28, 1952, that "the prevailing wartime conditions [had] to be taken into account," since these had created "a sensitive atmosphere toward criminals of every kind." The Special Court had determined "without any error in law" that the accused was in fact a "dangerous habitual criminal," although he was guilty of nothing more than a few love affairs. The defendant Kessler, former presiding judge of the Special Court and an unrepentant Nazi, had refused to budge an inch during his testimony: "I still stand today by the verdict I passed then." The court found in his favor and stated clearly in its decision that "application of the Blood Protection Law was without doubt lawful and correct at that time." In no way was it accurate to assert that the judges' brutal and unconventional tactic of combining the Blood Protection Law and the Law on Dangerous Habitual Criminals "represented a departure from the German tradition of an honorable judiciary."[4]

And in 1954 the same Kassel County Court dealt with the case of an informer ultimately responsible for several death sentences passed by the People's Court on grounds of (among other things) listening to illegal foreign radio broadcasts. Here the court determined there had been "no grave errors in procedure that might have invalidated one of these decisions."[5]

In 1971, after a six-year investigation (!), the Berlin County Court reached the conclusion that no objections could be made to the proceedings against the July 20 conspirators at the People's Court, although it was possible to get a direct impression of their "legality" from the film record that had been preserved. Though Hitler had publicly announced their forthcoming executions even before the verdict was reached, the court in 1971 could find no proof "that the members of the July 20 resistance movement had been murdered, or sentenced to death in what was merely a show trial, or that their trial had failed to fulfill the minimal requirements of correct legal procedure."[6]

In the case of Maurice Bavaud, who was executed in 1939 in connection with another unsuccessful attempt on Hitler's life, the same Berlin court, in order to condemn the accused again, had to employ the concept of "attempted crime" developed by the *Reichsgericht* for "racial sexual offenses." On November 9, 1938, the fifteenth anniversary of Hitler's beer hall putsch, Bavaud placed himself among the spectators of the parade in Munich with a small-caliber pistol in his pocket and waited in vain for the Führer to come within range. For this intent, he was sentenced to death by the People's Court on December 18, 1939. In 1955 his surviving relatives filed to have the case reopened. The Berlin County Court classified Bavaud's intent, which did not constitute a crime since it did not proceed beyond a preliminary act, not as attempted manslaughter but as "attempted murder." Bavaud could not have been charged with attempted murder under the German murder laws that have been in effect since 1941 (unless "base motives" were ascribed to him), and paragraph 2 of the Criminal Code states that if a law is altered between the time a crime is committed and the time of trial, then the court must use the milder form. Nevertheless, the court found in 1955 that "Bavaud was guilty of attempted murder. He attempted, with intent and premeditation, to take a person's life. Hitler's life is to be considered to enjoy the protection of the law as much as that of any other person, under the meaning of the regulations in paragraph 211 of the Criminal Code . . . Furthermore, actions that violate the law remain criminal offenses regardless of the individual motive behind the deed, a motive that may possibly be understandable." The Berlin Court offered proof of the fact that it still considered Bavaud's plan to take Hitler's life particularly reprehensible by not only sentencing him posthumously to five years in a penitentiary, but also expressly depriving him of his honor as a citizen for five years, although the law nowhere required this step.[7]

Then there was the case, mentioned above, of Chief Jürgens of the Düsseldorf Police, who tried to direct that no resistance be offered to American troops only a few hours before they entered the city, in order to prevent further bloodshed. For this he was sentenced to death in summary proceedings presided over by a drunken lieutenant colonel. On March 5, 1949, the Düsseldorf County Court found that Jürgens had "not presented what one would call the picture of an upstanding man and officer," and took the view that the summary death sentence "corresponded not only to the positive prevailing norms but also to general human expectations of what is permissible and necessary for protection of community norms." Even the hasty execution of Jürgens during the night, before the Americans took the city, seemed unobjectionable to the County Court: "If a step has been recognized as just and lawful, then it may also be carried out."[8]

The courts also showed an extraordinary lack of tact in their evaluations of the mass murders committed in the name of the euthanasia program. To name just one striking example, the Cologne County Court, in its decision of October 24, 1951, referred to the victims of the program as "burned out human beings," "creatures vegetating below the level of animals," and "people below the level of ciphers."[9]

There was hardly any decision handed down by a court between 1933 and 1945 that was too superficial, partisan, or inhuman for postwar judges to deny it the label "still defensible." A West German court has never summoned the courage to declare a single Nazi decision "null and void." Such reserve has been based not on uncertainty about the law—although German trial regulations do not officially recognize the concept of "voided" decisions—but rather on obviously political considerations. One case does exist in which the West Berlin *Kammergericht* overcame its legal scruples and pronounced several decisions "null and void," since they were marked "by a whole series of infringements against the most elementary principles of law." "That evidence was not taken according to criminal trial rules, that verdicts were based on only partially complete police records or informers' reports so that guilt could not be established on the basis of firm evidence, that the principle of public venue for the main proceedings was observed in only a few cases for the purpose of 'show trials,' that verdicts were determined in advance and according to preestablished guidelines, that the long or maximum penitentiary sentences or death sentences imposed stood for the most part in no just relation to the alleged offenses and contradicted every recognized principle of the rule of law in their excess"—all these circumstances led the *Kammergericht* to conclude on March 15, 1954, that "tolerating the decisions as merely flawed is out of the question . . . They are *ipso iure* and irreparably null and void."[10]

What decisions did the *Kammergericht* condemn so roundly in 1954? Were they the barbaric decisions of the People's Court, the Special Courts, or "mobile summary courts," in which people were sentenced on the basis of a joke, an affectionate gesture by an engaged couple, or an act of pity toward a starving prisoner of war? No indeed, the condemnation was aimed at decisions handed down in the "so-called German Democratic

Republic." Immediately after the war ended, thousands of prominent Nazis were interned in the Waldheim Camp near Chemnitz (now Karl Marx City); in 1950, for their participation in the crimes of the Third Reich, 3,000 of them were placed on trial before the Chemnitz County Court, which sent a panel of judges to Waldheim expressly for this purpose. The classification of the Chemnitz decisions as "absolutely and irreparably null and void" and the finding that "those so sentenced should be placed at no disadvantage before the law" were contained in a decision rejecting a plea from East German prosecutors for assistance in investigations. Had the *Kammergericht* not pronounced the Chemnitz decisions null and void, the Law on Legal Assistance of 1953[11] would have required the West German judicial authorities to cooperate with the East German courts. However, when it was a matter of convicting criminals from the past, the readiness of West German courts to be of assistance gave way to increased constitutional scruples.

The West German legal system always regarded the foundations on which sentences were based during the Third Reich as "valid law at the time," including the extremely harsh laws and "Führer's decrees" that often mandated the death penalty or gave judges a completely free hand in determining sentences, from a night in jail to death. The "point of departure" in these deliberations was, in the words of the Federal Supreme Court, "always the right of a nation to protect its own interests. Since time immemorial, nations have passed strict laws for their own security when they were engaged in a life-and-death conflict. The National Socialist government should not be categorically denied the right to pass such laws."[12] Even the strategic combination of the Blood Protection Law and the Blackout Regulations to convict Leo Katzenberger could "not be called injustice as such,"[13] in the opinion of the County Court of Nuremberg-Fürth of April 5, 1960. And in his oral opinion on the Rehse case, *Kammergericht* judge Ernst-Jürgen Oske offered several variations upon the Federal Supreme Court doctrine, such as: "Every government, even a totalitarian one, has a right to defend its own interests. No reproach may be made of the fact that in times of crisis, it resorts to extraordinary measures of deterrence."[14] Neither the Blood Protection Law nor the Decree on Asocial Elements, neither the special Wartime Criminal Regulations nor the Criminal Regulations Concerning Poles have ever been termed "null and void" by a West German court. In deliberations involving a key provision of the Special Wartime Regulations, the Federal Supreme Court even went so far as to state explicitly that the constitutional character of the provision had "been nowhere questioned in previous decisions."[15]

Nevertheless, the high court reached an entirely different conclusion in an advisory opinion dating from 1953. There the judges of the First Civil Panel found that "National Socialist legislation, which placed all fundamental rights at the mercy of the National Socialist regime and their oft-times criminal aims," violated "the supralegal validity of these fundamental rights and was thus null and void." This opinion dealt neither with the Blood Protection Law nor with the laws on national security, and it did not rehabilitate any victims of the Nazi dictatorship. What it did do was set aside, as "legally null and void," the provisions of the Civil Service Law of 1937 which would have deprived former Nazi civil servants in the Federal Republic of their "well-earned rights."[16]

31

A Latter-Day "Condemnation"
of Nazi Justice

In spite of widely varying assessments of the nation's recent past, all the political parties represented in the Bundestag (the Christian Democrats, the Christian Social Union, the Free Democrats, the Social Democrats, and the Greens), in a rare demonstration of unanimity, passed a resolution on January 25, 1985, declaring "that the institution known as 'the People's Court' was not a court in the true sense but an instrument of terror used to impose National Socialist dictatorship."

This gesture may have appeared to the general public as an uncompromising step toward closing a shameful chapter in German history, but on closer inspection it revealed itself as nothing more than an embarrassingly half-hearted measure. Press reports that the Bundestag had set aside the decisions of the People's Court were far from accurate. The West German legislature was still as unwilling to pass such a statute in 1985 as before; the formulation agreed upon was the far weaker phrase that "in the judgment of the German Bundestag, . . . the decisions of the People's Court [have] no legal validity. For this reason," the resolution continues, "the decisions were set aside through legislation in the states in the first few years after the war [that is, before the Federal Republic was founded in 1949] and through regulations of the powers of occupation, either expressly in the form of statutes or in court proceedings initiated by petition." [1]

Vague as this statement is, it still does not correspond to the facts. The Control Commission's Law Number 1 of September 20, 1945, did rescind twenty-five laws "of a political nature or establishing a state of emergency on which the Nazi regime was based," from the Law to Redress the Danger to the People and the Reich ("Enabling Act") to the police regulation requiring foreigners performing forced labor in Germany to wear special identifying badges. Later, the Commission's Law Number 11 of

January 30, 1946, added fourteen more laws and decrees to the list.[2] However, this list did not include all the laws permeated by the evil spirit of Fascism, nor did it address the question of what was to be done with all the sentences handed down while they were in force. All it did was to prohibit any further enforcement of these laws.

Proclamation Number 3 of the Allied Control Commission, dated October 20, 1945, did declare that "sentences passed for political or religious reasons under the Hitler government must be annulled."[3] Such a declaration did not set them aside, however, and these rather vague instructions to legislatures were later interpreted very differently in the different zones of occupation.

Before the founding of the Federal Republic, a *Länderrat* (States' Council) was formed in which all the states in the three western zones were represented. This council passed a law entitled "Reparation of National Socialist Injustice in Criminal Sentencing," which went into effect in 1946 and lifted sanctions on "political acts undertaken in opposition to National Socialism or militarism."[4] The law decreed further that convictions under typical Nazi statutes such as those mentioned in Laws 1 and 11 of the Control Commission could be set aside upon the filing of a petition by public prosecutors, the convicted persons themselves, or their surviving relatives. If the conviction had been based solely upon one of these laws, then it was to be considered automatically set aside; if other laws had been involved as well, then the sentence handed down during the Nazi era was to be reconsidered and fixed anew.

A second Law on Reparation of National Socialist Injustice in Criminal Sentencing, valid for all three western zones of occupation, was passed on April 5, 1947. It finally established that Special Court decisions "which appear excessively severe and therefore National Socialist in character when the crime and circumstances at the time are taken into consideration" were not to be set aside, but were to be merely "reduced to an appropriate level."[5] Furthermore, for a sentence to be reduced under this law, it was necessary to file a petition with a judge who would, as stated, take into account the circumstances at the time—that is, the extremely brutal political atmosphere that had played a role in thousands of death sentences.

In sum, the two laws left the assessment of whether sentences had been excessively severe to courts consisting largely of the judges who had passed them in the first place and were thus particularly inclined to take the former political atmosphere into account. Even in cases where the laws prescribed automatic annulment of a conviction, public prosecutors had to confirm that it had been set aside and had to remove it from their records;

this step frequently involved the victim in a long struggle, since prosecutors often simply refused to comply with the law.

Just as embarrassing as the Bundestag's lame resolution of 1985 was the story behind its passage. The Social Democratic Party had a majority in the legislature that would have enabled it to pass a law bringing to a close this bleak chapter in German history, and had held this majority for thirteen years before it presented the draft of a resolution entitled "Invalidity of the Decisions Handed Down by the Instruments of the National Socialist Dictatorship known as 'the People's Court' and 'the Special Courts.' "[6] The version finally passed merely stated that the Bundestag regarded "the decisions handed down by the institution known as 'the People's Court' as null and void from the beginning"; in other words, the decisions of the Special Courts were no longer included, although the resolution did call on the West German government to publish a report "on the question of the invalidity of the decisions passed by all the political Special Courts created . . . under National Socialist rule and to take appropriate action if necessary."

Federal minister of justice Engelhard responded with a firm refusal to set aside any decisions of the People's Court or the Special Courts. No argument was too silly to serve as an excuse; among others, he mentioned that declaring all the decisions of the People's Court null and void would lead to the "undesirable result" that even the (rare) acquittals would be voided. (Engelhard appeared to assume that voiding an acquittal was equivalent to a conviction.) He also argued that Special Court decisions should remain valid, at least, since "most convictions involved ordinary cases of major crime."[7]

These "arguments" clearly swayed the legal committee of the Bundestag. After only five meetings, the committee agreed to follow the minister's recommendations: it would not set aside a single judicial decision of the Nazi era. Thus, the absurd situation was created in which the federal legislature passed a resolution—unanimously—expressing its opinion that the existing legal situation was "intolerable" and at the same time refused to use the only means at its disposal—namely, new legislation—to end it.

Thus, after all attempts to make the judges of the Third Reich accountable for their actions had failed utterly, the victims were refused formal acknowledgment that their treatment had been unjust. Even though the act of declaring convictions from the Nazi era null and void would have had only symbolic significance, there was just as much symbolism in the insistence on retaining and upholding decisions from the People's Court and the Special Courts.

· 32 ·

An Attempt at an Explanation

How Was It Possible? This was the title of a book on the Third Reich by Alfred Grosser, a French authority on German affairs, who was, not surprisingly, unable to offer a conclusive answer. Where the crimes of Nazi jurists are concerned, the question has hardly ever been seriously investigated; the major surveys of the Third Reich have not gone into it in any depth. It is true that a great deal has begun to be written on the subject in the last few years, but the self-justifications and misinformation published after the war by participants have made an accurate assessment of the past difficult. And now, it seems, although a new and unprejudiced generation has the opportunity to deal with the subject, modern trends in scholarship stressing "theory production" tend to obscure more than they enlighten. One learns little about the crimes of Nazi jurists from observations such as that the "substance of ideological legitimation and the decision-making process of the authoritarian state [were] combined in a kind of model of expression,"[1] or that "the paradox of substantial decisionism . . . [was] the ideological counterpart to the structural chaos of the Nazi dictatorship.[2]

Ernst Fraenkel's book *Der Doppelstaat* (The Dual State)[3] has also contributed to the general confusion, largely because it is seldom read and is then misunderstood. When Fraenkel completed the manuscript in 1938, the Third Reich appeared to him to consist of a coexisting "normative state" and a "prerogative state." It was his intention to demonstrate that alongside chaos and arbitrary rule, there existed an area of the system which the Nazis left undisturbed and in which, in spite of all the social agitation of the National Socialist "Workers' party," they continued to pursue economic interests. Fraenkel never claimed that there was, alongside the excesses of the SS, SA, and the police in Hitler's Germany, a criminal justice system that respected the rule of law. He himself cited dozens of court cases to show how legal norms were forced to yield to political opportunism. The "double state" is a striking slogan but also easily misunderstood; Fraenkel certainly did not want to say that "on the one side the measures of the Fascists in the concentration camps and Gestapo torture chambers (the prerogative state) and on the other the normal functioning of the criminal justice system (a just state) together [formed] the double state." And it was by no means "positivism, with its rigid separation of justice and politics" that led to the legal system's being coopted;[4] on the contrary, this occurred precisely because of its total politicization. Those who accept such a simplified version of the "double state" theory are in effect joining in the effort to make the role of the judicial system seem more innocuous, an understandable undertaking on the part of those who are incriminated.

Another theory has been put forward on several occasions suggesting that the behavior of jurists during the Third Reich can be explained by the large degree of overlap between the ideas and attitudes of middle-class conservatives in the Weimar Republic and National Socialists. Although this hypothesis may be less spectacular than some that use fancy new terminology, it has the advantage of being based on fact. The intellectual affinity between conservatives and Nazis was expressed politically in October 1931 in the founding of the "Harzburg Front," a joint program for action. The program enabled the professional elite to identify themselves just enough with the Nazi regime to overcome any scruples they may have had about keeping their positions in the army, civil service, and judiciary. Apparently this theory ran counter to prevailing intellectual trends of the postwar period, however, which even younger scholars today ignore at their peril. For forty years, academics have been trying to draw a clear line of demarcation between conservatives (and their "positive" ethical values) and the Nazis (who were criminals), though this line has been trampled beyond recognition. They have even tried to turn Franz Gürtner, the longstanding minister of justice who left his stamp on most Nazi laws, into a kind of resistance fighter. Supposedly, by "holding out in office" he managed to prevent worse excesses. Gürtner's biographer, Eckehard Reitter, has described him as a "German Nationalist rooted in the National Liberal tradition" and has noted the many points at which his thinking coincided "with that of the National Socialists and the Bavarian People's party in Bavaria."[5] Gürtner provided key support for Hitler's career and used his influence to protect him after the Munich putsch attempt.[6] The Nazis' rise to power and their appalling crimes would not have been possible without the enthusiastic support and active cooperation of German nationalists and other conservatives in the military, civil service, and the courts, but after the Second World War this was a fact people were eager to forget.

Support for Hitler was played down as a mere bagatelle if it had been based not on National Socialist sentiments but on the German nationalist convictions that helped bring down the Weimar Republic with the "possible and in fact necessary strategy" of taking over the "valuable elements" of the Nazi movement "for the common goal of national revolution."[7] It is not only in the Gürtner biography mentioned above that the anti-democratic movement is presented as a basically admirable effort, with the sole flaw that it was undertaken in cooperation with Hitler. The fact that conservatives in high places made Nazi crimes possible, indeed participated in and defended them, emerges from such books only if one reads between the lines. No matter what offices conservatives held under the Nazis and what inconceivable crimes they helped to commit, as in the case of Gürtner, they have been credited until the present day with "taking the entire burden of guilt upon themselves, . . . always in the hope that they could effect change for the better."

Above and beyond this sort of justification for participation in the crimes of the Third Reich, certain of Hitler's derogatory remarks about the legal profession continue to be cited in its defense. It is true that he took a dim view of lawyers and had no use for treaties or statutes, let alone a constitution. Hitler did not even like his own decrees to limit his complete freedom of action. He detested lawyers as pen-pushers who filled whole volumes with tangled commands and prohibitions and always had their noses buried in ridiculous tomes. He once confided to a gathering of confidants that going to law school must turn every rational person into "a complete idiot," and that for his part he would "do everything he could . . . to make people despise a legal education."[8]

Such disparagement of "eggheads" was surely fueled by envy of those who had been able to attend universities on the part of a man who felt he had been deprived of many opportunities, but first and foremost it was an expression of his complete lack of sympathy for humanistic values, civilization, and the rule of law. It was no accident that the most frequently used words in his credo *Mein Kampf* are "harsh," "brutal," and "merciless." Hitler called for the use of "brute force" and "barbaric ruthlessness" against everything that displeased him. His avowed goals were "the victory of the stronger and the destruction or unconditional subjection of the weak," and he showed undisguised contempt for the "loathsome humane ethics" of Christianity and socialism, both of which speak on behalf of the weak and oppressed. In his eyes, this "so-called humanity" merely expressed "a mixture of stupidity, cowardice, and imagined superior knowledge."[9] The dictator considered that laws aimed at protecting the weak or placing restraints on the exercise of power (such as a government's) were actually criminal. The Jewish jurist Rudolf Olden once accurately characterized the Führer's attitude as follows: "The mystical process by which a state fetters itself, binds itself to the written word, first hands the weak a weapon and then submits to them—the essence of civilization—[was] detestable to him, seemed perverse and annoyingly contrary to the only order he understood."[10]

Of course, this characterizes not only Hitler's attitude but also the conception of law in the Third Reich and the attitude of its judges. Not only Nazis but all "nationally minded" jurists agreed in their hearts when Helmut Nicolai, the party's legal philosopher, praised the "legal temper of Bismarck's Germany" and the "manly character of a German political system," while attacking the whole "dirty gray brew of pacifism, belief in human nature, humanism, commercialism, self-debasement, international brotherhood, lack of honor, cowardice, . . . enlightenment, and democratic mob rule."[11] It was conservative jurists who often attested that the "new National Socialist view of the *Volk* and the state," with its links "to the German—that is, national [*völkisch*]—traditions in our forms of government and laws, . . . [was] conservative in the best sense."[12]

Justice as an ideal disappeared from Germany with the "elimination" (the most popular word in legal writings of those twelve years) of the Jewish, socialist, and democratic members of the legal profession, who made up one fifth of the total number and were the group at which Hitler's attacks were chiefly aimed. What remained was a mutilated and perverted sense of justice, characterized not by "positivistic miseducation" but by glorification of power, brutalization of the climate of opinion, and inhumanity, and which shared Hitler's aversion to all "legal-mindedness." He had always objected strongly to the German "mania for objectivity" and had demanded a "ruthless and fanatically one-sided attitude" toward all enemies, particularly those within the country's own borders. Adopting this approach to a large extent, German judges and legal scholars began to develop "constructions" of laws that left only their outer shell, and in many cases not even that. At the same time, however, these constructions were not necessarily "typically National Socialist," but simply conservative, authoritarian, anti-Enlightenment, and predemocratic in spirit. This explains their lasting success. Since many doctrines prevalent during the Third Reich had been conceived and propagated earlier by conservatives of the old school—and were far from being the exclusive property of fanatic Nazi party supporters—they did not fall into total discredit with the fall of the dictatorship and are in part still advocated today.

After May 8, 1945, virtually no other sort of jurist existed in Germany any more, nor had any other view of the law survived. With the people who had been driven out of the country or exterminated had gone their theories and ideas, their scholarly programs and plans. The lack of interest in rehabilitating them was matched by a lack of interest in studying their writings and thoughts. The legal profession of the Third Reich was not prepared to change its thinking, and those trained between 1933 and 1945 were probably not even capable of it. The resulting damage has made itself felt in the intellectual climate of German jurisprudence up to the present day, and has proved to be one of the most lasting inherited defects. All recollection of the great liberal German jurists of the nineteenth century, the socialist and democratic teachers of the Weimar Republic, and the legal ethos they propounded has been systematically rooted out of the last three generations of law students. For them, "the law" has become reduced to a canon of procedures—including those developed during the Third Reich, and even earlier—for destroying the "enemy," procedures which also proved ideally suited for rehabilitating the Nazis after the war.

Former County Court judge Hubert Schorn, who has striven like no other to absolve the Nazi legal profession of guilt, unwittingly exposed the basic dilemma of German jurists when he observed approvingly, "The proud history of the judiciary has always been permeated by a spirit of loyalty to state leadership and by the love with which service to the state was performed."[15] This statement is not entirely accurate, for judges were not always loyal to democratic governments. Nevertheless, it is still noteworthy that someone who wanted to rehabilitate the Nazi legal system should have stressed judges' loyalty to "state leadership" and not to the law.

It was this fixation on the government characteristic of such a large part of the judiciary that made it so easy for them to adapt to conditions in the Third Reich, and it also explains the one-sidedness of their assessments of cases with a political background. The higher courts in West Germany, in particular, continue today to make fine distinctions based on the "loyalty" of defendants.

The use of "left" and "right" as categories for examining court decisions involving politics is hardly new; it has been going on since the end of the First World War. The fact that such categories continue to suggest themselves as an obvious way of interpreting the data shows how little the profession has progressed beyond the "friend-foe" ideology of Carl Schmitt. A few last examples. When the writer and graphic artist Peter Paul Zahl produced an "international poster" to commemorate the first of May in 1970, it depicted a hand grenade surrounded by the names of several militant foreign liberation organizations with the slogan "Freedom for All Prisoners." He was charged with "inciting to criminal acts" under paragraph 111 of the Criminal Code. The Petty Court of Berlin-Tiergarten acquitted him on March 3, 1971, but prosecutors appealed the verdict. The Berlin County Court convicted him on April 17, 1972, and imposed a six-month prison sentence for having incited to the crimes of "freeing prisoners" and "illegal use of explosives." The court found that the poster supposedly created "a first and dominant impression of a call to attain political goals in the Federal Republic and West Berlin through the use of force and to free prisoners with the means glorified by the organizations cited, namely with force." The First Criminal Panel of the Berlin *Kammergericht* saw "nothing to object to" in the County Court's findings when it reviewed the case. In the eyes of this court, "common experience [showed] . . . that circles exist here . . . that can be encouraged by the use of such slogans," and the court concluded that the slogan "Freedom for All Prisoners" sufficiently fulfilled all "requirements for specificity as an incitement to criminal acts."[16]

In contrast, such specificity was found to be lacking in the various slogans smeared on walls and windows by a neo-Nazi, according to the decision handed down by the Third Criminal Panel of the Federal Supreme Court on March 14, 1984. The phrase "Death to Wehner and Brandt!" enabled even the Supreme Court judges "to recognize that the death of both politicians . . . is desired. However, the meaning of the words leaves it open as to whether death is to be achieved by a criminal act," since such slogans "do not incite to an act *expressis verbis*." Now, it turned out that the defendant had been a bit more specific in the slogan "Kill Cremer, Hang Brandt!" and the judges were forced to concede that he had indeed committed a "linguistic" incitement to "criminal behavior in regard to certain persons." But the Supreme Court was still not inclined to take too serious a view of the matter, since it was possible that the slogans were only "manifestations of discontent by an outsider," who merely "wanted to give expression to his displeasure with the politicians named."[17]

In the meantime, however, there are indications that a new climate of opinion is gaining ground, primarily in the efforts of younger judges and attorneys to unearth and restore long-buried democratic legal traditions in Germany. New developments in the conduct of criminal trials, new republican and democratic organizations formed by attorneys and judges, and—last but not least—several decisions (usually handed down by lower courts) show that once again there are jurists at work who feel an obligation to the law rather than to government authority. This book is dedicated to some of them.

Notes · Bibliography · Index

Notes

1. "Time to Raise an Outcry"

1. Hoffmann's comments on Jahn's trial are cited by Herbert Kraft and Manfred Wacker, eds., in E. T. A. Hoffmann, *Werke*, 4 vols. (Frankfurt: Insel Verlag, 1967), IV, 525.
2. Ibid., 526.
3. "Meister Floh," Ibid., 69–70.
4. Theo Rasehorn, "Preussen und der Rechtsstaat," *Recht und Politik* 12 (1981), 107.
5. Diether Huhn, "Oppositionelle Richter," *Deutsche Richterzeitung* 46 (1968), 82–83.
6. Ibid., 83.
7. Heinrich Heffter, *Die deutsche Selbstverwaltung im 19. Jahrhundert* (Stuttgart: K. F. Koehler, 1950), 341.
8. Quoted in Dieter Simon, *Die Unabhängigkeit des Richters* (Darmstadt: Wissenschaftliche Buchgesellschaft, 1975), 41.
9. Huhn, "Oppositionelle Richter," 82.
10. Diether Huhn, "Von der Standes- zur Klassenjustiz," in Raimund Kusserow, ed., *Richter in Deutschland* (Hamburg: Gruner & Jahr, 1982), 44.
11. Bernt Englemann, *Preussen: Land der unbegrenzten Möglichkeiten* (Munich: Bertelsmann, 1979), 271.
12. Huhn, "Von der Standes-zur Klassenjustiz," 44.

2. The Enforcement of Conformity

1. Eckart Kehr, *Der Primat der Innenpolitik*, 2nd ed. (Berlin: de Gruyter, 1976), 75.
2. Dieter Simon, *Die Unabhängigkeit des Richters* (Darmstadt: Wissenschaftliche Buchgesellschaft, 1975), 42.
3. Leo Kofler, *Zur Geschichte der bürgerlichen Gesellschaft* (1948; 3rd ed. Neuwied: Luchterhand, 1966), 565.

4. Ernst Fraenkel, *Zur Soziologie der Klassenjustiz* (Berlin: Laub, 1927), 10.
5. Kehr, *Der Primat der Innenpolitik,* 78.
6. Friedrich Karl Kübler, "Der deutsche Richter und das demokratische Gesetz," *Archiv für die civilistische Praxis* 162 (1963), 107–109.
7. Paul Laband, "Die Anträge auf Errichtung eines Staatsgerichtshofes für das deutsche Reich," *Deutsche Juristen-Zeitung* 6 (1901), cols. 1ff.
8. Paul Laband, *Das deutsche Kaisertum* (Strasbourg: J. H. E. Heitz, 1896), 29.
9. Heinrich Heffter, *Die deutsche Selbstverwaltung im 19. Jahrhundert* (Stuttgart: K. F. Koehler, 1950), 737.
10. Fraenkel, *Zur Soziologie der Klassenjustiz,* 12.
11. Cited in Kübler, "Der deutsche Richter und das demokratische Gesetz," 111n.
12. Max Reichert, "Die deutschen Gerichte der Zukunft," *Deutsche Richterzeitung* 4 (1912), 635.

3. The Judges of the Weimar Repulic

1. Johannes Leeb, "Dreierlei," *Deutsche Richterzeitung* 13 (1921), 131.
2. Dieter Simon, *Die Unabhängigkeit des Richters* (Darmstadt: Wissenschaftliche Buchgesellschaft, 1975), 49.
3. Excerpts from Simons' speech before the Society of Legal Studies in Munich were printed in the *Deutsche Juristen-Zeitung* 31 (1926), col. 1667.
4. Carl Schmitt, *Der Begriff des Politischen* (1927; new ed. Berlin: Duncker & Humblot, 1963), 27 and 33.
5. Otto Kirchheimer, *Political Justice: The Use of Legal Procedure for Political Ends* (Princeton: Princeton University Press, 1961), 62.
6. Wilhelm Hoegner, *Die verratene Republik: Geschichte der deutschen Gegenrevolution* (Munich: Isar Verlag, 1958), 36.
7. Felix Halle, *Deutsche Sondergerichtsbarkeit, 1918–1921* (Berlin and Leipzig: Franke Verlag, 1922), 16 and 26.
8. German League for Human Rights, *Das Zuchthaus als politische Waffe* (Berlin: Deutsche Liga für Menschenrechte, 1927), 20.
9. For information on the trials, see Karl Brammer, *Verfassungsgrundlagen und Hochverrat* (Berlin: Verlag für Politik und Wirtschaft, 1922), 13–84.
10. *Reichsgesetzblatt* (1920), 1487.
11. The verdict is cited in Brammer, *Verfassungsgrundlagen und Hochverrat,* 114ff.
12. Emil Julius Gumbel, *Verschwörer: Zur Geschichte und Soziologie der deutschen nationalistischen Geheimbünde, 1918–1924,* 2nd ed. (Heidelberg: Verlag Das Wunderhorn, 1979), 31ff.
13. Philipp Loewenfeld, *Das Strafrecht als politische Waffe* (Berlin: Dietz, 1933), 27.
14. See Heinrich Hannover and Elisabeth Hannover-Drück, *Politische Justiz, 1918–1933* (Hornheim-Merten: Lamuv Verlag, 1987), 63ff.
15. Brammer, *Verfassungsgrundlagen und Hochverrat,* 121.
16. The verdicts are printed in *Die Justiz* 3 (1927–28), 516ff.

17. L. Bendix, "Das Recht des Offiziers als amnestierten Hochverräters auf Pension," *Die Justiz* 2 (1926–27), 420.
18. *Entscheidungen des Reichsversorgungsgerichts,* vol. 4, p. 232; also cited in Deutsche Liga für Menschenrechte, *Das Zuchthaus als politische Waffe,* 142ff.
19. Cited in Hannover and Hannover-Drück, *Politische Justiz,* 146.
20. On the events in Munich, see Wilhelm Hoegner, *Hitler und Kahr, die bayerischen Napoleonsgrössen von 1923* (Munich: Birk-Verlag, 1928); and Hannover and Hannover-Drück, *Politische Justiz,* 145.
21. Hannover and Hannover-Drück, *Politische Justiz,* 146.
22. On the course of the trial, see K. Schwend, *Bayern zwischen Monarchie und Diktatur* (Munich: Pflaum-Verlag, 1954), 256ff.
23. State Archives, Munich, Staatsanw. Munich 3098, Decision 44.
24. Alan Bullock, *Hitler: A Study in Tyranny,* rev. ed. (New York and Evanston: Harper & Row, 1962), 121.
25. Hoegner, *Die verratene Republik,* 270–271.
26. Ibid., 272.
27. Ibid., 284.
28. Ibid., 265–266.
29. Ibid., 272.
30. *Reichsgesetzblatt* (1922), 585.
31. The decision of June 22, 1923, is printed in *Die Justiz* 1 (1925–26), 521ff.
32. Cited in L. Foerder, "Die 'Judenrepublik' in der Rechtsprechung," *Die Justiz* 1 (1925–26), 528; and Gottfried Zarnow (pseud. of Ewald Moritz), *Gefesselte Justiz: Politische Bilder aus deutscher Gegenwart* (Munich: J. F. Lehmann, 1932), II, 73.
33. Hoegner, *Die verratene Republik,* 265.
34. Ibid., 268.
35. Cited in Gustav Radbruch, "Offener Brief an Dr. O. Liebmann," *Die Justiz* 1 (1925–26), 196.
36. The decision is printed in *Die Justiz* 8 (1932–33), 119–120.
37. For more on the trial, see Peter Bucher, *Der Reichswehrprozess: Der Hochverrat der Ulmer Reichswehroffiziere* (Boppard a. Rhein: Boldt, 1967); and Procurator, "Rede und Antwort: Zum Hochverratsprozess gegen die Ulmer Reichswehroffiziere," *Die Justiz* 6 (1930–31), 62ff.
38. The decision of October 4, 1930, is printed in *Die Justiz* 6 (1930–31), 187ff.
39. The same panel attributed "base motives" to the Nobel peace laureate Carl von Ossietzky in his trial for treason; see Bruno Frei, *Carl von Ossietzky: Eine politische Biographie,* 2nd ed. (Berlin: Das Arsenal, Verlag für Kultur und Politik, 1978).
40. Cited in Hoegner, *Die verratene Republik,* 265.
41. W. Heine, "Staatsgerichtshof und Reichsgericht über das hessische Manifest," *Die Justiz* 7 (1931–32), 154ff. The "Boxheim Documents" are printed in Eike Hennig, ed., *Hessen unterm Hakenkreuz: Studien zur Durchsetzung der NSDAP in Hessen* (Frankfurt: Insel Verlag, 1983), 433ff.
42. Cited in Karl Dietrich Bracher, *Die Auflösung der Weimarer Republik* (Stuttgart: Ring Verlag, 1955), 383.

43. This law went into effect on July 16, 1919; see *Reichsgesetzblatt* (1919), 687.

44. *Allgemeine Staatslehre* (1900; 3rd ed. Berlin: O. Haring, 1914), 359.

45. Emil Julius Gumbel, "Landesverratsstatistik," *Die Justiz* 3 (1927–28), 386–387.

46. Emil Julius Gumbel, *Vom Fememord zur Reichskanzlei* (Heidelberg: Schneider, 1962), 70.

47. Cited in Emil Julius Gumbel, "Landesverrat, begangen durch die Presse," *Die Justiz* 2 (1926–27), 86.

48. Hugo Sinzheimer, "Die Legalisierung des politischen Mordes," *Die Justiz* 5 (1929–30), 69.

49. *Entscheidungen des Reichsgerichts in Strafsachen: Amtliche Sammlung* 62 (1928), 46.

50. Ibid., 65.

51. Thomas Mann, in a letter to Alfred Apfel of January 10, 1932, cited in Kurt Richard Grossmann, *Ossietzky: Ein deutscher Patriot* (Munich: Kindler, 1963), 208.

52. Gustav Radbruch, "Staatsnotstand, Staatsnotwehr und Fememord," *Die Justiz* 5 (1929–30), 127.

53. Carl Schmitt, *Staat, Bewegung, Volk* (Hamburg: Hanseatische Verlagsanstalt, 1933), 7.

54. Alfons Sack, *Der Reichstagsbrandprozess* (Berlin: Ullstein, 1934), 93.

55. Ibid., 94.

4. The Reichstag Fire Trial

1. *Reichsgesetzblatt* (1933), I, 35.

2. See the extensive evidence included in Walter Hofer et al., eds., *Der Reichstagsbrand: Eine wissenschaftliche Dokumentation* (Berlin: Arani, 1972), I, 224–225, 242, 247–248.

3. *Faksimilierte Neuausgabe* (Frankfurt: Röderberg-Verlag, 1978).

4. Fabian von Schlabrendorff, *Begegnungen in fünf Jahrzehnten* (Tübingen: Wunderlich, 1979), 171–172.

5. Robert Kempner, *Ankläger einer Epoche* (Frankfurt: Ullstein, 1983), 99–100.

6. *Reichsgesetzblatt* (1933), I, 83.

7. Ibid., 85.

8. Bruno Frei, *Carl von Ossietzky: Eine politische Biographie*, 2nd ed. (Berlin: Das Arsenal, Verlag für Kultur und Politik, 1978), 208ff.

9. See Ingo Müller, "Der berühmte Fall Ossietzky vom Jahre 1930 könnte sich wiederholen," in Hans-Ernst Böttcher, ed., *Recht, Justiz, Kritik: Festschrift für Richard Schmid zum 85. Geburtstag* (Baden-Baden: Nomos, 1985), 297ff.

10. Hans Joachim Bernhard et al., eds., *Der Reichstagsbrandprozess und Georgi Dimitroff: Dokumente* (Berlin: Dietz, 1982), I, documents 83, 87, 199, and 248.

11. Ibid., document 228.

12. Ibid., document 337.

13. Cited in Alfons Sack, *Der Reichstagsbrandprozess* (Berlin: Ullstein, 1934), 154.

14. *Reichsgesetzblatt* (1933), I, 151.

15. The court reporter's version of the proceedings is included in Georgi Dimitrov, *Reichstagsbrandprozess: Dokumente, Briefe und Aufzeichnungen* (Berlin: Verlag Neuer Weg, 1946).

16. Speech for the prosecution by the chief public prosecutor; printed in Sack, *Der Reichstagsbrandprozess,* 155ff.

17. See the decision printed ibid., 325ff. and 335.

18. Otto Kirchheimer, "Staatsgefüge und Recht des Dritten Reiches," *Kristische Justiz* 9 (1976), 43.

19. Cited in *Das Recht ab 1934* [monthly supplement to *Deutsche Justiz*] (1934), 19.

20. *Der völkische Beobachter* 358–360 (December 24, 1933).

21. Henry Picker, ed., *Tischgespräche im Führerhauptquartier, 1941–42* (Bonn: Athenäum Verlag, 1951), 241.

22. Decision in the rehearing of the Martinus van der Lubbe case of October 15, 1980; printed in *Strafverteidiger* 1 (1981), 140ff.

5. Jurists "Coordinate" Themselves

1. "Zum neuen Jahre," *Deutsche Richterzeitung* 25 (1933), 1.

2. See Robert Kuhn, *Die Vertrauenskrise der Justiz, 1926–1928* (Cologne: Bundesanzeiger, 1983), 109ff.

3. Hans Wrobel, "Der Deutsche Richterbund im Jahre 1933," *Kritische Justiz* 15 (1982), 325.

4. "Zeitspiegel," *Deutsche Richterzeitung* 25 (1933), 121.

5. Ibid., 122.

6. *Reichsgesetzblatt* (1933), I, 175–176.

7. *Deutsche Richterzeitung* 25 (1933), 156.

8. Friedrich Karl Kaul, *Geschichte des Reichsgerichts* (Glashütten/Taunus: Auvermann, 1971), IV, 54–55.

9. *Deutsche Richterzeitung* 25 (1933), 156.

10. Ibid., 189–190.

11. Ibid., 187.

12. Ibid., 258.

13. "Richter und Staatsanwalt im Dritten Reich," ibid., 280.

14. Gerhard Fieberg, *Justiz im nationalsozialistischen Deutschland* (Cologne: Bundesanzeiger, 1984), 37.

15. See the biographical sketch in E. Brandis, "Lebenslauf," in *Erwin Bumke zum 65. Geburtstag,* Festschrift (Berlin: von Decker, 1939), ixff.; and Dieter Kolbe, *Reichsgerichtspräsident Dr. Erwin Bumke* (Karlsruhe: C. F. Müller, 1975).

16. Kolbe, *Reichsgerichtspräsident Dr. Erwin Bumke,* 233.

17. Ibid., 109ff.

18. Hans Mayer, *Ein Deutscher auf Widerruf: Erinnerungen* (Frankfurt: Suhrkamp, 1982), I, 144.

19. Ernst Niekisch, *Das Reich der niederen Dämonen* (1953; new ed. Berlin: AHDE Verlag, 1980), 199.

20. *Deutsche Juristen-Zeitung* 39 (1934), cols. 945ff.

21. "Die deutschen Intellektuellen," *Westdeutscher Beobachter* 126 (May 31, 1933), 1.
22. Carl Schmitt, *Staat, Bewegung, Volk* (Hamburg: Hanseatische Verlagsanstalt, 1933), 45.
23. "Die deutsche Rechtswissenschaft im Kampf gegen den jüdischen Geist," *Deutsche Juristen-Zeitung* 41 (1936), col. 1193.
24. Ibid., col. 1197.
25. See Claus-Dietrich Wieland, *Staatsrechtler des neuen Reiches* (Stuttgart: Deutsche Verlagsanstalt, 1987).
26. Printed in the conference brochure, *Die deutsche Rechtswissenschaft im Kampf gegen den jüdischen Geist* 1 (1936), 15.
27. Schmitt, *Völkerrechtliche Grossraumordnung: Mit Interventionsverbot für raumfremde Mächte* (Berlin and Vienna: Deutscher Rechtsverlag, 1939), 87.
28. Robert Kempner, *Ankläger einer Epoche* (Frankfurt: Ullstein, 1983), 129.
29. Claus-Dietrich Wieland, "Carl Schmitt in Nürnberg," *1999: Zeitschrift für Sozialgeschichte des 20. und 21. Jahrhunderts* 2 (1987), 105.
30. *Frankfurter Rundschau,* December 16, 1966.
31. Arnold Schmitz, *Die Bildlichkeit der wortgebundenen Musik Johann Sebastian Bachs* (Mainz: Schott, 1950).
32. Hans Barion, ed., *Festschrift für Carl Schmitt zum 70. Geburtstag* (Berlin: Duncker & Humblot, 1959).
33. Hans Barion et al., eds., *Epirrhosis: Festgabe für Carl Schmitt* (Berlin: Duncker & Humblot, 1968).

6. The Legal System during the State of Emergency

1. Carl Schmitt, *Politische Theologie* (1922; 2nd ed. Munich and Leipzig: Duncker & Humblot, 1934), 181–182.
2. Ibid., 20.
3. Decision of May 31, 1935; see *Deutsche Richterzeitung* 27 (1935), 636–638.
4. In a decision of November 1, 1933; see *Deutsche Justiz* 96 (1934), 64.
5. The State Supreme Court (*Kammergericht*) was the only appellate court in Prussia for criminal cases.
6. Decision of July 12, 1935; see *Reichsverwaltungsblatt* (1936), 61–62.
7. *Deutsche Justiz* 97 (1935), 1831–32.
8. *Deutsches Strafrecht* 3 (1936), 429.
9. *Deutsche Verwaltung* 13 (1936), 385.
10. *Badische Verwaltungszeitschrift* (1938), 87.
11. *Deutsche Verwaltung* (1936), 385.
12. According to the decree of March 23, 1936 (printed in *Reichsgesetzblatt* [1936], I, 251), the only appellate courts for this type of "noncontentious" case were the *Kammergericht* in Prussia and the Munich Court of Appeals.
13. Decision of January 27, 1937; printed in *Jahrbuch für Entscheidungen der freiwilligen Gerichtsbarkeit* 15 (1937), 61–62.
14. Decision of November 25, 1935; printed in *Höchstrichterliche Rechtsprechung* 592 (1936).

15. Decision of April 15, 1937; see *Juristische Wochenschrift* 66 (1937), 2212.
16. "Werdendes Polizeirecht," in *Das Recht ab 1934* [monthly suppplement of *Deutsche Justiz*] (1938), 224.

7. Treason and Treachery

1. Cited in Martin Broszat, "National Socialist Concentration Camps, 1933–1945," in Helmut Krausnick et al., eds., *Anatomy of the SS State,* trans. Marian Jackson (New York: Walker, 1965), 407–408.
2. Ibid., 413.
3. Ibid.
4. *Reichsgesetzblatt* (1933), I, 136.
5. Decision of March 21, 1933; ibid., 135.
6. Decree of March 21, 1933; ibid., 134.
7. "Der nationale Zweck," *Deutsche Juristen-Zeitung* 38 (1933), 718ff.
8. Decision of the Fourth Criminal Panel of January 7, 1933, cited in Friedrich Karl Kaul, *Geschichte des Reichsgerichts* (Glashütten/Taunus: Auvermann, 1971), IV, 81.
9. Ibid., 82.
10. Cited ibid., 83.
11. See Wolfgang Abendroth, *Aufstieg und Krise der deutschen Sozialdemokratie,* 4th ed. (1964; Frankfurt: Stimme-Verlag, 1978), 68. See also Helga Grebing, *Geschichte der deutschen Arbeiterbewegung: Ein Überblick* (Munich: Nymphenburger Verlagshandlung, 1966), 215.
12. Decision of June 20, 1934; cited in Kaul, *Geschichte des Reichsgerichts,* 84.
13. Decision of June 8, 1934; ibid., 85.
14. Heinrich Hannover and Elisabeth Hannover-Drück, *Politische Justiz, 1918–1933* (Hornheim-Merten: Lamuv Verlag, 1987) 215ff.
15. Gerhard Schulz, *Die Anfänge des totalitären Massnahmenstaates* (Frankfurt: Ullstein, 1974), 476.
16. Ibid., 193.
17. *Reichsgesetzblatt* (1933), I, 479.
18. *Nationalzeitung Essen,* December 23, 1933; cited in Schulz, *Die Anfänge des totalitären Massnahmenstaates,* 474.
19. Hanno Drechsler, *Die Sozialistische Arbeiterpartei Deutschlands* (Meisenheim am Glan: Hain, 1965), 333.
20. *Reichsgesetzblatt* (1934), I, 769.
21. See the report in *Deutsche Justiz* 96 (1934), 1210–11.
22. *Deutschland-Berichte der Sozialdemokratischen Partei Deutschlands, 1934–40* (Frankfurt: Verlag Zweitausendeins, 1980), 827ff.
23. Walter Ulbricht, et al., *Geschichte der deutschen Arbeiterbewegung* (Berlin: Dietz-Verlag, 1966), V, 82.
24. Drechsler, *Die Sozialistische Arbeiterpartei,* 335.
25. Decision in the case of Aljets and sixteen other defendants of June 6, 1935 (File OIV 30/34).
26. Decision of June 7, 1934 (File St O 83/1934).

27. Decision of June 7, 1934, p. 25.
28. Decision of June 6, 1935, pp. 1–2.
29. *Oldenburgische Staatszeitung* of April 13 and July 2, 1935.

8. Purges at the Bar

1. Wolfgang Scheffler, *Judenverfolgung im Dritten Reich, 1933–1945* (Berlin: Colloquium Verlag, 1960), 14.
2. Josef Goebbels, *Der Nazi-Sozi: Fragen und Antworten für den Nationalsozialisten,* 4th ed. (Munich: F. Eher Nachfolger, 1932), 13.
3. Comité des Délégations Juives, ed., *Das Schwarzbuch: Tatsachen und Dokumente: Die Lage der Juden in Deutschland, 1933* (1934; rpt. Frankfurt: Ullstein, 1983), 85.
4. Ibid., 88.
5. Udo Reifner, "Freie Advokatur oder Dienst am Recht?" in Helmut D. Fangmann and Norman Paech, eds., *Recht, Justiz und Faschismus nach 1933 und heute* (Cologne: R. Theurer, 1984), 62.
6. From the preface to Heinrich Hannover and Elisabeth Hannover-Drück, *Politische Justiz, 1918–1933* (Hornheim-Merten: Lamuv Verlag, 1987), 13.
7. Henry Picker, *Tischgespräche im Führerhauptquartier, 1941–42* (Bonn: Athenäum Verlag, 1951), 210ff., 259–260.
8. Fritz Ostler, "Rechtsanwälte in der NS-Zeit," *Anwaltsblatt* 33 (1983), 54.
9. Decree of October 1, 1933, *Reichsgesetzblatt* (1933), I, 699.
10. Comité des Délégations Juives, *Schwarzbuch,* 180.
11. Ibid., 174.
12. Amtlicher Preussischer Pressedienst, April 5, 1933.
13. Comité des Délégations Juives, *Schwarzbuch,* 179.
14. *Juristische Wochenschrift: Organ der Reichsgruppe Rechtsanwälte des NS-Rechtswahrer-Bundes* 62 (1933), 1689–90.
15. Comité des Délégations Juives, *Schwarzbuch,* 187.
16. *Juristische Wochenschrift* 67 (1938), 2796.
17. *Reichsgesetzblatt* (1938), I, 1403.
18. *Juristische Wochenschrift* 67 (1938), 2796.
19. *Reichsgesetzblatt* (1935), I, 1478.
20. *Deutsche Rechtswissenschaft* 1 (1936), 96.
21. For an example, see the "Rechtsanwaltsbrief" in Heinz Boberach, ed., *Richterbriefe: Dokumente zur Beeinflussung der deutschen Rechtsprechung, 1942–1944* (Boppard a. Rhein: Boldt, 1975), 408.
22. *Entscheidungen des Reichsgerichts in Strafsachen: Amtliche Sammlung* 73 (1939), 127.
23. Lothar Künhe, *Der Verteidiger ohne fremdrechtliches Gewand* (Berlin: A. Sudau, 1937), 79.
24. Hanssen, "Die Stellung des Rechtsanwalts als Organ einer starken nationalsozialistischen Rechtspflege," *Deutsches Recht* 14 (1944), 355.
25. "Rechtsanwaltsbrief," cited in Boberach, *Richterbriefe,* 408.

26. *Erwin Bumke zum 65. Geburtstag,* Festschrift (Berlin: von Decker, 1939), 332.

27. Leupolt, "Der Deutsche Rechtsanwalt," in Wissenschaftliche Abteilung des NS-Rechtswahrerbundes, *Der deutsche Rechtsstand* (Berlin: Deutscher Recht-Verlag, 1939), 140.

28. Cited in Lothar Gruchmann, "Hitler über die Justiz," *Vierteljahrshefte für Zeitgeschichte* 12 (1964), 100.

29. Heinrich Henkel, "Die Gestaltung des künftigen Strafverfahrens," *Deutsche Juristen-Zeitung* 40 (1935), 531.

30. Alfons Sack, *Der Strafverteidiger und der neue Staat* (Berlin: Westkreuz-Verlag, 1935), 106.

31. See Hubert Schorn, *Der Richter im Dritten Reich* (Frankfurt: Klostermann, 1959), 116.

32. Cited in Ostler, "Rechtsanwälte in der NS-Zeit," 59.

33. *Reichsgesetzblatt* (1933), I, 528.

34. Decision of January 23, 1939; *Entscheidungen des Ehrengerichtshofs der Reichs-Rechts-Anwalts-Kammer (für Rechtsanwälte)* 33 (1940), 9.

35. Decision of November 1, 1937; *Entscheidungen des Ehrengerichtshofs,* vol. 31, p. 148.

36. Decision of January 23, 1939; *Entscheidungen des Ehrengerichtshofs,* vol. 33, p. 8ff.

37. Ibid., 12ff.

38. Decision of October 14, 1940; *Entscheidungen des Ehrengerichtshofs,* vol. 33, p. 122.

39. Decree on the amendments to the *Reichs-Rechtsanwalts-Ordnung* of March 1, 1943; *Reichsgesetzblatt* (1943), I, 123.

9. Nazi Jurisprudence

1. *Reichtags-Drucksache,* 4/1741.

2. Georg Dahm, *Nationalsozialistisches und faschistisches Strafrecht* (Berlin: Junker und Dünnhaupt, 1935), 24.

3. *Goltdammers Archiv für Preussisches Strafrecht* 103 (1933), xxxiv.

4. David Earl Sutherland, "On the Migration of Sociological Structures, 1933–1941," *Current Sociology* 22 (1974), 100.

5. Eduard Rabofsky and Gerhard Oberkofler, *Verborgene Wurzeln der NS-Justiz* (Vienna, Munich, Zurich: Europaverlag, 1985), 124ff.

6. Gerhard Schulz, *Die Anfänge des totalitären Massnahmenstaates* (Frankfurt: Ullstein, 1974), 497.

7. Reproduced in Ilse Staff, ed., *Justiz im Dritten Reich: Eine Dokumentation,* 2nd ed. (Frankfurt: Fischer Taschenbuch-Verlag, 1978), 147.

8. Cited in Peter Lundgren, *Wissenschaft im Dritten Reich* (Frankfurt: Suhrkamp, 1985), 10.

9. Cited in Ernst Niekisch, *Das Reich der niederen Dämonen* (1953; new ed. Berlin: AHDE Verlag, 1980), 193.

10. Carl Schmitt, "Nationalsozialismus und Rechtsstaat," *Juristische Wochenschrift* 63 (1934), 713.

11. Wilhelm Sauer, "Schöpferisches Volkstum als national- und weltpolitisches Prinzip," *Archiv für Rechts- und Sozialphilosophie,* vol. 27, p. 13.

12. Friedrich Schaffstein, *Politische Strafrechtswissenschaft* (Hamburg: Hanseatische Verlagsanstalt, 1934), 26.

13. Ernst Forsthoff, *Der totale Staat* (Hamburg: Hanseatische Verlagsanstalt, 1933), 13.

14. Ernst Forsthoff, *"Der deutsche Führerstaat* von Otto Koellreutter," *Juristische Wochenschrift* 63 (1934), 538.

15. Carl Schmitt, "Was bedeutet der Streit um den 'Rechtsstaat'?" *Zeitschrift für die gesamte Staatswissenschaft* 95 (1935), 199.

16. Schmitt, "Nationalsozialismus und Rechtsstaat," 716.

17. Otto Koellreutter, "Der nationale Rechtsstaat," *Recht und Staat in Geschichte und Gegenwart* 89 (1932).

18. Herbert Krüger, "Rechtsgedanken und Rechtstechnik im liberalen Strafrecht," *Zeitschrift für die gesamte Strafrechtswissenschaft* 55 (1936), 199.

19. See Roland Freisler's entry "Rechsstaat," in Erich Volkmar et al., eds., *Die Rechtsentwicklung der Jahre 1933 bis 1935–36,* in *Handwörterbuch der Rechtswissenschaft,* VIII (Berlin and Leipzig: de Gruyter, 1937), 572.

20. Schmitt, "Was bedeutet der Streit um den 'Rechtsstaat'?" 198.

21. Heinrich Henkel, *Strafrichter und Gesetz im neuen Staat* (Hamburg: Hanseatische Verlagsanstalt, 1934), 68.

22. Otto Koellreutter, "Das Verwaltungsrecht im nationalsozialistischen Staat," *Deutsche Juristen-Zeitung* 39 (1934), 626.

23. Hans Helfritz, "Rechtsstaat und nationalsozialistischer Staat," *Deutsche Juristen-Zeitung* 39 (1934), 433.

24. Forsthoff, *Der totale Staat,* 26.

25. Eberhard Finke, *Liberalismus und Strafverfahrensrecht* (Bonn: L. Röhrscheid, 1936), 18.

26. Paragraph 1, section 1 of the law.

27. Eduard Kern, "Grenzen der richterlichen Unabhängigkeit?" *Archiv für Rechts- und Sozialphilosophie* 27 (1933–34), 309.

28. Erik Wolf, "Das Rechtsideal des nationalsozialistischen Staates," *Archiv für Rechts- und Sozialphilosophie* 28 (1935), 349.

29. Carl Schmitt, *Staat, Bewegung, Volk* (Hamburg: Hanseatische Verlagsanstalt, 1933), 46.

30. Emil Niethammer, "Das Reichsgericht als Schrittmacher der Entwicklung des Strafverfahrens nach geltendem Recht und in Zukunft," *Deutsches Strafrecht* (1937), 135.

31. Schmitt, *Staat, Bewegung, Volk,* 46.

32. Wolf, "Das Rechtsideal des nationalsozialistischen Staates," 351.

33. Ibid., 351.

34. Wolfgang Siebert, "Vom Wesen des Rechtsmissbrauchs," in Georg Dahm et al., eds., *Grundfragen der neuen Rechtswissenschaft* (Berlin: Junker und Dünnhaupt, 1935), 209.

35. Friedrich Schaffstein, "Das Verbrechen als Pflichtverletzung," in Dahm et al., eds., *Grundfragen der neuen Rechtswissenschaft,* 120.

36. Georg Dahm, "Der Methodenstreit in der Rechtswissenschaft," *Zeitschrift für die gesamte Strafrechtswissenschaft* 57 (1938), 248.

37. Heinrich Lange, "Generalklauseln und neues Recht," *Juristische Wochenschrift* 62 (1933), 2859.

38. Georg Dahm, "Das Ermessen des Richters im nationalsozialistischen Strafrecht," *Deutsches Strafrecht* 1 (1934), 90.

39. Georg Dahm and Friedrich Schaffstein, *Liberales oder autoritäres Strafrecht?* (Hamburg: Hanseatische Verlagsanstalt, 1933), 19.

40. Hans Welzel, *Naturalismus und Wertphilosophie im Strafrecht* (Mannheim: Deutsches Druck-und-Verlagshaus, 1935), 73.

41. Georg Dahm, "Verbrechen und Tatbestand," in Dahm et al., eds., *Grundfragen der neuen Rechtswissenschaft*, 95.

42. Justus Hedemann, "Die Wahrheit im Recht," in Roland Freisler and Justus Hedemann, eds., *Kampf für ein deutsches Recht: Richard Deinhardt zum 75. Geburtstag* (Berlin: R. v. Decker, 1939), 7.

43. Karl Larenz, "Volksgeist und Recht," *Zeitschrift für deutsche Kulturphilosophie* 1 (1935), 47.

44. Carl Schmitt, "Der Weg des deutschen Juristen," *Deutsche Juristen-Zeitung* 39 (1934), 698.

45. Wolf, "Das Rechtsideal des nationalsozialistischen Staates," 348.

46. Rohling, "Stellung und Aufgabe des Staatsanwalts im künftigen Strafverfahren," *Deutsche Juristen-Zeitung* 40 (1935), 1348.

47. Cited in Heinz Boberach, ed., *Richterbriefe: Dokumente zur Beeinflussung der deutschen Rechtsprechung, 1942–1944* (Boppard a. Rhein: Boldt, 1975), 6.

48. Franz Gürtner and Roland Freisler, *Das neue Strafrecht,* 2nd ed. (Berlin: R. v. Decker, 1936), 143.

49. Wolfgang Naucke, "Die Aufhebung des strafrechtlichen Analogieverbots," *NS-Recht in historischer Perspektive: Kolloquien des Instituts für Zeitgeschichte* (Munich and Vienna: Oldenburg, 1981), 87.

50. Law of June 28, 1935; *Reichsgesetzblatt* (1935), I, 839.

51. Niekisch, *Das Reich der niederen Dämonen,* 96.

52. Gürtner and Freisler, *Das neue Strafrecht,* 163.

53. Schmitt, "Der Weg des deutschen Juristen," 693.

54. Heinrich Gerland, "Neues Strafrecht," *Deutsche Juristen-Zeitung* 38 (1933), 860.

55. Roland Freisler, "Der Wandel der politischen Grundanschauungen in Deutschland und sein Einfluss auf die Erneuerung von Strafrecht, Strafprozess und Strafvollzug," *Deutsche Justiz* 97 (1935), 1251.

56. Ibid., 1251.

57. Schmitt, *Staat, Bewegung, Volk,* 41.

58. Werner Brinkmann, "Die Parteigerichte als Schrittmacher einer volkstümlichen Strafrechtspflege," *Deutsche Richterzeitung* 27 (1935), 231.

59. Henkel, *Strafrichter und Gesetz,* 37.

60. Georg Küchenhoff, *Nationaler Gemeinschaftsstaat, Volksrecht und Volksrechtsprechung* (Berlin and Leipzig: n.p., 1934), 11.

61. Gürtner and Freisler, *Das neue Strafrecht,* 23.

62. Schaffstein, *Politische Strafrechtswissenschaft,* 25.

63. Wilhelm Sauer, *Grundlagen des Strafrechts* (Berlin and Leipzig: n.p., 1921).

64. Edmund Mezger, "Die materielle Rechtswidrigkeit im kommenden Strafrecht," *Zeitschrift für die gesamte Strafrechtswissenschaft* 55 (1936), 9.

65. *Scheffers Grundriss: Strafprozessrecht* (1943), 5.

66. Reichrechtsamt der NSDAP, ed., *Nationalsozialistische Leitsätze für ein neues deutsches Strafrecht* (Berlin: Deutscher Recht-Verlag, 1935).

67. Georg Dahm, "Gerechtigkeit und Zweckmässigkeit im Strafrecht der Gegenwart," in Paul Bockelmann et al., eds., *Probleme der Strafrechtserneuerung: Festschrift für Eduard Kohlrausch* (Berlin: de Gruyter, 1944), 11.

68. R. Peter, "Erb- und Rassenpflege im neuen Strafrecht," *Volk und Rasse* 12 (1937), 343.

69. Gürtner and Freisler, *Das neue Strafrecht,* 134.

70. Roland Freisler, "Schutz des Volkes, oder des Rechtsbrechers?" *Deutsches Strafrecht* (1935), 8.

71. Gürtner and Freisler, *Das neue Strafrecht,* 17.

72. Reichsrechtsamt der NSDAP, ed., *Leitsätze für ein neues Strafrecht,* 34.

73. Georg Dahm, "Verbrechen und Tatbestand," in Dahm et al., eds., *Grundfragen der neuen Rechtswissenschaft,* 103.

74. Schaffstein, "Das Verbrechen als Pflichtverletzung," ibid., 115.

75. Hans Welzel, "Über den substanziellen Begriff des Strafgesetzes," in Bockelmann et al., eds., *Probleme der Strafrechtserneuerung,* 109.

76. Wilhelm Sauer, "Wendung zum nationalen Strafrecht," *Der Gerichtssaal* 103 (1933), 1.

77. Welzel, "Über den substanziellen Begriff," 117.

78. Friedrich Schaffstein, "Ehrenstrafe und Freiheitsstrafe," *Deutsches Strafrecht* 1 (1934), 181.

79. Georg Dahm, *Gemeinschaft und Strafrecht* (Hamburg: Hanseatische Verlagsanstalt, 1935), 9.

80. Georg Dahm, "Die Erneuerung der Ehrenstrafe," *Deutsche Juristen-Zeitung* 39 (1934), 827.

81. Schaffstein, "Die materielle Rechtswidrigkeit im kommenden Strafrecht," *Zeitschrift für die gesamte Strafrechtswissenschaft* 55 (1936), 18ff.

82. Dahm, "Die Erneuerung der Ehrenstrafe," 823.

83. Erik Wolf, "Zur Stellung des Beschuldigten im Strafverfahren," *Zeitschrift der Akademie für deutsches Recht* 4 (1937), 178.

84. Friedrich Oetker, "Grundprobleme der nationalsozialistischen Strafrechtsreform," in Hans Frank, ed., *Nationalsozialistisches Handbuch für Recht und Gestzgebung* (Munich: Zentralverlag der NSDAP, Franz Eher, 1937), 1317.

85. NS-Dozentenbund, Gau Berlin, *Ansprachen und Vorträge* (1937), 33.

86. Friedrich Schaffstein, "Die Bedeutung des Erziehungsgedankens im neuen deutschen Strafrecht," *Zeitung für die gesamte Strafrechtswissenschaft* 55 (1936), 279.

87. Dahm, "Die Erneuerung der Ehrenstrafe," 826.

88. Ibid., 831.

89. Edmund Mezger, *Deutsches Strafrecht* (Berlin: Junker und Dünnhaupt, 1938), 72.

90. Dahm, "Gerechtigkeit und Zweckmässigkeit," in Bockelmann et al., eds., *Probleme der Strafrechtserneuerung*, 10.

91. Cited in *Frankfurter Rundschau* (May 24, 1986), 10.

92. Erich Schwinge, *Teleologische Begriffsbildung im Strafrecht* (Bonn: L. Röhrscheid, 1930).

93. Schaffstein, *Politische Strafrechtswissenschaft*, 11.

10. Civil Servants Become the Führer's Political Troops

1. Hans Gerber, *Politische Erziehung des Beamtentums im nationalsozialistischen Staat* (Tübingen: Mohr, 1933), 27.

2. Ibid., 31.

3. Law of January 26, 1937; *Reichsgesetzblatt* (1937), I, 41.

4. Oskar Fischbach, *Deutsches Beamtengesetz vom 26. Januar 1937: Textausgabe mit Erläuterungen* (Berlin and Leipzig: 1937), 22.

5. Ernst Rudolf Huber, *Verfassungsrecht des Grossdeutschen Reiches,* 2nd ed. (Hamburg: Hanseatische Verlagsanstalt, 1939), 445.

6. Erich Schultze, "Rechtsschöpferische Rechtsprechung des Reichsgerichts auf dienststrafrechtlichem Gebiet," *Erwin Bumke zum 65. Geburtstage* (Berlin: R. v. Decker, G. Schenk, de Gruyter, 1939), 105.

7. Cited in Schultze, ibid., 116–117.

8. Decision of May 16, 1940; *Entscheidungen des Reichsdienststrafhofs,* vol. 3, p. 22.

9. Ibid., 22.

10. Alfred Schulze et al., *Die Rechtsprechung des Reichsdisziplinarhofs* (1937), 73.

11. Decision of March 21, 1939; *Entscheidungen des Reichsdienststrafhofs,* vol. 2, p. 69.

12. "Dienststrafsenat beim Reichsgericht vom 27.7.1937," *Deutsche Justiz* 100 (1938), 1394.

13. Schulze et al., *Die Rechtsprechung des Reichsdisziplinarhofs,* 87.

14. Decision of May 29, 1940; *Entscheidungen des Reichsdienststrafhofs,* vol. 3, p. 40.

15. Decision of June 15, 1937; *Zeitschrift für Beamtenrecht* 8 (1937–38), 105.

11. Creation of the Concentration Camps

1. *Der Angriff,* February 20, 1934.

2. "Ersparnisvorschläge des Preussischen Richtervereins und Anregungen der Preussischen Staatsanwälte," *Juristische Wochenschrift* 61 (1932), 916–917.

3. Georg Dahm and Friedrich Schaffstein, *Liberales oder autoritäres Strafrecht?* (Hamburg: Hanseatische Verlagsanstalt, 1933), 22.

4. Friedrich Schaffstein, *Mitteilungen der internationalen kriminalistischen Vereinigung,* n.s. 6 (1933), 183.

5. *Reichsgesetzblatt* (1923), II, 163.
6. Decree of May 14, 1934; *Reichsgesetzblatt* (1934), I, 383.
7. Sozialdemokratische Partei Deutschlands, *Entwicklungstendenzen im deutschen Strafvollzug: Denkschrift* (Prague: n.p., 1935), 4.
8. Union für Recht und Freiheit, *Der Strafvollzug im Dritten Reich: Denkschrift und Materialsammlung* (Prague: n.p., 1936), 65.
9. Sozialdemokratische Partei Deutschlands, *Entwicklungstendenzen,* 6.
10. Martin Broszat, "Nationalsozialistische Konzentrationslager," Martin Broszat and H. A. Jacobsen, eds., *Anatomie des SS-Staates,* 2nd ed. (Munich: Deutscher Taschenbuch Verlag, 1979), II, 24.
11. Union für Recht und Freiheit, *Der Strafvollzug,* 73.
12. Ibid., 73.
13. Ibid., 7.
14. Ibid., 101.
15. Ibid., 77.
16. Ibid., 68.
17. For more on the Emsland camps, see Elke Suhr, *Die Emslandlager* (Bremen: Donat und Temmen, 1985).
18. Elke Suhr and Werner Boldt, *Lager im Emsland, 1933–1945* (Oldenburg: Bibliotheks- und Informationssystem der Universität Oldenburg, 1985), 18.
19. Sozialdemokratische Partei Deutschlands, *Entwicklungstendenzen.*
20. *Schweizerische Zeitschrift für Strafrecht* 40 (1935), 442ff.
21. Suhr and Boldt, *Lager im Emsland,* 26.
22. Suhr, *Die Emslandlager,* 80ff.

12. "Protecting the Race"

1. Adolf Hitler, *Mein Kampf,* 2 vols. in 1 (Munich: Zentralverlag der NSDAP, 1940), 313.
2. Helmut Nicolai, *Rassengesetzliche Rechtslehre: Grundzüge einer nationalsozialistischen Rechtsphilosophie* (Munich: F. Eher Nachfolger, 1932), 46.
3. *Archiv für die civilistische Praxis,* n.s. 19 (1934), 340.
4. Alfred Rosenberg, *Der Mythos des zwanzigsten Jahrhunderts,* 2nd ed. (Munich: Hoheneichen-Verlag, 1932), 569.
5. *Reichstags-Drucksache,* 4/1741.
6. *Nationalsozialistisches Strafrecht* (Berlin, 1936).
7. Minutes of the 37th meeting of the Criminal Law Commission, cited in Lothar Gruchmann, "'Blutschutzgesetz' und Justiz," *Vierteljahrshefte für Zeitgeschichte* (1983), 419.
8. Ibid., 420.
9. Ibid., 422.
10. Decision of July 12, 1934; *Entscheidungen des Reichsgerichts in Zivilsachen: Amtliche Sammlung* 145 (1935), 1ff.
11. Amtsgericht Bad Sülze, *Juristische Wochenschrift* 64 (1935), 2309.
12. Order of June 7, 1935, reproduced in Ernst Noam and Wolf-Arno Kropat,

Juden vor Gericht, 1933–1945: Dokumente aus hessischen Justizakten (Wiesbaden: Kommission für die Geschichte der Juden in Hessen, 1975), 62.

13. Königsberg County Court, August 26, 1935; in *Deutsche Justiz* 97 (1935), 1387.

14. Cited in Ernst Wolf's letter in the *Frankfurter Allgemeine Zeitung,* May 6, 1985.

15. *Deutsche Justiz* 97 (1935), 1086.

16. *Reichsgesetzblatt* (1935), I, 1146.

17. See Hans Wrobel, "Die Anfechtung der Rassenmischehe," *Kritische Justiz* 16 (1983), 349ff.

18. See Wrobel's list, ibid., 354ff.

19. *Juristische Wochenschrift* 62 (1933), 2041.

20. *Deutsche Justiz* 95 (1933), 818.

21. *Deutsche Justiz* 96 (1934), 134.

22. *Höchstrichterliche Rechtsprechung* 489 (1934).

23. "Recht, Richter und Gesetz," *Deutsche Justiz* 95 (1933), 694.

24. *Entscheidungen des Reichsgerichts in Zivilsachen,* vol. 154, p. 4; cited in *Juristische Wochenschrift* 63 (1934), 2613.

25. *Reichsgesetzblatt* (1938), I, 807.

26. Cited in Gruchmann, "'Blutschutzgesetz' und Justiz," 422.

27. Ibid., 425.

28. *Das Nürnberger Urteil* 20 (1946), 293.

29. Karl Dietrich Bracher, *The German Dictatorship,* trans. Jean Steinberg (1969; New York: Praeger, 1970), 253.

30. Martin Broszat, *The Hitler State,* trans. John W. Hiden (1969; London and New York: Longman, 1981), 284.

31. Report of December 3, 1935, Bundesarchiv R 22, no. 3133.

32. *Deutschland-Berichte der Sozialdemokratischen Partei Deutschlands,* 997.

33. Otto Koellreutter, *Grundfragen unserer Volks- und Staatsgestaltung* (Berlin: Junker und Dünnhaupt, 1936), 10.

34. Paragraph 5, section 1 of the administrative decree of November 14, 1935; *Reichsgesetzblatt* (1935), I, 1334.

35. Stuckart and Globke, *Kommentare zur deutschen Rassengesetzgebung* 1 (1936), 10–11.

36. Hans Pfundtner and Reinhard Neubert, *Das neue deutsche Reichsrecht: Ergänzbare Sammlung des geltenden Rechts seit dem Ermächtigungsgesetz* (Berlin: n.p., n.d.), no. 23, p. 8.

37. *Deutschland-Berichte der Sozialdemokratischen Partei Deutschlands,* 1019.

38. Decree of November 14, 1935; *Reichsgesetzblatt* (1935), I, 1334.

39. *Kommentare zur deutschen Rassengesetzgebung* 1 (1936), 112.

40. Decision of March 14, 1936; *Juristische Wochenschrift* (1936), 1397.

41. Decision of December 19, 1935; ibid., 730.

42. Paragraphs 131a and 137 of the Law on the Constitution of the Courts.

43. *Entscheidungen des Reichsgerichts in Strafsachen,* vol. 70, p. 375.

44. Ibid., vol. 72, p. 9.

45. Ibid., vol. 73, p. 94.
46. Decision of January 15, 1937; cited in Leppin, "Der Schutz des deutschen Blutes und der deutschen Ehre," *Juristische Wochenschrift* (1937), 3079.
47. Hans Robinsohn, *Justiz als politische Verfolgung* (Stuttgart: Deutsche Verlagsanstalt, 1977), 35.
48. Ibid., 23.
49. Heinrich Hannover and Günter Walraff, *Die unheimliche Republik: Politische Verfolgung in der Bundesrepublik* (Hamburg: VSA Verlag, 1982), 21.
50. Cited in Robinsohn, *Justiz als politische Verfolgung*, 66.
51. Ibid., 62.
52. Ibid., 62.
53. See the statistics ibid., 71.
54. Decision of the Hamburg County Court, cited ibid., 67.
55. Reproduced in Noam and Kropat, *Juden vor Gericht*, 124.
56. *Entscheidungen des Reichsgerichts in Strafsachen*, vol. 71, p. 70.
57. Cited in Robinsohn, *Justiz als politische Verfolgung*, 76.
58. County Court of Frankfurt/Main, cited in Noam and Kropat, *Juden vor Gericht*, 124.
59. Leppin, "Der Schutz des deutschen Blutes," 3080.
60. See the list in Robinsohn, *Justiz als politische Verfolgung*, 71.
61. *Entscheidungen des Reichsgerichts in Strafsachen*, vol. 71, p. 339.
62. Cited in Robinsohn, *Justiz als politische Verfolgung*, 41.
63. *Entscheidungen des Reichsgerichts in Strafsachen*, vol. 71, p. 28.
64. Ibid., vol. 73, p. 98.
65. *Juristische Wochenschrift* (1939), 93 (Reichsgericht).
66. *Juristische Wochenschrift* (1938), 447 (Reichsgericht).
67. *Entscheidungen des Reichsgerichts in Strafsachen*, vol. 73, p. 94.
68. Ibid., vol. 74, p. 404.
69. Ibid., 278.
70. Paragraph 43 II, 2b of the Criminal Code; Reinhard Frank, ed., *Das Strafgesetzbuch für das Deutsche Reich*, 18th ed. (Tübingen: Mohr, 1929–30).
71. *Entscheidungen des Reichsgerichts in Strafsachen*, vol. 53, p. 336.
72. Ibid., vol. 73, p. 76.
73. Ibid., vol. 74, p. 86.
74. The decision is reproduced in Noam and Kropat, *Juden vor Gericht*, 164ff.
75. *Reichsgesetzblatt* (1933), I, 995.
76. Ibid., 549.
77. The decision of April 20, 1943, is reproduced in Noam and Kropat, *Juden vor Gericht*, 168ff.
78. Decision of the Leipzig County Court, cited in Friedrich Karl Kaul, *Geschichte des Reichsgerichts*, (Glashütten/Taunus: Auvermann, 1971), IV, 149.
79. *Entscheidungen des Reichsgerichts in Strafsachen*, vol. 73, p. 146.
80. Bernd Schimmler, *Recht ohne Gerechtigkeit: Zur Tätigkeit der Berliner Sondergerichte im Nationalsozialismus* (Berlin: Wissenschaftlicher Autoren-Verlag, 1984), 96.
81. Robinsohn, *Juden vor Gericht*, 106.

82. The course of the trial is described by Jörg Friedrich, *Freispruch für die Nazi-Justiz: Die Urteile gegen NS-Richter seit 1948* (Reinbek bei Hamburg: Rowohlt, 1983), 269ff.

83. The decision is reproduced in Ilse Staff, *Justiz im Dritten Reich,* 2nd ed. (Frankfurt: Fischer Taschenbuch-Verlag, 1978), 178ff.

84. Cited in Ilse Staff, *Justiz im Dritten Reich,* 1st ed. (Frankfurt: Fischer Bücherei, 1964).

85. The decision is reproduced with a commentary in Martin Hirsch, Diemut Majer, and Jurgen Meinck, eds., *Recht, Verwaltung und Justiz im Nationalsozialismus* (Cologne: Bund-Verlag, 1984), 390–391.

86. *Deutsche Justiz* 98 (1936), 936.

87. Decision of May 27, 1937; *Juristische Wochenschrift* (1937), 3306.

88. Decision of September 14, 1937; ibid., 3306.

89. Decision of March 23, 1938; *Deutsche Justiz* 100 (1938), 905.

90. Decision of the Worms Petty Court of November 16, 1939; *Das Recht* [monthly supplement to *Deutsche Justiz*] 102 (1940), 295.

91. *Deutsche Justiz* 99 (1937), 1989.

92. Decision of August 12, 1939; cited in Ernst Fraenkel, *The Dual State: A Contribution to the Theory of Dictatorship,* trans. E. A. Shils (1941; rpt. New York: Octagon Books, 1969), 86–87.

93. See, for example, the decision of the Berlin County Court of May 14, 1934; *Juristische Wochenschrift* (1934), 1516.

94. *Juristische Wochenschrift* (1938), 2045.

95. Decision of November 7, 1938; ibid., 3242.

96. Ibid., 3248.

97. Decision of November 7, 1938; ibid., 3243.

98. The decision is reproduced in Noam and Kropat, *Juden vor Gericht,* 84ff.

99. Decision of November 25, 1933; *Deutsche Justiz* 96 (1934), 229.

100. Decision of February 28, 1934; ibid., 802.

101. Cited in Diemut Majer, *"Fremdvölkische" im Dritten Reich* (Boppard a. Rhein: Boldt, 1981), 247.

102. The decision of August 4, 1939, is reproduced in Noam and Kropat, *Juden vor Gericht,* 98–99.

103. Decision of September 4, 1940; ibid., 99–100.

104. Decision of February 4, 1940; *Deutsches Recht* (1940), 1326–27.

105. Decision of April 16, 1942; *Höchstrichterliche Rechtsprechung* (1942), 529.

106. Decision of County Labor Court of Düsseldorf of July 7, 1939; cited in Majer, *"Fremdvölkische" im Dritten Reich,* 689.

107. Decision of the Berlin County Court of November 7, 1938; *Juristische Wochenschrift* (1938), 3243.

13. The Courts and Eugenics

1. Cited in Diemut Majer, *"Fremdvölkische" im Dritten Reich* (Boppard a. Rhein: Boldt, 1981), 182.

2. Report in the *Völkischer Beobachter* of August 7, 1929.

3. *Reichsgesetzblatt* (1933), I, 529.
4. See Robert Gaupp, *Die Unfruchtbarmachung geistig und sittlich Kranker und Minderwertiger* (Berlin: J. Springer, 1925), 9ff.
5. Arthur Gütt, Ernst Rüdin, and Falk Ruttke, eds., *Gesetz zur Verhütung erbkranken Nachwuchses nebst Ausführungsverordnungen,* 2nd ed. (Munich: Lehmann, 1936), 55.
6. *Reichsgesetzblatt* (1933), I, 1021.
7. Cited in Union für Recht und Freiheit, *Der Strafvollzug im Dritten Reich* (Prague: n.p., 1936), 60.
8. Karl Binding and Alfred Hoche, *Die Freigabe der Vernichtung lebensunwerten Lebens* (Leipzig: n.p., 1920), 40.
9. See the survey of decisions in *Juristische Wochenschrift* (1935), 1865ff.
10. Ibid., 1873ff.
11. *Weser-Kurier,* July 16, 1980. See also Alexander Mitscherlich and Fred Mielke, eds., *Medizin ohne Menschlichkeit: Dokumente des Nürnberger Ärzteprozesses* (Frankfurt: Fischer Taschenbuch-Verlag, 1981).
12. See the statistics in N. Schmacke and H.-G. Güse, *Zwangssterilisiert* (Bremen: Brockkamp, 1984), 87.
13. Decision of the Jena Hereditary Health Court of Appeals of May 23, 1935; *Juristische Wochenschrift* (1935), 1870.
14. Ibid.
15. Gütt, Rüdin, and Ruttke, *Gesetz zur Verhütung erbkranken Nachwuchses,* 94.
16. Decision of the Jena Hereditary Health Court of Appeals of December 20, 1934; *Juristische Wochenschrift* (1935), 1870.
17. Jena Hereditary Health Court of Appeals, May 23, 1935; ibid.
18. Jena Hereditary Health Court of Appeals, March 21, 1935; ibid.
19. Darmstadt Hereditary Health Court of Apppeals, April 8, 1935; ibid., 1867–68.
20. Decision of November 29, 1934; ibid., 1870.
21. Hans Luxemberger, *Psychiatrische Erblehre und Erbpflege,* part 1 (1938), 7.
22. Arthur Gütt, Ernst Rüdin, and Falk Ruttke, *Gesetz zur Verhütung erbkranken Nachwuchses,* 1st ed. (1934), 83.
23. Cited in *Weser-Kurier,* July 18, 1980.
24. Zweibrücken Hereditary Health Court of Appeals, May 20, 1935; *Juristische Wochenschrift* (1935), 1866.
25. Gütt, Rüdin, and Ruttke, *Gesetz zur Verhütung erbkranken Nachwuchses,* 2nd ed. (1936), 94.
26. Decision of April 18, 1935; *Juristische Wochenschrift* (1935), 1869.
27. Jena Hereditary Health Court of Appeals, May 23, 1935; ibid., 1870.
28. Jena Hereditary Health Court of Appeals, November 29, 1934; ibid.
29. Darmstadt Hereditary Health Court of Appeals, April 8, 1935; ibid., 1867.
30. Berlin Hereditary Health Court of Appeals, January 17, 1935; ibid., 1873.
31. Berlin Hereditary Health Court of Appeals, November 22, 1934; ibid., 1874.
32. Berlin Hereditary Health Court of Appeals, March 9, 1935; ibid., 1873.
33. Decision of February 18, 1935; ibid.

34. On August 8, 1939; *Reichsgesetzblatt* (1939), I, 1560.
35. Heinz Boberach, ed., *Meldungen aus dem Reich: Auswahl aus den geheimen Lageberichten des Sicherheitsdienstes der SS, 1939–1944* (Neuwied: Luchterhand, 1965) III, 800.

14. The Euthanasia Program

1. Franz Gürtner, ed., *Bericht über die Arbeit der amtlichen Strafrechtskommission* (Berlin: F. Vahlen, 1935), special section, 258.
2. Cited in K. Dörner, "Nationalsozialismus und Lebensvernichtung," *Vierteljahrshefte für Zeitgeschichte* 20 (1972), 138.
3. H. Puvogel, *Die leitenden Grundgedanken bei der Entmannung gefährlicher Sittlichkeitsverbrecher* (1937), 34.
4. See Ernst Klee, *"Euthanasie" im NS-Staat* (Frankfurt: S. Fischer, 1983), 66ff.
5. Bundesarchiv R 22, no. 3379.
6. Bundesarchiv R 22, no. 3355.
7. A facsimile is printed in Peter Przybylski, *Zwischen Galgen und Amnestie: Kriegsverbrecherprozesse im Spiegel von Nürnberg* (Berlin: Dietz, 1979), 16.
8. Lothar Gruchmann, "Euthanasie und Justiz im Dritten Reich," *Vierteljahrshefte für Zeitgeschichte* 20 (1972), 261.
9. Ibid., 262.
10. The meeting is described in Helmut Kramer, "Oberlandesgerichtspräsidenten und Generalstaatsanwälte als Gehilfen der NS-Euthanasie," *Kritische Justiz* 17 (1984), 29–30.
11. Eugen Kogon, Adalbert Rückerl, and Hermann Langbein, *Nationalsozialistische Massentötungen durch Giftgas: Eine Dokumentation* (Frankfurt: S. Fischer, 1983), 57ff.
12. Diemut Majer, *"Fremdvölkische" im Dritten Reich* (Boppard a. Rhein: Boldt, 1981), 184.

15. "Defenders of the Law"

1. See the survey in Friedrich Karl Kaul, *Geschichte des Reichsgerichts* (Glashütten/Taunus: Auvermann, 1971), IV, 184–185.
2. Ibid., 222.
3. Alfred Klutz, *Volksschädlinge am Pranger: Eine Aufklärungsschrift im grossdeutschen Freiheitskampf* (Berlin: H. Hillger, 1940), 12.
4. Kaul, *Geschichte des Reichsgerichts*, 231.
5. Ibid.
6. Decree of September 1, 1939; *Reichsgesetzblatt* I, 1683.
7. Decision of May 22, 1942; *Hochstrichterliche Rechtsprechung* 593 (1942).
8. *Entscheidungen des Reichsgerichts in Strafsachen*, vol. 74, p. 271.
9. An offense according to paragraph 366 of the Criminal Code at that time.
10. See *Entscheidungen des Reichsgerichts in Strafsachen*, vol. 74, p. 239.
11. Decision of April 8, 1940; ibid., 166.
12. Decision of May 20, 1940; ibid., 199.

13. Decree of December 5, 1939; *Reichsgesetzblatt* (1939), I, 1378.
14. Verden County Court, cited in *Entscheidungen des Reichsgerichts in Strafsachen,* vol. 74, p. 281.
15. Decision of September 12, 1940; ibid.
16. The case is discussed in detail in Hans Robinsohn, *Justiz als politische Verfolgung* (Stuttgart: Deutsche Verlags-Anstalt, 1977), 111ff.
17. Decision of April 4, 1935; *Entscheidungen des Reichsgerichts in Strafsachen,* vol. 69, pp. 183–184.

16. Arbitrary Decisions in Everyday Life

1. *Deutsche Richterzeitung* 26 (1934), app. 455.
2. Decision of April 14, 1937; *Juristische Wochenschrift* 66 (1937), 2311. The decision of the *Reichsarbeitsgericht* of March 13, 1935, is similar; see *Deutsche Richterzeitung* 27 (1935), suppl. 411.
3. Decision of March 31, 1936; *Deutsche Juristen-Zeitung* 41 (1936), 771.
4. Decision of June 5, 1936; *Zentralblatt für Jugendrecht und Jugendwohlfahrt* (1936), 281.
5. Decision of April 15, 1935; *Das Recht ab 1934* [monthly supplement to *Deutsche Justiz*] (1935), 8015.
6. Decision of February 26, 1938; *Juristische Wochenschrift* 67 (1938); 1264.
7. See the case discussed in Richterbrief 3, in Heinz Boberach, ed., *Richterbriefe* (Boppard a. Rhein: Boldt, 1975), 48–49.
8. *Verkehrsrechtliche Abhandlungen* (1937), 319.
9. Decision of April 24, 1934; *Deutsche Richterzeitung* 26 (1934), app. 365.
10. Decision of July 1, 1934; ibid., app. 556.
11. Decision of April 3, 1941; *Entscheidungen des Reichsgerichts in Strafsachen,* vol. 75, p. 193.
12. Decision of September 22, 1938; *Juristische Wochenschrift* 67 (1938), 2957.

17. The People's Court

1. *Mein Kampf* (1940), 610.
2. *Reichstags-Protokolle,* vol. 425, p. 2424.
3. *Reichsgesetzblatt* (1934), I, 341.
4. *Völkischer Beobachter,* July 31, 1934.
5. Cited ibid.
6. "Der Volksgerichtshof—das Reichsstrafgericht?" *Zeitschrift der Akademie für Deutsches Recht* (1935), 91.
7. *Das Recht ab 1934* [monthly supplement to *Deutsche Justiz*] (1935), 518.
8. Law of April 18, 1936; *Reichsgesetzblatt* (1936), I, 369.
9. Wolfgang Idel, *Die Sondergerichte in politischen Strafsachen* (Schramberg: n.p., 1935), 36.
10. See the report in *Deutsche Justiz* 99 (1937), 1935.
11. *NS-Rechtsspiegel* 2 (1938), no. 6.

12. "Stellung und Aufgabe des Volksgerichtshofs," *Das Recht ab 1934* (1939), 486.

13. Cited in B. M. Kempner, *Priester vor Hitlers Tribunalen* (Munich: Rütten & Loenig, 1966), 444.

14. See Walter Wagner, *Der Volksgerichtshof im nationalsozialistischen Staat* (Stuttgart: Deutsche Verlagsanstalt, 1974), 23–24.

15. The statistics are given in Heinz Hillermeier, *"Im Namen des deutschen Volkes": Todesurteile des Volksgerichtshofs* (Neuwied: Luchterhand, 1980).

16. The full text of the decision is included in Wilhelm Raimund Beyer, *Rückkehr unerwünscht* (1978; rpt. Munich: Deutscher Taschenbuch Verlag, 1980), 185ff.

17. The case is documented by Helmut Heiber, "Zur Justiz im Dritten Reich: Der Fall Eliáš," *Vierteljahrshefte für Zeitgeschichte* 3 (1955), 275ff.

18. Henry Picker, ed., *Tischgespräche im Führerhauptquartier, 1941–42* (Bonn: Athenäum Verlag, 1951), 212.

19. See the plan for assignment of cases in Hillermeier, *"Im Namen des deutschen Volkes,"* 152.

20. Entry for January 23, 1943; cited in Heiber, "Zur Justiz im Dritten Reich," 277.

21. Bundesarchiv R 22 GR 5/457.

22. *Deutsche Justiz* 104 (1942), 397.

23. Decision of February 27, 1940; *Deutsche Justiz* 102 (1940), 939.

24. Cited in the first decision of the Berlin County Court of July 3, 1967, in the case of Hans-Joachim Rehse; *Deutsche Richterzeitung* 45 (1967), 394.

25. Cited in Martin Broszat, "Zur Perversion der Strafjustiz im Dritten Reich," *Vierteljahrshefte für Zeitgeschichte* 6 (1958), 438.

26. The case is documented in Wagner, *Der Volksgerichtshof im nationalsozialistischen Staat,* 291.

27. Cited in *Deutsche Richterzeitung* 45 (1967), 390.

28. Bill cited in Hillermeier, *"Im Namen des deutschen Volkes,"* 73.

29. Ibid., 96.

30. William L. Shirer, *The Rise and Fall of the Third Reich* (New York: Simon and Schuster, 1960), 1070.

31. Manfred Messerschmidt, *Die Wehrmacht im NS-Staat* (Hamburg: Decker, 1969), 373.

32. The scene from the film *Geheime Reichssache* is also described in Shirer, *The Rise and Fall of the Third Reich.*

33. Kempner, *Priester vor Hitlers Tribunalen,* 67.

34. M. Hofer, ed., *Der Nationalsozialismus: Dokumente, 1933–1945* (1982), 356.

35. Hillermeier, *"Im Namen des deutschen Volkes,"* 97; see also the report by the prison pastor H. Poelchau, *Die letzten Stunden* (1949), 107.

36. Werner Johe, *Die gleichgeschaltete Justiz* (Frankfurt: Europäische Verlagsanstalt, 1967), 116.

37. The decision is printed in Ilse Staff, ed., *Justiz im Dritten Reich: Eine Dokumentation* (Frankfurt: Fischer Taschenbuch-Verlag, 1978), 210ff.

38. *Deutsches Recht* (1945), 73.

39. See the bibliography in Gert Buchheit, *Richter in roter Robe: Freisler, Präsident des Volksgerichtshofes* (Munich: List, 1968), 287ff.
40. Michael Freund, *Deutsche Geschichte* (Gütersloh: Bertelsmann Lexicon-Verlag, 1974), 1441–42.

18. Summary Courts of the "Inner Front"

1. See the various decrees on special courts cited in Felix Halle, *Deutsche Sonder-gerichtsbarkeit, 1918–1921* (Berlin and Leipzig: Franke Verlag, 1922). See also the Law on the Protection of the Republic of August 21, 1922 (Reichsgesetzblatt [1922], I, 585), and the Emergency Decree of October 6, 1931 (Reichsgesetzblatt [1931], I, 537).
2. *Reichsgesetzblatt* (1933), I, 136.
3. Ibid., 537.
4. E. Noack, "Formalismus im Strafprozess," *Deutsches Recht* (1934), 357.
5. "Der nationalsozialistische Strafprozess," in Hans Frank, ed., *Nationalsozial-istisches Handbuch für Recht und Gesetzgebung* (1935; rpt. Munich: Zentral-verlag der NSDAP, 1937), 1478.
6. Cited in Richterbrief 2, in Heinz Boberach, ed., *Richterbriefe: Dokumente zur Beeinflussung der deutschen Rechtsprechung, 1942–1944* (Boppard a. Rhein: Boldt, 1975), 17.
7. Introduction to Alfred Klütz, *Volksschädlinge am Pranger* (Berlin: H. Hillger, 1940), 5.
8. *Reichsgesetzblatt* (1939), I, 1658.
9. Cited in Werner Johe, *Die gleichgeschaltete Justiz* (Frankfurt: Europäische Ver-lagsanstalt, 1967), 91.
10. Klütz, *Volksschädlinge am Pranger*, 13.
11. *Reichsgesetzblatt* (1940), I, 565.
12. Decree of September 4, 1939; *Reichsgesetzblatt* (1939), I, 1609.
13. Decrees of October 17 and November 14, 1939; *Reichsgesetzblatt* (1939), I, 2055 and 2222.
14. Klütz, *Volksschädlinge am Pranger*, 12.
15. The decision is printed in W. Koppel, *Ungesühnte Nazijustiz* (1963), 15–16.
16. Klütz, *Volksschädlinge am Pranger*, 13.
17. Paragraph 14 of the Decree on Jurisdiction of November 20, 1938.
18. O. Rietzsch, "Die Stellung der Sondergerichte in der Strafrechtspflege," cited in Johe, *Die gleichgeschaltete Justiz*, 91.
19. Decrees of the Reich Ministry of Justice; *Deutsche Justiz* (1940), 233, 795. See also Bernd Schimmler, *Recht ohne Gerechtigkeit: Zur Tätigkeit der Berliner Sondergerichte im Nationalsozialismus* (Berlin: Wissenschaftlicher Autoren-Verlag, 1984), 13.
20. Cited in Johe, *Die gleichgeschaltete Justiz*, 92.
21. See the numbers cited ibid., 106.
22. Instructions issued by the Reich Ministry of Justice on July 5, 1943, cited ibid., 105.
23. Ibid.

24. The decision is printed in Koppel, *Ungesühnte Nazijustiz,* 16.
25. Johe reaches this conclusion in his analysis of Special Court decisions, *Die gleichgeschaltete Justiz,* 107.
26. Diemut Majer, *"Fremdvölkische" im Dritten Reich* (Boppard a. Rhein: Boldt, 1981), 734.
27. *Deutsches Recht* (1941), 2473.
28. Cited in Helmut Krausnick, *Hitlers Einsatzgruppen* (Frankfurt: Fischer, 1985), 50.
29. *Deutsches Recht* (1941), 2474.
30. See Majer, *"Fremdvölkische" im Dritten Reich,* 735ff.
31. The various decrees are cited ibid.
32. *Reichsgesetzblatt* (1941), I, 759.
33. A remark made on October 2, 1939, cited in Imanuel Geiss and Wolfgang Jacobmeyer, eds., *Deutsche Politik in Polen, 1939–1945* (Opladen: Leske & Budrich, 1980), 14.
34. The German Criminal Code for Poland, *Deutsche Justiz* 104 (1942), 25.
35. The decision is printed in Ilse Staff, ed., *Justiz im Dritten Reich; Eine Dokumentation* (1964; 2nd ed. Frankfurt: Fischer Taschenbuch-Verlag, 1978), 191–192.
36. The decision is printed in Koppel, *Ungesühnte Nazijustiz,* 23.
37. Ibid., 14.
38. Ibid., 16.
39. See Raul Hilberg, *The Destruction of the European Jews* (1961; rpt. New York: Octagon Books, 1978), 150–151.
40. The decision is printed in Koppel, *Ungesühnte Nazijustiz,* 41ff.
41. "Zweifelsfragen im Polenstrafrecht," *Deutsche Justiz* 104 (1942), 226.
42. Christoph Schminck-Gustavus, "NS-Justiz und Besatzungsterror," in Norman Paech and Gerhard Stuby, eds., *Wider die "herrschende Meinung"* (Frankfurt and New York: Campus, 1982), 34.
43. *Reichsgesetzblatt* (1941), I, 797.
44. The decision is printed in Wolfgang Koppel, *Justiz im Zwielicht* (Karlsruhe: published by the author, 1963), 24ff.
45. Letter of February 2, 1942, cited in Majer, *"Fremdvölkische" im Dritten Reich,* 769.
46. Edmund Zarycki, *Tätigkeit des Nazi-Sondergerichts in Bydgoszcz* (1976), 208–209.
47. The case is documented in Eduard Rabofsky and Gerhard Oberkofler, *Verborgene Wurzeln der NS-Justiz* (Vienna, Munich, Zurich: Europaverlag, 1985) 73.
48. Documented in B. M. Kempner, *Priester vor Hitlers Tribunalen* (Munich: Rütten & Loenig, 1966), 196ff.
49. Documented in Christoph Schminck-Gustavus, *Das Heimweh des Walerjan Wrobel: Ein Sondergerichtsverfahren, 1941–42* (Bonn: Dietz, 1986).
50. Documented in Rabofsky and Oberkofler, *Verborgene Wurzeln der NS-Justiz,* 73ff.
51. Cited in Peter Alfons Steiniger and Kazimierz Leszczynski, *Fall 3* (Berlin: Deutscher Verlag der Wissenschaften, 1969), 186.

52. The text is printed in Peter Przybylski, *Zwischen Galgen und Amnestie: Kriegsverbrecherprozesse im Spiegel von Nürnberg* (Berlin: Dietz, 1979), 40.
53. Cited in Lothar Gruchmann, "'Nacht- und Nebel'- Justiz," *Vierteljahrshefte für Zeitgeschichte* 29 (1981), 359.
54. Ibid.
55. Elke Suhr, *Die Emslandlager* (Bremen: Donat und Temmen, 1985), 177.
56. Cited in Steiniger and Leszczynski, *Fall 3*, 177.
57. Ibid., 180.
58. Cited in Suhr, *Die Emslandlager*, 178.
59. Cited in Steiniger and Leszczynski, *Fall 3*, 182.

19. "Correcting" Decisions

1. Henry Picker, ed., *Tischgespräche im Führerhauptquartier, 1941–42* (Bonn: Athenäum Verlag, 1951), 213.
2. *Archiv für Rechts- und Sozialphilosophie* 27 (1933–34), 309.
3. *Völkischer Beobachter,* December 24, 1933.
4. Cited in Martin Broszat, *The Hitler State,* trans. John W. Hiden (London and New York: Longman, 1981), 335.
5. Ibid., 343, note 9.
6. Bundesarchiv R 22, no. 3356.
7. See the list in Broszat, *The Hitler State,* 335.
8. Bernd Schimmler, *Recht ohne Gerechtigkeit: Zur Tätigkeit der Berliner Sondergerichte im Nationalsozialismus* (Berlin: Wissenschaftlicher Autoren-Verlag, 1984), 120.
9. *Völkischer Beobachter,* October 16, 1939; cited ibid., 121.
10. Cited in Broszat, *The Hitler State,* 334.
11. Ibid.
12. Walter Wagner, *Der Volksgerichtshof im nationalsozialistischen Staat* (Stuttgart: Deutsche Verlagsanstalt, 1974), 47.
13. Werner Johe, *Die gleichgeschaltete Justiz* (Frankfurt: Europäische Verlagsanstalt, 1967), 160.
14. Gerhard Schulz, *Die Anfänge des totalitären Massnahmenstaates* (Frankfurt, Berlin, Vienna: Ullstein, 1974), 204.
15. Diemut Majer, *"Fremdvölkische" im Dritten Reich* (Boppard a. Rhein: Boldt, 1981), 649.
16. See Helmut Heiber, "Zur Justiz im Dritten Reich," *Vierteljahrshefte für Zeitgeschichte* 3 (1955), 283.
17. Cited in Broszat, *The Hitler State,* 334–335.
18. *Reichsgesetzblatt* (1934), I, 529.
19. Broszat, *The Hitler State,* 336.
20. Printed in Ilse Staff, ed., *Justiz im Dritten Reich* (1964; 2nd ed. Frankfurt: Fischer Taschenbuch-Verlag, 1978), 106ff.
21. Werner Best, *Die deutsche Polizei* (Darmstadt: Wittich, 1940), 18.
22. The case is documented in Friedrich Karl Kaul, *Geschichte des Reichsgerichts* (Glashütten/Taunus: Auvermann, 1971), IV, 195ff.

23. *Reichsgesetzblatt* (1934), I, 91.
24. The minutes are printed in Ilse Staff, ed., *Justiz im Dritten Reich,* 1st ed. (Frankfurt: Fischer Taschenbuch-Verlag, 1964), 117.
25. Peter Alfons Steiniger and Kazimierz Leszczynski, *Fall 3* (1969), 198.
26. Cited in H. Wagner, "Die Polizei im Faschismus," in Udo Reifner and Bernd-Rüdeger Sonnen, eds., *Strafjustiz und Polizei im Dritten Reich* (Frankfurt and New York: Campus, 1984), 167.
27. *Reichsgesetzblatt* (1943), I, 372.

20. The Legal Officers' Corps

1. Adolf Hitler, *Mein Kampf,* 2 vols. in 1 (Munich: Zentralverlag der NSDAP, 1940), 588.
2. Cited in Manfred Messerschmidt, "Deutsche Militärgerichtsbarkeit im Zweiten Weltkrieg," in Hans Jochen Vogel, ed., *Die Freiheit des Anderen: Festschrift für Martin Hirsch* (Baden-Baden: Nomos, 1981), 111.
3. *Reichsgesetzblatt* (1933), I, 264.
4. Erich Schwinge, *Militärstrafgesetzbuch: Kommentar,* 5th ed. (1943), 2.
5. Cited in Messerschmidt, "Deutsche Militärgerichtsbarkeit," 116.
6. Otto Hennicke, "Auszüge aus der Wehrmachtsstatistik," *Zeitschrift für Militärgeschichte* (1966), 445.
7. Messerschmidt, "Deutsche Militärgerichtsbarkeit," 137.
8. Otto Hennicke, "Über den Justizterror in der deutschen Wehrmacht am Ende des Zweiten Weltkrieges," *Zeitschrift für Militärgeschichte* (1965), 716.
9. Hennicke, "Auszüge aus der Wehrmachtsstatistik."
10. *Entscheidungen des Reichskriegsgerichts* 2, no. 23; cited in Messerschmidt, "Deutsche Militärgerichtsbarkeit," 123.
11. Ibid., 133.
12. The case is described ibid., 131; and in Ulrich Vultejus, *Kampfanzug unter der Robe: Kriegsgerichtsbarkeit* (Hamburg: Buntbuch, 1984), 69.
13. The case is described in Messerschmidt, "Deutsche Militärgerichtsbarkeit," 135.
14. Note to paragraph 50 of the Military Criminal Code, in Schwinge, *Militärstrafgesetzbuch: Kommentar.*
15. Ibid., 7.
16. The case was presented in the *Frankfurter Rundschau,* September 11, 1986.
17. Rudolf Absolon, ed., *Das Wehrmachtsstrafrecht im 2. Weltkrieg* (1958), 90ff.
18. Vultejus, *Kampfanzug unter der Robe,* 69–70.
19. *Reichsgesetzblatt* (1945), I, 30. Summary courts had existed since November 1, 1939; see Absolon, *Das Wehrmachtsstrafrecht,* 198ff.
20. The case is documented in the decision of the Aschaffenburg County Court of December 6, 1948; *Justiz und NS-Verbrechen* 3, pp. 625ff. (case no. 105).
21. The case is documented in Jörg Friedrich, *Freispruch für die Nazi-Justiz* (Reinbek bei Hamburg: Rowohlt, 1983), 140–141.
22. *Der Spiegel* 32 (1972), 148.
23. Cited in Vultejus, *Kampfanzug unter der Robe,* 102.

21. Resistance from the Bench

1. *Deutsche Justiz* 97 (1935), 1685–86.
2. Curt Rothenberger, *Der deutsche Richter* (1943), 53.
3. Hubert Schorn, *Der Richter im Dritten Reich* (Frankfurt: Klostermann, 1959), 176.
4. Fritz Hartung, *Jurist unter vier Reichen* (Cologne: Heymann, 1971), 98.
5. Schorn, *Der Richter im Dritten Reich,* 187. Several later criminal trials dealt with the murders of Sack and von Dohnanyi. See the decision of the Augsburg County Court of October 15, 1955, and the decision of the Federal Supreme Court of June 19, 1956; *Justiz und NS-Verbrechen* 13, no. 420.
6. See the excerpts from his personnel file in Friedrich Karl Kaul, *Geschichte des Reichsgerichts* (Glashütten/Taunus: Auvermann, 1971), IV, 266.
7. Ger van Roon, *Widerstand im Dritten Reich: Ein Überblick* (Munich: Beck, 1979), 131 and 136.
8. Gerhard Ritter, *Carl Goerdeler und die deutsche Widerstandsbewegung* (Stuttgart: Deutsche-Verlags-Anstalt, 1954), 346.
9. Schorn, *Der Richter im Dritten Reich,* 191.
10. Compare the documentation in Lothar Gruchmann, "Ein unbequemer Richter im Dritten Reich: Aus den Personalakten des Dr. Lothar Kreyssig," *Vierteljahrshefte für Zeitgeschichte* 32 (1984), 463ff.
11. Ibid., 470.
12. Schorn, *Der Richter im Dritten Reich,* 281.
13. Ibid., 291.
14. Ibid., 139.
15. Arthur Brandt, *Der Tscheka-Prozess: Denkschrift der Verteidigung* (1925; rpt. Hamburg: Attica, 1979).
16. See the excerpts from his personnel file in Kaul, *Geschichte des Reichsgerichts,* 297–298.
17. Cited ibid., 233.
18. See Kaul's statistics, ibid., 221.
19. Martin Hirsch, Diemut Majer, and Jurgen Meinck, eds., *Recht, Verwaltung und Justiz im Nationalsozialismus* (Cologne: Bund-Verlag, 1984), 547.
20. Gerhard Fieberg, *Justiz im nationalsozialistischen Deutschland* (Cologne: Bundesanzeiger, 1984), 54.
21. *Braunbuch: Kriegs- und Naziverbrecher* (1968), 113.
22. Walter Wagner, *Der Volksgerichtshof im nationalsozialistischen Staat* (Stuttgart: Deutsche Verlagsanstalt, 1974), 799.
23. Statistics cited in Bernd Martin, "Zur Untauglichkeit eines übergreifenden Faschismus-Begriffs," *Vierteljahrshefte für Zeitgeschichte* 29 (1981), 71–72.

22. Collapse and Reconstruction

1. *Military Government Gazette,* Germany, United States Zone, Issue A (June 1, 1946), 1.
2. R. Wenzlau, *Der Wiederaufbau der Justiz in Nordwestdeutschland* (Königstein: Athenäum, 1979), 98.

3. Gerhard Erdsiek, "Chronik der Rechtsentwicklung," *Deutsche Rechtszeitschrift* 1 (1946), 23.
4. H. Kesselböhmer, cited in Wenzlau, *Der Wiederaufbau der Justiz,* 121.
5. Friedrich Karl Kaul, *Geschichte des Reichsgerichts* (Glashütten/Taunus: Auvermann, 1971), IV, 239.
6. M. Stolleis, "Rechtsordnung und Justizpolitik, 1945–1949," in Norbert Horn, ed., *Europäisches Rechtsdenken in Geschichte und Gegenwart* (Munich: Beck, 1982), I, 191.
7. *Official Gazette of the Control Council for Germany,* 2 (November 30, 1945), 27.
8. Wenzlau, *Der Wiederaufbau der Justiz,* 103.
9. Jörg Friedrich, *Die kalte Amnestie: NS-Täter in der Bundesrepublik* (Frankfurt: Fischer Taschenbuch-Verlag, 1984), 40.
10. Wenzlau, *Der Wiederaufbau der Justiz,* 103 and 130.
11. Cited ibid., 137.
12. Bernhard Diestelkamp, "Rechts- und verfassungsgeschichtliche Probleme der Frühgeschichte der Bundesrepublik Deutschland," *Juristische Schulung* 21 (1981), 492.
13. National Archives, Washington D.C., RG 59, pp. 321ff.
14. Justus Fürstenau, *Entnazifizierung: Ein Kapitel deutscher Nachkriegspolitik* (Neuwied: Luchterhand, 1969), 221.
15. Lutz Niethammer, "Zum Verhältnis von Reform und Rekonstruktion," in Wolf-Dieter Narr and Dietrich Thränhardt, eds., *Die Bundesrepublik Deutschland: Entstehung, Entwicklung, Struktur* (Königstein/Taunus: Verlagsgruppe Athenäum, 1979), 33.
16. Lutz Niethammer, *Die Mitläuferfabrik: Die Entnazifizierung am Beispiel Bayerns* (Berlin: Deitz, 1982), 595.
17. Cited in Joachim Perels, "Die Restauration der Rechtslehre nach 1945," *Kritische Justiz* 17 (1984), 360.
18. Günther Krauss, "Die Verfassung Deutschlands, 1945–1954," *Die öffentliche Verwaltung* 7 (1954), 580.
19. Cited in Perels, "Die Restauration der Rechtslehre," 362.
20. Cited in Friedrich, *Die kalte Amnestie,* 273.
21. Wackerzapp (CDU), cited ibid., 280.
22. Heinemann (CDU), ibid.
23. Menzel (SPD), ibid.
24. Kleindienst (CDU), ibid.
25. *Bundesgesetzblatt* (1951), I, 307.
26. Ibid., 980.
27. *Entscheidungen des Bundesverfassungsgerichts,* vol. 3, p. 58.
28. *Entscheidungen des Bundesgerichtshofes in Zivilsachen,* vol. 13, p. 265.
29. Ibid., 299.
30. *Entscheidungen des Bundesverfassungsgerichts,* vol. 6, p. 132.
31. Ibid., 167.
32. *Bundesgesetzblatt* (1961), I, 1557.
33. *Bundestags-Protokolle,* 3rd session, vol. 49, p. 9710.

34. Ibid., 9582.
35. Cited in Ulrich Vultejus, *Kampfanzug unter der Robe* (Hamburg: Buntbuch, 1984), 85.

23. Restoration in the Legal System

1. *Stuttgarter Zeitung,* November 30, 1960.
2. Jörg Friedrich, *Die kalte Amnestie: NS-Täter in der Bundesrepublik* (Frankfurt: Fischer Taschenbuch-Verlag, 1984), 25–26.
3. R. Wenzlau, *Der Wiederaufbau der Justiz in Nordwestdeutschland* (1979), 309.
4. From the introduction to the *Festschrift zur Eröffnung des Bundesgerichtshofes in Karlsruhe* (Karlsruhe: C. F. Müller, 1950).
5. "Die Tradition des Reichsgerichts," ibid., 27.
6. *Deutsche Richterzeitung* 32 (1954), 251–253.
7. *Juristenzeitung* 9 (1954), 680.
8. Helmut Heiber, "Zur Justiz im Dritten Reich: Der Fall Eliáš," *Vierteljahrshefte für Zeitgeschichte* 3 (1955), 282.
9. Peter Alfons Steiniger and Kazimierz Leszczynski, *Fall 3* (Berlin: Deutscher Verlag der Wissenschaften, 1969), 256–257.
10. See the obituary in *Deutsche Richterzeitung* 54 (1976), 90.
11. Wolfgang Koppel, *Justiz im Zwielicht* (Karlsruhe: published by the author, 1963), 123.
12. See his commentary in *Die Strafrechtsnovellen, 1933–34* (1934), 137.
13. H. Kramer, "Die Aufarbeitung des Faschismus durch die Nachkriegsjustiz in der Bundesrepublik Deutschland," in Helmut D. Fangmann and Norman Paech, eds., *Recht, Justiz und Faschismus nach 1933 und heute* (Cologne: Theurer, 1984), 210.
14. Eduard Rabofsky and Gerhard Oberkofler, *Verborgene Wurzeln der NS-Justiz* (Vienna, Munich, Zurich: Europaverlag, 1985), 77ff.
15. See the minutes of the meeting taken by Adolf Eichmann; Nuremberg Document NG-2568, photocopy at the Institut für Zeitgeschichte in Munich.
16. Testimony before the Wolfenbüttel Petty Court, December 10, 1969 (Az: Ss 88/68, p. 7).
17. For information on the careers of these men in the Ministry of Justice, see *Handbuch der Justizverwaltung* (Berlin, 1942). See also *Handbuch der Justiz* (Hamburg, Berlin, Bonn) for the years 1953, 1954, 1958, 1960, 1962, and 1964.
18. See the information given in Wolfgang Koppel, *Ungesühnte Nazi-Justiz* (1960), 68ff.
19. See the alphabetical list given in Koppel, *Justiz im Zwielicht.*
20. Christoph Schminck-Gustavus, *Das Heimweh des Walerjan Wrobel: Ein Sondergerichtsverfahren, 1941–42* (Bonn: Dietz, 1986), 20–21.
21. The document announcing the closing of the investigation (Az: 1 Js 112/60) is printed in Koppel, *Ungesühnte Nazi-Justiz,* 62.
22. Otto Schweling and Erich Schwinge, *Die deutsche Militärjustiz in der Zeit des Nationalsozialismus* (Marburg: Elwert, 1977).
23. *Der Spiegel* 32 (1972), 147ff.
24. R. Strecker, ed., *Dr. Hans Globke* (Hamburg: Rütten & Loenig, 1961), 94.

25. *Deutsche Justiz* 98 (1936), 587.

26. See Strecker, *Dr. Hans Globke.*

27. Strecker documents Globke's career after the war; see ibid., 5–6.

28. Hans Robinsohn, *Justiz als politische Verfolgung* (Stuttgart: Deutsche Verlags-Anstalt, 1977), 154.

29. See the lists in Koppel, *Ungesühnte Nazi-Justiz,* 68ff.; and idem, *Justiz im Zwielicht,* 41ff.

30. *Entscheidungen des Bundesgerichtshofes in Strafsachen,* vol. 9, p. 302.

31. See Koppel, *Ungesühnte Nazi-Justiz; and idem, Justiz im Zwielicht.* See also the answer of the West German government to a parliamentary inquiry into the judicial system under the Nazis, November 26, 1986; *Bundestags-Drucksache* 10, no. 6566, pp. 20–21.

32. Michel Anders, *Die Sippe der Krähen* (Frankfurt: Eichborn, 1981), 46.

33. Cited in *Braunbuch* (1968), 139.

34. Adalbert Rückerl, *Die Strafverfolgung von NS-Verbrechen, 1945–1978: Eine Dokumentation* (Heidelberg: Müller, 1979), 172.

35. See *Braunbuch,* 172.

36. Cited in Kramer, "Die Aufarbeitung des Faschismus," 77.

37. Cited in Lutz Lehmann, *Legal und opportun: Politische Justiz in der Bundesrepublik* (Berlin: Voltaire, 1966), 16.

38. Information provided by the West German government, *Bundestags-Drucksache* 10, no. 6566, p. 23.

39. See the article in *Stuttgarter Zeitung,* March 13, 1971.

40. *Braunbuch,* 378.

41. *Hochverrat und Staatsgefährdung: Urteile des Bundesgerichtshofes,* vol. 1, p. 246.

42. *Entscheidungen des Bundesgerichtshofes in Strafsachen,* vol. 23, p. 46.

43. *Der Spiegel* 13 (1985), 180.

44. Heinrich Hannover and Günter Walraff, *Die unheimliche Republik: Politische Verfolgung in der Bundesrepublik* (Hamburg: VSA Verlag, 1982), 12ff.

45. Kramer, "Die Aufarbeitung des Faschismus," 79.

46. Decision of February 6, 1975; *Entscheidungen des Bundesverwaltungsgerichts,* vol. 47, p. 359.

47. Excerpts from the decision are printed in Robinsohn, *Justiz als politische Verfolgung,* 23.

48. Decision of May 29, 1975; *Entscheidungen des Bundesverfassungsgerichts,* vol. 39, p. 334.

49. Kramer, "Die Aufarbeitung des Faschismus," 79.

50. Willi Geiger, *Die Rechtsstellung des Schriftleiters nach dem Gesetz vom 4. Oktober 1933* (Darmstadt and Leipzig: Buske Nachfolger, 1941), foreword and pp. 9 and 39–40.

51. *Entscheidungen des Bundesverfassungsgerichts,* vol. 39, p. 349.

24. Coming to Terms with the Past

1. Gustav Radbruch, "Richterliches Prüfungsrecht," *Die Justiz* 1 (1925–26), 16.

2. Carl Schmitt, "Legalität und Legitimität," *Verfassungsrechtliche Aufsätze aus den Jahren 1924–1954* (Berlin: Duncker & Humblot, 1958), 344.

3. Forsthoff, *Der totale Staat* (Hamburg: Hanseatische Verlagsanstalt, 1933), 32.
4. Decision of the Wetzlar Petty Court of June 17, 1935; printed in Ernst Noam and Wolf-Arno Kropat, *Juden vor Gericht, 1933–1945* (Wiesbaden: Kommission für die Geschichte der Juden in Hessen, 1975), 61ff.
5. *Entscheidungen des Reichsgerichts in Strafsachen*, vol. 72, p. 9.
6. This was one of the passages that led to public controversy between Hochhuth and Filbinger.
7. Strictly speaking, Jahrreiss appeared at the trial only as a witness; see Peter Alfons Steiniger and Kazimierz Leszczynski, *Fall 3* (Berlin: Deutscher Verlag der Wissenschaften, 1969), 156.
8. Hubert Schorn, *Der Richter im Dritten Reich* (Frankfurt: Klostermann, 1959), 31.
9. Hermann Weinkauff, *Die deutsche Justiz und der Nationalsozialismus* (Stuttgart: Deutsche Verlagsanstalt, 1968), I, 69.
10. See under the heading "Rechtsstaat," in E. von Becherath, ed., *Handwörterbuch der Sozialwissenschaften* (Stuttgart: G. Fischer et al., 1964), VIII, 770.
11. Eberhard Schmidt, *Lehrkommentar zur Strafprozessordnung*, 2nd ed. (Göttingen: Vandenhoeck & Ruprecht, 1964), Randnummer 409.
12. Schmitt, "Legalität und Legitimität," 345.
13. "Naturrecht und Rechtspositivismus," in Werner Maihofer, ed., *Naturrecht oder Rechtspositivismus?* (Bad Homburg: Gentner, 1962), 23.
14. Hans Welzel, *Naturalismus und Wertphilosophie im Strafrecht* (1935), 76.
15. Günther Küchenhoff, *Nationaler Gemeinschaftsstaat, Volksrecht und Volksrechtsprechung* (Berlin and Leipzig: 1934), 56.
16. Günther Küchenhoff, *Rechtsbesinnung: Eine Rechtsphilosophie* (Göttingen: O. Schwartz, 1973), 68–69 and 582.
17. Decision of March 28, 1952; printed in Klaus Moritz and Ernst Noam, eds., *NS-Verbrechen vor Gericht, 1945–1955: Dokumente aus hessischen Justizakten* (Wiesbaden: Kommission für die Geschichte der Juden in Hessen, 1978), 323.
18. Schorn, *Der Richter im Dritten Reich,* 32.
19. Ibid., 139.
20. Hermann Weinkauff, "Der Naturrechtsgedanke in der Rechtsprechung des Bundesgerichtshofes," in Maihofer, ed., *Naturrecht oder Rechtspositivismus?* 557.
21. *Entscheidungen des Bundesgerichtshofes in Zivilsachen*, vol. 11, app. 34.
22. Weinkauff, "Der Naturrechtsgedanke."
23. *Entscheidungen des Bundesgerichtshofes in Zivilsachen*, vol. 6, pp. 208ff. (Grand Panel in Civil Cases); see also vol. 11, app. 1, and vol. 13, pp. 265ff.
24. Weinkauff, *Die deutsche Justiz und der Nationalsozialismus,* 179.
25. Ibid., 180.
26. Ibid., 188.
27. P. Sieber von Groote, *Die Frauenfrage und ihre Lösung durch den Nationalsozialismus* (Berlin: Verlag der NSDAP, 1933), 13.
28. Adolf Hitler, *Reden und Proklamationen, 1932–1945,* ed. Max Domarus (Würzburg: Domarus, 1962–63), I, 450.

29. "Germanisches Frauentum in unserer Zeit," *Der Schulungsbrief* 4 (1937), 93–94.

30. Weinkauff, "Der Naturrechtsgedanke," 559.

31. *Entscheidungen des Bundesgerichtshofes in Zivilsachen,* vol. 11, app. 34.

32. *Amtsblatt der Militärregierung* (British Zone), 1.

33. *Reichsgesetzblatt* (1944), I, 339.

34. See the report on the conference (which took place December 3–6, 1946, in Wiesbaden), in *Süddeutsche Juristenzeitung* (1947), 219.

35. W. Dallinger, *Süddeutsche Juristenzeitung* (1950), 731.

36. K. S. Bader, "Die Wiederherstellung rechtsstaatlicher Garantien im deutschen Strafprozessrecht," *Festschrift für H. Pfenninger* (1956), 7.

37. *Bundestags-Drucksache,* vol. 4, p. 178.

38. R. Wenzlau, *Der Wiederaufbau der Justiz in Nordwestdeutschland* (1979), 27.

39. E. Kern, "Die Wiederhestellung der Rechtseinheit auf dem Gebiet der Strafgerichtsverfassung und des Strafverfahrens," *Monatsschrift für Deutsches Recht* 4 (1950), 586.

40. *Deutsches Strafrecht* 4 (1937), 125ff.

41. *Deutsche Rechtszeitschrift* (1946), 11ff.

42. Lutz Niethammer, "Zum Verhältnis von Reform und Rekonstruktion in der US-Zone," in Wolf-Dieter Narr and Dietrich Thränhardt, eds., *Die Bundesrepublik Deutschland: Entstehung, Entwicklung, Struktur* (Königstein/Taunus: Verlagsgruppe Athenäum, 1979), 51.

43. See the documentation in *Demokratie und Recht* 8 (1980), 355.

44. Norbert Schmacke and Hans-Georg Güse, *Zwangssterilisiert* (Bremen: Brockkamp, 1984), 143.

45. Law of June 18, 1974; *Bundesgesetzblatt* (1974), I, 1297.

46. The resolution passed by the *Bundestag* on November 29, 1979, and the decision of the Kiel Petty Court are documented in *Demokratie und Recht* 14 (1986), 339ff.

47. *Monatsschrift für Deutsches Recht* 1 (1947), 75.

48. Decision of June 7, 1946; *Süddeutsche Juristenzeitung* (1946), 120.

49. Decision of April 15, 1946; ibid., 96.

50. Ibid., 118.

51. *Schleswig-Holsteinische Anzeigen: Justizministerialblatt für Schleswig-Holstein* (1946), 4.

52. Law of March 18, 1943; *Reichsgesetzblatt* (1943), I, 169.

53. Decision of July 30, 1947; *Monatsschrift für Deutsches Recht* 2 (1948), 27.

54. *Entscheidungen des Reichsgerichts in Strafsachen,* vol. 72, p. 164.

55. Decision of January 10, 1947; *Monatsschrift für Deutsches Recht* 1 (1947), 136.

56. Wording of 1871; *Reichsgesetzblatt* (1871), 127.

57. Franz von Liszt, *Lehrbuch des deutschen Strafrechts,* 9th ed. (Berlin, 1899), 348.

58. *Reichsgesetzblatt* (1943), I, 339.

59. See A. Dalcke and K. Schäfer, *Strafrecht und Strafverfahren,* 35th ed. (1950), note B to paragraph 240.

60. Wording of 1953; *Bundesgesetzblatt* (1953), I, 735.

61. Decree of May 29, 1943; *Reichsgesetzblatt* (1943), I, 339.

62. Decision of June 26, 1946; *Süddeutsche Juristenzeitung* (1946), 120.
63. Law no. 1 of May 20, 1945; *Amtsblatt der Militärregierung* (British Zone), 35.
64. *Entscheidungen des Bundesgerichtshofes in Strafsachen,* vol. 1, pp. 81 and 308.
65. Thus, the penalties for trespassing (paragraph 123) were one day to three months in 1871, but one month to one year in 1986; for duress (paragraph 240) one day to one year in 1871, but one month to three years in 1986; for shoplifting or pilfering (old version of paragraphs 370 and 242) one day to six weeks in 1871, but one month to five years in 1986.
66. Fritz Hartung, *Jurist unter vier Reichen* (Cologne: Heymann, 1971), 123.

25. The Opposition Goes on Trial Again

1. *Reichsgesetzblatt* (1934), I, 341.
2. Laws no. 1 (September 20, 1945), no. 11 (January 30, 1946), and no. 55 (June 20, 1947).
3. Franz Gürtner and Roland Freisler, *Das neue Strafrecht,* 2nd ed. (Berlin: R. v. Decker, 1936), 136.
4. *Bundestags-Drucksache,* vol. 1, no. 1307, p. 27.
5. Josef Schafheutle et al., *Die Strafrechtsnovellen von 1933 und 1934* (1934).
6. *Bundestags-Protokolle,* 1st session (July 9, 1951), 6297.
7. Ibid. (July 11, 1951), 6476.
8. "Der publizistische Landesverrat," *Neue Juristische Wochenschrift* (1963), 6.
9. *Bundestags-Protokolle,* 1st session (March 16, 1950), 1593.
10. *Bundestags-Drucksache,* vol. 1, no. 563.
11. *Bundestags-Protokolle,* 1st session (March 1, 1950), 1794.
12. Ibid., 1788.
13. Decision of March 9, 1956; *Entscheidungen des Bundesgerichtshofes in Strafsachen,* vol. 9, p. 101.
14. W. Ammann, "Die Problematik des vorverlegten Staatsschutzes," in Carl Nedelmann et al., eds., *Kritik der Strafrechtsreform* (Frankfurt: Suhrkamp, 1968), 122 and 126.
15. Alexander von Brünneck, *Politische Justiz gegen Kommunisten in der BRD, 1949–1968* (Frankfurt: Suhrkamp, 1978), 230.
16. Ibid., 278.
17. This remark, made by Maihofer during a television broadcast in 1965, is cited in Lutz Lehmann, *Legal und opportun: Politische Justiz in der Bundesrepublik* (Berlin: Voltaire, 1966), 108.
18. Ibid., 203 and 206.
19. Landesarbeitsgericht Munich, *Der Betrieb 1958,* p. 1188.
20. Von Brünneck, *Politische Justiz gegen Kommunisten,* 296.
21. Ibid., 294.
22. *Der Spiegel* 28 (1961), 25.

26. Law Schools

1. See the table in Wolfgang Scheffler, *Judenverfolgung im Dritten Reich, 1933–1945* (Berlin: Colloquium, 1960), 68.
2. C. Ehmann, "Eine Rückberufung der Verjagten unterblieb," *Frankfurter Rundschau* (September 26, 1985), 9.
3. L. Elm, *Hochschule und Neofaschismus* (East Berlin: Akademie-Verlag, 1972), 31.
4. Ehmann, "Eine Rückberufung der Verjagten."
5. See H. Wrobel, "Otto Palandt zum Gedächtnis," *Kritische Justiz* 15 (1982), 1ff.
6. Walter Hamel, "Die Polizei," in Hans Frank, ed., *Deutsches Verwaltungsrecht* (Munich: NSDAP, 1937), 395.
7. Walter Hamel, *Die Bedeutung der Grundrechte im sozialen Rechtsstaat* (Berlin: Duncker & Humblot, 1957), 30 and 64.
8. In P. Bockelmann et al., eds., *Probleme der Strafrechtserneuerung* (Berlin: de Gruyter, 1944), 109.
9. Hans Welzel, *Das deutsche Strafrecht* (Berlin: de Gruyter, 1947), 2.
10. Ibid., 153.
11. Ibid., 23.
12. Ibid., 78.

27. Punishing Nazi Criminals

1. Cited in *Kriegsdokumente über Bündnisgrundlagen, Kriegsziele und Freidenspolitik der Vereinten Nationen*, Veröffentlichungen des Instituts für Internationales Recht an der Universität Kiel (Hamburg: Verlag Robert Mölich [1946]), I, 26.
2. *Reichsgesetzblatt* (1933), I, 134.
3. The case is documented in Martin Broszat, "Siegerjustiz oder strafrechtliche Selbstreinigung?" *Vierteljahrshefte für Zeitgeschichte* 29 (1981), 498.
4. *Monatsschrift für deutsches Recht* 1 (1947), 64; and *Süddeutsche Juristenzeitung* (1947), 326.
5. Law no. 13 (November 25, 1949), in *Amtsblatt der Alliierten Hohen Kommission*, 54.
6. Law on the Granting of Immunity of December 31, 1949; *Bundesgesetzblatt* (1949), I, 37.
7. *Bundestags-Protokolle*, 1st session, vol. 13, p. 1499.
8. Cited in Arnulf Baring, *Aussenpolitik in Adenauers Kanzlerdemokratie* (Munich: Oldenbourg, 1969; new ed. 1971), I, 152.
9. *Bundestags-Protokolle*, 1st session, vol. 13, p. 1503.
10. Adalbert Rückerl, *Die Strafverfolgung von NS-Verbrechen, 1945–1978: Eine Dokumentation* (Heidelberg: Müller, 1979), 125.
11. Law of July 17, 1954; *Bundesgesetzblatt* (1954), I, 203.
12. Cited in F. Kruse, "NS-Prozesse und Restauration," *Kritische Justiz* 11 (1978), 119.

13. Rückerl, *Die Strafverfolgung von NS-Verbrechen,* 140.
14. Law of May 30, 1956; *Bundesgesetzblatt* (1956), I, 437.
15. *Bundestags-Drucksache,* vol. 7, p. 130.
16. "Im Namen des Volkes," in Helmut Hammerschmidt, ed., *Zwanzig Jahre danach: Eine deutsche Bilanz, 1945–1965* (Munich: Desch, 1965), 308.
17. Meeting 117 of the third Bundestag, May 24, 1960; printed in Deutscher Bundestag, *Zur Verjährung nationalsozialistischer Verbrechen* (Bonn, 1980), I, 21.
18. Ibid., 110.
19. Statute of Limitations for Criminal Offenses, *Bundesgesetzlbatt* (1965), I, 315.
20. Ninth Law to Alter Criminal Statutes, August 4, 1969; *Bundesgesetzblatt* (1969), I, 1065.
21. Through the law of August 9, 1954; *Bundesgesetzblatt* (1954), I, 729.
22. *Bundesgesetzblatt* (1955), II, 405.
23. Article 3, section 3b.
24. *Entscheidungen des Bundesgerichtshofes in Strafsachen,* vol. 21, p. 29.
25. *Bundestags-Drucksache,* vol. 7, p. 130.
26. Michael Ratz, ed., *Die Justiz und die Nazis: Zur Strafverfolgung von Nazismus und Neonazismus seit 1945* (Frankfurt: Röderberg-Verlag, 1979), 173.
27. Cited in B. Maier, "Das deutsche-französische Abkommen vom 2. Februar 1971," *Neue Juristische Wochenschrift* (1975), 471.
28. *Bundesgesetzblatt* (1968), I, 503.
29. Meeting 236 of the fifth Bundestag, June 11, 1969; see Deutscher Bundestag, *Zur Verjährung nationalsozialistischer Verbrechen* (Bonn, 1980), II, 398.
30. H. Schröder, "Der Paragraph 50 StGB und die Verjährung bei Mord," *Juristenzeitung* 24 (1969), 132.
31. First Reform Law on the Criminal Code, June 25, 1969; *Bundesgesetzblatt* (1969), I, 645.
32. *Entscheidungen des Bundesgeichtshofes in Strafsachen,* vol. 22, pp. 375ff; also *Neue Juristische Wochenschrift* (1969), 1181.
33. Report of the Federal Minister of Justice, *Bundetags-Drucksache,* vol. 4, p. 3124.
34. For more on their activities, see Helmut Krausnick, *Hitlers Einsatzgruppen* (Frankfurt: Fischer Verlag, 1985), 82–83 and 121ff.
35. *Reichsgesetzblatt* (1941), I, 549.
36. Cited in W. Schulze-Allen, "Die Praxis der Verhinderung von Verurteilungen und Strafverbüssungen," in Ratz, ed., *Die Justiz und die Nazis,* 96.
37. Deutscher Bundestag, *Zur Verjährung nationalsozialistischer Verbrechen: Dokumentation zur parlamentarischen Bewältigung des Problems* (Bonn, 1980).
38. Sixteenth Law to Alter the Criminal Code, July 16, 1979; *Bundesgesetzblatt* (1979), I, 1046.
39. *Justiz und NS-Verbrechen: Sammlung deutscher Strafurteile wegen nationalsozialistischer Tötungsverbrechen, 1945–1966,* vol. 8, p. 439 (case 281a).
40. Ibid., vol. 9, pp. 61ff. (case 299).
41. Ibid., vol. 13, pp. 320–321 (case 420a).

42. Ibid., vol. 15, p. 232 (case 465a).
43. Cited in Jörg Friedrich, *Die kalte Amnestie* (Frankfurt: Fischer Taschenbuch, 1984), 237.
44. Ibid., 224.
45. *Entscheidungen des Reichsgerichts in Strafsachen,* vol. 74, p. 78.
46. Ibid., vol. 63, p. 215.
47. *Entscheidungen des Bundesgerichtshofes in Strafsachen,* vol. 8, p. 293.
48. Ibid., vol. 18, p. 87.
49. *Justiz und NS-Verbrechen,* vol. 21, pp. 270ff. (no. 594b).
50. Ibid., vol. 21, pp. 345ff. (no. 594c).
51. Cited in E.-W. Hanack,"Zur Problematik der gerechten Bestrafung national-sozialistischer Gewaltverbrecher," *Juristenzeitung* 22 (1967), 333 and 331.
52. Freidrich, *Die kalte Amnestie,* 399.
53. Ibid.
54. Ernst Klee, *Was sie taten—was sie wurden: Ärzte, Juristen und andere Beteiligte am Kranken- oder Judenmord* (Frankfurt: Fischer Taschenbuch, 1986), 210.
55. Ibid., 209.
56. Az: 2 Ks 2/74.
57. Alfred Grosser, *Germany in Our Time: A Political History of the Postwar Years,* trans. Paul Stephenson (New York: Praeger, 1971), 219.
58. Bauer, "Im Namen des Volkes," in Hammerschmidt, ed., *Zwanzig Jahre danach,* 308.
59. Cited in Richard Henkys, *Die nationalsozialistischen Gewaltverbrechen* (Stuttgart: Kreuz-Verlag, 1964), 346.
60. *Bundesgerichtshof* (Az: StR 55/55); cited in Rückerl, *Die Strafverfolgung von NS-Verbrechen,* 144.
61. *Justiz und NS-Verbrechen,* vol. 21, p. 271 (no. 594b).
62. Ibid., vol. 21, pp. 345ff. (no. 594c).
63. Ibid., vol. 21, pp. 266–267 (no. 594a).
64. *Der Spiegel* 28 (1979), 54.
65. Ibid., 53.
66. Ulrich-Dieter Oppitz, *Strafverfahren und Strafvollstreckung bei NS-Gewaltverbrechen* (Ulm: Braunland, 1976; 2nd ed. 1979), 368.
67. Decision of July 28, 1970; cited ibid., 369.
68. Grosser, *Germany in Our Time,* 218.
69. See Hamm Court of Appeals, *Neue Juristische Wochenschrift* (1970), 2126.
70. Oppitz, *Strafverfahren und Strafvollstreckung,* 380.
71. Grosser, *Germany in Our Time,* 219.
72. *Der Spiegel* 18 (1974), 57–58; and 50 (1980), 187.
73. *Frankfurter Allgemeine Zeitung,* October 3, 1974.
74. *Der Spiegel* 18 (1974), 60.
75. Decision 2 Wg 185/186/70 is reproduced in Peter Przybylski, *Zwischen Galgen und Amnestie* (Berlin: Dietz, 1979), 177–178.
76. Cited in Jörg Friedrich, *Freispruch für die Nazi-Justiz* (Reinbek bei Hamburg: Rowohlt, 1983), 30.

28. The Deserving and the Undeserving

1. Decree of February 13, 1924; *Reichsgesetzblatt* (1924), I, 62.
2. Amended versions of Paragraphs 1232 RVO and 9 AVG; *Bundesgesetzblatt* (1957), I, 45 and 88.
3. Law of June 9, 1965; *Bundesgesetzblatt* (1965), I, 476.
4. Decision of November 24, 1965; *Entscheidungen des Bundessozialgerichts*, vol. 24, p. 106.
5. Decision of July 16, 1970; *Zeitschrift für Beamtenrecht* (1971), 26.
6. Cited in Ulrich Vultejus, *Kampfanzug unter der Robe* (Hamburg: Buntbuch, 1984), 85.
7. Hans Robinsohn, *Justiz als politische Verfolgung* (Stuttgart: Deutsche Verlags-Anstalt, 1977), 160.
8. Ibid., 161.
9. Ibid.
10. Paragraphs 4ff. of the Federal Reparations Law of September 18, 1953; *Bundesgesetzblatt* (1953), I, 1387.
11. Cited in Norbert Schmacke and Hans-Georg Güse, *Zwangssterilisiert* (Bremen: Brockkamp, 1984), 155.
12. Both cited in H. Dux, "Entschädigung, aber kein Ende der Diskriminierung," *Demokratie und Recht* 8 (1980), 264.
13. Decision of January 7, 1956; *Rechtsprechung zur Wiedergutmachung* (1956), 113.
14. The case is documented in Dieter Galinski and Wolf Schmidt, eds., *Die Kriegsjahre in Deutschland, 1939–1945* (Hamburg: Verlag Erziehung und Wissenschaft, 1985), 121ff.
15. *Rechtsprechung zur Wiedergutmachung* (1962), 70.
16. Law of May 26, 1952, in the transcription of October 10, 1954; *Bundesgesetzblatt* (1955), II, 405.
17. Paragraph 1, section 4 of the Federal Reparations Law of September 18, 1953.
18. Law of December 23, 1936; *Reichsgesetzblatt* (1936), I, 1128.
19. Cited in Dux, "Entschädigung, aber kein Ende der Diskriminierung," 266.
20. Decision of June 27, 1961; *Entscheidungen des Bundesverfassungsgerichts*, vol. 13, p. 50.
21. Alexander von Brünneck, *Politische Justiz gegen Kommunisten in der BRD, 1949–1968* (Frankfurt: Suhrkamp, 1978), 297.
22. Decision of April 13, 1959; *Rechtsprechung zur Wiedergutmachung* (1959), 391.
23. Decision of June 9, 1965; *Rechtsprechung zur Wiedergutmachung* (1965), 513.
24. Decision of March 5, 1970; *Rechtsprechung zur Wiedergutmachung* (1970), 403.
25. Documented in Joseph Eduard Drexel, ed., *Der Fall Niekisch: Eine Dokumentation* (Cologne: Kiepenheuer & Witsch, 1964); and also in Fabian von

Schlabrendorff, *Begegnungen in fünf Jahrzehnten* (Tübingen: Wunderlich, 1979), 75ff.

26. Alfred Kantorowicz, *Die Geächteten der Republik: Alte und neue Aufsätze* (Berlin: Verlag Europäische Ideen, 1977), 41.
27. Jurgen Rühle, ed., *Alfred Kantorowicz* (Hamburg: Christians, 1969).

29. Jurists on Trial

1. *Trials of War Criminals before the Nuremberg Military Tribunals* (Washington, D.C.: U.S. Government Printing Office, 1951), III, 31.
2. Ibid., 31.
3. Ibid., 32–33.
4. Ibid., 1086.
5. Peter Alfons Steiniger and Kazimierz Leszczynski, *Fall 3* (Berlin: Deutscher Verlag der Wissenschaften, 1969), 110.
6. *Trials of War Criminals before the Nuremberg Military Tribunals*, III, 984–985.
7. See the numerous examples cited in Heribert Ostendorf and Heino ter Veen, eds., *Das "Nürnberger Juristenurteil": Eine kommentierte Dokumentation* (Frankfurt and New York: Campus, 1985), 34ff.
8. Jörg Friedrich, *Die kalte Amnestie* (Frankfurt: Fischer Taschenbuch, 1984), 254.
9. *Der Spiegel* 6 (1965), 34.
10. *Der Spiegel* 19 (1965), 66.
11. *Braunbuch* (1968), 117.
12. Peter Przybylski, *Zwischen Galgen und Amnestie* (Berlin: Dietz, 1979), 157.
13. Adalbert Rückerl, in Akademie Bad Böll, *Protokolldienst* 13 (1981), 35.
14. Decision of December 7, 1948; cited in Jörg Friedrich, *Freispruch für die Nazi-Justiz* (Reinbek bei Hamburg: Rowohlt, 1983), 150.
15. *Entscheidungen des Obersten Gerichtshofs der Britischen Zone in Strafsachen*, vol. 1, p. 217.
16. *Entscheidungen des Bundesverwaltungsgerichts*, vol. 6, pp. 132–133.
17. *Entscheidungen des Bundesgerichtshofes in Strafsachen*, vol. 9, p. 302.
18. Jörg Friedrich mentions seventeen convictions, but this list is by no means complete. See Friedrich, *Freispruch für die Nazi-Justiz*, 442.
19. Decision of the Flensburg County Court of March 30, 1948; *Justiz und NS-Verbrechen*, vol. 2, p. 397 (51a).
20. Decision of the Wuppertal County Court of October 29, 1948; ibid., vol. 3, p. 325 (no. 92).
21. Decision of the Berlin County Court of November 1, 1947; cited in Friedrich, *Freispruch für die Nazi-Justiz*, 443.
22. Decision of the Düsseldorf County Court of April 23, 1949; *Justiz und NS-Verbrechen*, vol. 4, p. 431 (no. 135a).
23. Both cases are documented in Friedrich, *Freispruch für die Nazi-Justiz*, 445.
24. Ibid., 246.
25. *Entscheidungen des Bundesgerichtshofes in Strafsachen*, vol. 9, p. 302.
26. Radbruch, "Gesetzliches Unrecht und übergesetzliches Recht," *Süddeutsche*

Juristenzeitung (1946), 104; and "Urteilsanmerkung," *Süddeutsche Juristenzeitung* (1947), 634.

27. On the discussion about crimes against humanity, see *Süddeutsche Juristenzeitung* (1947), 135.

28. "Justiz als Symptom," in Helmut Hammerschmidt, ed., *Zwanzig Jahre danach: Eine deutsche Bilanz* (Munich: Desch, 1965), 227.

29. Printed in Klaus Moritz and Ernst Noam, eds., *NS-Verbrechen vor Gericht, 1945–1955* (Wiesbaden: Kommission für die Geschichte der Juden in Hessen, 1978), 308ff.

30. Bundesgerichtshof, *Monatsschrift für deutsches Recht* 6 (1952), 695.

31. Printed in Friedrich, *Freispruch für die Nazi-Justiz,* 164.

32. Decision of June 30, 1959; *Justiz und NS-Verbrechen,* vol. 16, pp. 581ff. (no. 494b).

33. Decision of July 23, 1970; ibid., vol. 16, p. 578 (no. 494a).

34. Decision of February 4, 1952; cited in Friedrich, *Freispruch für die Nazi-Justiz,* 128.

35. Cited in Friedrich Karl Kaul, *Geschichte des Reichsgerichts* (Glashütten/Taunus: Auvermann, 1971), IV, 221; see also *Braunbuch* (1968), 121.

36. Decision of February 16, 1960; *Neue Juristische Wochenschrift* (1960), 975.

37. Decision of June 24, 1964; *Deutsche Richterzeitung* (1964), 313.

38. By B. M. Kempner (Munich: Rütten & Loenig, 1966).

39. Excerpts of the decision are printed in *Deutsche Richterzeitung* (1967), 390.

40. Excerpts are printed in Friedrich, *Freispruch für die Nazi-Justiz,* 461–462.

41. Decision of June 28, 1956; *Entscheidungen des Bundesgerichtshofes in Strafsachen,* vol. 9, p. 302.

42. The full text of the decision is printed in Friedrich, *Freispruch für die Nazi-Justiz,* 463ff.

43. *Entscheidungen des Bundesgerichtshofes in Strafsachen,* vol. 9, p. 305.

44. See P. von Feldmann, "Die Auseinandersetzung um das Ermittlungsverfahren gegen Richter und Staatsanwälte am Volksgerichtshof," *Kritische Justiz* 16 (1983), 306 and 310.

45. Friedrich, *Freispruch für die Nazi-Justiz,* 457.

30. Injustice Confirmed

1. *Justiz und NS-Verbrechen: Sammlung deutscher Strafurteile,* vol. 9, p. 367 (no. 310).

2. The decision is printed in Jörg Friedrich, *Freispruch für die Nazi-Justiz* (Reinbek bei Hamburg: Rowohlt, 1983), 181.

3. *Justiz und NS-Verbrechen,* vol. 16, p. 495 (no. 494).

4. Kessler's remarks and the decision are included in Klaus Moritz and Ernst Noam, eds., *NS-Verbrechen vor Gericht, 1945–1955* (Wiesbaden: Kommission für die Geschichte der Juden in Hessen, 1978), 321ff.

5. Decision of November 16, 1954; excerpts are printed in Friedrich, *Freispruch für die Nazi-Justiz,* 428ff.

6. Decision of March 12, 1971; cited in Jörg Friedrich, *Die kalte Amnestie* (Frankfurt: Fischer Taschenbuch, 1984), 289.
7. Decision of December 12, 1955; ibid., 290. The decision was reversed in 1956 by the *Kammergericht.*
8. Cited in Friedrich, *Freispruch für die Nazi-Justiz,* 119 and 121.
9. Cited in Ernst Klee, *Was sie taten—was sie wurden* (Frankfurt: Fischer Taschenbuch, 1986), 210.
10. *Neue Juristische Wochenschrift* (1954), 1902.
11. *Bundesgesetzblatt* (1953), I, 161.
12. Decision of June 19, 1956; *Justiz und NS-Verbrechen,* vol. 13, p. 331 (no. 420).
13. Cited in Friedrich, *Freispruch für die Nazi-Justiz,* 279.
14. Cited in Michel Anders, *Die Sippe der Krähen* (1981), 40.
15. *Deutsche Richterzeitung* (1964), 313.
16. Advisory opinion of June 8, 1953; *Entscheidungen des Bundesgerichtshofes in Zivilsachen,* vol. 11, apps. 81ff.

31. A Latter-Day "Condemnation" of Nazi Justice

1. *Bundestags-Protokolle* (10th session), 8761, in connection with Bundestags-Drucksache, vol. 10, no. 2368, p. 2.
2. *Amtsblatt der Militärregierung* (British Zone), no. 5, p. 35.
3. Ibid., 34.
4. *Sammlung der Länderratsgesetze* (1950), 67.
5. Ibid., 69.
6. *Bundestags-Drucksache,* vol. 10, no. 116.
7. *Recht: Informationen des Bundesjustizministers* (1983), 103.

32. An Attempt at an Explanation

1. W. F. Haug, "Zum Verhältnis von Gewalt und juristischer Ideologie im deutschen Faschismus," *Demokratie und Recht* (1984), 459.
2. H. Rottleuthner, "Substantieller Dezisionismus," in Rottleuthner, ed., *Recht, Rechtsphilosophie und Nationalsozialismus* (supp. 18 of *Archiv für Rechts- und Sozialphilosophie*), 20 and 35.
3. Ernst Fraenkel, *The Dual State: A Contribution to the Theory of Dictatorship,* trans. E. A. Shils (1941; rpt. New York: Octagon Books, 1969).
4. U. Wesel, "Denn sie wussten, was sie tun," *Vorgänge* 4–5 (1983), 148.
5. Ekkehard Reitter, *Franz Gürtner: Politische Biographie eines deutschen Juristen, 1881–1941* (Berlin: Duncker & Humblot, 1976), 220.
6. Gustav Radbruch, "Des Reichsjustizministeriums Ruhm und Ende," *Süddeutsche Juristenzeitung* (1948), 57.
7. Reitter, *Franz Gürtner,* 220.
8. Henry Picker, ed., *Tischgespräche im Führerhauptquartier, 1941–42* (Bonn: Athenäum Verlag, 1951), 211 and 213.

9. *Mein Kampf,* 2 vols. in 1 (Munich: Zentralverlag der NSDAP, 1940), 371.

10. Rudolf Olden, *Hitler* (Amsterdam: Querido Verlag, 1935), 223.

11. Helmut Nicolai, *Grundlagen der kommenden Verfassung* (Berlin: Hobbing, 1933), 19.

12. Otto Koellreutter, "Das Verwaltungsrecht im nationalsozialistischen Staat," *Deutsche Juristen-Zeitung* (1933), 625.

13. *Mein Kampf,* 201.

14. Ibid., 370.

15. Hubert Schorn, *Der Richter im Dritten Reich* (Frankfurt: Klostermann, 1959), 100.

16. The decision of May 30, 1973, is printed in Erich Fried et al., eds., *Am Beispiel Peter Paul Zahl* (Frankfurt a.M.: Sozialistische Verlagsauslieferung, [1976]); the decision of the court of first instance is cited.

17. *Entscheidungen des Bundesgerichtshofes in Strafsachen,* vol. 32, p. 310.

Bibliography

Compiled by Detlev Vagts

The following works may be useful to those readers who would like further information relating to the issues in this book but who cannot consult the German literature that is cited in the notes.

The general structure and development of the German legal and judicial system are described in the *Manual of German Law*, written for officers of the British occupation forces in Germany by E. J. Cohn and Martin Wolff (London: H. M. Stationery Office, 1950; 2nd ed., 1968).

Nazi changes in the system are described in Karl Loewenstein, "Law in the Third Reich," *Yale Law Journal* 45 (1936), 779–815. Changes made during the U.S. occupation are described in "Law and the Legislative Process in Occupied Germany," *Yale Law Journal* 57 (1948), 724–760, 994–1022.

For information on aspects of the German legal profession during the Third Reich, see Max Rheinstein, "Law Faculties and Law Schools: A Comparison of Legal Education in the United States and Germany," *Wisconsin Law Review* (1938), 5–42; Burke Shartel and Hans Wolff, "German Lawyers: Training and Functions," *Michigan Law Review* 42 (1943), 521–527; Hans Wolff, "Criminal Justice in Germany," *Michigan Law Review* 42 (1943), 1067–1088, and 43 (1943–44), 155–178.

A translation of the German penal code, with amendments to that time, was prepared by Vladimir Gsovski and published by the U.S. Library of Congress in 1947 as *The Statutory Criminal Law of Germany*. For a more recent format, see Gerhard O. Mueller and Thomas Buergenthal, *The German Penal Code of 1871* (South Hackensack, N.J.: F. B. Rothman, 1961).

A basic document, used extensively by Ingo Müller, is the record in United States vs. Altstoetter et al., the so-called Jurists' Trial conducted by an American military court at Nuremberg in 1946. See *Trials of War Criminals before the Nuremberg Military Tribunals under Control Council Law No.*

10, Nuremberg, October 1946–April 1949 (Washington, D.C.: U.S. Government Printing Office, 1951), vol. III.

For a detailed biography of Carl Schmitt, see Joseph Bendersky, *Carl Schmitt: Theorist for the Reich* (Princeton: Princeton University Press, 1983).

Robert Lifton, *Nazi Doctors: Medical Killing and the Psychology of Genocide* (New York: Basic Books, 1986) looks at the role of the medical profession in the Nazis' euthanasia campaign. Robert Proctor, *Racial Hygiene: Medicine under the Nazis* (Cambridge, Mass.: Harvard University Press, 1980) examines the medical profession more broadly. Geoffrey Cocks, *Psychotherapy in the Third Reich: The Göring Institute* (New York: Oxford University Press, 1985) describes the encounter of that profession with Nazism.

Three books about the Nazi state and its organization include some treatment of the legal system: Karl Dietrich Bracher, *The German Dictatorship,* trans. Jean Steinberg (New York: Praeger, 1970); Richard Grunberger, *A Social History of the Third Reich* (London: Weidenfeld and Nicolson, 1971); and Franz Neumann, *Behemoth: The Structure and Practice of National Socialism* (New York: Oxford University Press, 1942).

James Tent, *Mission on the Rhine: Reeducation and Denazification in American-Occupied Germany* (Chicago: University of Chicago Press, 1982), describes that chapter in German-American history.

Index